RIGHT
IN HER
SOUL

RIGHT IN HER SOUL

The Life of
Anna Louise Strong

Tracy B. Strong
and Helene Keyssar

RANDOM HOUSE

New York

*We gratefully acknowledge permission from the following individuals to reprint
material over which they have control:* Seema Rynin Allan, Rewi Alley, James Aronson,
Cedric Belfrage, Jack Chen, Elsie Fairfax-Cholmeley, Stephanie Hicks Craib, John K.
Fairbank, Frederick V. Field, Frances Putnam Fritchman, Lement Harris, Huang Hua,
Rose Lavoot, Ma Hai-teh, Sidney Rittenberg, Social Welfare Archives of the University
of Minnesota (David Klaasen, Curator), Franklin D. Roosevelt, Jr.,
Peter Steffens, Anne Pierson Tobey.

Library of Congress Cataloging in Publication Data
Strong, Tracy B.
Right in her soul.
Bibliography: p.
Includes index.
1. Strong, Anna Louise, 1885–1970. 2. Journalists—
United States—Biography. 3. Radicals—United States—
Biography. I. Keyssar, Helene. II. Title.
PN4874.S74S8 1983   070'.92'4 [B]   83-42755
ISBN 0-394-51649-4

For our children

Foreword

Wee shall finde that the God of Israell is among us, when tenn
of us shall be able to resist a thousand of our enemies, when
hee shall make us a prayse and glory, that men shall say of
succeeding plantacions: the lord make it like that of New England: for wee must Consider that wee shall be as a Citty on a
Hill, the eies of all people are uppon us; so that if wee shall
deale falsely with our god in this worke we have undertaken
and so cause him to withdraw his present help from us, wee
shall be made a story and a by-word through the world, wee
shall open the mouths of enemies to speake evill of the wayes
of god and all professours for Gods sake; wee shall shame the
faces of many of gods worthy servants, and cause their prayers
to be turned into Cursses upon us till we be consumed out of
the good land whether wee are goeing.

> —John Winthrop, *Christian
> Charitie. A modell hereof.*

So many deeds cry out to be done,
And always urgently;
The world rolls on,
Time presses.
Ten thousand years are too long,
Seize the day, seize the hour!

> —Mao Tse-tung, "Reply to
> Comrade Kuo Mo-jo"

Anna Louise Strong was born in 1885 in a two-room parsonage in Friend,
Nebraska. She died in 1970 in Peking, China, where she was buried with
full honors in the Revolutionary Martyrs Cemetery. During the years
between, she bore witness to most of the upheavals of our century. From
1919 until her death she followed the revolutionary uprisings in Russia,
Mexico, Spain and China, writing millions of words to try to persuade
her fellow Americans that the social transformations occurring in these
lands were to be celebrated rather than feared.

No one who met Anna Louise Strong ever forgot her. She traveled on
a journalist's visa, but she was determined to shape the news as well as
to report it. She organized labor, marched with revolutionary armies and
participated in the events she described in her writings. Her intelligence

and candid commitment to the left as well as her diligence won her the attention and often the trust of leaders around the world. She knew Trotsky well, dined in the White House with Eleanor and Franklin Roosevelt, and with Stalin's blessing edited the first English-language newspaper in the Soviet Union. In the years before 1949 she carried news from Chou En-lai and Mao Tse-tung to the West, and during the sixties her *Letters from China* provided the West with a unique perspective on Vietnam, the Cultural Revolution and other major developments in the Far East.

She understood the challenges of the twentieth century in worldwide terms, but the country she most passionately hoped to save was her own. Throughout her life she remained quintessentially American, and in a peculiarly American tradition, her radicalism had a strong evangelical tinge. She learned the gospel of political and spiritual reform in childhood from her father, a Congregational minister, and she followed it unswervingly ever after. "By words and life," she remembered, "he taught me that neither money nor fame nor human opinion are to be counted against being 'right in one's soul.' "

Tall and statuesque, with riveting blue eyes and a voice that could cut across a room full of conversation, Anna Louise commanded attention by her presence as well as by her deeds. Always a maverick among the American "Reds," she cleared her own path but cherished association with any who shared even a small part of her vision. She did not so much join the American left as repeatedly make herself over into a member. As a leader in the child welfare movement in the years before World War I, she came to know many of the men and women who were attempting to change or remedy the inequities of American society. Lincoln Steffens, Roger Baldwin, Jane Addams, Owen Lovejoy, Norman Hapgood, Ben Lindsey, Luther Gulick, "Mother" Ella Bloor, Emma Goldman and Max Eastman were among her early companions in the struggle to reconstruct America. During and after World War I, her leadership of the labor movement in Seattle and her support of the newborn Soviet Union solidified her ties to the Reds in progressive American politics. But Anna Louise was a remarkably solitary traveler, and for the next fifty years, as she journeyed repeatedly from the United States to Russia, China and Europe, her role in the American left became increasingly complex.

More constant in her life were her bonds with strong women. After the premature death of her brilliant and independent mother, she turned to Jane Addams, Florence Kelley, Lillian Wald and Julia Lathrop for friendship and guidance. Later it was women like Alexandra Kollontai,

Soong Ch'ing-ling and Eleanor Roosevelt to whom she was most drawn. Much of her best writing focuses on women, and her life vividly illuminates the sorrows and satisfactions that were inseparable from her attempt to free herself and others of the constraints imposed upon women.

Anna Louise Strong was my grandfather's older sister, and throughout my childhood and adolescence I was aware that my great-aunt was a famous person, about whom some of my other relatives preferred not to talk. I met her only once, in 1951, when I was eight years old and returning from the Far East with my mother, brother and sister. My parents were missionaries, and my father had remained behind for a few more months. Anna Louise, who was then in the United States, met our plane in Los Angeles. I remember a large, gruff woman who paid no attention to me, even though she had never seen me before. She wanted to speak with my father, and when she discovered that he was not there, she cried, "If I had known, I wouldn't have come," and marched away. She had no use for general impressions of China or social niceties; my father was worth the effort because she saw him as a particularly astute and politically trustworthy observer. The rest of us were merely family.

In 1960, when I was a freshman at Oberlin College, an instructor whose father had been one of her friends persuaded me to write to her. She was again in China. Her response astonished me. She wrote a four-page single-spaced letter that began: "It is incredible to me that I have a great-nephew old enough to be in Oberlin, but since you give the right passwords and mail through the secret channels, I shall take your word. In the momentary shock, I feel as old as the T'ang dynasty." She gave detailed answers to all my questions and invited me to "come again."

Two years later I rather shyly inquired about the possibilities of making her a visit; she was receptive, but for personal reasons I dropped the idea temporarily. In 1967, now a graduate student, I suggested it again. At that time, the great storm of the Cultural Revolution was breaking over China. Unbeknownst to me, Anna Louise wrote to friends of hers in the town where I was living as well as to my parents seeking confirmation that I would not embarrass her politically or personally. She received the appropriate assurances, but to her distress she was unable to obtain permission for me to come. Three years later she died.

The missed opportunity troubled me, and in 1972 I began research for an article on Anna Louise. It soon became apparent that no one essay could do her justice. A year and a half later I wrote to her executor in Peking, Frank Coe, that I wanted to come to China to learn more of her life there. He told me to wait for the political climate to change. In 1980, my wife, Helene Keyssar, and I went to Peking for two months. The quantity and complexity of the material we discovered made clear that writing a book about Anna Louise would take both our best talents, and we agreed to become co-authors.

—Tracy B. Strong

Acknowledgments

Anna Louise Strong's published writings include over thirty books and innumerable articles. We estimate that for over sixty years she published an article a week. In addition, her letters and diaries from childhood on were saved. She was touched and awed to discover after her father's death that he had carefully collected every piece she published and every public reference to her he could find. She herself preserved not only copies of manuscripts, publications, and incoming letters but carbons of even the most trivial letters she sent out.

In her journalism, one finds an exemplary figure whose trail is better traced than is her character. A similar persona, still more model than substance, appears in her autobiography, *I Change Worlds*, which narrates the first forty-nine years of her life. Her early poetry, her one published play, *The King's Palace*, and her novel, *Wild River*, give a key to her emotions. Still another dimension is revealed in her unpublished manuscripts, which include interviews with such major historical figures as Mao Tse-tung, fragments of a second volume of autobiography, and what she called "explosions," her self-censored assaults on the governments she publicized. Finally, it is in her extensive and continuing correspondence with hundreds of people that one finds her private self most fully revealed.

Of the two major Anna Louise Strong collections, the one in the Suzzallo Library at the University of Washington in Seattle contains most of her files until 1931, some materials from the thirties, forties and fifties, and an extensive file of her field notebooks and manuscripts from her sojourn in China in 1946 and 1947. The other main collection of her work is in the Peking Library in China and contains her papers from 1958 until her death. There are over thirty cartons in Seattle and twenty in China. There also are, or were, eight file drawers of material in the Soviet Union. We were unable to discover if these still exist, let alone gain access to them.

We also consulted other library archives, notably the Philip Jaffe archives at Emory University, the Social Welfare Archives at the University of Minnesota, the Peace Collection at Swarthmore College, the Raymond Robins archives at the State Historical Society of Wisconsin, the Roger Baldwin archives in the Seeley Mudd Library at Princeton University, the American Board of Missions archives at Houghton Library in Harvard University, and the archives of her father and brother, both in the University of Washington. A number of her friends and relatives in this country gave us access to their private files.

The intelligence services of the United States spent an enormous amount of time keeping track of Anna Louise Strong. Her mail was regularly intercepted and copied, her telephones tapped, her movements followed. Through the Freedom of Information Act we obtained almost 6,000 pages from the FBI files, another 500 from other government agencies, 1,000 from the Federal Communications Commission, and about 100 from the Bureau of Investigation, the predecessor to the FBI. Despite the active presence of the government censor, these files allowed us to fill in many gaps.

Crucial to our endeavor were our interviews with those who knew her, worked with her, fought with her and loved her. In this country a loose network of older American radicals, many of them now forgotten, gave generously of their time and memories. We talked with over fifty individuals in the United States and corresponded with as many more. The second largest number of her friends is in the People's Republic of China. During our 1980 visit we interviewed all those still alive who had known her. Some of the more than thirty people with whom we spoke in China had known her as far back as her first visit to Canton in 1925. Sources for specific information and a list of all those interviewed appear at the end of this book. Our gratitude for this assistance is immeasurable.

Her surviving relatives provided information that only they could know. Without them, we might never have seen how much Anna Louise remained the child of her genealogy, despite her efforts to escape it.

To our children and friends who have patiently endured our absence and Anna Louise's looming presence, we offer our thanks beyond words. Carol Axel and Richard Numeroff took care of our children while we went to China. Jane Geddes made it possible for us to finish this book in less than a lifetime.

To the Committee on Research at the University of California at San Diego, the Faculty Research Fund of Amherst College, the Faculty Research Fund of Smith College, the East Asian Research Center of the University of Pittsburgh, and the American Philosophical Association we are indebted for financial assistance that supported our work.

We have been helped by the staffs of a number of excellent libraries: the Suzzallo Library at the University of Washington, the Peking Library, the University of Minnesota Library, Emory University Library, the Seeley Mudd Library, and Swarthmore Library. We would like to thank Richard Berner and Karyl Wynn in Washington, Li Xun-da at the Peking Library, and Dorothy Green at the Sophia Smith Collection of Smith College for particular help.

Our trip in China would not have been the success it was without the ability and intelligence of Guo Ze Pei, Zhang Xue Ling, and the staff and officers of the Chinese People's Association for the Friendship with Foreign Nations.

In this country, Jeremy Paltiel provided important help and information about China and the U.S.S.R.; the staff of the political science and communications departments of the University of California at San Diego, especially Monica Paskvan, gave more than asked.

Most especially, Robbins Strong and Tracy Strong, Jr., provided readings and help without which we would never have been able to start or complete this work.

A biography of Anna Louise Strong cannot help but tempt its authors to analyze the history of the twentieth century. In writing this book, one of our most difficult tasks was to subordinate our own voices to that of Anna Louise. Our editor, Anne Freedgood, taught us to write Anna Louise's story. She also taught us more about the act of writing than we ever imagined we had to learn. We offer her both gratitude and admiration.

Anna Louise said of her 1935 autobiography that it had done more for her than it might ever do for any of her readers. The same might be said of this book for its authors.

Tracy B. Strong
Helene Keyssar
Encinitas, California

Contents

RIGHT IN HER SOUL

1

Lao Tai-tai

There is one thing I fear—
  Not death, nor sharp disease,
Nor loss of friends I hold most dear,
  Nor pain, nor want—not these.

But the life of which men say:
  "The world has given him bread;
And what gives he to the world as pay
  For the crust on which he fed?"

I would pour out strength, and then
  When I have no strength to give,
No use, no share in the lives of men
  Who toil, and fight, and live—

Then let the end come fast,
  Whatever my past success;
That I may not cumber the ground at last,
  Nor linger in uselessness.

       —Anna Louise Strong,
       "The Toiler's Fear," 1906

Hurrah for a ride as fast
As my new sled will go,
Hurrah for the end at last
The plunge in the soft white snow.

       —Anna Louise Strong,
       "Hurrah for Santa Claus," 1896

On Saturday, March 28, 1970, an eighty-four-year-old American woman lay in a private room in the north wing of the Fan Di hospital in central Peking. Except for a blue sweater, carefully folded on a small table near the patient's bed, there was no color in the room. The patient herself was as pale as the walls and sheets. Westerners who visited her were suddenly reminded that, for the Chinese, white was the color of death.

Only her firm, broad jaw seemed to defy her surroundings. She had always hated dependency, and even here she reserved her strength to assert herself. Shortly after her admission to the hospital earlier that week, the doctors had inserted an intravenous tube in her arm to provide the nourishment and medication she was refusing at home. An hour later she had yanked it out, refusing to be "tied down." For over seventy years, she had come and gone as she pleased, but for some time now she had been afraid that her life might end in a room like this, surrounded mostly by people whose language she had never learned to speak. "At least I want to be able to ask for a glass of water," she had written the previous November to her great-nephew in the United States. So she had begun to make plans to return to the country that had always remained hers. In the hospital she spoke repeatedly of the coming journey, but the prospect of seeking permission from the U.S. Department of State was anathema to her; at least IV bottles and whispered words she did not understand were confrontable enemies.

And here she was well treated. In Peking, in the midst of the Cultural Revolution, she was surrounded by little luxuries and gestures of kindness such as she had not experienced since she was a child. She had returned to Peking at the age of seventy-two because, she had written to friends at the time, China stood at the forefront of world revolution. But she also knew how well the Chinese treated an old and honored friend. There were always thermoses of cold water and warm tea for her, a specially constructed bed to ease the pain in her legs and the right friend brought to her at the right moment to assuage her loneliness.

Here she was not only respected but admired. China was one of the few countries that still treated her as a special person; she did not need to remind the Chinese leaders that she had been first in more places and at more world-shaking events than anyone could remember. At home, in the United States, she would be simply Anna Louise Strong, a burdensome, often ill-tempered old lady, a dimly remembered radical. In Peking she had Chinese names, names of honor and respect. Long ago, in Chungking in 1940, a professor friend had given her a Chinese name to mark the occasion of her third visit to China. "Anna Louise Strong," he had said, "the giving of a name is very important in China; it reflects and shapes who you are. We will call you Shih Teh-lang, 'especially brilliant about history.'" She had been Shih Teh-lang for twenty-five years until during the 1960s a new appellation had gradually taken its place. In deference to her age, and always with a tone of affection, the Chinese now called her by the name once used for a mandarin's wife, Lao Tai-tai, the "honored old one."

Her friends, foreign and Chinese, had been particularly careful during the week she had been in the hospital to pay her the kind of attention they knew she enjoyed. Early that morning Kuo Mo-jo, the distinguished poet and calligrapher, now the president of the Academy of Sciences, had paid a call. The nurses quickly spread the news among the hospital staff and noted that Lao Tai-tai had glowed. A little later Yang Tzao, an agronomist at Red Flag Commune outside Peking, and his wife, Joan Hinton, arrived. Anna Louise had known Yang Tzao in Yenan when he still had his Western name, Sid Engst. He looked like the midwestern farmers she had known as a child, and sometimes he reminded her of her Soviet husband, Joel, who had been a deputy minister of agriculture in Russia during the last years of his life. The "honored old one" did not say much to her visitors. She had trouble swallowing and speaking. Yet her doctors' orders to avoid speech chafed her. She was not about to let the "dictatorship of the doctors" replace that of the proletariat, she informed her old friend Dr. George Ma when he cautioned her against too much talk.

As afternoon drew on, Anna Louise began to watch the door, impatient for the arrival of more friends. She saw the door open, and her face glowed with pleasure as she recognized her visitor. The man before her had grown increasingly handsome with each of his seventy-two years. His dark full brows framed lustrous eyes, and the late-afternoon shadow (for which he was often teased) gave further dimension to his broad, mobile face. His Communist party name, Small Mountain, suited him well.

Premier Chou En-lai stood for a moment in the doorway, trying to conceal his distress and surprise. The slight figure in the bed bore little resemblance to the imposing woman he had known, entertained, scolded and worked with for over thirty years. When he had last seen her, the previous October on National Day, her movements had been labored, but her will was unshaken. He recalled that she had written him an irate letter the previous December, insisting that one of her grandnephews be allowed to enter China despite the ban on Americans during the Cultural Revolution; he made a mental note to grant the young man permission immediately.

Chou En-lai had just learned of Anna Louise's refusal to eat or to take medication. Before going to her room, he had consulted with the director of the hospital and with her own physician, who was vice-chairman of the Department of Medicine. The doctors had somewhat nervously informed him that she was a "difficult patient"; for a long time she had resisted coming to the hospital at all. She had acquiesced only after her physicians had told her that her weight loss was becoming serious enough to require treatment. She had an infection in her lung and a failing heart. Any attempt to swallow set off fits of violent coughing; the doctors were not sure why. Meals took over an hour, and Anna Louise consumed very little. They had, the director explained carefully, tried to persuade her of the need for food and medication, but she rejected them violently. They had not wished to assault her dignity by forcing upon her treatment she so adamantly opposed. The premier was openly incensed. He told the doctors that he should have been informed long ago and that he would now speak to her himself.

He went to the bed and took Anna Louise's hand. Mao Tse-tung's dense and earthy wit, grounded in peasant tales and the Chinese classics, had often left her puzzled and unsure, but Chou En-lai's charm had never failed to dispel her gloom or impatience. In those strange and exalted days in Yenan in 1946 and 1947, she had sought Chou out like a schoolgirl pursuing a movie star. She had been sixty-one when she had played bridge with him in Yenan, but she had flirted with him over her cards with the transparency of a nineteen-year-old.

Now, in the hospital, he spoke a few words of greeting and then, in his sternest voice, said, "Anna Louise, I command you to eat. And furthermore, I order you to take medication, and to do exactly as the doctors tell you." Anna Louise looked at him and nodded. "I will try," she whispered. His face softened, and he said again to her what he had said in Yenan twenty-three years earlier: "You have important things to do for us and for the rest of the world." He left the room.

In the corridor he was met by the nurses and doctors. He ordered them to provide every possible treatment for Shih Teh-lang; she would now accept their ministrations. Then he went to Frank Coe, who had been waiting in an anteroom. Coe had come to China in 1957 to advise the Chinese on international finance. He had met Anna Louise the first week of her return to China in 1958, and from that time on he had been her most trusted advisor as well as, more recently, her designated executor. Chou wanted to know if Coe knew the whereabouts of Anna Louise's grandnephew, John Strong; could an urgent message reach him? Coe thought that John was somewhere in Southeast Asia. He would make every attempt to contact him. "Find him," the premier ordered, "and get him here immediately." Then he stopped to see the hospital director. "If there is any change in her condition, at any hour, day or night," he told him, "call me immediately."

After Chou's visit, Anna Louise seemed stronger than she had in days. She had work to do, she told the Coes, and she counted, as she had for many years, on Frank's help. Her readers in the United States and all over the world were awaiting her seventieth *Letter from China*, and there had already been too long a delay since the previous one. In the whisper that was all that remained of her voice, she urged Frank to tell her the most recent news so that she could begin to shape in her head the words for the next *Letter*, which would go out in four languages to 40,000 subscribers.

The next morning she was weak but in good spirits. Talk of the premier's visit was all over the hospital. Now that Anna Louise was receiving blood transfusions her condition was stable. During the day, many of the country's leaders came for brief visits, and as the light dimmed, a group of Anna Louise's close friends gathered down the hall from her room. Later none of them would recall sensing that she was about to die. Perhaps because it was Easter Sunday, perhaps because they knew that their presence comforted her, they kept a quiet vigil outside her room.

At about six-thirty Frank and Ruth Coe began their nightly walk to the hospital. Ruth had visited earlier in the day, but since they had been seeing Anna Louise each night after supper, they were afraid that a break in the pattern would confuse or trouble her. When they reached the hospital, they found everything in chaos. At 7:00 P.M., there had been a sudden change in Anna Louise's condition. With a startling burst of energy she had sat upright in bed, looked slowly and firmly about the room, and asked in a clear voice: "Is it possible?" Then she collapsed. Shortly afterwards her heart stopped beating. For the next hour the doctors applied heart massages, artificial respiration and injections.

In a room down the corridor, Anna Louise's friends waited. Across the city another friend waited as well. When his patient's heart stopped, Dr. Li went to the director of the hospital, Dr. Fang. Remembering his orders, Dr. Fang immediately telephoned Chou En-lai, who told the doctors to try every treatment possible. In the meantime, the premier said, he would be working in his office, but he would keep his telephone line open. Any further changes should be conveyed to him immediately over the open line.

At 9:30, the attending physicians took another electrocardiogram. The line on the graph was flat. They tried more massage, more injections. At 11:00 P.M., Chou En-lai finally accepted Dr. Fang's pronouncement that Anna Louise Strong was dead.

It is the Chinese custom for friends and relatives of the deceased to pay their last respects to the body immediately after death. Dr. Fang opened the door to Anna Louise's room. One by one her friends entered and filed past the bed. Despite the days of weakness and the years of increasing bad health, no one had really imagined her absence. More than once in her life she had changed worlds, as her autobiography attested, but with each change and each new decade she seemed to gather strength. From the early days of the labor movement in Seattle through the Soviet Revolution to the Spanish civil war, again and again to China, and repeatedly back to the United States, she had been a phoenix who derived new life from each defeat, disappointment, and success. It was oddly fitting, thought one of her friends, that so far from home, so removed from her Christian origins, Anna Louise had still managed to die on Easter Sunday.

In a long first-page obituary the next day, the *New York Times* identified Anna Louise Strong as "the American who spent most of her life extolling the virtues of Communism," and went on to say: "Generations of Americans, Europeans, Asians and Africans have read Miss Strong's firsthand, highly personal accounts of pro-Communist movements all over the world. In recent years, her descriptions of Mao Tse-tung swimming or dining, for example, offered China-watchers insights into the hidden, mysterious life of political Peking. This unusual woman . . . served a curious function in the usually secretive Communist world." The anonymous *Times* reporter seemed caught between admiration for Anna Louise's "fierce motivation that kept her active virtually until her death" and suspicion of that same devotion, which was described as "not so much intellectual as emotional." The *Times* also quoted O. Edmund Clubb, who had served as American consul general in China from 1947 to 1950: "She sold Communism to the world, and the Communists rightly loved her for it."

Clubb was only partially correct. Despite her thirty years of service to the U.S.S.R., there was no mention of Anna Louise's death in either *Pravda* or *Izvestia*. In China, however, it was an occasion for public mourning. Radio Peking broadcast the news throughout the day following her death; lengthy obituaries in the *People's Daily* and the English-language Hsinhua News Agency referred to her as "the noted American progressive writer" and included a summary of a memorial speech by Kuo Mo-jo that proclaimed: "Comrade Strong was a fine daughter of the American people and a genuine and devoted friend of the Chinese people. She sought progress all her life and knew well whom to love and whom to hate. . . . Her passing away is a loss not only to the American people but also to the people of China and other countries."

It was her relationship to China and not to America that most obituaries emphasized. Few failed to mention that she had had closer contacts with top Chinese leaders than almost any other foreigner and that many of these leaders attended her funeral. Mark Gayn, the Asian specialist on the *Toronto Star*, noted that "Miss Strong's name was familiar to hundreds of millions in China" because of the inclusion in the works of Mao Tse-tung of her 1946 interview in which Mao argued that "all imperialists are paper tigers." That interview had become "one of the keystones of Maoist doctrine," Gayn recalled, and Anna Louise had been given due credit for eliciting and publicizing the concept. On the streets of Peking, parents would point out Anna Louise to their children as "the Lao Tai-tai of the paper tiger interview," and mention of her name would elicit a glimmer of recognition in even the most remote regions of China.

Most American newspapers, with no such audience for their obituaries, took a stance similar to that of the *New York Times* and identified Anna Louise as a propagandist for world communism who "glorified" the Soviet Union and China. Even in Seattle, where her name had once been well-known, the *Seattle Times*, grouping her with John Reed and "Big Bill" Haywood as "certified saints in Red mythology," lamented in an editorial "what a woman of her brilliance, drive and public spirit might have accomplished for her native America or her city of Seattle had she not become an early and lifelong convert to the Communist religion."

It was not until several weeks after her death that her supporters began to be heard. William Hinton, who had worked in rural China after the revolution, began his memorial in the *National Guardian* with a protest against the *New York Times* for calling Anna Louise "an ardent apologist": "Would that we had 10,000 'apologists' who could see the world as clearly as she saw it and popularize their knowledge as effectively." After an eloquent summary of Anna Louise's "commitment to the workers and peasants, the oppressed and exploited people of the world," Hinton asked, "What other American, what other citizen of the world, has surpassed Anna Louise Strong in clarity of vision and enduring commitment?"

There was also a memorial service at the First Unitarian Church in Los Angeles, the church that had given her shelter and companionship during her desperately lonely times in the 1950s. Pastor Stephen Fritchman's text was taken from the thirty-fourth chapter of Ezekiel: "I will make a covenant of peace with them; I will break their yoke and liberate them from their oppressors." Barbara Nestor, one of the charter members of the American Communist party, matched Fritchman's text with Anatole France's epitaph for Émile Zola: "Envy him his destiny and heart, which made his lot that of the greatest—he was a moment in history." LaRue McCormick, Anna Louise's friend from the fifties, recalled Thoreau's words: "For every thousand who hacked away at the branches of evil, there was one who hacked at the roots." Anna Louise, she asserted, "was one of those people who hacked at the roots. I think this is why we loved her so much."

Speaking for the Black Panther party, Ray Masia Hewitt said, "We see a very real need that in the future, when tribute is paid to Anna Louise Strong, more and more people, especially younger people who are not as aware as they think, who are not as aware as they are vociferous, come to see what the woman's life was about and her concern for people both here in America and abroad." He urged all people, "the New Left and the Old Left, the radicals and the liberals, . . . to use Anna Louise Strong as a standard."

In all the obituaries and memorials, however, there were few attempts to examine the pain that made Anna Louise not just a standard but a rich and instructive human being. As her friend Betty Rottger said at the Unitarian service, "She knew herself better than most people realized. She knew what she had given up in order to do the job she had set herself. She once said to me that she would dearly love to have one of our puppies, but she had observed that dogs took on the characteristics of their masters, and she would never want to live with a dog like herself."

Anna Louise's endeavors, as Lincoln Steffens once wrote to her, were both lonely and exemplary: "To make and cross a bridge from one age to another is something that was never before done in any other transition in history." Anna Louise never doubted the righteousness of her path, but she also knew its challenge. While she traveled around the world for half a century with an ease that awed even her critics, her soul remained in America, where she could find neither shelter nor peace. Throughout her life she called to her native land to take up her journey. Like her pioneer forefathers, she was always in search of new frontiers: "Every map sent back helped those who followed," she wrote midway through her life. "I must mark down the steep bits and the morasses and the places where I have managed to get through."

2

Conspicuous Origins

Mamma was continually saying: "Into the valley of death plunged
the six hundred." That seems to be her favorite quotation, for
she is always saying it when we go down a mountain.

—Anna Louise to her diary, July 1896

Throughout her life Anna Louise Strong was haunted by her ancestors
and at the same time proud of her origins. Her parents' marriage had
united two families—the Tracys and the Strongs—who claimed ancestors
among the first settlers in the American colonies. Both families arrived
in New England in the 1630s and moved from place to place, founding
and leaving towns, always building, always determined to be their own
masters. Elder John Strong founded the town of Windsor, Connecticut,
and then, in 1660, was invited to Northampton, Massachusetts, where
he became a leading businessman and the ruling elder of the church. On
Anna Louise's mother's side, her heritage included such well-known colonial families as the Russells and the Lords. In her autobiography, *I
Change Worlds*, Anna Louise pays particular attention to her ancestor
John Russell, "who founded the town of Hadley, Massachusetts, and who
bragged in his old age of the years when he had hidden in his house the
two regicides, Goffe and Whalley, when the officers of England's king
were seeking them." Her family, she implies, had a long history of rebel-
lious gestures against illegitimate authority, but they had a longer one of
uprightness and virtue. They were frugal, careful in business as in life,
not averse to gaiety but always serious. Both sides of the family supported
institutions of higher learning: Elder John sent yearly contributions to
Harvard College, and Samuel Russell, son of John Russell, initiated the
first activities of Yale College in his own library. Both Strongs and Tracys
were leaders of their local churches; men from both families fought in the
War of Independence.

Her ancestors on both sides continued to be restless and in constant search of new frontiers. In 1793 her great-grandfather, John Stoughton Strong, left Connecticut for Marlboro, Vermont, where with his wife, Tamar, he became a prominent farmer and opened a successful business in potato whiskey and applejack. In 1813 they migrated again, this time to Ohio to found the town of Strongsville. The Tracys followed the Strongs westward a few decades later, and by the 1860s Anna Louise's grandfather Frederick Tracy had become a rich and successful senior partner in a wholesale grocery chain in Ohio. Prosperity enabled both families to provide their children with excellent educations; no distinction was made between sons and daughters in this regard.

It was at Oberlin College that Ruth Maria Tracy met Sydney Dix Strong in 1880. Sydney was in his senior year, Ruth Maria was a freshman. He was a slender man with delicate features and deep-set eyes that seemed to maintain a gentle yet quixotic expression; the elements that would later lead acquaintances to call him a "saint" were already present. A brilliant student, during his college years he had become an ardent advocate of Darwin's theory of evolution. Ruth Maria was even better at her studies than Sydney, especially in philosophy and political economy. She was a striking rather than a conventionally pretty woman, with dark hair pulled tautly away from an intense, mobile face, and a substantial frame. The two were instantly attracted to each other; they must also have been struck by the remarkable coincidences in their family histories. Sydney's own mother, Ruth Maria Dix, who had died when he was five years old, had the same given names as his future wife. Lyman Whitney Strong, Sydney's father, had been educated at Western Reserve College, and then, like Ruth Maria Tracy's father, had become a successful Ohio merchant.

By the end of their one shared year at Oberlin, the two had reached three decisions: they would marry; Ruth would first complete her Oberlin degree; Sydney would study for the ministry. On November 20, 1884, the wedding took place, and the bride and groom immediately departed for a world tour, which took them not only to Europe but also to Greece, Palestine and Egypt—all biblical places they wanted to know firsthand. The trip was financed by two thousand dollars that Sydney had just inherited, and his family was distressed by the impracticality of the expenditure.

Ruth Maria was six months pregnant when they returned from their trip and was not entirely happy to settle in a two-room wooden frame house in the tiny prairie town of Friend, Nebraska, where Sydney was quickly taken up by the duties of the ministry. Their first child was as impatient as her parents to embrace life. Anna Louise Strong was born a week earlier than had been expected, on November 24, 1885, thereby occasioning the first of the thousands of extraordinary letters she would receive in her lifetime. From Mansfield, on November 25, Ruth Maria's father, Frederick Tracy, wrote to his granddaughter:

My very dear Granddaughter,
While this is my very first letter to you, I regret that in writing it I must express some dissatisfaction at your strange conduct or at least your want of thoughtfulness.—
    You should know that your Grandma Tracy has been thinking of you a great deal these weeks that are past and finally notwithstanding she is quite an old lady, she has started upon a long journey of two days and nights in the cars, in order that she might be present to introduce you to your Mother and Father and the many friends in this world you will make, I trust, during the coming years. And now while she is flying over the prairies of the west as fast as a lightning train can take her, your Father informs me you have already made your introductory speech to them, without the formality of your Grand-mother's introduction—Now which you will allow me to say this was not just the proper thing to do, we will excuse you this time for your great considera-tion in coming a *girl* and *not* a *horrible boy*.—If you had been a boy, I am sure I do not know what I would have said, but as it is, I congratulate you on your arrival and that you have brought with you a good strong pair of lungs and whenever you feel uncomfortable or neglected you will use them and while Mama may think you very noisy and want you to keep more quiet, you need not pay any special attention to her request at least for the present but keep in mind for the coming few weeks it is your privilege to keep not only Papa-Mama-Grandma, but all the friends that come to see you busy caring for your little wants, for by and by the times will change and then you will necessarily keep quiet and do all you can for the comfort and pleasure of those who now do so much for you.
    With renewed congratulations on your safe arrival and trusting your life may be grand and that you may ever be as great a comfort to your Papa and Mama as they have been to theirs, I am most lovingly,
                                                    Your Grandpa
                                                            Tracy

Grandpa Tracy's letter is an eerily prophetic document. Anna Louise would receive countless other letters over the years remarking on her "strange conduct," chastizing her for a "want of thoughtfulness" and not-ing her lack of propriety. Her "great consideration in coming a girl and not a horrible boy" seems to have marked her permanently, but created more conflict than her grandfather foresaw. She would eventually articu-late this at the end of *I Change Worlds:*

I had been trained as a woman to "want to be wanted." I had been trained
by one professor after another to "allow myself to be stirred." I had been
trained by my religion to wait adoringly for a will that was "higher." Even as
a child, I had been trained to be "good"—interesting yet never obtrusive—
in the hope that everybody would like me. To be liked, desired, wanted by
parents, playmates, sororities, men, editors, had been the goal of life. To
desire, to want—food, sex or an evening's conversation—had been improper.
I had been trained to expect a god and then serve him. And what a good
little slave they had made of me!

Actually, there is little evidence that Anna Louise was trained in pas-
sivity. The earliest family anecdote of her childhood, a story she relates
in her autobiography, is a tale of conquest and indomitable spirit. She was
less than a year and a half old when a sudden cyclone lifted her from the
front yard into the air, like Dorothy in *The Wizard of Oz*, and deposited
her in a cow pasture some distance away. As Anna Louise later reported
the incident, "When they found me I was somewhat worried by the cows
but not at all by the cyclone; clearly I continued the pioneer tradition and
found the storms of nature friendlier than the whims of living creatures."

As a young girl, Anna Louise was precocious, daring, outspoken and
tactless. If family lore is correct, she not only talked well at an exceptionally early age but paid keen attention to language. When her family
moved to Mount Vernon, Ohio, in 1887, she "corrected the grammar of
a woman on the train, saying: 'My mother says you mustn't say *ain't*.' "
Since Anna Louise's brother, Tracy, was born in Mount Vernon on August
6, 1887, she could not have been more than twenty months old at the
time. In 1961, at the age of seventy-five, she recalled the incident in a
letter to her friend Helen Tompkins and reflected that it showed that
"even then I was bent on being unpopular."

In *I Change Worlds* Anna Louise attributes her fearlessness, her naive
optimism and her loneliness to the teachings and exemplary lives of her
parents. She describes her father as "the only man I ever knew who
almost always follows the ethics of Jesus; he can die for a faith but cannot
renounce an ideal." Her descriptions of her mother are even more idyllic;
she was not only "very beautiful and able," but was a "comrade to her
husband," an "educator to her children," and a social worker who accomplished all these duties "graciously and well." "From neither of my parents did I ever hear a harsh or unjust word; if they blamed or punished,
it was only after careful inquiry showed me the reason for my punish-
ment." Yet in the letter to Helen Tompkins written twenty-six years after

I Change Worlds, Anna Louise began to admit that something was askew in her perfectly serene and rational upbringing:

> I am quite aware that sometime in quite early childhood I became convinced that my best bet was to be clever, or shall one put it, that I could get attention by my brains, if in no pleasanter way. . . . Whether this was because siblings came along who were cuter, or because my father had the same unconscious sex feelings for me that I noted later when mother died, I could probably not unearth, as you note, without analysis, for which it is rather late.

Anna Louise may have thought her brother and sister were more attractive than she, but photographs do not confirm this. On the contrary, she seems to have been strikingly beautiful as a child. She inherited her father's wide-set almond-shaped blue eyes, high cheekbones and sensuous mouth. Her younger sister, Ruth, more distinctly resembled their mother, and since Anna Louise perceived her mother as a great beauty, she may have envied her sister's physical inheritance. But nothing in the childhood photographs suggests that Ruth was the obvious beauty of the family. If any of the children could have made such a claim it would have been Anna Louise herself.

She was not an ordinary child. She wrote Latin words as early as English ones. By the age of four she was reading and writing well, and by six she was writing verse. Anna Louise attributed much of this early development to her mother's attention to her education. She recalled to Helen Tompkins that "Mother read me to sleep with Scott's *Lady of the Lake* when I could understand only the rhythm and a few of the more sonorous words." And while her father began to take her to lectures and church Latin classes by the time she was six, it was the instruction in star constellations and the study circle her mother organized during her preschool years that Anna Louise emphasizes in her autobiography. Her younger siblings, Tracy and Ruth, were gradually admitted into the study circle, and mealtimes became occasions for family vocabulary lessons, but neither of the younger children received the kind of intense academic instruction during early childhood given to Anna Louise. At an early age Ruth took on domestic chores and developed skills with her hands that had never interested Anna Louise; it was Tracy and Ruth who milked the family cow. By the time she entered school, Anna Louise had taken over much of the responsibility of instructing the younger children. Well into her adolescence, she continued to lead her brother through his studies and to tease him, somewhat enviously, for his preference for mischief and play over serious learning.

In 1891, shortly before Anna Louise's sixth birthday, the family moved from Mount Vernon to Cincinnati. With a modest increase in income from Sydney's new ministry and assistance from Ruth Maria's relatives, they were now more comfortable financially. Ruth Maria employed a woman to wash the family clothes, and she and Sydney bought a house with an authentic parlor and a bedroom for each of the children.

Anna Louise was sent to the nearby public school. In *I Change Worlds* she writes that she "still remembers the bewildered shock when I met the harshness of the public school in Cincinnati, where a teacher jerked my ear and shook me violently for the crime of having on my own initiative filled my inkwell when it was empty." But her memory is a bit too innocent. Her parents later recalled that she was a problem child throughout her early schooling, and that in both Cincinnati and Oak Park, where the family moved when Anna Louise was ten, she was a source of difficulty to her teachers and schoolmates. Her skills in reading and writing were so far ahead of her classmates' that she was bored, restless and unwilling to accept the unhesitating discipline then customary in such schools. Used to impressing others with her brains, she tended to correct her instructor and to speak out of turn. After months of tension, her mother resumed teaching her at home. Within the year, however, Ruth Maria had persuaded the best private school in Cincinnati to admit Anna Louise as a scholarship student.

Academically the new school was a success. Anna Louise completed all eight grades of elementary school before she was eleven. But she did not mature as quickly in her social behavior and continued to have difficulty making friends. As an adult, she carried with her the memory of a remark made to her mother by the headmistress: "Your daughter is a real 'love-child'; she has evidently always known kindness. She always expects people to like her and assumes that they have kind motives. Even when girls are unkind she invents better excuses for them than they can invent themselves." Anna Louise later commented that while she and her mother considered the words a compliment, they should perhaps have been taken as a warning against the danger of expecting only kindness in a world that contained so much evil. The headmistress may also have been warning them of the danger in Anna Louise's refusal to acknowledge her tendency to antagonize others her own age.

Ruth Maria began during the years in Cincinnati to develop her own work of organizing women's clubs intended to heighten women's aspirations and to improve their conditions as well as to cleanse urban life of alcohol, prostitution, political corruption and other "social diseases." She was determined, according to Anna Louise's memories, to make her oldest daughter equally independent. By the age of seven Anna Louise was making frequent shopping excursions on her own to downtown Cincinnati; when she was eight, her mother sent her alone by train to visit her grandparents in Mansfield, Ohio.

The journey to Mansfield was a marvelous adventure for Anna Louise and occasioned her first letter to her parents, which she typed on her grandfather's machine. After an apology for not writing immediately upon her arrival, she describes her activities so as to confirm that she is being as responsible as her parents might wish. Her delight in her new activities is very much that of an eight-year-old girl, but her warning to her mother not to "get as tired as she had been when they were packing" has an odd tone of an enforced new maturity.

A similar precocity appears in the poetry that Anna Louise wrote during the same period. "Niagara Falls," dated August 4, 1894, is a narrative account, in six heavily rhymed stanzas of four lines each, of a trip she took with her family. It manages both to capture an image of a place and to sustain the presence of the speaker. The poem emphasizes the pleasure in danger that her mother encouraged in Anna Louise throughout her childhood. This attempt was followed by numerous rhymes written during her eighth and ninth years, most of which were composed either to alleviate boredom or as a gift to a relative. By the time she was ten, she was beginning to experiment with form and to use her poems to instruct the reader. "Some More, Some Less," written in January 1896 for family worship, foreshadows the political poetry she would one day write:

> "The people murmur," said Moses one day,
> For fear that some should fall by the way;
> "Tonight from heaven will I rain bread
> Enough for each," the Lord then said.
> Some more, some less.
>
> They did not measure the manna that fell,
> In order that each might perfectly tell
> If he had as much as his neighbor had:
> Oh, no! that might have made some feel sad.
> Some more, some less.
>
> This is the way God's mercies fall—
> Some more, some less, but some to all.

None should wish to have more than his friend
Each has enough to last to the end.
Some more, some less.

It is a short leap from the last lines of this to the creed Anna Louise would embrace as an adult, "From each according to his ability, to each according to his need." She learned the essence of such teachings from her father. In his progressive Christian idealism, Sydney was turning his attention increasingly to the political issues around him.

In July 1896 the Tracys took Ruth Maria and Anna Louise on another of their extensive vacations. Sydney had gone to Europe to work and study, leaving the family behind because of both financial anxieties and Ruth Maria's desire for a more relaxing time than her husband had in mind. From their letters, it appears that the couple had also decided that they needed a period apart from each other. Ruth Maria gladly accepted when her parents offered her an excursion and arranged for the younger children to spend the next few months with nearby friends.

After a train ride from Cincinnati to Detroit, the party took the steamer *Alberta* through the Great Lakes, then a train west to Banff and Lake Louise. Anna Louise began a diary on July 11, the first day out of port, and wrote in it faithfully throughout the next two months of travel. It was usual for young people, especially females, to keep diaries, and her mother encouraged the practice. What is unusual is that the tone and contents of Anna Louise's diary consistently reflect a conception of an audience other than herself. The stories that she collected as the family continued from Banff to Vancouver, Vancouver to Portland, then on to San Francisco and Hawaii, were the beginning of her attempt to preserve and bring back experiences for others not as fortunate as she.

In the diary Anna Louise also began to construct a self-portrait that has notable resemblances to the persona of her adult writings. At Tacoma, Washington, she suddenly found herself in a context that made her uncomfortable. The family had arrived at half past eight, too late for dinner at the hotel where they were to spend the night. In search of an evening meal, Anna Louise related, "We were directed by a man on the street to the 'people's restaurant.' When we were inside we found that it was a place for workingmen, while half the tables were occupied by Chinese and Negroes. There could be no backing out and we sat down to the table which we did not like though we had the place of honor." It is unclear whether the notion of a "people's restaurant" is Anna Louise's own or that of the man on the street; what is apparent is her unease in this working-class context. Yet she also understood and accepted the impossibility of leaving the restaurant. She did not understand, nor did she need to, whether the principle derived from Christian ethics or political consciousness; in her family the two were inseparable.

Ruth Maria heard little from Sydney during the trip. Her letters to him express both passionate longing for his presence and concern about the emotional distance that had come between them. Her dreams, she wrote to Sydney, "have not been happy ones, and I always wake up with the thought that I am in the way at home and that things go smoother when I am not there. I am afraid my coming home this time is not going to be any happier than previous days." The fault, she asserted in numerous letters, was unquestionably with her. Everyone she encountered spoke of her husband's "perfect" character and she agreed: "It seems to me, darling, if I could only be the wife you ought to have that you would be the most useful man I know of. I never have known a man with more character, and more unselfish or more noble and free from all little narrow thoughts. But, somehow, the distance between us seems to grow wider and wider and I seem an outsider. We don't seem one as we once did."

Ruth Maria's greatest consolation, she told her husband, was Anna Louise, who had been "behaving like an angel" and impressing her mother anew with her brightness. During the two months of the vacation, Anna Louise wrote at least twenty poems; her mother applauded the work by typing up those she considered best along with portions of the diary. Ruth Maria also encouraged Anna Louise's growing political awareness. "She never sees a company of men talking politics," she wrote Sydney, "that she doesn't join them and is as interested as you ever saw her over a fairy book." On one occasion Anna Louise became involved in a debate on the silver question with four men, one of whom presented a fierce argument for free silver. A vote was called, but the "silver man" protested that the gold side had not yet made its arguments. "No," said Anna Louise. "It needs none. It is self-evident." She was sufficiently sophisticated about the issues that some months later, on the eve of the 1896 presidential election, she composed an allegory for Ruth's bedtime story about the "knights" McKinley and Bryan and the "Princess Columbia" who had been imprisoned for four years by the giant "Hard Times."

While Anna Louise, her mother and her grandparents continued on to Hawaii, Sydney returned to Ohio to prepare for another move. To Ruth Maria's distress, he had accepted a new parish in Oak Park, Illinois, a town just outside of Chicago. The position offered considerably more money, and Sydney was restless. Ruth Maria had written her husband that she strongly preferred to remain in Cincinnati, where she had been happier than anywhere in her life; she wanted Sydney to approach the church elders in Cincinnati for a salary raise, but he ignored her urgings. When Anna Louise and her mother arrived home, they were immediately immersed in moving the household to Oak Park. Two weeks before her eleventh birthday, in the fall of 1896, Anna Louise entered Oak Park High School, from which she would graduate four years later.

At school Anna Louise studied Latin and Greek, chemistry and algebra; at home her training continued, not just in the Christian ethics so important to her parents but also in the relation of these to the society in which she lived. Her father's sermons repeatedly emphasized the worldliness of the Christian message, not at the expense of Christ's divinity but always in the sense that the teachings of the Gospel were to be lived in everyday life. After the move to Oak Park, Ruth Maria's involvement in the organization of socially conscious women's societies increased and frequently took her to the mining towns of southern Illinois. Anna Louise remembered later that her mother would return depressed and laden with lessons for her daughter: "Some people are hard and greedy and grab much more than their share; they refuse to hear the rights of others. Many people suffer because of them, yet nobody punishes them. You must never, never grab more than your share."

Ruth Maria was determined that her oldest daughter know and acknowledge the people who had little and suffered unjustly. Just as she had sent her at age seven into the downtown world of Cincinnati, so, soon after the family moved to Oak Park, she began sending her to Chicago on various tasks. By the time Anna Louise was twelve, she was conducting sewing classes, arranged by her mother, in settlement houses on Chicago's West Side. Although Anna Louise claims in her autobiography that as a child she was insulated in a middle-class world, her parents, especially her mother, took care to expose her to a variety of cultures and of economic and class situations.

For many of the Strongs' neighbors in Oak Park, the town was a welcome escape from the invasion of Chicago by black families from the South. Such an attitude was abhorrent to Ruth Maria, whose Oberlin education had left her with a deep commitment to the achievement of equality for blacks. Anna Louise never forgot her mother's anger at a fleeting glimpse of her daughter's innocent prejudice. Ruth Maria had run into a classmate from Oberlin, a black woman named Molly Church, on the street, and had embraced her; Anna Louise was introduced and pulled away with obvious discomfort. "As soon as the woman left, my mother reproved me, saying that if I had any feeling against people on account of the color of their skin, these were bad feelings which I must at once overcome."

Ruth Maria also taught her daughter to sew and embroider and attempted to teach her to cook, though she soon gave this up as hopeless. Since music and singing were an important part of the Strongs' daily lives, Anna Louise was taught to play the piano, and by the time she was twelve she had begun to compose simple songs. Nor were the ordinary desires of childhood ignored. If anything, Anna Louise, Tracy and Ruth were overindulged. The Christmas Anna Louise was eleven, she wrote four jingles as her present to her grandmother. The image of Christmas in the Strong household conveyed by these verses is one of tables overflowing with candy, cake and peanuts, of a Santa Claus with lots of presents, and of grandparents, aunts, uncles and cousins gathered for fun and celebration. The puppy the children had been requesting appeared that Christmas, as did the "fast sled" that Anna Louise had been coveting.

The children were also encouraged to enjoy the pleasures of the outdoor world. They played football and basketball, hiked and swam, and their attention was drawn to the fragrance of flowers, the subtle changes in a winter sky, the colors of a sunset. Most of Anna Louise's poems written during her eleventh and twelfth years are lyrical odes to the natural beauty around her. But in the spring of her eleventh year, the fact of her ultimate separateness from nature first made her aware of her loneliness in the world. She wrote of herself:

> She threw herself around the lilac bush, but the lilac bush remained aloof, tantalizingly beautiful and never to be reached. She threw herself on the ground and clutched the roots, digging her face into the soft grass of spring. There was comfort in the hardness of the earth, but the essential desolation remained. The ecstasy of the day was like a pang from which a naked new baby is born. For the first time she knew herself an individual creature, cut off from the world of which she had been a part. She wanted painfully to get back.

In the summer of 1897 Anna Louise had her first experience abroad. On the Fourth of July the family departed for England. The passage through customs fascinated Anna Louise, as did the contrasts between life in England and life in the United States. In an essay later published in a church youth magazine, she detailed the "pulsing and jamming" as passengers waited to debark in Liverpool. She was impressed by the careful examination of each party's baggage. Her account of the journey to England and Scotland was that of a student who had carefully attended to a good lesson; the trip itself appears to have been at least in part planned for the instruction of the children. Once outside London, the children were taken bicycling in the Lake Country and brought to the cathedral in which Sir Walter Scott was married. The journey ended in Edinburgh, where they saw the original *Waverley*, the first copy of the Bible in the English language and "several other things." Anna Louise appears to have been somewhat bored by the whole venture. She concludes her published essay on a note of relief at the return home: "I felt as though, after all, America is the best place to live, though a trip to foreign lands is very inviting."

In the fall of 1897 Anna Louise started to write occasionally in French and published a poem in the high school magazine. Later in the year Ruth Maria expressed dissatisfaction with Anna Louise's essays for English class. When Anna Louise wrote up an interview for an assignment, her mother told her to redo it; a well-written interview, her mother declared, should begin with a physical description of the person and the context of the interview; then the reader would have a vivid image. On another occasion that year, Ruth Maria reprimanded her daughter for acquiring insufficient information from a stranger who had appeared at the door. "When someone comes to the door," Anna Louise was told, "one must always ask who? what? when? and why?" Ruth Maria was rarely unreservedly pleased with her daughter's performance. As Anna Louise moved into adolescence, she was being instructed not only in the skills of journalism, as she later noted, but in the inseparability of intimacy, criticism and personal attention.

The more immediate results showed in the extensive diary that she kept during the family's stay in France and Switzerland in the summer and fall of 1898. Ruth Maria and the children departed in June, leaving Sydney behind to join them at the end of July. A main purpose of the trip was to improve the children's French; accordingly, after they had found a large, cheap flat in Lausanne, a neighbor, Mme. Raymond, was employed as tutor. Not a moment was lost. In addition to studying French, the Strongs went swimming and hiking, visited sites of interest, attended local festivals and generally explored every inch of the neighboring terrain. Ruth Maria also did considerable maneuvering to get Anna Louise admitted to a summer school for teachers at the Université de Lausanne. Anna Louise was taken aback by her mother's insistence. For the first time there is a note of hesitation in her journal about the propriety of her mother's aggressively demanding behavior. She observed that one of the university students, a German schoolteacher, was "thoroughly indignant at the brass of Americans," and mused that "this is the first time that Mama has wanted me to appear older than I am. She is afraid that I will not get in if I don't."

Ruth Maria pushed hard and thirteen-year-old Anna Louise was admitted. She was soon able to understand passing conversations in French, and she proudly recalled following a Sunday sermon. She profited doubly because the pastor confirmed her own belief that "there is much falseness in common politeness." Others might have wished that she had not understood so well.

Many of Anna Louise's observations in her diary during this period reveal a growing sexual awareness that both disturbed her and separated her from her siblings. She was struck by the "queer bathing suits" of the Swiss. The tops of women's suits were as "low as an extremely fashionable ball dress," and the bloomers were "very tight." The men's suits were even more provocative: they "would almost go on the blade of a knife and leave room for something else." It was because of the revealing nature of bathing suits, she concluded, that men and women were not allowed to bathe together. Anna Louise did not explain, at this point, how she knew what Swiss men wore bathing, but a few paragraphs later she returned to the subject of men's clothing in general: "The men don't look nearly as nice as in America. They are dirty and unkempt, with their crooked slouch hats and their tangled beards." Because of this, she decided that Switzerland was "very nice to stay in for a while," but she would not like to live there.

While Swiss men caused Anna Louise one kind of half-conscious irritation, her sister was becoming a clearer source of tension. The diary is replete with indications of annoyance at Ruth. When the family went hiking, Ruth held them back; on a mountain climb, "Ruth had to be helped down all the way"; each time Anna Louise took Ruth to the local pool to teach her to swim, Ruth became more afraid and finally was banned from the pool after losing her head and yelling. Anna Louise's description of Ruth's birthday party on July 24 marks another gesture of separation. It was a party for the "little girls." Anna Louise no longer saw herself as a little girl; she was, after all, passing for a teacher at the university.

With Papa, however, she was still happy to be a child, and she anxiously awaited his arrival. But Papa, to her surprise, now became dizzy on difficult climbs and preferred quiet afternoons of reading or excursions to the castle at Chillon. By early October, when the family departed for

Paris, Anna Louise was eager for the excitement of a city. She was not pleased, once they arrived in Paris, to be placed in still another school and tutored, in addition, in Latin and Greek. She complained repeatedly in the diary that the Paris school was boring and wasteful, and she finally managed to escape by acquiring a series of bad colds that kept her bedridden for over a week before the family left for New York.

In December she began her senior year of high school, and in order to prepare herself for college and satisfy her own yearnings to live "a thousand lives" she took on much more than the usual academic load. She found it stupid to accept at thirteen the limited fate of being "just one person." She wanted to be "a North Pole explorer, and an airman, and a great writer, and a mother of ten—one child wasn't worth the time." She managed over the years to accomplish only one of those lives, but in her senior year she succeeded remarkably well in all her academic undertakings, including the addition of German to her Latin, Greek and French. Her favorite course was English, taught by a Miss Farrell, the first of a series of woman teachers whom Anna Louise would idolize. Miss Farrell's slightest gesture of praise inspired Anna Louise for days; Miss Farrell's gestures of affection toward others drew pangs of envy. The book that most impressed Anna Louise that year was Edward Bellamy's *Looking Backward*, with its "economic basis in publicly owned wealth and equal division of goods."

At seventeen and eighteen her classmates were obsessed with fantasies of romance and sexuality; barely fifteen when she graduated, Anna Louise had not yet begun to sort out the attractions and repulsions of flirtations with boys—or girls. She took with her from that year "a painful feeling . . . of generally not being wanted." From a forbidden novel, Marie Corelli's *A Romance of Two Worlds*, she had extracted a vision of a "perfect soul-mate" who lived on a distant planet and would come to her bidding in her dreams.

Although she was academically prepared to enter college, neither her parents nor her teachers felt she was old enough for the social life she would find there. She was not, however, to be kept unproductively at home. Instead, Ruth Maria planned to send her to Germany for a year. There was a suitable boardinghouse in Hamelin run by two older women who would provide adequate supervision and assistance. Anna Louise began intensive German lessons in the spring and in July 1901 departed for Hamelin with her mother.

Every day after Ruth Maria left her in Hamelin, Anna Louise wrote letters that she conceived of as both an obligation to her family and friends and a journal. Repeatedly, toward the beginning of her stay, she admonished her father to keep these letters. He did so faithfully. They provide an extraordinarily detailed account of that year; more than any of her journals, they are characterized by a candor that appears in few of her other writings.

She complained of the "eternal chaperoning of the two Fräuleins." She wanted to go sit at the edge of the woods and half read, half study, but "we must not go near the wood but stay where we can see but not enjoy its tantalizing shade." She told her father that she was nonetheless respectful of the restraints and understood that "they can't help looking at things in a different way." Subsequent letters to her mother disclosed her duplicity. She took every opportunity she could to stretch if not break the rules, and she was only occasionally ashamed of the latitude she was taking.

The impulse behind Anna Louise's new disobedience was no mystery. She had discovered boys, or, as she boasted in letter after letter to her mother and Miss Farrell, they had discovered her. Soon after her arrival in Hamelin, two young men, Leo and Heinrich, became remarkably attentive to her. By early August their attentions occupied most of her thoughts and much of her letters to her mother.

"Really, Mamma," she wrote on August 4, "I think I need your watchful care as a guard against flirtation. I have in my room four roses from three different boys." She went on to tell Mamma two long stories about encounters with Leo and Heinrich in which she was clearly not so much the innocent victim as her initial plea would indicate. One of these stories related how, having become aware of a peculiar whistle that was used as a code between the two boys, she decided to imitate it. She stole outside with a female cohort, Lotty, and whistled "The Last Rose of Summer." The next day, she heard Leo whistling "The Last Rose of Summer" near her window, and roses arrived. In the same letter Anna Louise told her mother of a strange trick that Heinrich had taught her: "You wet the back of your hand, brush it briefly with a thistle, then swing your arm in circles—lo and behold, blood rushes to your hand." Heinrich, Anna Louise hastened to assure her mother, was a "very studious boy." Just what he studied was not mentioned.

Anna Louise ended the letter to her mother with an unabashed assertion of her newly discovered womanhood. "All this boy stuff," she wrote, "is no problem for Lotty, who is only fourteen, and still wears short dresses, but for me it's horrible." Four days later, however, Anna Louise's "horror" became outrage that she was forbidden by one of the fräuleins to go for a 5:00 A.M. unchaperoned walk in the woods with Heinrich.

Daily incidents encouraged Anna Louise in the confident exercise of her rapidly developing independence. She reassured her parents that she was keeping careful accounts of her finances and even managing to save a portion of her funds to donate to charity. She reported the compliments she was receiving on her facility with the German language, and mentioned specifically people who had sought her out because they had heard how clever she was. She also took care to note how diligently she was studying and to mention that she frequently played hymns on the piano for her companions, knitted, crocheted, sewed and made lace. And she found time to make fudge and cream candies with nuts for the girls. All who tasted her creations were "impressed and pleased."

In mid-September, after receiving a letter from Tracy mentioning that he was now taking geometry, she wrote back that this information made her feel "as old as the hills." She then launched into three pages of advice on how to handle both geometry and its instructor. From the distance of her greater years and far removed, she petted Tracy fondly: he was, she reminded him, her "baby brother," about whom she bragged to her German friends. "The people here have fallen in love with you," she informed him.

By the end of September, Anna Louise had written over four hundred pages of letters, mostly to her parents, a few to her siblings, a few to grandparents and many to Miss Farrell. Only gradually did the compulsion to record every detail of her life abroad diminish. This occurred in part, her letters suggest, because daily life was settling into a routine, but also because her relationships with the local young men were no longer as flattering as they had been initially. She attributed the ebb in their attentiveness to her own coolness and restraint. The young men were "fickle" and easily distracted by the "foolish flirtations of other girls." She was relieved that her mother was soon to arrive to take her on a trip to Italy.

Once the trip to Italy commenced in mid-October, Anna Louise's letters, mostly addressed to her father, resumed their earlier vitality. Each city that she and her mother visited was more enthralling than the previous one: "Rome was a queenly Zenobia who commanded attention and homage as a tribute. Florence, Cleopatra-like, merely opened her arms, displayed her beauty, and I couldn't resist." Venice wholly seduced her. "Venice is ideal," she wrote to Papa. "At night, especially, it is an aerial palace just out of fairyland," so perfect that she expected it to be struck by a burst of lightning and "burnt up by the glory and intense fire."

But it was in Rome that she had her most complicated experience. Shortly after they arrived, it became apparent to Anna Louise that her mother was determined to arrange an audience for her with the Pope. For Anna Louise, Ruth Maria's maneuverings were as disturbing as the meeting that eventually occurred. Ruth Maria had sent money ahead to secure tickets, but mysteriously the money had either not arrived or not been acknowledged at its appropriate destination. Ruth Maria did not accept this error lightly or straightforwardly. She marched into the office of the Vatican secretary, announced that she had not received the expected tickets and informed the secretary that she would prefer to give her money to the American College in Rome and would promptly do so if tickets were not forthcoming. Anna Louise described to her father the subsequent drama: the secretary apparently understood no English. Nonetheless, he leaped from his chair, discerned the message and assured Ruth Maria that she would have her money returned. She also immediately received two tickets for an audience with Pope Leo XIII.

The audience itself awed and perplexed Anna Louise. "What business had we with the Holy Father? What was he to us?" she asked half rhetorically in her letter to her father. It troubled her that for Protestants like herself and her mother, seeing the Pope was "almost like sightseeing" and not fair to Catholics. Despite this hesitation, the meeting impressed her. She described every detail and was much taken with the physical appearance of the Pope, whom she noted had a "tired expression and thin hands" and whose "gorgeous whiteness was sprinkled with color." The radiance of the man and the ceremony did not entirely assuage her discomfort. She closed her letter to her father with the pained remark that it "would have had deeper religious significance for us if we hadn't remembered how we had practically bought our way in."

After Rome, she and her mother went on to Vienna, but Anna Louise found it boring, and she was not unhappy to return to Hamelin in mid-November while her mother returned to Oak Park. The family had determined that she should enter Bryn Mawr College in the fall of 1902 with a full year's advanced credit, and she began to write to her father for advice on her studies. She assured him she had no anxieties about her ability to handle the work at Bryn Mawr with ease, but her letters reflect a variety of apprehensions about recognition. She received a letter from a "Bryn Mawr prize winner" who had received better grades than she on the entrance tests; she determined to study even harder during the spring months and take the tests again. She wrote to her grandmother that she wished "there was some study in which I could do decidedly better than the other girl." In February of 1902 the youth magazine *American Weekly* published two of her stories about her trip to Italy. She was delighted and gleefully projected her future as a writer, but soon afterwards she received another letter from Margaret Franklin, the "prize winner," who reported continued success in her studies. Anna Louise blamed her own slower-paced academic endeavors on Germany: "There's too much ability in Germany to take things easily. It makes me wonder if there is any force in the universe as strong as inertia."

By late March, Anna Louise was worried about inertia of a different sort. "The girls will all call me 'fatty' when I get home. And the worst of it is, if I weigh 140 pounds at sixteen, what will I weigh at twenty-five? I am doomed alas to be a heavy-weight, and all my tears are of no avail. I fear that I must get married. Portly wives are splendid looking (at least some people say so) but a fat teacher—did you ever see one? Possibly my anxieties will wear me down. Let's hope for the best."

She made plans to travel to Berlin and Paris on her own in June and lost ten pounds worrying about these trips, then regained the weight eating chocolates. No one, least of all her mother, called her fatty when she finally rejoined her family in Paris, for she carried her weight easily on her five-nine frame, but as her first day at college approached, she worried less each day about her academic credentials and more about what she would look like to her classmates.

3

Adolescence
and the Kingdom of
God on Earth

It seemed to me that I could see the influence of Christ reaching out in all the lands and that the reign of love had begun.

—Anna Louise to her diary on hearing a performance of Handel's *Messiah,* December 1902

The soul asks first for pleasure
And then excuse from pain,
And then, the little anodynes
That deaden suffering.

—by Emily Dickinson.
Copied in Anna Louise's
diary, October 31, 1905

Anna Louise did not enter Bryn Mawr that fall. The choice of a college had been a matter of considerable debate between her parents, and in the early summer of 1902, while he was a visiting preacher at the First Congregational Church of Oberlin, Sydney quietly reached a decision:

My darling wife:
I am going to write you about AL's coming to Oberlin. I fear that you will not like it, . . . yet I should not be true to you or her if I did not speak freely about what is the highest welfare of our children, their training and education. . . . There is a community life here that she would not find anywhere else—I mean by that a combination of school, home and church. . . . AL would have this *entrée* to the best homes and people at once. . . .

I have thought of [the social life], and while using wisdom such as becomes parents, I think it is best not to worry. Those who *plan* not to have their daughter meet a husband, generally fail. . . . I think that AL would be sen-

sible to the fact that she was beginning her education, that a career was before
her because of her exceptional talents, if not spoiled by early alliances. Also,
I think that she would obey us in spirit and in letter (as we have always stood
for her freedom) in not encouraging social advances. . . .

With great love,

Ruth Maria accepted her husband's compromise that Anna Louise
transfer to Bryn Mawr after her freshman year, and Anna Louise thus
became the third generation of her family at Oberlin College. Her grandmother, Anna Lord, had graduated from Oberlin in 1839, with the second
coeducational class, a socially radical gesture at the time. Anna Louise
moved into a room with a balcony in Talcott Hall across from Tappan
Square, the central common green, named after Arthur Tappan, yet
another of her ancestors who had attended the college.

Her early education stood her in good stead. She received advanced
credit in French, English composition and German, was granted sopho-
more standing and promptly enrolled in Bible 3, an upper-division course
taught by one of the great teachers of the college, Edward Increase
Bosworth. In addition, she took analytical geometry, advanced English
composition, Greek 1, Shakespeare and ornithology and did exceptionally
well in all of them except ornithology.

She also found time to participate actively in the literary society, to put
together a book of *Songs of Oberlin*, to compose "Fair Oberlin," an ode
to the college still sung today in assemblies, and to protest the social
restraints on women students. She resented the 8:30 P.M. curfew. When
she discovered that the girls were also not to be allowed to participate in
the late-evening torchlight parade celebrating the inauguration of a new
president, she was angry enough to get permission to organize a similar
parade and reception the following Saturday; to her open pleasure, almost
all of the participants were women. She wrote another song for the
occasion exalting the leadership of the new president.

But in private Anna Louise was enduring all the agonies of adolescence. Her anxieties about eating and perplexities about men became
matters of daily challenge. During her first semester, her classmates
discovered that Anna Louise would do almost anything for chocolates.
"To eat or not to eat—that was the question," she wrote in her diary
shortly before Christmas 1902, recounting with wry pride the events of
two days before:

> Whether twas better thus to swallow down
> A bottleful of catsup and obtain

The Huylers offered me by "Skeeter" Jones
To eat, aye there's the rub, perchance to eat
For in that act who know what pains may come
When I have finished up that bottleful.

Her classmate, "Skeeter" Jones, had publicly offered her one pound of Huyler chocolates if she would consume an entire bottle of catsup at the noon meal. She found the offer irresistible and to the collective mirth of the diners finished off the whole bottle. When she appeared for supper, her first request was to ask Mr. Jones if he would "please pass me the bottle of catsup." That evening she took the chocolates to the literary society and passed them around as tokens of her triumph.

Throughout her life, chocolates were magical tokens in all of Anna Louise's dealings with others. She would share them with those in her favor, use them as bribes and deny them to those she disliked. Huang Hua, who was to become one of China's major leaders, wrote to Anna Louise in 1946 thanking her profusely for the Oh Henry! bars that she had brought in by the boxful to the central committee of the Chinese Communist party in Yenan; at the same time she threatened to cut off the supply to a friend unless he helped her with some translations. Periodically, on Anna Louise's request, her secretary in China would hide the box of chocolates to prevent Anna Louise from finishing them off. Chocolates were the fact and symbol to Anna Louise of an indulgence in which she could engage and with which she could be selectively generous. Her upbringing made it impossible for her to drink, or indeed to swear; chocolates were a passion no one had thought to forbid.

Anna Louise thought seriously about her future during her first year at Oberlin, trying to find a way of life that was singularly her own and would also further the good of humanity. In her diary she never spoke of becoming a housewife and living an ordinary life. Neither of her parents made a distinction between what they thought and believed and what they did. Whatever Anna Louise accepted as her own ideals would also have to be her activity. Missionary work was suggested by her family and encouraged at Oberlin, which each year sent two of its graduates to work in Shansi province in Northern China.

She had, however, too many doubts about who she was to commit herself wholeheartedly to such work, and in the middle of December of her freshman year, she acknowledged her frustrations with her hopes and life plans in a lengthy "idealized bit of autobiography," which strangely foreshadows her future:

Ever since her childhood when she had lain for hours in the tall grasses reveling in the mysteries of Grimm's fairy tales, she had wondered at the stupidity of people to whom the fairies had granted that oft-given blessing— three wishes. "When my fairy appears, I will have my answer ready and it will be something fine," she had said. At last, on the eve of her seventeenth birthday when she sat on the balcony of Talcott Hall gazing up at the cold brilliance of Orion, her fairy appeared. "You have one wish. Take one week to think." Then the fairy vanished into the chill sparkle of the snow-edged trees and the girl began to think.

She had great ambitions, this maiden of seventeen, and fairly high ideals. She knew enough to know that wealth cannot bring happiness, and she entertained that wish for only a moment. But she held her breath as she thought of fame, no, not of fame but of genius. Even if her works were never known, if her works must go down to future generations marked "anonymous" or were even attributed to someone else, what joy to feel that they would go down to future generations. . . . Why not be the greatest poet, the greatest artist, and the greatest musician that the world has ever known, all rolled into one? and what if happiness did not go with it. . . . Is not greatness better and more noble? She thought of this wish for a long time and her heart throbbed with its suggestion of power.

Then, as the calm of evening deepened in her soul, the eternal stars seemed to say, "Is it worthwhile. . . ? Is it great enough for you? . . ." But she answered full of hope: "It would be worthwhile . . . to have helped a few human beings to a larger view of life . . ." But a reply came back from the night: "Would you do more good in that way than you can now? Are you not put into the world fitted for just what you ought to do? If God had needed a genius for the furtherance of his plan, could he not have made you one? Does not the fact that you do not possess those talents show that they would interfere with the work you are meant to do?" And the girl sighed, "It is so."

Then her thoughts turned to a wish which she had often felt. Why not ask that others should feel toward her exactly as she felt toward them? What unrequited friends it would save.

She rejected this choice on the grounds that if all her love and friendship were requited, there would be nothing to do with the surplus she felt in herself and love would be "a mere barter."

She decided at last that she would choose something, not merely for her own enjoyment and glorification, but for the betterment of the world. "I have it now: the way in which I can best serve the world is to improve myself and give myself. I will wish for something which will strengthen my character, increase my powers, and in so doing I will give the most to the world."

The last wish was in turn declared inadequate when she realized that this meant that she would become an "automatic machine" and her duty would lose "all value if it were the only course open to me." Kant, her philosophy teacher reminded her, shows that virtue cannot be easy. Anna Louise followed the narrative of her idealized self through the week. On Friday the heroine went to the freshmen prayer meeting happy. She had discovered her wish. It was that the "real things should seem real." Yet even this Hegelian version of the Second Coming was not to be. For at prayer meeting, she heard a classmate ask a question:

> "What is the reason for the seeming unreality of the spiritual life?" "Ah!" she thought with exultation. "It won't be unreal to me." As in a dream she heard Professor Bosworth's . . . closing sentence. "When a strong will comes in contact with a weaker one, the strong one dare not be present all the time for fear of overwhelming the personality of the weaker. We need moments of unreality for the full development of our individual character." The young woman gave a little gasp. Was it true? Then what a terrible wish she had been about to make.

Finally, in Anna Louise's account, the fairy returns and inquires what the wish is to be. Loftily the girl answers that she is satisfied and has no wish to make. But the fairy will not let her off: if one has a wish, one must make use of it. Life must be used. Frightened, she gasps:

> "What shall I do . . . that will do the least harm?" A thought came over her. She smiled, . . . then under sudden impulse she raised her head: "Give me," she said, "a box of chocolate almond Allegrettis."

Knowingly or not, in this fragment, Anna Louise had confronted and rejected most of the standard ethical postures of the West. Her assurance was not much tempered by self-doubt. While she was bent by anxieties about who she was, no *arguments* could change the perfection of her self-conception. She was often profoundly hurt by others' perceptions of her, but untouched in her sense of self.

She came to feel that Oberlin was too transcendentally perfect a place to reveal her vocation in the world. When on her seventeenth birthday she made a trip into Cleveland to visit her grandmother for Thanksgiving, she confronted in her diary the illusory quality of her first months at College:

> Oberlin is a sort of idealized world where one finally comes to believe that the earth is rapidly improving, that things are coming out all right, and that tho' there are lots of bad people, they are getting better as fast as they are able. One likewise gets the impression that smoking and drinking are really of rare occurrence. What an awful change it was for me to go to Cleveland

and ride for half an hour thro' the streets lined with saloons in a car filled with the smell of tobacco. My heart sank into my shoes and I thought: Oh dear me, how very far off the millennium is! Why does it have to take so long?

Oberlin was so perfect, and so much like the world her parents had given her, that there appeared to be no way for her to make an impact. Anna Louise eagerly anticipated her transfer to Bryn Mawr, where her father hoped she would "take hold and organize the girls," for a "few earnest, bright, straightforward girls could in a few years improve the higher life of Bryn Mawr for fifty years." The presence at Bryn Mawr of her best friend Helen Wyeth made it all the easier.

In April 1903 her parents embarked for southern Africa as part of a delegation to evaluate the missions there. Anna Louise, Tracy and Ruth were left in the care of family friends in Prairie Depot, Illinois; that summer Anna Louise waited on tables at a resort in Lakeside, Ohio, for three dollars a week, plus tips. She fretted, then made her peace with the notion of tips, of getting something for nothing but good behavior. Everything was chaos: the cooks repeatedly got drunk or quit or both; the waitresses were expected to pick up all the slack and took most of the blame. "The life here," she confessed to her diary, "is my first experience with fighting and drinking and swearing. It simply makes my heart sick."

The end of summer brought some relaxation. She went to visit her Aunt Sarah Spitzer, Sydney's older sister, who was married to an important banker in Toledo. In a letter to her parents Anna Louise could hardly contain her exultation in her sudden luxuries: "Whew! I never knew what it meant to be rich. I am getting my head turned. . . . Oh, the change, from Lakeside Hotel (waiting on table) to Toledo (automobiling)! I didn't tell anyone about the 'waiting.' It may have been false pride." Despite these indulgences, she was disoriented by the experiences of the summer and wrote to her parents in Africa that she felt like "a wanderer on the face of the earth." On the way to Bryn Mawr, she made the mistake of stopping at Oberlin. She left feeling guilty that she was not returning. More people had liked her than she had realized.

She entered Bryn Mawr as a junior and found herself again alone. She immediately resented the lack of close relations between students and professors, especially male professors, "for fear of the talk it would cause." The possibility of staying out until 10:00 P.M. was an improvement, but she could no longer repair to the gymnasium roof, where she had been assured of privacy at Oberlin. Classes were no harder than the previous year, and she noted with matter-of-fact pleasure a grade of high honors in a trigonometry entrance test. She confided to her diary that Bryn Mawr was not as irreligious as she had previously feared, which paradoxically made it less important that she be there.

Her parents were due back from Africa in the middle of October. Three weeks before her eighteenth birthday, Anna Louise's world was irrevocably changed. On November fifth she wrote in her diary:

> Just one month since I last wrote in you, my journal. Oh why couldn't I have known all that was to happen. Just one month ago! It seems years and years, it seems like a different life. And it is a different life, for that which meant almost the most to me in life is gone. I cannot realize that when I made my last entries, I was expecting to go to New York to meet Papa and Mama; I was expecting to bring them down to Bryn Mawr; I thought of how Mama would admire my room, my new clothes, and all the trivial things for which I had time, then. And she would laugh when I told her what a tyrant Ruthie was, and would say that she had better stay at home hereafter. Oh dear, I can't go on with this, or I shall lose my self-control. On Wednesday evening, three weeks ago last night, I received word by telegram from Tracy that Mama had died of heart failure.

Ruth Maria had contracted typhoid in Africa and had died between Port Said and Naples on the return trip. After getting the news, Anna Louise went immediately to New York, where she and Tracy met the steamer on October 28. Ruth remained in Prairie Depot. With their father and their mother's body, the two older children rode out to Mansfield, where Ruth Maria was buried in the Tracy plot.

The death of her mother was "almost the most important thing in the world" and at first marked a strengthening of Anna Louise's religious faith. She noted on her eighteenth birthday that she was now "no longer afraid of life, for I know that, whatever happens, He will not let me go." But the death also made her realize that she was not going to be a missionary. She looked around her and found that she had no chance to be like her mother: she was not able to bring even her classmates closer to God. But to refuse to be a missionary was not to escape the sense of being sent and of having or wanting a mission. The call was in the family; her work, however, was not to be *in* the church.

Her mother's sacrificial death fixed in her mind a perfected ideal of marriage, and she could only conclude that her father had been psychologically crippled by his wife's death. For Anna Louise, her parents's relationship had exemplified the "soul-mates" idealized in Marie Corelli's *A Romance of Two Worlds*, a view she held for the rest of her life. In 1959 she wrote to a friend:

> My parents gave me a surrounding full of love. They were love [*sic*] in the old
> Victorian sense. . . . I have since known that this also has drawbacks, for
> when Mother died, Father could never again become a whole person. . . .
> His brain worked on for decades, but in emotions he was never a whole
> human being. . . . He had made a single human being with her. . . . And
> the result of this on me was that I never wanted to love as completely as they
> did, lest I lose myself and be left only part of a person when the other died.

In addition to this vision of a perfect marriage, Ruth Maria left her
children a stark challenge and burden: the achievement of social justice
depended on people, and most immediately her children, becoming
"good enough." But for Anna Louise, to be "good enough" meant to excel
at *everything* and to receive applause for that excellence. After her mother's death, the external voice that had pressed her to be best at every
task was silent; the death was at once a release and a source of anxiety. In
May, despite her feeling that she had been a "hermit" since her mother's
death, she was asked to give the Class Day Speech and prepared a talk
that was both comic and self-mocking:

> Only yesterday, I received a note from the Ivory Snow concern asking for
> some rhymed advertisements. They wanted something that would catch the
> eye from sheer lack of sense, and my work seemed to them very promising.
> And in this morning's mail, I got a letter from the manufacturers of Mother
> Winslow's Soothing Syrup. She had heard that I was a precocious infant of
> three years who wrote melancholy verses, and she was sure a bottle of her
> syrup would completely cure me.

She also became less self-consciously pleased with the excellence of
her academic performance and wished that her friends could do as well
as she. And she began to have regular severe headaches.

The next year she transferred back to Oberlin as a senior. It was nearer
home where, as the oldest child, she was needed by her father and her
siblings, but more important, it was her mother's college. As an old
woman, she would vehemently recall that she had hated the "snobbery"
of Bryn Mawr women. One of her most vivid memories of Bryn Mawr
was of President M. Carey Thomas' pronouncement to the Bryn Mawr
college assembly "that education was useful to women because, if they
did not find happiness in marriage, they would have outside interests."
The concept of education for women as a protection against the assaults
of boredom was an insult to Anna Louise's sensibility and a direct attack
on all that her mother had taught her. At Oberlin, at least, learning and
labor were united, for both men and women.

Anna Louise's college years set the pattern for her personal relationships. She wanted them to be strong and intense, but she did not want to be dependent on anyone. In her diary entry for March 11, 1905, her senior year at Oberlin, she permitted herself some reflections "with regard to crushes. . . . They thrive on uncertainty, and are very bad in [their] nervous effects on the crushed one." She admonished herself that "people don't want you to care for them too much, or perhaps I should say too intensely." If there were to be strong friendships, they must be "sane." She gave an example of her own "insanity." "On the night of the big bonfire celebrating our debate with Wesleyan, I stood at one of the windows. Now the rest of the people at the window were watching the fire and commenting on it." But Anna Louise spent her time "watching the light of the fire on a certain person's face." That was "insane," she decided. "If I had watched the fire and asked her once or twice how she liked it . . . I would have been sane." "Self-control and courage," she concluded, "are two of the essential virtues."

Most of her crushes were on women, and most of them proved to be both threats and disappointments. She wrote poems to her female friends of a passion so intense that she found herself "disgusted" with their sentiments. Worried that her "nerve-wracking" infatuations were leading her "to behave like a regular heathen, . . . as if God wasn't capable of taking care of my affairs," she tried to rationalize the failure of others to return her passion: "If I care for someone else and they aren't terribly wild about me—well what then? It's probably good for me, or it wouldn't happen. This is my final conclusion. I am going to be more philosophic and more Christian."

The most important relationship that she formed at Oberlin was with a faculty member, Florence May Fitch, some ten years her senior. It was her face that Anna Louise had fixed on in the light of the bonfire. Miss Fitch was one of the five women faculty members at Oberlin and the only one not a language teacher. Her deep bright eyes were framed by rimless glasses perched a short way down her finely chiseled nose, and with her slightly pointed ears and oval face, the overall effect was of a wise elf. She had graduated from Oberlin and, like Anna Louise, had studied in Germany, where she had taken a Ph.D. in philosophy at the University of Berlin in 1903. There were few academic positions open to women at colleges and universities. Oberlin offered her a position as an instructor in philosophy and secretary to the president. The following year she became dean of college and graduate women and associate professor of philosophy. She never married.

Miss Fitch, as Anna Louise always referred to her, was intellectually rigorous, thoughtful and independent. Throughout Anna Louise's last semester at Oberlin, most of her diary entries included an allusion to Miss Fitch and often a lengthy discussion of what had been happening between them. Anna Louise's closest college friend, Helen Hampson, was also enamored with Miss Fitch, and the three would go for long walks and expeditions.

On one occasion they drove to the Vermillion River, about ten miles north of Oberlin. Anna Louise's pleasure was undermined by her conviction that Helen and Miss Fitch would be happier alone, and she ostentatiously went off by herself to gather flowers.

If relations with Miss Fitch were less requited than she wished, relations with most of her male classmates were hopeless. After a skating party at the Rockefeller Rink she wrote: "I can truthfully say that it is the first party at which I have not enjoyed myself." Having previously disliked girls who could not go to parties without escorts, she found herself depressed to be without a partner: "I felt for the first time my dependence upon the other sex." She tried to compensate for her loneliness by an exaggerated focus on the skating, but "upon going too fast, I was told by a girl to keep out of the way. . . . If a girl be pretty and popular," she sadly concluded, "she need not know how to skate, for she will have plenty of men to teach her. Men do not care for self-reliance in women; they like soft creatures who hang on to their arms and give them all the credit of good skating."

Very few men are mentioned in her Oberlin diary or in her letters from this period. The one exception is Paul Leaton Corbin, whom she met the second term of her first year. He was a senior, on his way to becoming a missionary with the Oberlin program in Shansi. He had a reputation as a campus poet and was one of Anna Louise's few intellectual equals. Paul and Anna Louise walked and talked often. Among the poems he sent her was one called "The Covenant of Blood." It described a man and woman in love who marry and on their wedding night cut each other's veins, drink each other's blood and are found dead the next morning, still intertwined.

Paul, however, was engaged to a woman named Miriam Locke, who arrived in April 1903 in preparation for the marriage. Anna Louise tried hard to become Miriam's close friend, but Miriam understandably demurred. "Isn't it queer how we like people anyway," Anna Louise wrote. "I would give a great deal to know her better, to be a real friend, but one can't control those things. I thought that one could, that by gifts and attentions and being with a person one could hurry up friendship, but it won't work that way. It takes time, and it sometimes seems as if Providence had a considerable share in it. Sometimes we are with nice people for a very long time and want to harmonize and can't and sometimes we suddenly feel a liking for someone, a feeling that we belong together. And then, queerest of all, sometimes the other person doesn't have that feeling."

There was more than a touch of pathos in the "queerest of all." Anna Louise resisted the social skills that might have eased her interactions with others. She was irked at a providence that insisted on interfering with the exercise of her will. She sought to control even friendships by insisting that every instant be full of meaning. She recognized this in herself, but she seemed unable to change. In her diary, toward the end of her last year at Oberlin, she marked off a "conclusion about human nature": "People like you, not for what you do for them, but for what you graciously permit them to do for you." After wishing that she could profit from this understanding, she sadly concluded, "I shall probably continue overwhelming my friends with gifts until the end of time."

Paul Corbin and Miriam were married, and a subscription was collected to send them off to China.

> Only in memory now
> Lives the light that gleamed thro' tempest strife
> Naught know I of the world of men.
> But I know that love is stronger than life
> And since I love, I know, someday, somehow,
> That we shall meet again.

Anna Louise called the poem "Auf Wiedersehen" and inscribed it on the back of a picture of herself that she sent to the newlyweds. When she reprinted it as "Au Revoir" in a collection called *Storm Songs*, she changed the fourth line to "I know of love that is stronger than life."

On January 22, 1903, she analyzed in her journal her feelings for Paul and her difficulties in expressing them. Then she wrote:

Faith Brown [a classmate] said a queer thing after reading the above. "Anna Louise, I don't want you ever to marry. At least not until late in life. I want you to write and not be bothered with domestic cares." "Ah," but I reminded her, "you know that they say that no one can write until he has loved." "Well, then you might as well do that and then be disappointed." "Or he might die," I said, "and I have always felt that sorrow would numb me." "It would at first, but afterwards you might write better." "All right," said I, "let's hope for the best. Maybe he'll die."

It was best, Anna Louise decided, to be attached and not attached, married and not married. The contradiction led her repeatedly into depression, and the depressions to an insistence that her will become stronger:

> May 20, 1905. I hereby forswear this long three weeks fit of the blues. . . . It is wicked and useless as well as unpleasant. Beginning last night I determined to have no more headaches, to get tired no more, and in short to resume that ancient "joy of living" which this year has so sadly deprived me of. This resolve may seem a little like Christian Science, but let me explain. By headaches I mean the particular headaches brought on by crying; they must go. By "tired" I mean the state in which I am after a night spent in feeling miserable. I am going to stop.

Her headaches did not stop. She finished her studies nevertheless and graduated summa cum laude and Phi Beta Kappa. She was nineteen years old.

Thanks to the publication of *Storm Songs* shortly before she left Oberlin, Anna Louise was offered a position as journalist for the *Advance*, a fundamentalist Protestant paper published in Chicago. The *Advance* was edited by a Dr. Adams, who hired bright young women upon their graduation from college and promptly exploited them. According to Anna Louise: "I wrote tirelessly. Every weekly issue contained fairy tales by me on the children's pages, stories on the women's page with a good moral for youth, reports on the Ministers' Federation and the Women's Church organizations, half a dozen book reviews, an original column called 'From a Woman's Window,' expressing an ironic, feminist viewpoint, and another column of synthesized news from other presses entitled 'More About Women.' " She wrote under four pseudonyms.

At home she composed many poems (many of which were published) and wrote letters, took care of her father when he was in town and still managed to pay attention to her brother Tracy and his fiancée, Edith Robbins. In her less structured moments, she complained about her sister Ruth's spendthrift habits, took long walks, visited friends and worried about her relationship with Miss Fitch. She had repeated headaches.

For at least eighteen months after Anna Louise's graduation, Miss Fitch remained the center of her emotional life. She returned a number of times to Oberlin to see her, and her accounts of these meetings suggest that Miss Fitch showed irritation at Anna Louise's passion. After one trip in early October, Anna Louise confronted Miss Fitch in a long, ingenuous letter:

> How can we ever be friends? Isn't friendship founded, as President King says, on mutual self-revelation and answering trust? But I have revealed and revealed myself to you till I felt naked and ashamed to the world (do you know what a terrible thing that is?), and I do not even know if you believed me or not. Verse was the only way I *could* speak; it is dreadfully hard for me to show affection and most people, I fear, cannot understand a revelation in verse. . . .
>
> You *never* made any "revelation" to me—except once. That was on my first trip back to Oberlin. I paid a heavy price for it, for I showed you everything I had ever felt about you and that was one of the hardest things I have ever done. But when you put your arms around me and kissed me, I was repaid. That night I had a few hours of the greatest joy I had ever known. And I trusted your revelation so implicitly even though you said so little. I wish I hadn't, for when I came back again, you didn't seem so glad to see me, and when I came the third time and you sent me home, I wanted to die.

By the end of the letter, she felt purged. She concluded by declaring that she no longer spent all her time thinking about Miss Fitch and was taking interest "much more in other persons."

On March 8, 1906, seven months after she was hired, Anna Louise was fired from the *Advance*. Her diary records: "No reason given. I find that the last four women helpers have all left after six months. It's the policy of the paper during the slack season after getting in all the subscriptions." She was genuinely shocked at her dismissal, but there had in fact been friction between her and Dr. Adams well before March. Increasingly, articles about which Anna Louise felt excited were turned down, the most important of which was an account of a lecture by Jack London where he referred to "the Russian anarchists as his comrades."

Her father had been urging her to attend graduate school, and she now applied to the University of Chicago. After speaking with the president and the dean, she was not only accepted but informed that there would be "no difficulty in the matter of a scholarship." She worked out a course of study that combined psychology, English literature and philosophy; the focus was to be the influence of religion on literature. Her regular work at the *Advance* ended on the last day of March. On April 2, she started classes at the University of Chicago.

Back in school, Anna Louise found herself in her familiar role of the brilliant female student. Her father urged her to write a commentary on Kant, and she was soon being invited to the head table for banquets in

the honor of visiting celebrities. She was ambivalent about her intellectual
success. In a letter written but not sent to Miss Fitch, she observed: "It
seems to me I am on the wrong track. I don't want to be a Ph.D.; I don't
want to be a college professor; I don't want to be a freak." Part of the
problem, she concluded, was that she "craved affection." After one party
where she greatly enjoyed being "bossed around" she wrote in her diary:
"I hate being independent and running myself—and yet it's just what I
seem built to do. If only I could find someone who would understand me
completely and 'run me.' "

Anna Louise's loneliness was increased that fall by the sudden departure of her father from Oak Park to Seattle, where he took up a new
parish on Queen Anne Hill. During much of the previous year, he had
been keeping company with Mrs. Ginevra Smith, a divorcée of about
forty. Word got out, and despite the fact that the engagement was broken,
he was forced to resign from his parish. Anna Louise very much liked
Ginevra and was privately disturbed at the broken engagement. Tracy,
however, was so shocked that he refused to be in the same room as his
father's fiancée. Henceforth Tracy would keep a close eye on his father's
relationships with women. He repeatedly saw to it that his father remained a widower, and, inadvertently, that his elder sister remained the
woman in their father's life.

With her father in Seattle, Anna Louise was by herself for the first
time in her life. She was an adult, on scholarship, in a town where she
had no family. Her journal entries for the year 1907 were entered immediately below those for the corresponding day the previous year. Miss
Fitch almost disappeared from mention. Headaches were fewer, except
on special occasions. Anna Louise resigned herself to being a dedicated
student, even though, she remarked wistfully, she occasionally "longed
for the fleshpots of Egypt."

Philosophers became her inner circle: "Laotze I always think of as a
most charming, gentle-souled old man. . . . Hegel, I hate for his conceit
and coldness, but he's lots of fun to tease people with when he's tired of
being good and wants to be frivolous. And he has a certain fascination; I
live in mortal dread that I may be like him in some ways, for I love
paradoxes. They have the same aesthetic effect as wit." At their center,
she insisted, was God, and He was so primary that *all* other individuals
were reduced to the same secondary plane. She did not, however, adhere
wholly to her own dogma. Next to God, there was Kant. The *Critique of
Pure Reason* was first on her agenda every day as she carefully made her

way through the entire work, picking out for special annotation those passages that emphasize the centrality of human agency in experience.

By March 1907, less than a year after she started graduate work, Anna Louise was ready for her master of arts examinations. Her diary entry for March 13 reads: "And so the exam is over and I get my M.A. at the next convocation." She thought, however, that her achievements were too easy and lacked seriousness. She felt herself to be a "jumble of selves" and wondered in the beginning of a new diary if there was anything more to life than "playing to an audience." She feared that there was not.

She spent the summer in the "big free West" with her father and brother, returning to Chicago in early September determined to become something more than a scholar. She still planned to complete her Ph.D., but for a time she "wanted to come up hard against life and the facts of life." "I'm going to work in a factory—Sprague-Warner's. . . . And I have a room all engaged—on Halsted." She had in fact had difficulty finding a "safe" tenement flat to rent. Halsted Street was in a district to which she would not normally have gone, and she had finally chosen the apartment with the help of a friend, Florence Towne, a kindergarten teacher who had "been around these places so much" that she could tell "by instinct whether a house was decent or not." Anna Louise was, as she admitted to herself and Florence, "plain scared," even though "there is no reason why one should be more afraid of poor folks than rich ones."

Sprague-Warner's was a canning plant for fruits and vegetables. Bill, the record keeper, signed her up for $5.50 a week. " 'Where did you work before?' he asked. 'Nowhere—I've just come to Chicago,' was my perfectly true and eminently satisfactory answer." Anna Louise was sent up to the third floor, given an apron and put to work washing tins and applying orange-colored apple butter labels. "A hum of conversation" permeated the room in which four women worked at each of ten tables. "My nearest neighbor was an elderly Scotch woman, a fact which I ascertained by her accent. But no sooner had I found this out than one of the other girls said to me 'Are you English?' 'No,' I answered. 'She talks like it, doesn't she?' appealed the girl to the fourth member of our crowd. 'She has some queer kind of accent,' was the other's noncommittal reply." "What nationality are you?" was the next question. When Anna Louise responded, "American," the girls stared at her as if doubting what she meant by the term. "My mother and father were both born in this country," Anna Louise said flatly. And with that, the matter was momentarily settled.

But it did not take long for Anna Louise to be found out. It was easy, she remarked to her diary, to begin a "personal conversation," and her new friend and partner, Agnes, soon drew from her the information that she was from the West and a Sunday-school teacher ("How did you know?" asked Anna Louise, astonished, only to be told the obvious: "There is something about the way you look"). Agnes also discovered the important information that the boss remembered Anna Louise's name, as he well might have, since he was an acquaintance of her father's. Anna Louise redeemed herself from the taint of her otherness by rapidly learning the ropes: if not busy, appear to be; don't worry too much about getting things clean; watch out for Bill's advances.

She was happy in her new environment. She moved with enthusiasm into the life of the urban working class and admired the women with whom she worked, who preferred independence to marriage "until they fell in love." Her poems of this period are naively exuberant, exuding the passion of someone for whom the work was temporary—"playing," as she had put it earlier. Intensity of feeling toward the factory was safe precisely because her stay there would be short, but there is authenticity in the tone of her response to the working-class world. She had little time for self-doubt and self-pity in her new role, and despite the obvious differ- ence in background between her and her companions, she felt less iso- lated, more connected to others than she ever had before. With the women in the factory, she probed the mysteries of men and marriage more concretely than she had been able to with her acquaintances in graduate school. And the factory allowed her to meet and flirt with various men, including one who wished that the girls were "more social- ist" and would spread their favors out equally.

She was twenty-two years old. Flirting with men and talking to other women about those flirtations were not trivial matters to her. Inter- spersed in her diary between accounts of city life are frequent references to her own confusions about romance and marriage. She occasionally wished of a man that he were a girl, for "men are so embarrassing," and she clung to the idea that her marriage would have to be like that of her parents—one of perfectly symbiotic soul-mates. At the same time she worried increasingly that such a marriage might be incompatible with a Ph.D. She recognized that her brash, direct intelligence and her need for solitude were obstacles to just the kind of marriage she envied in others' lives.

It is no wonder that Anna Louise thought of herself as a "jumble of selves" during this period. She was at once a pious middle-class young woman, an outstanding doctoral student and a worker in a canning factory, and she desperately needed some context in which the contradictions in her life could be relieved. She found it in Hull House, one of the most important American settlement houses.

According to the dictionaries of the time, a settlement house was "an establishment in the poorer quarter of a larger city, where educated men and women live in daily contact with the working class." Its mission was to transplant the mores and skills of young, college-trained Americans, particularly women, into the ghettos. Anna Louise had been going to Hull House even before working at Sprague-Warner's; in fact, people there had encouraged her to take the factory job. During the late summer of 1907 she began to go the settlement house more frequently, and on September 22 she described with considerable pride an invitation to have supper with Jane Addams, the director and cofounder of Hull House. Addams, a nationally known social worker, was herself slowly moving from a personal politics of goodwill to a more socially based vision of the United States. She was twenty-five years older than Anna Louise, a logical role model and replacement for Ruth Maria.

During that fall and winter Anna Louise became increasingly concerned about the effects the American economic system was having on its workers. She began to see the false optimism in her perception, just a few months before, of the "joy of the common lot." The last stanza of her poem "The Song of the City," often omitted in reprints, conveyed her bleaker vision of the lives of workers:

> They are worn and spent with labor
> They are tossed aside again.
> And the city is calling, calling,
> For the lives of other men.

When classes resumed at the University of Chicago, she regretfully gave up her factory job, moved back to her own flat and spent most of her evenings at Hull House. She began teaching Descartes to undergraduates and found that it was neither more nor less rewarding than teaching Sunday school. Academic successes flocked her way. An article on "The Relation of the Subconscious to Prayer" was accepted by the *American Journal of Religious Psychology and Education*. She amplified the same ideas in another article, "Some Religious Aspects of Pragmatism," which appeared in April 1908 in the *American Journal of Theology*.

The notions of self, God, prayer and process that appeared in her academic articles were the foundations for her Ph.D. dissertation. By winter she had moved into Hull House and was spending most of her time working on the thesis, which she entitled "A Consideration of Prayer from the Standpoint of Social Psychology." The self, she argued, was "essentially social," and emerged at those points where instincts failed to gain satisfaction; hence the self developed mainly from conflict and frustration. "Complete adjustment depersonalizes the world; moreover, complete adjustment passes over very quickly into unconsciousness, but there are always new problems." It followed that unless there were new problems, there would be no self. The necessity to seek new challenges—the "pioneer spirit" of her ancestors—shone forth as the center of what it meant to be a person. Prayer, she argued, was a means to the "establishment of the self," and not a plea to God to make the world right. When the dissertation was published, it was dedicated "to my father and mother, from whose life and spirit I know more of the reality of prayer than all analysis can teach."

She defended her dissertation before the combined faculties of philosophy and theology—a departure from the conventional private defense before the thesis committee—and her public performance was impressive. "Then I left the lecture hall and grabbed my gold cape and rushed to an open square of darkness in the 'Midway' to throw myself down on the snow. I dug my face into the cold, white softness till I reached the buried grass, and I turned and threw a kiss to the stars. 'You loveliness,' I cried, 'I've been proving the funniest things about you. I hope you enjoyed that nice debate.' I felt a little worried lest I find my stars receding, lest God might be annoyed at the impertinent freedom with which I 'had to' treat him to win that discussion. So I put a good face on it—bluffing God!"

4

The Containment
of Multitudes

There are many things which can be accomplished better by
giving up the strain of conscious choosing and allowing the
subconscious and habitual activities to work out the end un-
hampered by the efforts of the mind which only serve to confuse action.

> —Anna Louise Strong in her Ph.D. dissertation, "A
> Consideration of Prayer from the Standpoint of
> Social Psychology," 1908

The newfound wilderness became for me a passion; I began to
seek out more and more difficult climbs, new peaks to conquer. . . . How could I explain the ecstasy that arose out of
physical pain and exhaustion that the human will subdued,
that new mysticism of the adventurer conquering the uncon-
querable forces of desolate nature.

> —Anna Louise Strong in *I Change Worlds*

Anna Louise still did not know what she wanted to do after graduation.
In part she was awaiting the appearance of the right man. Her work,
whatever it was, would tide her over until *he* appeared, and would become tangential to what he did. In the meantime, the attractions of Hull
House were not enough to keep her in Chicago, and she decided to join
her father in Seattle. Sydney had become a respected leader in a city
known for its progressive politics, and soon after her arrival she and he
conceived of a project that would challenge and satisfy them both. Called
"Know Your City," it was an attempt, as reported miles away in the Oak
Park, Illinois, newspaper, to make "citizenship conscious (and this includes women), of bringing out constructive criticism and giving publicity
to Christian social ideals."

Anna Louise did most of the organizing. Sydney directed her to the appropriate people and institutions, and she set up lectures, discussions and walking tours aimed at acquainting the town's citizens with unexplored opportunities for work and pleasure. "Know Your City" was such a success in Seattle that it quickly spread to other Western cities. For more than a year Anna Louise was kept busy traveling and organizing these projects and running her father's household. In addition, she and her father wrote and edited a series of "Bible Hero Classics," whose purpose, she explained, was "to make this generation as acquainted with Abraham, David, Paul and the others as they were with Alexander, Caesar, and King Arthur." This project was also a considerable success. The pamphlets found their way into Sunday school classes and YMCAs all over the country.

All this was merely temporizing, however, as is most apparent in the play she published in 1908, *The King's Palace*. In one of the few apparently gratuitous passages of *I Change Worlds*, she calls attention to this play: "I published also a rather useless short drama describing the shocked idealism of a young girl who sees the world and refuses to enter it." "Useless" as *The King's Palace* may have been in any public sense, Anna Louise's repeated revisions of the script, beginning while she was at Chicago, and her decision to publish it at this point suggest some personal investment in her dramatization of a young woman's difficulties leaving the protected "king's palace" of childhood for the adult world of marriage and independent work. The heroine of *The King's Palace* is named Elise, and Elise's father is a sad and saintly man, even more impractical than Sydney.

Anna Louise and her father visited Japan in the summer of 1909, but on their return she found herself bored with her work and more uneasy with her role as the woman in her father's house. That winter she left for an indefinite stay in New York City. She was ready, she wrote to her father, for the "proper job, if I find it, but [I'm] not anxious. I shall see the shows and the social work, and take it, at worst, as an educational sojourn."

She lived in Greenwich House, a settlement house on Jones Street in what was becoming known as Greenwich Village. Her natural move at this point would have been into social work, as it had been for the most progressive elements in the middle-class still working within the political system. Florence Kelley, Homer Fowkes, Lillian Wald, Owen Lovejoy, Sydney Hillman, Norman Thomas, Roger Baldwin—all had associations with organized social work and settlement houses. Anna Louise's experience at Hull House gave her an easy entry into this world, but she did not throw herself into their activities. She thought of herself now as a writer as well as a social activist, and social work provided little outlet for her writing. Nevertheless, it was with the most prominent social-work organization in the East that she eventually found a position.

The Russell Sage Foundation, established by Mrs. Russell Sage with a family fortune, combined the settlement-house ideology with enough money to make a difference on a large scale. The director of the Child Hygiene Department was Luther Gulick, an important figure in the social-work movement and the founder of the modern science of public administration. One of Anna Louise's new friends, Florence Kelley, a sharp-witted early socialist, a settlement-house organizer and the translator of Engels, knew Gulick and recommended Anna Louise, who was soon at work writing a report on hygiene in normal and high schools.

Anna Louise's letters to her father at this period are enthusiastic over her work and her life in New York. Her father was not as pleased as she. He was now fifty-two years old, his wife was dead, and his attempt at remarriage had not only failed but cost him the pastorship of an important midwestern parish. Tracy had just announced his engagement, Ruth was in college at Oberlin, and the threat of losing all his children suddenly became real. Whatever its attractions, Seattle was not the center of things. His church there was small, and his increasingly progressive views limited his congregation. Filled with self-doubt, he thought of taking up another line of work, and both Anna Louise and Tracy had to tell him explicitly that it would not be desirable for him to live with Tracy and his wife after their marriage.

He then began to plan a long European tour on which he expected Anna Louise to accompany him. He asked her to make the arrangements, since she was in New York, and with her indomitable efficiency, she got a 40 percent reduction on his ticket, made certain that he would return in time for her brother's wedding, and returned to her own work.

One source of her enthusiasm in her new job was Luther Gulick. He was twenty years older than she, happily married with four children, but he took a great liking to Anna Louise and kept her out of positions in which she would have to be a lieutenant to someone else. "You are made to do your own work," he told her. "You have it in you to do." Anna Louise reported this and similar statements to her father with the excitement of someone who has found at least the start of a path through life.

The more Anna Louise praised Gulick, however, the more Sydney warned her against becoming too attached to him, finally urging her not to see him at all. Again and again Anna Louise felt obliged to close her letters with the reminder to her father that "I admire you more than any man I've known."

Gulick introduced Anna Louise to political ideas more radical than any she had previously encountered except in books: "He told me that there were any number of rich men in New York who were giving or planning to give money in large amounts for welfare work, and that some of them were doing it with the definite purpose of staving off socialism, which is more dangerous here to capital than *we* realize. He told me that he had heard them say so. On the other hand, he said, most of the social workers who are using that money *are* socialists. So it's a mighty interesting situation all the way around, and a time when it's worthwhile living and working. He added that he wanted most of the things that the socialists did, but that he wasn't a political socialist." Through Gulick, Anna Louise's circle of acquaintances grew rapidly. She had dinner with Felix Adler, the founder of the Society for Ethical Culture; she met and impressed Owen Lovejoy of the National Child Labor Committee. Florence Kelley moved to New York from Chicago to become head of the National Consumer's League, and she and Anna Louise spent much of their time together.

To her father's distress, Anna Louise's life was becoming what she called bohemian. The same experiences informed both her political and emotional education, and she took a slightly perverse delight in detailing them to her father: "There are many places . . . where one can drop in any hour of the evening before ten, unannounced, and without having met half the people there assembled—and find one's self in a half-hour exchanging views on life and death, peace and war, negroes, japanese, socialism, marriage, with people whose last names one doesn't even know, but who hand out inner reactions, intellectual and emotional, quite frankly."

Of all the new notions that Anna Louise encountered among her New York friends, those she most resisted were challenges to the vision of marriage which her parents had given her. Tracy wrote that their father was again thinking of marriage, this time to a Seattle pediatrician. Tracy was deeply opposed to the union, and when Anna Louise wrote to her father, she was equally adamant: "I strongly advise against marriage with the person you wrote about. As I said before, the disadvantages from the point of view of prudence are too great to give way unless under the pressure of a very strong affection." Then, as if to complete a bargain, she agreed to seek no more work from Luther Gulick.

Her father may have had some reason for his anxiety about Anna Louise and Gulick. It was almost certainly Gulick to whom she tersely referred as a source of pain in *I Change Worlds*: "I had fallen in love with a married man and had a nervous breakdown from the strain of repelling him." She spoke of the affair as "a ghastly accident which could happen to anyone." However, she was in fact seeing sexuality everywhere and was ill-prepared to do anything but fend it off. She wrote her father:

> I do know that I got some good-looking clothes abroad [in Japan] and I get quite a number of compliments on them. I also know that I often attract attention in a crowd of social workers, as being younger, enthusiastic, etc. I have experienced already certain advantages and certain disadvantages from this fact. The advantages consist in the ease with which some high-up people grant me interviews, consultations, etc. after they have once met me. . . . Now, my dear father, it is running blindfold into danger for me not to realize just what is or may be happening when a man looks at a young girl in a certain indescribable manner and grows suddenly gracious. It occurs too often to be ignored. New York is a frightfully overstimulated place.

Anna Louise was not inflating the positive impression that her physical appearance made on others. Her grandmother's bribes for good posture had served her well, and she carried her five feet, nine inches and one hundred and fifty pounds with exceptional grace. She not only liked buying "good-looking" clothes but carefully selected styles that showed her body to advantage; she took care to choose colors that complemented her startlingly blue eyes and light hair. She also had the kind of translucent, high-colored skin that made others want to touch. In her mid-twenties she was unquestionably an attractive woman.

She delighted in her physical appearance, but she also wanted to be taken seriously in her work, and she did not find the two easily compatible. A succession of young men and potential suitors appeared in her life. The most tenacious was Judge Ben Lindsey, a prominent reformist judge from Denver who had established the first juvenile court system in the United States. Sixteen years older than she, the combination of his slight physical stature and relentless political courage had earned him the nickname of "Bull Mouse." His most recent book, *The Beast*, an exposé of political corruption and child labor in Colorado, was causing a national stir when he and Anna Louise met in the fall of 1910. He courted her earnestly, but she resisted anything beyond simple friendship. Their easy camaraderie and shared interests were not the great passion she longed for, and when he indicated erotic interest, she felt her intellectual identity threatened.

As her visions of marriage and romance became increasingly vague, her work began to take on definition and focus. In September 1910 Owen Lovejoy offered her a position on the National Child Labor Committee. Neither Lovejoy nor anyone else was precisely sure what they wanted her to do, but they thought of her as a person whom it was important to have around. Despite this uncertainty and the fact that she had been with the Russell Sage Foundation for only six months, she accepted Lovejoy's offer. The National Child Labor Committee was a progressive, independent organization dedicated to improving the welfare of children, especially in urban settings: its central task was education through research, exhibits and lobbying, to "show all the forces in the city which affect the welfare of the child."

Her first months with the National Child Labor Committee were disappointing. Ostensibly, her job was to take exhibits all over the United States, to speak and educate local communities to the dangers of child labor and to raise questions wherever she went about hygiene, birthing practices, infant mortality and delinquency. But support for this large project did not materialize rapidly enough to satisfy her. She concluded that Owen Lovejoy was a dreamer—able to conceive of projects but not to carry them through. By December she had made plans to go to Seattle for at least an extended Christmas vacation.

On her way to the train, she ran into Walter L. Harvey, a member of the committee's executive board. Harvey had reluctantly agreed to take over the organization of the exhibit project, and he promptly offered Anna Louise the position of his assistant, at $170 a month. "It will bring me in touch with all sides of the entire exhibit," she wrote to her father, apologizing for not coming to Seattle as planned.

Her first task was to coordinate the various elements of the agency around a number of standard exhibit formats. She started out using stereopticon shows, but they did not seem to her sufficiently dramatic. There was, however, another medium available, motion pictures, which had only recently become part of American culture. Anna Louise immediately had a number of one-reelers shot that covered the problems at hand. *Starting Baby Right*, *The Man Who Learned*, and *Visiting Nurse* were among her favorites because they were both entertaining and educational. *The Fly Pest*, a melodramatic study of ignorance, disease, flies and their eradication, was, she proclaimed, the "dandiest." The free moving pictures drew such large crowds that at one point she was ironically accused of ignoring the welfare of the children who had to stand in long lines to gain entry.

The exhibits were a great success wherever they went, and Anna Louise could rightfully claim credit for them. She prefaced each with an open meeting to articulate local concerns and then planned the emphasis of the exhibit accordingly. The involvement of local citizens was crucial to her scheme. Administratively, on the other hand, she took command in the imperious manner that was to become her trademark. Once given the authority to make her own program, she focused entirely on the job and treated the other people involved as mere instruments to get the work done. It was with a tone of genuine surprise that she wrote to her father on February 18, 1911, just after the success of the New York exhibit:

> I have just been up against it good and proper. There's a fierce light that beats around a throne, you know. I've been accused of being unbearably rude and unmannered, making enemies for the exhibit, etc. A whole lot of the accusation was due to the tenseness of the whole work, a lot more to jealousy, most of the rest to misunderstanding. But when I go around in a fit of abstraction, forgetting to say good morning or good evening, etc. etc. it does hurt people. . . . The Gulicks handed me out a good long discourse on the subject last evening, because they thought I was worth saving.

Anna Louise apologized all around and tried to take the matter to heart. But her thoughtlessness toward others was based on the assumption that everyone around her had the same feelings she had and was in unspoken harmony with her. The existence of such a harmony, she said to a friend, "is what God is—or could be."

She was well on her way to reconstructing her theology in a manner that would reconcile her upbringing, her behavior toward others and her work. There were worlds to be conquered—or constructed—and it was clear to Anna Louise that one could have one's soul only if one had the world at the same time. It was these beliefs, coupled with her continuing urge to write, that separated her from women like Jane Addams. Her closest friends knew that Anna Louise was not cut out to be a social worker. "She had a philosophical-ethical outlook on social forces and larger ideas than doing good to disadvantaged people," one of them recalled.

She continued, nonetheless, with her work for the Child Welfare Exhibit Program, and in the fall of 1911 everything once again seemed right with the world. She finally made it clear to Ben Lindsey that she would not move from the friendly to the personal, and after an initial depression at his withdrawal from the relationship, she felt free to concentrate on her job. She was now in charge of the program in name as well as in fact. She threw herself into the Kansas City exhibit with renewed energy, and the result was the most successful show to date. Thirteen thousand people came to the exhibit, and "thousands more couldn't get in."

During her first days in the city, she met Ruth White, a woman of her own age who was the daughter of a prominent lumber industrialist. Before long, she was referring to Ruth as her closest friend. Ruth was head of the Standards of Living and Minimum Wage Committee for Kansas City. She acquainted Anna Louise with the city, and the two women helped each other to solve the daily difficulties that arose in their work. As their conversations became more intimate, they discovered that they were both searching for a political vision that would overcome the chaos they saw in the world. Their friendship was cemented when, after a few days apart, they found that they had each arrived at the same answer—socialism.

The man who confirmed this conclusion was Dante Barton, director of the industrial relations conditions committee for the Child Welfare Exhibit Program, a journalist for the *Kansas City Star* and an old friend of Ruth's. Anna Louise later described him as a wise left-wing Merlin to whom she and Ruth went to receive the magic words that would open the doors to socialism. In fact Anna Louise was Dante Barton's boss, and more important, neither Ruth nor Anna Louise was as naive about socialism as Anna Louise's accounts of this period suggest. Dante was, however, a good teacher. The two women had come to him because they thought he could help them make "socialism come true." Instead of welcoming them, he told them bluntly that the Socialist party would never let them in. But he had the patience and intelligence to talk to them of the realities of the class struggle—of strikes and violence and years of defeat before there might be any hope of changing the world.

He sent them to the Socialist party headquarters, where a worker repeated what Barton had already said: they should take their visions back to the middle-class world in which they lived and try to change things there. Shortly before midnight, after the closing of the Kansas City exhibit on November 3, 1911, Anna Louise cabled her father:

> Exhibit very complete and fine much enthusiasm Mrs. Kelley says she never saw exhibit anywhere that was so ruthlessly truthful. Much more radical than

the others but the executive committee will stand for it thanks for telegram please come by the way I'm turning socialist better come and see about it.

Her political transformation derived in part from her new position as boss which put her in touch with aspects of administration of which she had been only dimly aware before. She had to fire people who had no choice but to join the ranks of the unemployed. Recalling one such instance with a draftsman whom she admired, Anna Louise wrote, "How did it chance that I, a girl in my twenties, and in no way related to this man, had the power to refuse him the right to a living? His wife, his babies had nothing to say about it; but I, an outsider, had. What monstrous thing was this?"

Kansas City redefined and expanded Anna Louise's world. As she traveled the country to whatever city called her, her dream became not the homestead and forty acres of her pioneer ancestors but a society "where work and job and wages were public matters." In such a society, living for everyone would be efficient and "waste and chaos would be banished."

Shortly after the Kansas City exhibit, she was invited to organize a program in St. Louis as consultant to the research division of the St. Louis School of Social Economy. On the board of directors was Roger Nash Baldwin, a young man from a prominent Boston family who had moved to St. Louis after his graduation from Harvard Law School and was "looking around for people who had answers to poverty and injustice." Among his close associates were socialists, social workers, anarchists, Protestant preachers and a Catholic priest. Baldwin was also the chief officer in juvenile court and had just started to work with the Civic League.

He and Anna Louise were taken with each other from the moment that she burst into his office. Roger thought her one of the prettiest women he had ever met, and the combination of her beauty, intelligence and political conviction fascinated him. Anna Louise was equally attracted to Roger's elegant physique; she rarely spoke of him without referring to his good looks. They also soon discovered other ways in which they were strikingly compatible. In one of their first conversations, Roger asserted that he did not want a "normal" household kept by a conventional wife. Anna Louise was relieved and entranced. For the first time, she had fallen in love with someone with whom it was possible to contemplate marriage. Roger respected the demands of her work but relished their time together as much as she. They took long walks in the countryside, rejoicing in each other's knowledge of birds and flowers, spent evenings reading and sharing books, met and liked many of the same people.

Despite the acknowledged attraction between them, they were sufficiently self-conscious and middle-class to proceed cautiously with public plans for their future together. "We had gone pretty far in our relations when we told our families," Roger later recalled. In the spring of 1912, six months after she had met Roger, Anna Louise wrote to her father: "If you are really interested in examining into the antecedents (as I know you are) of the attractive young men I know, you might look up Roger N. Baldwin. . . . He is a very attractive youth of twenty-eight, chock full of social consciousness, but rather short on religion. If he should take it in his head to go after me, I should find some difficulty in resisting." In the meantime, Roger took Anna Louise home to meet his parents.

Sydney did not take long to respond. His next letter admonished Anna Louise to "avoid physical contact." Anna Louise countered by quoting Roger: "He told me that he had never before had a kiss that seemed so 'peaceful and natural.' " Sydney was not reassured. Another alarmed father-to-daughter letter followed. Just prior to Anna Louise's first mention of Roger, her sister Ruth had become engaged to Charles Niederhauser, a Seattle high school teacher. Ruth had not asked Sydney's permission to marry Charles, and her gesture of independence provoked disapproval from her siblings and great resentment from Sydney. Anna Louise had no desire for more of the same. She took care to inform her father of each small step in her romance. It was only the largest decisions that she ignored or diminished. But her father's anxiety about his daughter was not to be assuaged. He responded to each new piece of information with probing letters and telegrams. Was Anna Louise sure that Roger was not trying to "get" her? The euphemism covered a multitude of possible sins, all insidiously vague. Anna Louise responded that there was nothing to fear, for although she had indeed kissed Roger, she believed that a physical act did not in itself *mean* anything.

To her father's insistence that she would be humiliated if she allowed physical affection before there was permanence, she responded: "I can't feel any difference between this kiss last Sunday and the friendly kisses I've given girls. Same motive, same effect. . . . Moreover, I have often received kisses from a few girls (whom I was comforting on account of disappointments in love) which had a whole lot of thrill and actual 'sex feeling' in them."

The Sunday kiss had come after a long walk "scrapping about religion." Anna Louise detailed the walk and the kiss in obsessive length. Although she had by now known and liked Roger for six months, a kiss was still an unusual event for her. "You were perfectly right," she wrote to Sydney, "in saying that the kiss would be repeated. It has been, twice in the two weeks since then. And during and after each time I felt, not as if I had been degraded, but as if I had been put on a pedestal and worshiped."

Between themselves, Anna Louise and Roger had made a commitment to marry. They thought of themselves as formally engaged. Neither attempted to hide the decision, but they hesitated to make a public announcement or to set a wedding date. While they waited, conflict grew between them. Anna Louise saw the engagement as a time to make Roger over. She was no longer an active churchgoer, but she remained religious in what Roger called a "large sense.'" She was still her father's daughter, and it was difficult for her to imagine marrying a man "with whom she could not say her prayers at night"—whether or not she was actually saying them. Even more distressing to Anna Louise was that Roger smoked and drank occasionally. Roger thought that Anna Louise had made "reform a condition of marriage," and he rejected this attitude as "an invasion of personality."

Their sexual relationship and Roger's noxious habits became linked. They talked and wrote about going to bed together before they married. Roger was more candid and eager about this than Anna Louise, who, while she did not wholly reject the possibility, was inexperienced and mindful of her father's warnings. Roger recalled it ruefully: "We always kissed and hugged each other. She lay in my arms, but I wouldn't say that she was cozy. It wasn't as heated or as comfortable as that—more formal." He suspected that if he gave up smoking and drinking, she would agree to their making love, but he was not about to change his habits and assumed that after they were married the sexual tensions between them would disappear. Anna Louise also thought that they would work out the problems in their physical relationship, but the closer she became to Roger, the more troubling she found his indulgences.

They tried hard, nonetheless, to make the relationship work. Anna Louise took Roger to Ohio for Thanksgiving to meet her aunt and uncle. He found her relatives so straitlaced that Anna Louise seemed loose by comparison. They laughed together about Anna Louise's puritanical background. There were more visits by and to Roger's family. Then, despite Sydney's continuing letters of protest, Roger decided to confront his future father-in-law in person. He went to Seattle and spent three days with him. To their mutual surprise, they liked each other, at least as friends. Sydney had checked up on Roger's family background and found that the young man was of good ancestry and training. His only black marks were his protests against organized Christianity. After seeing and talking with Roger, Sydney admitted that he was a "fine fellow." Roger was even more admiring of Sydney; he found him to be a "true saint," gentle, kind and firm.

Throughout December, Roger and Anna Louise continued to think of themselves as officially engaged. Tension between them was eased by repeated separations. Both of their jobs necessitated frequent trips to other cities. Anna Louise organized a very successful exhibit in Montreal followed by one in Cleveland and another in Washington, D.C. The more success she had, the more opportunities came her way. When Anna Louise and Roger were apart, they wrote to each other at least once a day, happily sharing the details of their work and the growth of their affection for each other.

When she was away, Anna Louise liked being in love. Each time she returned to Roger, however, she provoked another discussion of the issues that separated them. By the end of 1912, she saw these differences not just as annoying habits but as metaphysical distinctions. At one point Roger claimed to believe in the ultimacy of liberty, to which Anna Louise responded, "Liberty for what?" "I know," she retorted further, "that liberty is an empty term unless it means that the human race shall at last be free . . . to respond to the great laws."

Roger wanted to enjoy being in love with Anna Louise, but his fiancée left little space for such pleasure. "There's a jolly irresponsible pagan in me that's going to get killed," he told her. "I guess he isn't much use, old junk—but he's a happy, carefree, inoffensive creature and I hate to see him die." He tried hard "to acquire a soul" and to change his behavior. But it was not enough. He saw that the deep portion of his self that turned toward anarchism and preferred the free to the good or even the right could never be at ease with someone as powerful as she. During the winter and spring of 1913 he felt increasingly that he was being forced to choose between remaining who he was and becoming what Anna Louise and her genealogy of Puritans required him to be. He chafed at Sydney's continuing interference and began to feel that the real question was whether he could marry both Anna Louise *and* her father. Anna Louise was not above pitting the two men against each other. In May she wrote to her father: "Roger's quite jealous of you. He says *he* doesn't want to control my judgment, but he hates to see any one else doing it."

In the late fall of 1912, in the midst of facing the complexity of her engagement to Roger, she had been offered a job at the headquarters of the new U.S. Children's Bureau in Washington, headed by a friend from Hull House, Julia Lathrop. She was not enthralled with the offer. It was a move up the national ladder of power and public prominence, but she was suspicious of centralized authority, and she knew from her friend at the Russell Sage Foundation, Leonard Ayres, that those in control of the social-work network already felt threatened by the power she had wrested from the establishment. "You see," Ayres told her, "you're not a social worker. You've never studied in the New York School of Philanthropy. . . . There are in New York certain experts who know how every community should be run and what every charity should do. They have a system as scientific as mathematics." Anna Louise's belief that the welfare of children had to be dealt with in the context of the minimum wage, working conditions, trade unions and compensation for work-related accidents was not part of that system, and by now she knew it.

She also knew that Washington was developing its first big set of bureaucracies, and rules about everything were proliferating. Rather than reject the offer, however, she proposed to Julia that a committee consisting of Jane Addams and Anita McCormick Blaine be appointed nominal supervisors of the exhibit program, with Anna Louise left free to run the exhibits as she pleased. Julia promised to pursue the idea, and Anna Louise left to set up a previously scheduled exhibit in Providence, Rhode Island.

Providence was sufficiently stodgy to make Anna Louise eager to return to Washington. Roger was in Boston for Christmas, but their plans for the holidays had been left vague, and Anna Louise wrote to her father just before Christmas with a perverse glee that "he has not yet communicated with me." Encouraged by what appeared to be an estrangement between his daughter and her fiancé, Sydney again pressed Anna Louise to join him in Seattle and help him with his work. When that plea failed, he asked her to take another trip with him to Japan at the beginning of April. She hedged on this as well.

Anna Louise did not want to move to Seattle, but she was accomplishing little in her position in Washington. In name at least, she was now working for three organizations—the Russell Sage Foundation, the National Child Labor Committee and the U.S. Children's Bureau, but none of them had enough of the right work for her. By June she felt too frustrated to remain in Washington and agreed to take a trip with Roger in the Appalachian mountains. It turned out to be a time filled with mutual affection. Anna Louise was, however, shocked by the conditions she found in the countryside. Like many progressives she had thought that the source of social problems in families was syphilis, "feeblemind-edness" and illegitimacy, all afflictions that could be cured by education and improved habits. Now she saw that poverty gave rise to the abject-ness of the people, and she concluded that the only solution was a change in the class structure, the source of poverty.

On her return to Washington in July, everything seemed to go wrong, and by fall she had begun to accept the fact that neither her professional nor her personal desires were likely to be fulfilled. She and Roger had good moments as well as bad, but the struggle was taking a heavy toll on both of them. Anna Louise told Roger that she would not marry him, then wrote to her father that she cried herself to sleep every night. She tried changing her mind: "Even last Sunday, I *offered* to marry him and to try not to notice things in which we disagreed. When he wouldn't trust me to do it, the world seemed to stop and then to go smash." Roger finally told her that he had to break off the relationship. Her criticisms of him had shattered his work and his self-respect. The path he chose, Anna Louise self-righteously informed her father, was to have "a perfectly respectable affair with a married woman."

With Roger and marriage no longer issues to be directly dealt with and her work in a state that she saw as stagnant, Anna Louise's life was at an impasse. On November 8, 1913, she sent a three-page letter to the national committee analyzing the impotence of her job. It was not a resignation, but it contained an offer to resign.

While she was waiting for an answer, she started west, stopping at Oberlin, at her Aunt Sarah's in Dayton, and at cities that were potential sites for exhibits. Her records contain no response from the national committee, and she did not resign. Neither did she spend much time working for the national committee. She went to New York, took up residence in the College Settlement House and began doing research for Julia Lathrop. The chief glory of this research was that the best way to do it was by driving a car. This was the beginning of her love affair with automobiles.

In March she received a letter from the Countess of Aberdeen pre-senting "her compliments to Mrs. Anna L. Strong and . . . venturing to write . . . to ask if Mrs. Strong could possibly come to Ireland and organize a Child Welfare Exhibition for the Women's National Health Exhibition at the forthcoming Civic Exhibition in Dublin." Flattered and eager for any escape, she solicited her sister Ruth's aid in putting together an appropriately elegant wardrobe and sailed for Dublin at the end of May. She arrived in an Ireland torn by the strife of home rule.

Writing to her father, her grandparents and anyone she could think of on the stationery of the vice-regal lodge, she detailed every point of etiquette at Lady Aberdeen's, the endless meals, who sat with whom, and who wore what. She reveled in the formality and precision of the arrangements. She went to Catholic services, admired the number of devout men she saw in church and wrote some Irish nationalist songs. She also mounted the child welfare exhibit.

In her spare time she immersed herself in a crash course in Irish history and came out strongly against the pro-British separatism of Protestant Northern Ireland. She greatly admired her hostess, ignoring the fact that Lady Aberdeen's politics were royalist and English rather than Irish nationalist. On August 2 she addressed a group of three hundred and fifty Irish volunteers in a field five miles from the vice-regal lodge. The volunteers were still an illegal body, and after the speech, she found herself interrogated by a police sergeant suspicious that she might have something to do with the gunrunning from America to County Kerry.

When she was not giving speeches, she was writing fervent articles for the *Westminister Gazette*. She had at least the grace and good breeding not to sign these articles, "as that would be embarrassing for Lady Aberdeen." The pieces were subsequently published in *On the Eve of Home Rule*, a book that set the style characteristic of her mature work. Although she relied heavily on quotations from her informants, she was herself a definite presence in the book, taking the reader with her to see and hear what she saw and heard. The strategy of the opening, a quotation from her Irish driver, was to establish American connections to Ireland: " 'Sure, it's the fine time fo ye to be comin' to Ireland now, with the Home Rule and all soon upon us. And is it from America ye are, now? It's the best half of County Mayo is in America. Sure, I had an uncle myself that was a senator from Philadelphia, and I never got a ha'penny out of him.' "

Anna Louise returned home the third week of August 1914, when almost all ships had been commandeered as war transports. Ireland had been wonderful, except that she had gained twelve pounds. She was not eager to return to her job as director of exhibits or to the tension within her family. While she had been away, Ruth and her husband Charles had moved out of Sydney's house, and her father was nervously trying to find someone to run the household.

Family problems took up much of Anna Louise's time upon her immediate return, but these seemed trivial in the context of World War I. "This war is one thing I can't grasp," a frustrated Anna Louise wrote to her father. "When I do, it seems to make all individual effort useless."

She went back to the U.S. Children's Bureau to a job that proved less and less exciting. One of the few benefits of her return was meeting David Thompson, chief of the Legislative Reference Bureau of the Library of Congress. Julia Lathrop introduced them, Anna Louise thought, in the hope of "setting them up," but it took three meetings before Anna Louise was interested in pursuing even a friendship with David. English by birth, he was a naturalized citizen, eleven years older than she, and a widower who lived with his sister. It was a quiet romance. David was gentle and undemanding and contrasted sharply with Roger. So did Anna Louise's feelings: "It seems a pity that he isn't a girl, as he seems in need of having his head rubbed and being petted."

Sydney quickly sent his daughter a list of questions about her new beau. Anna Louise assured her father that David passed all the tests that Roger had failed. He was "sweet, gentle, restful, considerate"; he had no "bad habits." Anna Louise was conscious of her continuing desire for a hero who would sweep her off her feet, but she was also lonely, restless, and disquieted by images of herself as a spinster. It took her weeks to confess to her father that David was not a practicing Christian and "would consider it a black lie to have the church perform any rites over him— funeral or wedding." It also turned out that he smoked, although only a pipe.

Anna Louise turned to Julia Lathrop for advice and was told that it would be a perfectably acceptable marriage. As soon as she had spoken with her friend, she regretted sharing the confidence, for the conversation seemed to settle the matter and Anna Louise felt imprisoned by the quick conclusion. Sydney responded with a convincing barrage of arguments against widowers—a subject on which he claimed authority—and Anna Louise became increasingly nervous, tense and frustrated. After three letters from her father, she estimated that the chances that she would marry David had moved from five in ten to one in ten. "I feel at present I would cheerfully promise not to see him again, if that would stop your worrying," she wrote to Sydney.

David eventually convinced her that true spirituality was possible without being a Christian. "Never in recent years do I remember any one who has so stirred and stimulated the spiritual side of me," she proclaimed in a letter announcing that she was coming to Seattle for Christmas. But her mother had also taught her that the true test of love was the feeling that you could not live without someone, and with David that feeling was never there.

She went from Seattle to San Diego to mount an exhibit, then on to

San Francisco for another. She took time off to climb to the top of Mount Tamalpais to see the sun rise and to hike in the redwood forests. Years before, she had worried about marrying someone with whom she could not say her prayers at night; now she worried about marrying someone with whom she could not climb a mountain: "A man who can get into a physical condition because the altitude of the Grand Canyon affects his head and the heat of Southern California exhausts him is not exactly the person I want for first choice! I am relieved to find that he doesn't want it either."

Her relationship with David now finished, she began a serious romance with mountains. During a stop in Portland for an exhibit, she joined the Mazamas, a mountaineering group, and organized the first post-season climb of Mount Hood. But she could not stay on the mountains forever. Her father, who had been industriously seeking employment for her in Seattle, eventually turned up a position running a girls' school. Anna Louise rejected it on the ground that she no longer thought she could enforce the conventions of proper behavior. She teased her father with the possibility that she might marry a forest ranger in order to organize women's outdoor clubs.

In October 1916 she made one last trip to the West Coast for the National Child Labor Committee and then resigned. She moved in with her father at the house he had bought next door to Tracy. Ruth and her husband lived nearby. To give Anna Louise plenty of space and privacy, Sydney moved out of his own bedroom on the second floor to an extra room on the first floor. They took meals with Tracy and Edith. Edith remembered to the end of her life that Anna Louise always "acted as if such fare were her due and never helped with the house or the dishes."

5

A Glimmer
on the Hills

And I think: Man
Has so few years
And so many problems,
It is best to UNDERSTAND each other.
WHY do we try so hard
To KEEP from understanding?
There is so little light
Each soul may offer
In the great puzzle
Of engulfing DARKNESS,
Why do we seek to HIDE
That LITTLE LIGHT,
When all of them together
Flaming GOLDEN
Might make us truly
A CITY of LIGHT,
Set high on many hills.

—Anna Louise Strong, "A City of Light"
  in *Ragged Verse*

By 1916 Seattle was one of the most progressive cities in America. With the defeat of populism and western silver in 1896, it had become a focus for American radicals seeking new opportunities. Eugene Victor Debs, the founder of the Social Democratic party, and Henry Demarest Lloyd, the economist and author, had started a series of small semi-utopian communities around Puget Sound which were loosely federated as the Brotherhood of the Cooperative Commonwealth. Edward Bellamy, whose utopian romance *Looking Backward* Anna Louise had admired in her teens, helped start the colony Equality on Padilla Bay, just off the Seattle coast.

In addition to the utopians, more practical socialists of all persuasions flocked to the Northwest. Since the turn of the century, young industries and a new work force had made the West fertile organizing ground for the Industrial Workers of the World, the most radical force in American labor at that time. The Wobblies, as they were universally known, were committed to the proposition that "the working class and the employing class have nothing in common." They were anarchist rather than Marxist and dedicated to the formation of a single union of wage earners rather than to a series of unions organized along craft or industry lines. In theory and in general practice they were opposed to any form of discrimination based on race, nationality or sex; class made the only difference.

Anna Louise found Seattle an ideal place for her talents. With her family as a secure base, she turned all her attention to the public world. Her work in the child welfare movement had given her a considerable reputation in progressive circles. In addition, she benefited from her father's prestige among the liberal and pro-labor forces in the city. She had hoped to run for the state legislature, but when she found herself petitioned by several hundred progressives, most of them women, she became a candidate for the school board instead. Supported by a coalition of labor unions, college-educated civic leaders, women's groups, and the federation of ministers, she promised to introduce "human and educational values" into school board discussions. This required, she asserted in her speeches, "a woman's point of view." She promised to oppose the "interests," a shadowy collection of those who put personal gain ahead of the public welfare; "I stand for stimulating the widest possible use of our school buildings for community centers," she wrote in her platform, "that we may get full return from the millions invested and that the schools may be real centers of public education." On Sunday, December 3, 1916, just a week after her thirty-first birthday, banner headlines in the *Seattle Intelligencer* and other papers saluted her easy victory. Seattle progressives were delighted.

School-board positions were unsalaried, and her colleagues were all well off. Anna Louise usually found herself a minority of one, able to sway only unimportant issues in her direction. Much of the business of the board was taken up with voting appropriations for "gas and heating contracts, new buildings in important new areas," about which, Anna Louise was quick to confess, she knew little. Nor did she learn. She refused to participate fully in school politics, much as she had refused to become a conventional administrator for the child welfare committee. Instead, she became involved in broader and more controversial issues.

On May 1, 1916, the International Shingle Weavers Union, a member of the American Federation of Labor (AFL), had called a strike throughout most of the Northwest. By August it had been won or called off in almost every city except Everett, Washington, home of the Jameson mill. Shingle weaving was among the most dangerous of jobs: the workers had constantly to reach around the cutting blades to turn the shingles so that they were cut evenly on all sides. If the weaver did not catch cedar asthma from the dust that penetrated even the sponge tied over his mouth, it was only a matter of time until he lost a hand or an arm to the whirling saws. On August 19 a group of thugs hired by the Jameson millmen savagely beat the eighteen pickets walking the line. Shortly thereafter the police in Everett began to enforce an "ordinance" passed by the city council prohibiting speechmaking downtown. Since 1914, free-speech questions and the right to address groups in public had been major issues to the unions. The Everett ordinance was tantamount to shutting off union organizing. With this, the IWW joined forces with the shingle weavers.

This was the background for what became known as "Bloody Sunday," November 5, 1916: the Everett Massacre. The IWW called a rally in Seattle for two in the afternoon, and the assembled crowd marched to the docks and boarded the steamer *Verona* for the thirty-mile trip up the bay to Everett. As the steamer approached the far shore, the passengers, singing "Hold the Fort," could see only three men assembled on the dock.

A large crowd had in fact come to accompany them to the meeting place but had been kept off the dock area. One of the three men waiting for the boat was the sheriff of Everett, who forbade the passengers to come ashore. When the Wobblies disregarded his warning, volley after volley of rifle fire broke out from two hundred deputies hidden behind the warehouse and from others on an opposite dock and in an adjoining tugboat. Eleven Wobblies were killed and two deputies died; thirty-one Wobblies were wounded. All the men on the *Verona* were arrested and charged with conspiracy and murder. They were formally indicted on December 26, 1916.

Anna Louise used her eastern connections to arrange to cover the trial for the *New York Evening Post*. The trial of the first defendant, Thomas H. Tracy, started on March 7, 1917. Her daily reports to the *Post* started with a quote from the prosecution or one of the state's witnesses. The rest of the story would subtly but devastatingly demolish the prosecution's position. On May 5, after twenty hours of debate, the jury returned a verdict of not guilty, and for Anna Louise the American system as well as

Thomas Tracy had been vindicated. Although she claimed to have been only a reporter of these events without "consciously taking sides in the struggle," Anna Louise's files contain a broadside requesting funds for the defendants that appears to have been typed on her machine and is corrected in her hand.

The trial over, Anna Louise spent considerable time with the IWW leaders in Seattle; she was also immediately faced with other political decisions. On April 2, 1917, after Germany announced a resumption of unlimited submarine warfare and after the discovery of a telegram offering the southwestern states to Mexico should she enter the conflict on Germany's side, President Wilson appeared before Congress requesting a declaration of war. To Anna Louise, as well as to many others, the announcement of a state of war was the last step in an unwelcome process. Anna Louise had been working with her father, an ardent pacifist, for over six months on "anti-preparedness" campaigns. Her reasons for her involvement were vague. In her letters from this period, she evinced little explicit commitment to the pacifist cause. But she did see the war as what the "interests" sought, and so she was against it.

Before 1917 it was respectable to wish to keep America out of the European war; indeed most liberals, including the mayor of Seattle, Ole Hanson, were of that persuasion. With the declaration of war, pacifism became illegal; Anna Louise's brother Tracy was jailed briefly until alternate work was found for him. Anna Louise had been conducting street polls that initially showed strong antiwar sentiment; suddenly they swung in the opposite direction.

Anna Louise's friends in the labor movement, notably Hulet Wells and Sam Sadler, remained pacifist and anti-conscription. Their names were signed to an anti-conscription leaflet that appeared shortly before the declaration of war. Anna Louise had been present at the meeting authorizing the pamphlet, although she did not sign it, and she became a main witness for the defense at the trial of the signatories, arguing persuasively for the legitimacy of the pamphlet *when it was written*. The jury returned a hung verdict.

The declaration of war on April 6, 1917, marked the beginning of Anna Louise's disaffection with the American political system. "Nothing in my whole life," she wrote, "not even my mother's death, so shook the foundations of my soul. . . . 'Our America' was dead! . . . The people wanted peace; the profiteers wanted war—and got it." She shared these feelings with Roger Baldwin when he came through the city on his efforts for the American Union Against Militarism. He told Anna Louise of his own plans to resist conscription. The memories between them were strong. "We both kind of wanted it back and toyed with it again," Roger recalled much later. "But it didn't come off." Baldwin returned to New York; Anna Louise turned to nature for solace. She fled "from the problems of human society I could not face" to the summer camp she had organized on the slopes of Mount Rainier. There she spent the summer of 1917, conducting hikes on glaciers, busy with the problems of pack trains, commissaries, and avalanches.

When she returned to Seattle in early September, she began to frequent the left-wing meeting halls of Seattle and to write for the radical IWW-oriented paper, the *Seattle Daily Call*, under the pseudonym of "Gale." Added to her nationwide reporting of the Everett trial and her testimony for Wells and Sadler, this act branded her as a "bolshevik," and action was started to remove her from the school board. It would probably have gone nowhere had Anna Louise not immediately confirmed her dangerously radical status.

Among her friends was a young woman named Louise Olivereau, who during the summer of 1917 had had a job as a typist in an IWW hall. On her own initiative she had mailed circulars to all Seattle men who were drafted, suggesting resistance to conscription. During a raid on the hall in September, copies of the leaflet were found in her desk and she freely admitted having sent out over two thousand. Indicted under the Espionage Act as a dangerous subversive, she was an easy target: thirty years old, well-educated, single, with no apparent family or connections, and gentle in manner. She insisted on conducting her own defense and asked Anna Louise to sit with her during the trial. Despite the urgings of other friends to think of her own position, Anna Louise did so as an act of friendship. Louise "rushed on jail like a moth on a flame," and when she was found guilty, so, by association, was Anna Louise.

The movement to recall Anna Louise from the school board immediately gained momentum. The key issue became the "no conscription" leaflet issued by the meeting three weeks before the enactment of the Selective Service Act. Anna Louise tirelessly pointed out that because it occurred *before* the act she had committed no crime and the attempt to link her to *illegal* antidraft activities was calumny, but the more she insisted on the chronology, the more she was judged to be a dangerous radical. An article she had written the previous year for the social-work journal *Survey* on "The Verdict at Everett" was repeatedly cited as proof of her connections to the dreaded IWW. As evidence of her patriotism, Anna Louise circulated almost 30,000 leaflets and copies of her poems, including one "dedicated to President Wilson, as an effort to express the ideal he has uttered for my country."

The labor unions did what they could to raise money and muster support for her. The petition circulating among longshoremen read:

> Regarding the recall of Anna Louise Strong, I think that we should take some actions to keep our ranks in the field and *brothers* who have children in the schools should give this a good thought *so* any one who wishes to help can come to the window and give whatever they feel able towards the Campaign fund and vote against the Recall.

The establishment papers in Seattle refused to cover Anna Louise's side of the story; one paper would not even take paid advertisements. On March 6, 1918, the recall election was held. Most of those voting against her came from the newer middle-class districts; her support was predominantly among the working class and older Seattle gentry. Anna Louise lost by 25,000 to 21,000, a narrower margin than expected. Her impressive showing emboldened her to urge in her resignation statement that the school board replace her with another woman.

The defeat nevertheless diminished her commitment to Seattle. She wrote Leonard Ayres on March 9 that she found herself "freer than ever before": "If you run across any place in Washington where I could do something, please let me know." From New York, Roger Baldwin sent her a note containing the right question.

> Dear Louise:
> I am glad you made the fight just as openly and as fearlessly as you did. Time will justify the strength of those of us who do not yield to blind authority and mob opinion. Congratulations and thanks; —your fight belongs to us all.
> What are you going to do?

What was Anna Louise going to do? She apparently quietly joined the IWW and continued to write articles for the *Daily Call*, most of them attempting to make vivid to Seattle workers events of international importance. She interviewed Michael Grusenberg, a Russian on close terms with Lenin who, on his way back to the Soviet Union to participate in the building of the world's first socialist state, stopped to talk with Anna Louise about the politics of the various Russian immigrant groups in America attempting to return to the new Soviet state. Shortly after this interview, Anna Louise's work on the *Call* came to an end. A gang of "patriots" wrecked the printing presses. Now the only left-wing publication of note in Seattle was the weekly *Seattle Union Record*.

The *Union Record* was an unusual paper. It soon became a daily and was for a time the only general circulation daily in the country owned and operated by a trade union—the Seattle branch of the American Federation of Labor. The editor was Harry Ault, himself a socialist, as his father had been before him. Ault had taken over the job in 1915, and with the demise of the *Call* had pushed the circulation of the *Union Record* from 3,000 to 25,000. He was quick to see that Anna Louise would be an important asset to the paper and offered her a choice of positions. She suggested that she be made editor of the features department and be paid not a personal salary but a salary for the entire department. She would then be in charge of allocating the funds, a control she had never had in the welfare movement.

Given the freedom to organize her contribution to the paper as she wished, she created a complex role for herself. She reported on international events of importance; she wrote occasional pieces of news analysis; she helped determine editorial policy; and she contributed a regular poem to the editorial page. Her signed contributions during the summer of 1918 included three articles on China; one on "What is an anarchist anyway?" (in reference to a proposed law requiring the deportation of all anarchists); a discussion of political developments in Russia; an analysis of the politics of Meyer London, the only socialist member of Congress; an essay arguing that art was important as long as it was available to the common man; an interview with suffragette Jeannette Rankin; and an analysis of the Seattle schools. Her reporting was good, but it was the poems signed "Anise" that made her reputation. These appeared as many as five times a week and were later published under the title of *Ragged Verse*, an accurate description of their assertive, unmannered style. One poem written during the Christmas season of 1918 expressed a hope so constant that she chose to reprint it fifty years later, fifteen months before her death in Peking.

THE TURN OF THE YEAR

I

Now
Is the turn of the year
At Christmas-time!
These are the darkest days
When the Summer's dead leaves,
Beaten by the rain,
Tossed by the wind,
Are rotted down

At last
Into NEW SOIL
For plants that are to be.
Now
Is the time when the SUN
Turns north again,
Bringing the glad new SPRING!
Oh, there are many days
Of winter yet to be,
The coldest of the year,
The windiest of the year—
Days when the earth
Seems FROZEN
And the promise of SPRING
Seems dead!
There will be long months
Of waiting;
But the turn of the year
Has come!
And THIS
Shall be known
As the sign;
That day by day
The DARKNESS lessens
And day by day
The LIGHT grows more!

II

Now
Is the turn of the age—
EARTH'S Christmas-time!
These are the darkest years.
When the old forms of thought,
The old customs,
The old systems,
Are beaten at last to dust,
SOIL for the world to be!
Now is the time when HOPE
Turns north again,
Bringing the glad new Spring!
Oh, many will be the years
Fierce with tempest;
Many will be
The bleak MIDNIGHTS;
And many the sunless mornings
When Winter seems ruler forever
And the promise of Spring

Seems DEAD!
There will be long years
Of waiting;
But the turn of the age
Has come!
And this shall be taken
As the sign;
That the light of TRUTH
And mutual KNOWLEDGE
Has flashed
From nation to nation;
And day by day
The darkness lessens;
And day by day
The LIGHT grows more!

Unabashedly derivative, her poems drew with equal ease from religious sources, well-known literary works and contemporary events. Her proclamation that the turn of the age had come was a response to what she saw around her. The American troops sent to Europe were not the only way in which the United States had dropped its isolationist veil. Europe had also come to America. All over the country the middle and upper classes were increasingly concerned that the same political and economic forces that had overthrown the czar and were convulsing the rest of Europe were also at work in the United States. Pamphlets from the socialist parties in Petrograd (soon to be Leningrad) and issues of the New York monthly *The Masses* circulated quickly from New York to Chicago to Seattle; across the country, workers and capitalists paid wary attention to the news of the closer revolution in Mexico. IWW halls were persistently raided, meetings of foreign-born radicals were disrupted, and movements to deport "troublemakers" gained momentum. The Bureau of Investigation kept careful lists of those with "radical tendencies." While Woodrow Wilson was trying to make the world safe for democracy, world history was threatening the dominant classes at home.

In no place was this more apparent than in Seattle. Like much of the West Coast, Seattle had profited enormously from war production. Large amounts of money had been poured into the Emergency Fleet Corporation headed by Charles Piez, and more than a quarter of all the ships produced were built in Seattle. To accomplish such a task required a rapid expansion of the labor force, and the shipyard unions had grown enormously. The shipyards were, according to the proud recollection of

James A. Duncan, head of the central labor council, 100 percent union-
ized.

To lure workers during the war, the Seattle yards had offered higher
wages than were available elsewhere on the West Coast. The highest
wages, at the Skinner and Eddy yard, had become the standard by which
wage contracts were now being judged in the industry. This created
problems in labor supply along the rest of the coast. In August 1917 a
shipbuilding labor adjustment board was established with the avowed aim
of bringing the Seattle union into line. The eventual offer was well under
the union demands, but during the war no strikes were possible.

From her vantage point as features editor of the *Union Record*, Anna
Louise paid careful attention to the increasing tension among the Seattle
workers. The language of labor politics came quickly and easily to her.
She attended meetings to learn about developments in Russia and, according to the informant for the Bureau of Investigation, led the crowd in
cheering the "Bolsheviki." Under Harry Ault and Anna Louise, the *Union
Record* was the only paper in the United States to publish *Soviets at
Work*, Lenin's address in April 1918 to the Congress of Soviets. The text
of the speech was published in New York by the Rand School, and Anna
Louise had been quick to recognize its importance. She cut the scholarly
annotations from the Rand edition, and, after the initial publication in the
Union Record, put out an edition with her own introduction and explan-
atory headings. Twenty thousand copies were sold on the West Coast.
When the central labor council of Seattle withdrew from the chamber of
commerce the next month, Anna Louise wrote the supporting editorial
for the *Union Record*: "Utopia is coming all right, but it is coming through
the absorption into the working class of all classes and the final mastery
of the world by the workers of the world."

For Anna Louise and for the workers in Seattle's shipbuilding industry,
as well as for steelworkers, miners, railroad workers and hundreds of
thousands of others across the nation, Armistice Day heralded the end of
one kind of war and the beginning of another. Throughout the arduous
negotiations of the previous year, Seattle's shipyard workers had been
waiting for this moment. On December 10, 1918, after an appeal and an
apparent refusal by Charles Piez in Washington to agree to direct negotiation between unions and employers, the decision to strike was voted
by more than the required two-thirds majority of union members. Piez
did not yield. Then a telegram messenger "mistakenly" delivered a telegram from Piez intended for the Metal Trades Association (the employers)

to the Metal Trades Council (the unions), threatening the owners with the loss of their steel allocation unless they held firm. Political indignation among the workers exploded, and the shipworkers went on strike.

In January the labor leaders of Seattle were temporarily distracted from the shipyards by an event that had attracted international attention—the Chicago convention to free Tom Mooney. Mooney, a militant unionist, had been accused, almost certainly falsely, of participating in a bomb explosion in San Francisco. The year before he had been condemned to death. With the end of the war, domestic and international pressure had led Wilson to commute Mooney's sentence to life imprisonment. Labor forces mobilized in late 1918 to try to force a new trial or a full pardon. On January 14, 1919, under the auspices of the Chicago Federation of Labor, a great gathering of Wobblies, as well as American and foreign socialists, assembled in Chicago to discuss tactics. With the shipyards still on strike, most of the labor council, including Anna Louise, went to Chicago. The discussion turned to the idea of a general strike by all workingmen and -women. The IWW and the French syndicalists present were much in favor of this approach; AFL socialists like Harry Ault were far more hesitant, worrying about possible union-busting and armed repression.

In the midst of the debate, word came from Seattle that the Metal Trades Council had voted to call for a general strike on January 21. Stunned, the Seattle leaders immediately left for home. Anna Louise later doubted that the general strike would have been called had the leaders been in Seattle. Once home, Ault and the others realized they had to throw in with the membership and go ahead with the strike. Votes in union locals were running sixteen to one in favor. The leadership did succeed in postponing the strike until February 6, so as to permit more effective organization.

Although Anna Louise was certainly not responsible for the general strike, she had helped to create the context that allowed it to occur. Her recall from the school board had inspired and united workers and intellectuals, and her writing for both the *Call* and the *Union Record* had informed and aroused many readers. In her public speeches, her private conversations with unionists, and her daily poems and articles, she had encouraged the people of Seattle to believe that their city could lead the nation in beating the old system to dust. When she returned from Chicago, she was engulfed in the tide of popular sentiment. Her editorials and poems in the *Union Record* give no sense of a plan or direction, but mark the flood of events. On January 31 she wrote about "Organizing

Random House: *Strong*

Iron and Steel" and contributed a poem, "In the New Day." The February 1 paper included an account of the Mooney convention, and in the same day's evening edition—events were moving so fast that the *Union Record* was publishing two editions—there was another poem and an editorial by Anna Louise that proclaimed: "Charles Piez has to be taught a lesson."

On Sunday, February 2, a general strike committee was elected, composed of more than 300 delegates from 110 unions. It immediately met to authorize special services for garbage pickup, hospital care, milk delivery and other necessities. The workers planned to run the city by and for themselves. Seattle unions did not want simply to stop capitalism: they wanted to supplant it. A steering committee of fifteen was selected and the date of the strike affirmed: February 6.

The middle classes in Seattle were highly apprehensive. A general strike was not only unprecedented in American life but called to mind the chaos and revolution of European countries. The *Seattle Star*, usually sympathetic to the cause of labor, panicked completely. On February 4 it warned workers:

> You are being rushed pell mell into a general strike. You are being urged to use a dangerous weapon. . . . It isn't too late to avert the tragic results which are sure to come from its use. . . . Confined to Seattle or even confined to the Pacific coast as a whole, the use of force by Bolsheviks would be, and should be, quickly dealt with by the army of the United States. These false Bolsheviks haven't a chance to win anything for you in this country, *because this country is America—not Russia.*

On the same day, the *Union Record* published two pieces by Anna Louise, neither of which set any minds to rest. The first was a poem entitled "Some Rapid Educating"; the end of the poem predicted:

> On Thursday
> We shall have stopped the works
> And taken them over.
>
> WHAT
> Shall we do with our town?
> Shall we leave it alone
> Till it falls into pieces
> And SOMEBODY ELSE
> Does SOMETHING?
> Or shall WE do SOMETHING?
> Plan it and organize it.

And START it again
Bit by bit as we choose,
FIXED
In the way WE WANT IT?

Even more explicit than the poem was the front-page editorial by Anna Louise, "On Thursday at 10 A.M." For her, the workers were setting off like pioneers, unsure of their destination, but with their sights on the property of the higher classes instead of on virgin land:

There will be many cheering and there will be some who fear.
Both of these emotions are useful, but not too much of either.
We are undertaking the most tremendous move ever made by LABOR in this country, a move which will lead—NO ONE KNOWS WHERE!
We do not need hysteria.
We need the iron march of labor.
LABOR WILL FEED THE PEOPLE.
Twelve great kitchens have been offered, and from them food will be distributed by the provision trades at low cost to all.
LABOR WILL CARE FOR THE BABIES AND THE SICK.
The milk-wagons and the laundry drivers are arranging plans for supplying milk to babies, invalids and hospitals, and taking care of the cleaning of linen for hospitals.
LABOR WILL PRESERVE ORDER.
The strike committee is arranging for guards, and it is expected that the stopping of the cars will keep people at home.
A few hot-headed enthusiasts have complained that strikers only should be fed, and the general public left to ensure severe discomfort. Aside from the inhumanitarian character of such suggestions, let us get this straight—
NOT THE WITHDRAWAL OF LABOR POWER, BUT THE POWER OF THE STRIKERS TO MANAGE WILL WIN THIS STRIKE.
What does Mr. Piez of the Shipping Board care about the closing down of Seattle's shipyards, or even of all the industries of the northwest? Will it not merely strengthen the yards at Hog Island, in which he is more interested?
When the shipyard owners of Seattle were on the point of agreeing with the workers, it was Mr. Piez who wired them that, if they so agreed—
HE WOULD NOT LET THEM HAVE STEEL.
Whether this is camouflage we have no means of knowing. But we do know that the great eastern combinations of capitalists COULD AFFORD to offer privately to Mr. Skinner, Mr. Ames and Mr. Duthrie a few millions apiece in eastern shipyard stock.
RATHER THAN LET THE WORKERS WIN.
The closing down of Seattle's industries, as a MERE SHUTDOWN, will not affect these eastern gentlemen much. They could let the whole northwest go to pieces, as far as money alone is concerned.
BUT, the closing down of the capitalistically controlled industries of Seattle, while the WORKERS ORGANIZE to feed the people, to care for the babies

and the sick, to preserve order—THIS will move them, for this looks too much like the taking over of POWER by the workers.

Labor will not only SHUT DOWN the industries, but Labor will RE-OPEN, under the management of the appropriate trades, such activities as are needed to preserve public health and public peace. If the strike continues, Labor may feel led to avoid public suffering by reopening more and more activities.

UNDER ITS OWN MANAGEMENT.

And that is why we say that we are starting on a road that leads—
NO ONE KNOWS WHERE!

Anna Louise's editorial became the most famous piece of writing to come out of the strike and remains one of the best-known documents of the American labor movement. Unfortunately, her open enthusiasm for uncharted territory did not help the cause of the strike. Supposedly the editorial had been approved by Harry Ault and the Metal Trades Council. In fact, Ault later recalled, he had demanded extensive changes in an earlier version and had let this one slip through because he was overtired. The tone of Anna Louise's editorial was influenced by Lenin's writings, but she had overlooked a key portion of his argument. Lenin had indeed said that the future could be thought of only as a question mark. He had, however, envisioned a highly organized and theoretically self-conscious party at the vanguard of the workers. No such organization existed in Seattle; if anything, the council was following the membership. Happily ignoring all such matters, Anna Louise set her faith in the semiorganized "natural" instincts of the working class. Life would go on, she thought, but the workers would now be in control.

The editorial had two political consequences, which together produced a devastating effect. On the one hand, it was so powerful that it impeded further discussion of the aims of the strike among the workers, the executive committee and the labor council. On the other, it served to convince the middle-class public of Seattle and newspapers across the country of a "Revolution in Seattle." The issue was no longer Charles Piez and the "interests," but the American system of government.

It was only a short step to the conclusion that the strikers were bolsheviks and anarchists. The day after Anna Louise's "On Thursday" editorial, the *Seattle Star* responded bluntly:

Under Which Flag?

The general strike is at hand. A general *showdown*—a showdown for all of us—a test of Americanism—a test of *your* Americanism. . . . A part of our community is defying our government, and is, in fact, contemplating changing that government, and not by *American methods*.

The two days before the strike were spent preparing for child care and milk deliveries. Public meals had to be organized, since no stores would be open. Provision was made to serve 30,000 meals a day in public dining halls. Ambulances and fire engines were allotted to appropriate committees. At 10:00 A.M. on Thursday, February 6, 1919, the strike bells sounded, and all work in the city stopped. Miraculously, everything went precisely as Anna Louise had claimed it would in her editorial. Important services were maintained; order was preserved; meals were prepared and served. Anna Louise had hoped that a spirit of communal endeavor and discussion would sweep the city as the workers took control and that the whole city might become a giant Hull House. For a while that seemed to be happening.

But there was one thing the strikers had not taken into account. Now that there was no need for stepped-up wartime production, the government could easily afford simply to let the strike drag on. By Saturday, February 8, the executive committee recognized this and by a vote of thirteen to one recommended the cessation of the strike and the opening of negotiations.

The mayor of Seattle, Ole Hanson, saw the opportunity to make a national reputation as the man who had "stopped the revolution" and, after consultation with Washington and eastern big business, refused to settle for anything but unconditional surrender. The 300-delegate general strike committee was also not prepared to yield and voted down the recommendation of the executive committee. The strike continued through Tuesday, February 11, by which time it had become apparent that its purpose had vanished. Anna Louise greeted its conclusion with a poem, "Trusting the People."

Ironically, Anna Louise accepted the middle-class verdict about the strike. She could account for its failure only as a defeat of "reds" by the dominant class interests. She did not then, nor ever in her later life, think there was anything un-American about being on the side of the reds. But she did conclude that intelligence, organization and goodwill could no longer be counted on to educate those who had less vision or who were scared or selfish. Clear planning and the seizure and use of power were also necessary. From this time on, she thought that she had lost the chance to claim America for herself simply by force of example, effort and goodwill.

She did not abandon her communal vision, however, but began to look to the land where the revolution appeared to have succeeded. If the triumph of right and virtue—the "revolution"—had not occurred in Seattle, it must have been because Seattle was, as the *Star* had said, in America and not in Russia. Whereas before the strike much of her editorial writing about distant lands had been about China—always the land for the missionary impulse—it was now more and more about the Soviet Union.

News of the extraordinary events in Russia was not hard to come by in Seattle: not only were there Lenin's writings, but in December 1917 a Russian boat, the *Shilka*, had arrived in port. Lenin himself had instructed the *Shilka*'s crew to carry the news of the new Soviet world to the workers in Seattle, and the Russian seamen had been enthusiastically received by Seattle dockworkers. Moreover, as Anna Louise wrote, "Reporters who had seen the Russian Revolution occasionally drifted into Seattle on lecture tours." There was Raymond Robins, once a top executive of the International Red Cross; Louise Bryant, an American socialist writer and the wife of John Reed; Wilfred Humphries and Albert Rhys Williams, sympathetic non-Communist eyewitness observers of the bolshevik revolution. Anna Louise spent many private hours with each of these lecturers, and the central labor council established a Bureau of Russian Information headed by her.

After the strike she threw herself into writing the history of the general strike. In April the entire editorial staff of the *Union Record* was arrested for attempting to "incite, provoke and encourage resistance to the United States . . . by presenting and purporting to advance the interests of laborers as a class and giving [them] the complete control and ownership of all property . . . through the abolition of all other classes of society described as 'capitalists' [or] the 'master class' . . . and of using the post office to distribute indecent and unmailable matters." Anna Louise was set free on $2,000 bail provided by Liberty Bonds of the boilermakers' union.

The indictment turned out to be a legal disaster for the government. Not only was there inadeaquate evidence to support the charges but in fact the strike leaders had been downright timid. When the evidence was brought forward, it was clear that they had been responsible for maintaining order in the city. Furthermore, the possibility of losing 40,000 labor votes from the Democratic party to the newly formed *Union Record*–backed Farmer-Labor party was apparently a sufficient threat for Washington to start pulling the appropriate strings. The case was dropped in early January 1920, a month after it had gone to the bench of Judge Jeremiah Neterer.

Anne Louise's radical reputation was, however, now firmly established nationwide. In April 1919 her brother-in-law, Charles Niederhauser, was fired from his teaching position as a covert German (the name sufficed) and as a relative of the notorious Anna Louise. The Niederhausers moved to Tacoma. Sydney was now known as the "Red Reverend" and saw his parish attendance fall off sharply; he accepted a six-month leave to take a church in Melbourne, Australia. When Luther Gulick's book *A Philosophy of Play*, on which Anna Louise had worked so hard and lovingly, appeared in 1920, a prudent acknowledgment substituted a pseudonym for Anna Louise's name: "It is most fortunate that Miss Anna L. von der Osten, who worked with Doctor Gulick in the original preparation of the manuscript, has generously given her time to the final preparation of the manuscript."

Anna Louise was still living in her father's house, and even before his departure for Melbourne, the house had become a center for political discussion. Anyone of interest coming through Seattle might very well wind up there, as did Lincoln Steffens, Upton Sinclair, Louise Bryant, and various Japanese dignitaries. So indeed did Frank Vanderlip, president of the National City Bank of New York. Anna Louise interviewed him for the *Union Record* and invited him to a supper her sister-in-law cooked. Vanderlip was so impressed with Anna Louise that he invited her to stay with him when she came to New York.

After Sydney left, Tracy sold his house and moved his family—he now had three children—into their father's house at 508 Garfield Street with Anna Louise. There were tensions. Anna Louise wrote to her father: "I am to have breakfasts with them and pay for them; I also arranged with Johanna [the maid] to sweep my room and do my washing for so much a week; Tracy will pay $25 a month rent and all housekeeping bills."

She continued to work on the *Union Record*, but much of the old fire was gone. She organized a drama club for labor, reported on other people's reporting, and wrote columns and more "ragged verse" about other places. She even knitted a pair of slippers that she brought to Roger Baldwin when she visited him in prison in New York, where he was in the sixth month of a sentence for evasion of conscription. "It was," Roger recalled, "as maternal as she ever got."

Back in Seattle, she still floundered. It was clear that this was not the place for a great work, but it was not clear where she might go. She seemed to have exhausted the possibilities of the United States. Two events precipitated her rebirth. A movement known as labor capitalism had arisen inside the ranks of labor. Union funds were used to start or take over laundries, theaters, groceries, even banks. The *Union Record* began to derive much of its advertising revenue from these enterprises. The whole affair split the ranks of Seattle labor. Anna Louise was caught in the middle: she liked Henry Ault, who was still editor of the *Record*, but she didn't like the control the advertisers were beginning to exert over editorial policy. She came under attack from "people she used to like" who now threatened to "run her name in the mud."

At this point, Lincoln Steffens returned to Seattle from a visit to the U.S.S.R. He was nineteen years older than Anna Louise, but after his last visit their names had been linked for a short while. Now, however, he was in love with a young Englishwoman, and he and Anna Louise met as friends in Blanc's Café. He spoke of the Soviet Union, where, he claimed, "with no government and no police force . . . there was order."

Steffens made Anna Louise realize the impossibility of reconciling the quarreling factions on the *Record*. "You must join one side or another," he told her, "or be torn in pieces by both." But there was another alternative: she could go to the Soviet Union as both a social worker and a part-time newspaper reporter on special assignment. Steffens suggested she contact the Quakers, the group most deeply involved in relief work in eastern Europe; she did, and was taken on to do publicity for the American Friends Service Committee.

Her decision to go was impetuous. In the middle of April she was busy making arrangements for the rent from her brother. On May 7 she wrote to her father: "The only people who can get any real fun out of life are either the frankly selfish folks who don't care what happens to the world; and the real Bolsheviks who see quite clearly that the Revolution is coming tomorrow to make all things right." A "very sudden announcement" appeared in the *Record* announcing her departure.

She acquired credentials as a reporter from the *Union Record*, as a free-lancer for both the *Nation* and the *Reporter*, and as a delegate from the northwestern United States to the Vienna meeting of Jane Addams' Women's International League for Peace and Freedom. She also planned to go to England for the Labour party conference.

In New York her new friend Frank Vanderlip put her in touch with American businessmen interested in Europe, and she changed her sailing reservations at the last minute to go on the same ship with the men who were on their way "to make the world safe for capitalism." "They are fine fellows," she wrote to her father, "unselfish (in the sense that they are planning for the business interest in the world, instead of for private gain or national gain), well meaning and mostly ignorant." None of them had the vision that Anna Louise required. "There isn't one of them who really dreams of making the world *better* than it was before the war. All they venture to dream is that it shall begin to commence to get back somewhere closer to where it was."

On the ship she also met Richard Waldo, who had just taken over as editor of the prestigious *Hearst's International* magazine. The Hearst News Service was one of the most vigorous news agencies, with a staff of progressive, intelligent young reporters, many of them with muckraking backgrounds. *Hearst's International* sought to promote international peace through understanding, and boasted contributors such as Rudyard Kipling, H. G. Wells and George Bernard Shaw. She was taken with Waldo ("He is terribly dynamic; believes that the chief end of man is to 'get things done' "), and by the end of the trip they had worked out an arrangement whereby Anna Louise would also receive credentials from *Hearst's* and would give them first refusal on six articles.

She arrived in Germany on July 5, 1921. Inflation had hit Europe east of the Rhine, and she was astonished at how far her money went. "The [German] government just keeps on printing this paper money ad lib!" she wrote her father. "And the value of it keeps on going down." By the last week in July her "mad career," as she called it, had taken her to Warsaw. For the Friends she wrote a series of pamphlets and reports on local conditions, especially in the countryside. Poland had had a good harvest but was suffering greatly from inequities of distribution. The AFSC handed out farm tools to peasants who had none and took care of refugees, many of them from across the Russian border. The experience gave Anna Louise her first sustained contact with dirt and disease: "One night . . . we slept in an open field of a malarial village near the Western border, and another night . . . we did not even try to sleep because the bedbugs in the Baranowicze railway station were so thick that even sitting down was torment and we walked the platform all night long."

Her supervisor and companion in Poland was Florence Barrow, a thin, gentle Englishwoman who had worked with refugees in Russia until the Allies ordered her out after the signing of the Brest-Litovsk Treaty between Russia and Germany. Anna Louise realized that Russia was where Florence longed to be and confided to her her own intention to go there. As soon as she could, Anna Louise contacted Mitchel Rubenstein, secretary of the Soviet embassy in Warsaw. It turned out that he had read her verses in the *Record* while he was an émigré in the United States before the Revolution; he promised her a visa for whenever she could come.

The only difficulty was her commitment to the Friends. The home office of the American Friends Service Committee was reluctant to grant any of its representatives permission to go to the U.S.S.R. Anna Louise worked on Florence Barrow, insisting daily that the most important thing one could do for world peace was to report truly and accurately the conditions of the famine in Russia. Barrow finally agreed and gave her permission without referring the question back to the home office in Philadelphia. Anna Louise took the train the next day to Minsk and then to Moscow. She was just in time, for within three weeks all Quaker activity was placed under the American Relief Administration headed by the U.S. secretary of commerce, Herbert Hoover, who immediately secured a pledge from the Quakers that all relief workers would be approved by him.

6

Crossing the Bar

There was no further west for me to go, so I went to Moscow.

—Anna Louise Strong in an interview
with Julia Older, *Hartford
Courant*, December 10, 1933

As soon as one has made up one's mind that the struggle in
Russia is not in essence different from elsewhere, that there
are the same old enemies of greed, private interest, etc., then
one begins to discover real advantages in Russia. I think I have
told you how amusingly the Greenwich villagers become disillusioned with Russia, while the dear conservative Quakers want
to settle there for life.

—Anna Louise to her father, November 1922

When Anna Louise arrived in Moscow late in August 1921, the Soviet
Union was, for the first time in its young history, mainly occupied with
internal problems. Despite the aid of the American Expeditionary Forces,
the counterrevolutionary White Russian armies had finally been defeated
both in the north at Murmansk and in the south in the Crimea. Lenin's
overtures to Western governments for recognition had fallen on deaf ears,
but in response to a plea from the writer Maxim Gorky, England, France
and the United States had agreed to supply food to the famine-stricken
areas of the Volga basin; in return, the U.S.S.R. recognized the debts of
the previous regimes, though not the principle of indebtedness.

Anna Louise arrived with a portable typewriter and reams of paper; a
large basket of food including many chocolate bars, which, she had been
warned, would be irreplaceable; a flashlight, which soon burned out; and
every conceivable credential. Officially she was a publicist for the American Friends Service Committee, now under control of the American
Relief Administration; a correspondent for four separate journals; and the
envoy of the labor council to any meeting that might require a fraternal

delegate from overseas. She recalled Lenin's statement, which she had circulated to workers of Seattle three years earlier: all that the Revolution required was conscientious and efficient workers. That, at least, she was sure she was.

After securing lodging at Quaker House, headquarters of the AFSC, she set off to pursue her dual vocations of publicizing the Friends' relief effort and reporting on the Revolution. She went from one government agency to another, offering to print whatever news they thought worthy of notice. To her frustration, no one told her anything, and she was passed along with little more than evasive grunts. It was a great relief when Arthur Watts, the head of Quaker relief work, offered her the chance to get out of the city and go to where news were being made.

The heart of the Russian famine was the town of Samara (later renamed Kuibyshev), some 600 miles southeast of Moscow, at the juncture of the Volga and Samara rivers on an almost treeless steppe. A middle-sized town in normal times, it was now swollen well beyond its capacities by the famine in the surrounding area. The Quakers sent two freight cars of provisions, and Anna Louise accompanied them. It took more than ten days to cover the distance because of frequent long stops for fuel.

Bread had run out a few days before Anna Louise reached Samara, and people were eating loaves made of a mixture of grass, bark and straw. The few who still had possessions were exchanging them at exorbitant prices for the produce that a few outlying farmers occasionally brought into the black market. The two boxcars of food that came with Anna Louise provided merely psychological benefit, a reminder of what food was and a sign that more might arrive. Hygiene was practically nonexistent; there was a typhus epidemic. Freezing temperatures made it impossible to do more than strip the dead of their clothes, which were passed on to the living, and then stack the bodies like cordwood in areas reserved for that purpose.

Anna Louise's first instinct was to share her food with the starving. Her letters in 1921 reflect a poignant realization of the moral problem that confronts all relief workers. To be fed, even if not sumptuously, in the middle of general famine, did not sit right with her. But she soon learned the discipline of the cadre and kept her food to herself, especially the chocolate bars.

She threw herself into her two full-time jobs. By day, she organized the relief effort, particularly for the children. By night, she wrote of the effort for the Friends and the *Record* and occasionally for *Hearst's*. By the time her interpreter, Sonia, appeared, Anna Louise had already made

arrangements with the local authorities for the distribution of food from
the two boxcars. "Sonia," she recalled, "was horrified; she warned me
that even doctors and teachers were robbers and must properly be controlled by the Samara Executive Committee." So many refugees were
pouring in that nearly every day a new home for abandoned children had
to be opened. In the midst of the despair she found hope: "I marveled
how the organized life of human society persisted through death and
chaos. Normal life asserted itself through discipline and education; and
the forms it took were new forms, fixed by the revolution. Fixed by these
creators in chaos who held nothing impossible, and who, organizing, held
on through every famine."

At Samara, Anna Louise learned a lesson she never forgot: "creation in
chaos" could be accomplished by people working their hearts and souls
out, often without reward or notice. "The [outer] Russian offices were
chaos, clogged with sluggish people who made no pretense of being
interested. But somewhere behind them were men in the inner offices,
working early and late, wearing themselves out, men who made the
whole thing work. These men did not care, like those clerks, for their
own cup of tea, their own food, their own jobs; to them every job of the
Soviet power was close and dear."

Her reports to the Friends were much like those that had been so
successful with the child welfare exhibits program. Published as pamphlets, her stories of the victories and defeats of particular famine victims
had an impact; the Quakers, somewhat to the distress of the ARA, continued to raise substantial funds on their own, as well as to distribute
whatever came through the United States government. Anna Louise sent
all her reports by cable from a telegraph office where no one spoke
English and only one clerk knew the Latin alphabet. It was not until
months later that she learned that her cables had reached the *Record* and
Hearst's as well as the Friends.

Her experience at Samara was brief, intense and pure. After four
weeks her head began to ache so badly that she was unable to work. Five
days later, it was discovered that she had typhus. Her first reaction was
one of relief. Typhus was beyond her control; it even served as an "initi-
ation fee" into a world she was now entitled to call hers. Five other
members of the ARA were stricken at the same time, and one of them
died. Anna Louise herself was very sick. A dedicated nurse named Mary
Pattison, on her second tour of duty in Russia, took expert care of her.
Though Anna Louise does not appear to have known it, Mary caught the
disease, probably from Anna Louise, and later died of it.

For almost a week Anna Louise was delirious and relived her life and her hopes in bizarre nightmares:

All night a nightmare of wild Cossacks pursued me, shouting "You can't resist" as I tottered over desert sands. I woke in a rage of utter exhaustion. What was the use of a doctor who couldn't even give you a night's decent sleep? "It would serve that doctor right if I went crazy," was my last vindictive thrust of consciousness. Almost immediately I did go crazy, escaping from Samara in a soft warm airplane.

I dropped in the Coliseum in Chicago and began to tell thousands of people about the famine. They must hurry, hurry with food! I saw my sister's face in the meeting but I could not stop to see her, I must take my report to London. I couldn't land in Fetter Lane in front of the Quakers' office; the streets were too dangerous for taxis. So I hunted for Miss Frye on the third floor of her country house, but the labor troubles on the second floor made it hard to get up and down. The water made my throat taste cottony; I was surprised that they had such bad water in England. Once they gave me a lemon that cut deliciously through the cotton; they brought it in a suitcase from London. But when I asked for more, the transport was blocked to Turkestan. What crazy excuse was that?

Her delirium retraced her steps for the last thirteen years, except for the times when she was with her father in Seattle. She wrote Sydney only after she was out of danger. "I passed the crisis, when you die or you don't, and came to, quite without pain, but very weak. Typhus gives an awful jolt to your nervous system and general strength and leaves you very flat. After you start to get better you discover what has been left to you in the way of complications. A death from typhus would not be a bad one, but getting well from it is awful trouble. I first had a few days of acute neuritis, shooting pains in my left side. Then that stopped and in a couple of weeks I had reached the stage where I could walk unaided to the bathroom or veranda; I had my reservation for Moscow; then this thrombosis developed in my leg. . . . You have to lie down and wait while your leg swells and goes down again, and you don't dare move for fear of dislodging a clot that might go to the heart and stop the works." She was finally taken to Moscow on the private train of Fridtjof Nansen, the head of the International Red Cross and erstwhile arctic explorer, and convalesced until the beginning of February.

The news of Anna Louise's illness convinced Sydney that there was no time to waste in getting on with the "great family project" he dimly had in mind. He sent her four copies of the same letter insisting that she join him, and all four copies arrived over the next two months, increasing Anna Louise's pride in the Russian postal system. But the anxieties expressed in the letter produced an effect opposite to the one Sydney intended. The Friends, already under pressure from Hoover to make sure that they engaged in no politics, had indicated to Sydney that his daughter's reporting for the press was perilously close to advocacy. She was now writing that justice and social virtue required concerted, centralized, authoritative action by the government. Sydney wrote that America was "still touchy" about Russian news and asked that she tone down her reporting. Her response was characteristic:

> I fear that you will be still more worried about other things I have sent to the
> *Record* and I herewith give you leave to censor them all. But you must
> remember that I owe a duty not only to the Friends, but to a large public of
> the *Record*. . . . I made it quite plain to the Friends before I left that I must
> send frequent letters to the *Record*. They knew my labor connections and
> accepted me with them. Incidentally, a letter from Jennie Matyas tells me
> that "the Friends are getting quite popular through me." So you must realize
> that there are two sides to every question and it doesn't pay to be apologetic.

She went on to describe the depth of her attraction to the Soviet Union. The "spiritual stimulus" was much greater than in America. "Here, whatever their failures, they are giving their lives and effort to one of the biggest experiments the world has ever seen. They may not work it out on the lines originally laid down; in fact, if one thing is sure, it is that no one can have a complete idea of what it will become; but at least they have the capacity to face facts, to recognize their mistakes, to accommodate themselves to reality, and to make concessions without losing sight of their original goals." What intrigued her most was the ordinary life in Russia, people's struggles with "oil, coal, transport, wheat . . . and so on." She was eager, she added, to learn Russian.

She had found a unique point of view. Most foreign journalists were treating the Soviet Union as the result of a simple coup d'etat and lived in the expectation—for some, the hope—of another upheaval. They tended to not take seriously or ignore the efforts being made to transform the fabric of ordinary existence and productivity. Few people in the West grasped the depth of the Bolshevik project. Those like John Reed who had written positively of the Revolution stressed the new political structure, the military, and the leadership. No one knew much yet about running a socialist or communist government; Marx himself had proclaimed that ideas could be tested only in practice. Surrounding Lenin were a group of highly competent, independent men and women who were about to experiment with divergent ideas. By focusing on changes in industry, agriculture, education, and especially the roles of women and children, Anna Louise hit upon the most important and difficult task for the Revolution. She was also able to avoid paying much attention to what had offended her in Seattle, the ebb and flow of political rivalry.

"Believe you me," she informed her father some weeks after she had arrived back in Warsaw to complete her convalescence, "the communists you meet in Russia, whatever their faults, are not lazy folk living off their views of life. They are people sobered by heavy responsibility under which only the hard-working Puritanical sort survived. . . . The Puritanism meant is not at all temperance for its own sake, but temperance because excess interferes with efficiency." She had discovered in the U.S.S.R. a group of women and men exactly like those her father had praised week after week from his pulpit. That they were not Christian paled before their valor and constancy.

In Warsaw, Anna Louise finished the six-month contract with the Friends, but her thoughts remained in Russia, and her attention was focused on finding a way to return. She received another note of chastisement from the home office and a complaint from the Friends' headquarters in Philadelphia that she was not sending enough publicity fliers. In Seattle, Sydney got a telegram from Herbert Hoover defending the ARA's claim that clogged ports at Petrograd made it impossible to send more foodstuffs to Russia; the telegram was a rebuttal to Anna Louise's public insistence that the United States was acting only in self-interest. Anna Louise recognized at once that the way was being paved for a refusal to renew her contract. She angrily retorted that she had sent out more material than any of the previous publicists and that Philadelphia was playing politics with her reports.

She saw no clear way of getting back to Russia, but had no intention of returning to Seattle. During her absence, Tracy had made a reputation for himself as boys' work secretary of the YMCA for the state of Washington and was now considering a position at the headquarters of the World Alliance of YMCAs in Geneva. Ruth was living in a small town in central Washington, and Sydney seemed inclined to return to Melbourne if Anna Louise would not commit herself to a collective project with him. Seattle was no longer the family home.

Just before she left Russia, Anna Louise had spoken with Ludwig E. Katterfield, the representative of the American Communist party in Moscow, about becoming a correspondent for a loose association of labor and left-wing publications known as the Federated Press. He had offered her $25.00 a week plus transportation costs—the "communist wage." Uncer-

tain whether this was enough to draw her back to Moscow, she decided
to go to London to complete her convalescence and consider her options.

The American embassy in Warsaw, however, had received orders not
to return her passport and to notify the State Department as soon as she
applied for her exit visa. Enraged, she contacted two influential friends,
C. F. France, the brother of the progressive senator from Maryland Joseph
France, and E. A. Filene, the Boston businessman whose department
stores had developed a form of worker participation. She hinted to Filene
that if she had her passport, she could arrange a special Russian tour for
a visiting group of American businessmen. Pressure was brought to bear,
her passport was returned, and she left immediately for London. There
Richard Waldo offered her a regular salary to file reports on Russia to
Hearst's International magazine, which had become one of the most
prestigious journals covering international affairs.

In answer to a dismayed letter from her father asking if she meant to
settle permanently in Europe, she wrote that if she were to settle, it
would be in Moscow. She assured him that this was not an ill-conceived
decision:

> In any event, I shall do nothing hasty, and nothing without coming home
> first. That is to say, I shall join no communist organization or anything that
> would be illegal in the United States; I shall keep my independence as a
> correspondent. And it is quite possible that on my return to Russia, I may
> find a closer look destroys the illusion. The lack of language is a difficulty, and
> it is an impossible language. So I am really not thinking of becoming a real
> Russian as much as I am thinking of working towards a position of authority
> on Russian affairs for the English-speaking world.

She arrived back in Moscow on June 6, 1922, and by June 16 was
established in the Hotel Metropol, which was about five minutes from
the Kremlin and reserved mostly for government and official workers.
Her acquaintance Dalina Suchanova, a party member who had an important position in the state publishing house, had offered to let her share
her rooms there, since Dalina's husband was often in Berlin on assignment.

Almost instantly, Anna Louise became a star reporter for *Hearst's* and
a model practitioner of a new kind of international journalism. She had
extraordinary energy, skill as a writer, and a keen sense of the issues that
most concerned the Russian people and might also interest Americans:
How did the people get food, find an apartment? What was happening
to families, especially to women and children? How were the steel mills

going to be made to work? For Anna Louise, Russia was a country redeemed by a thousand small acts of heroism rather than by the feats of a
leader. She chronicled the incompetence she encountered and rejoiced
in those who responded to it by redoubling their efforts. She gave Americans a new and living image of the Soviet Union, written in a seductively
transparent style that never lost a certain prairie canniness. Her writing
was what contemporary journalists call soft news, with the focus not on
the crisis of the day but on the contexts and issues that might give a
perspective to hard news events.

In early August, someone, probably Dalina, introduced her to Leon
Trotsky, then war commissar and the leading figure on the party central
committee after Lenin. Anna Louise was struck by his flamboyant and
heroic style and by the iron-willed discipline he was bringing to the
reorganization of Soviet industry. Her account of these impressions was
translated into Russian and published in *Izvestia*.

The Trotsky interview strengthened her conviction that Russia was the
place to make a commitment, and she decided to investigate mines in
Karelia on the Arctic Circle with the idea of investing in them. Disappointed by the chaos she found there, she went to Berlin to meet her
father, who was on his way home from Australia. They spent most of
October together in Berlin and Cologne and at some quiet resorts in
between. Anna Louise raised the possibility of his living in Moscow for
part of the year. Sydney did not immediately embrace this plan, but he
accompanied her back to Moscow in November and stayed with her for
about a month. He did not like what he saw. The procedures associated
with the expansion of the free market under the New Economic Policy
(NEP) convinced him that the same old structures of exploitation would
be reestablished. Besides, the heating was inadequate. He returned to
Germany.

In December, Anna Louise attended the meeting of the Red Trade
Union International (Profintern) as the delegate of the Seattle labor union
council. With credentials signed by Lenin himself, she was not only
granted an advisory voice at the congress but received similar standing at
the concurrent meeting of the Communist International and sat somewhat coyly for a group photograph of the English-speaking delegates.

She had just turned thirty-eight. With her carefully bobbed dark-blond
hair, striking height and proud stance, she commanded immediate attention, most particularly from Trotsky. He had not forgotten their earlier
meeting, and this time he did not let her slip away. Within a few days he
had asked her, she wrote her father, "to teach him English, coming by

appointment several times a week." She did not mention that Trotsky, who had lived in the United States and Canada for a short period, already spoke some English. He proposed that he give her Russian lessons in return, to which she demurred on the ground that this would take too much of his time. "I told him that the conversations would give me enough information on things in Russia, and enough contacts, to be worth a great deal to me. Then he said that any time I wanted to go anywhere in Moscow, and needed an automobile, I should call up his office."

Trotsky was very direct. He asked her details of her past life and of her experience in the labor movement in the United States. Anna Louise interpreted this to her father as evidence of his concern with conditions in the United States. Before long she was visiting him at his office four or five times a week, and he was telling her intimate details about his childhood and his relations with his father. She began to plan a biography.

The automobile materialized as promised, and Anna Louise did not hesitate to use it. The grand old matriarch of radical American politics, "Mother" Ella Bloor, arrived in Moscow with her attractive thirty-five-year-old son, Harold Ware, and a group of American farmers who had come to help with agricultural questions in the Soviet Union. When they made contact with Anna Louise, she obtained the Trotsky automobile to take them out to see schools in Sokolniki, a suburb of Moscow. Trotsky was certainly, as she wrote to her father, "going to be very very much worth knowing."

Under Trotsky's tutelage, Anna Louise's political education accelerated. Against her hopes for a workers' revolution in Germany, Trotsky argued that the chances were "nine to one that there would be a compromise of some sort" between big capitalism and the workers. No one could be sure, he told her, that such an agreement would come about, for the German government was very stupid in its alternating defiance and weakness in response to working-class demands. But if it did, a general conflict—into which Russia would inevitably be drawn—might ensue. Trotsky dimly foresaw the dynamics that would eventually result in National Socialism and World War II; Anna Louise took it all in, not quite sure what to make of it, but impressed with the brilliance of his vision of world history.

Rumors began to circulate about the attractive American correspondent and the war commissar. The American community in Moscow assumed that Anna Louise was having an affair with Trotsky. At the very least, she had the kind of infatuation for him that she often had for those with power. Trotsky, of course, was neither celibate nor monogamous.

When her father asked about Mrs. Trotsky, Anna Louise answered breezily that in Russia wives led their own lives. A friend from the time remembers that Anna Louise "enjoyed her English lessons very much" and wanted Trotsky to marry her.

Her relationship with Trotsky provided her with a reason for remaining in the Soviet Union. "Physical condition is excellent," she wrote her father. "I really think in Russia I am much less nervous and cross than I used to be at home. Perhaps that is because I have so few human contacts! But I don't feel lonely either. I wish often that I knew more Russians, and once in a while it seems to me that I am stuck in a little room all by myself way off from everyone I know. But when I stop to consider, I realize that I never have any acute attacks of lonesomeness, leading to real weeping spells, as I sometimes had at home. And while naturally I have slight ups and downs in my estimation of myself and the world, I spend more of my time gasping at my good luck than in any other mood!"

Trotsky was ill during the first part of 1923, "on account of general brain fatigue," according to Anna Louise. Actually, he had contracted malaria and was sent to a dacha some twenty miles south of Moscow, with orders from his doctor to confine his reading to French romances. Anna Louise reported the prescription with a note of flirtatious banter: "He laughed when he told me this, and I told him that I hoped that he would not consider it his duty to come back with a book written on modern French romance, based on the reading of a hundred of them, as he did with Russian literature after his last vacation in the Crimea." She hoped to be permitted to visit Trotsky because, she told her father, this would mean that she would go in an "auto-sled," a "new Russian patent," that would take her the twenty miles over snows too deep for automobiles and too long and strenuous for sleighs.

She did not get the chance to visit Trotsky, but she did receive an invitation from Christian Rakovski, a member of the central committee of the Communist party and chairman of the Ukrainian Soviet, to visit the "Pittsburgh of Russia," the Donets region, center of coal and steel production for western Russia. Trotsky, who returned to Moscow at the end of January, strongly urged her to accompany Rakovski, and she seized the opportunity. She traveled in Rakovski's private railroad car, sharing a compartment with a woman official, and reveling in the lack of apparent class distinctions: "I noticed that . . . when Rakovski called down the aisle for the porter it was 'Tovarich Provodnik—Comrade porter.'" On the way, Rakovski filled her in on a project that Trotsky had mentioned to her. The Trotsky group in the central committee was trying an experiment in industry. "They took over," she wrote, "a series of unprofitable factories, on a contract which makes them responsible for all failure, but which gives all the profits to the state. What they gain is freedom to act without red tape." She did not know at the time that this "experiment" was the source of a major conflict between Lenin and Trotsky which was making possible the advance of Stalin and his allies Lev Kamenev and Grigori Zinoviev.

In the Ukraine coal mines, half a mile under earth, Anna Louise met a gang of American miners who had come over to help with production and to escape the unemployment besetting American mines at this time. She immediately interviewed them and analyzed their lot for an article. They worked harder than the Russians but were "too concerned" with production. Their buying power was less than in the United States, but they had guaranteed work. How did they get along with their Russian comrades? " 'Not very well,' they admitted. 'The more intelligent ones, the communists and union officials, are glad we are here, because we are bringing up production. But the others—they would like to see us go tomorrow. They don't like our speed; they don't like our extra wages.' " (The Americans were paid by the carload, precisely the kind of piecework unions were striving to eliminate in the United States.)

Throughout the trip she worried about her father, who had remained in Europe and become involved in various pacifist movements in Germany. Inflation had reached unprecedented proportions, and there was agitation and unrest throughout Germany. "Please don't kill yourself and make me feel that I invited you around Europe to such an end!" she wrote him. But she also advised him not to return to Seattle. She hoped that what he saw in Germany made him better disposed toward Russia. "I am interested," she wrote, "in knowing the effects of Germany on you mentally. I remember once how, when Tracy and I got into a fist fight, it was mother who wanted to stop us, for fear that we would get hurt, and you who realized that we must see it through, though you were in theory the pacifist and she wasn't. I wonder if you won't see a time in the Ruhr when revolution will seem less of an evil and even less violent than the day-by-day life of the people."

Upon her return from the Ukraine, she continued to see Trotsky occasionally, but she no longer had the daily meetings that had structured her days during the winter. In her loneliness she turned to Mother Bloor's son, Hal Ware, who had accompanied her on a number of trips to agricultural sites in the Ukraine, and who seemed to share her sense of the similarities between Russians and Americans. She confided to a number of friends that she would probably marry him. A few people hinted that he might already be involved with Jessica Smith, an enterprising young woman who, like Anna Louise, had originally come to the Soviet Union with the AFSC. A letter to Sydney in early April 1923 suggests that her friends' hints had had some effect:

> You have to get used to a new attitude of mind on the part of young people, Father. Even I myself do not entirely agree with you, but I make my manner of life conform far more to your ideas than to my own, simply because I know what a tragedy the whole thing is for you. But there are times when *I rather regret this intense clinging to the absolute ideal of married life* [her italics]; and realize that the time will come when you will not be here and I shall be very lonely, and that I might have had children of my own if I could be content to give up the demand for absolute certainty beforehand and start on a married life which might or might not prove permanent, but which would at least be worthwhile while it lasted. I get such chances occasionally—they are not men for whom I would give up my own work and be content to follow their fortune in whatever land they might go; but they are interesting men who would be good comrades and make life much richer.

In the end, she went on to say, the only thing wrong with Roger Baldwin had been that he was a "bit selfish"; however, "most men were."

Other Americans in Moscow were also lonely, and many of them were planning to leave Russia, bringing back tales of the failures of socialism in yet another land. "The first arrivals expected a worker's paradise and were swiftly disillusioned by the ruined land they found. . . . They assumed that goodwill and efficiency would speedily carve out a place for them." The Soviet government was making efforts to avoid the potential anarchy of foreign talent. Foreign workers were admitted only as part of a commune, an organized group supplied with its own machines, equipment, food, clothing, and goals. Most of the communes failed, but from among the participants who lasted, who could not be defeated by either the rigors of the climate or the rigidity of the bureaucracy, Anna Louise began to draw some friends.

What was needed, she decided, was an institution on the model of Hull House that bridged the gap between Russians and Americans and created a network among Americans abroad. The impetus to organize a "Russian-American Club" was strengthened by the support of two new friends, Mikhail and Fanya Borodin. Mikhail Markovich Borodin had just returned from six months in an English jail, where he had been imprisoned as a Bolshevik agent. He was acquainted with all the top party leadership and was a protégé of Lenin's. Actually, as they soon discovered, Anna Louise and Mikhail had met before, in Seattle, in early 1918, when he was Michael Grusenberg. Borodin had lived for many years in the United States and had remained there after the Revolution to organize the screening of the thousands of emigrés who wanted to return to the new Russia. He had left for the Soviet Union through Seattle, accompanied by Krasnoschekov, an old Chicago friend of Anna Louise, who was now chief of the Industrial Bank in Moscow.

Borodin fascinated her. Tall and imposing, with deep-set eyes and a drooping mustache, he looked like what he was, a longtime, dedicated underground Bolshevik. He had an extraordinary range of knowledge and facility with several languages; he could quote statistics of grain harvests, province by province, and recite long passages from Shakespeare in English. Mikhail had met and married his Latvian wife, Fanya, while studying at Valparaiso University in Indiana. In America he had also lived for a time at Hull House; Jane Addams had been a reference on his subsequent visa application.

Anna Louise inspired Mikhail and Fanya with her idea of a Russian-American Club, and by June they had obtained a five-room cottage thirty-five miles from Moscow to serve as a temporary clubhouse. Anna Louise quickly realized, however, that the dacha was too small and too inaccessible for the Russian-American Club, and she began looking for a more suitable place. By this time she could get along passably well in Russian. She discovered that the ARA would soon be vacating a building known as the Blue House and decided this would make a good site for the club. She persuaded the head of the ARA mission to donate the Blue House furniture to the new clubhouse. In addition to its thirteen bedrooms and staff "used to American ways," the house was to contain a reading room and information service, an engineers club, and a network of guides and interpreters. Anna Louise established a tentative executive committee, with Fanny Borodin as chair. Then, having virtually announced the impending opening of the club to anyone who would listen, she informed Borodin, Trotsky and Trotsky's brother-in-law Kamenev, who had just been made a vice-president of the U.S.S.R., that everything was set. Borodin, who had been distracted from the project by his own new assignment—he was secretly preparing to depart for China—expressed delight that things had gone so well. Kamenev seemed supportive. And Trotsky only added the suggestion that she include American businessmen as well as those inclined toward socialism among her potential guests. She was confident that the club was assured.

Her enthusiasm was boundless. She urged her father to come to Russia for a longer visit than his previous one; he could deliver sermons on the relation between social justice and religion! She thought that her brother might have a good chance to organize boys' clubs and teach some of his newly developed techniques for the creative use of recreation to the Red Army. Her brother-in-law, Charles Niederhauser, could come and organize high schools.

She shared these hopes with Tracy when he came to Moscow in early July, and he encouraged her. In turn, she put him in contact with his potential counterparts in the U.S.S.R. Tracy never seriously entertained the possibility of staying in Russia, but at one of the meetings with Soviet youth work leaders, he suggested the name he had used in Washington, Pioneers, as a designation for the ten- to fourteen-year-olds, and the Soviet leaders adopted it. Anna Louise and Tracy talked at length about Tracy's future, and by the end of the visit he had decided to accept the offer to join the World Alliance of YMCAs in Geneva.

On July 15, in the midst of Tracy's visit, "permission for the club [was] categorically refused by the Department of the Interior, which licenses organizations, on the ground that they cannot allow prominent American businessmen and senators to maintain an organization here while America refuses to recognize Russia." She wired Trotsky at once, but he was again ill and out of Moscow. New overtures to Kamenev were to no avail. Borodin tried to comfort her: "It was a good idea, the way we started it," he assured her. "You pushed it and it was needed and some of it will come through. Not now—it may be too soon, and perhaps not in the same form. As for you personally, I understand just now you are completely broken. When you have been broken twenty times more, you will be fit to live in Soviet Russia." When she next attempted to reach Borodin, he had vanished.

She began to have severe and constant headaches and was relieved when Tracy left Moscow on July 26. Her depression was in great part anger at herself. She took the failure of the club as a sign that she had not managed to change from a middle-class American who thought in terms of efficiency into a person who thought first in terms of the collective. "Russia," she averred, "is really very anxious for American ideas and methods, in industry, education and all along the line." Since others had received buildings for factories, rent-free, on the condition that they raise the capital to start production, Anna Louise began to envision another project—a center that would propagate American ideas of education, especially those of John Dewey.

At the end of September 1923, she left Moscow. For the first time in over two years, she was on her way to the United States, where her father had set up a lecture tour for her. She stopped in London and met with the newly elected Labour members of Parliament—"good folk, but lacking the nerve to seize a situation." She took tea with H. G. Wells one day and Bertrand Russell the next and found to her pleasure that she had a one-track mind. "Nothing interests me except Russia and the various people connected with it. People here seem futile, lacking in any real reason for living."

The most productive part of her sojourn in London was a meeting with Horace Liveright of the publishing firm of Boni and Liveright. The various articles she had written for *Hearst's* added up to a book. All that was lacking was a publisher and a title. Liveright not only agreed to publish the book but also thought up the title, *The First Time in History*.

She stayed on in London to revise the manuscript, and while the result was not a great book, it was lucid and informative, honest in its recognition of difficulties the new Russia faced, and optimistic about the future. There was a three-page introduction by Leon Trotsky praising Anna Louise for having been "able to see, or perhaps at the very beginning to feel," the struggle against age-old ignorance and slavery in favor of "higher forms of life." This was the theme with which Anna Louise closed the book: a "common consciousness" that would change mankind as much as the evolutionary move from animal to human being.

Before leaving London, she wrote an article for *Hearst's* describing Lenin as a prophet and ruler who "commands the inner thoughts and loyalties" of his people. During her return home, Lenin died of a lingering illness. She wrote another article, which appeared in the April 1924 issue of *Hearst's* on "Russia's Leading Politician: J. V. Stalin." This article was the first extended discussion of Stalin in the American press and proclaimed categorically that "as far as Lenin can be said to have any successor, Stalin inherits his place." Anna Louise saw that Stalin's organizational skill had given him the edge over Trotsky; Stalin had attained preeminence by always occupying the middle position in every conflict.

In the United States, Anna Louise went quickly to Washington, where she met with Senator William Edgar Borah, who was then holding hearings on the Soviet Union. From there she made her way westward, speaking in New York, Cleveland, Oberlin and Chicago. She had planned to arrive in Seattle by February 9 or 10, but to her delight she was in constant demand. Her old contacts—Jane Addams, Lillian Wald at the Henry Street Settlement, Wilbur Thomas at Quaker headquarters—greeted her as a celebrity. She savored every moment, as did the Bureau of Investigation, which was now opening her mail and trailing her around the country. After a week in Hull House she finally arrived in Seattle ten days later than she was expected. She lectured almost every night of her short stay and left hurriedly for further engagements in Chicago, Boston, and New York, much to the irritation of her father, who had come back to Seattle to await her return. As soon as she departed, he wrote her a curious letter, asking her what he was to do and pointing out that at one time *he* had been the one asked to speak around the country. Anna Louise wrote back:

> I have still one general line of advice—to get a regular JOB. . . . But then there is another question—your whole personal life. I can't help feeling that it was a great pity that nothing happened years ago between you and Mrs. [Ginevra] Smith. She had dinner with me last night, and remarked that she understood that you might come to Chicago, and . . . said: "Once, for six years of my life I cared more for your father than I have ever cared, or expect to care for any other human being.". . . . I can't help feeling, as I always have, that it was your absorption in your children, and especially in me, which prevented you from finding some solution to your own personal life. I also feel, though this will seem farfetched to you, that it has been your intense interest in all my relations which has checked *my* getting married.

After barely two months in the United States, she left for London, Berlin, Warsaw and Moscow. The late April blossoms that greeted her return to Moscow evoked an initial celebratory mood. Her high spirits vanished, however, when she discovered that in her absence Hal Ware, whom she had decided would indeed make her a good husband, had married Jessica Smith. She held no grudge against Jessica, who had become one of her own friends during that spring, but she wrote to her father that it now seemed unlikely that she would get married at all. She had put on enough weight by the time she returned to Moscow for her friends to comment, and she continued to gain steadily after her arrival.

In early June, while she was still looking for long-term living arrangements, she was approached by Ruth Fischer, the Russian wife of an old Bolshevik who had lived many years in exile. Prior to her return with her husband to the Soviet Union, Ruth had been prominent in the German Communist party. For several years she had worked as a go-between for Soviet governmental organizations and Quaker relief work and had on her own started an agricultural commune for older children in her hometown of Khvalynsk. The civil war of 1918–22 had left tens of thousands of children homeless. The younger ones were placed in foster homes as fast as possible, but the older ones constituted a seasonal nomadic group, coming into homes for winter shelter, running away again in the spring. They formed the nucleus of a potential social problem: all of them were vagabonds and most survived through petty theft. The commune for these adolescents, which Ruth Fischer had named the John Reed Children's Colony, was in danger of foundering from lack of support from the regional authorities. Ruth turned to Anna Louise as a possible source of help from the outside world. Five thousand dollars was needed for supplies, rebuilding the old convent which served as the main living quarters, and acquiring farm machinery.

Anna Louise embraced the project with the skills she had learned in the child welfare program. She set up a committee, printed a pamphlet describing the situation and sent copies to her father, requesting him to seek support for this "self-help project." Only then did she remember the lessons of the Russian-American Club and get around to the source of the problems the colony had been encountering: "I have learned the reason John Reed had such hard sledding was that it wasn't started in the orthodox way at all. Mrs. Fischer wanted it for her hometown, to look after the homeless famine orphans. And her hometown, Khvalynsk, was too small and distant to receive the immediate notice of Saratov [the administrative oblast], which had a lot of other projects on hand. So she started it herself by main force and nearly killed herself during the winter trying to get food, etc., for it. However, that's nothing against the colony, except that now, in getting a bigger place we must take it up properly with the provincial authorities and go with the current instead of against it."

With her father's help, Anna Louise raised several thousand dollars. In an appreciative gesture, Ruth Fischer put in a good word for her with the central committee, and suddenly an apartment became available in the Hotel Continental, normally reserved for the use of high officials of the Communist party. The party central executive committee also gave her credentials from the children's committee. For the first time she had an official role in the Soviet Union.

At John Reed, Anna Louise encountered situations for which she had no solution and which did not respond to her abilities to raise money. At one point the children fired the cook "because they could do it alone." She was initially pleased with this form of self-help, but a closer look revealed growing anarchy. "The older girls make good bread, but when the younger ones are on the job, there is war in the camp and unpleasant comments from the boys. When all you eat is rye bread and soup made from cabbages and potatoes and a little fat, you want those things decently cooked. And when you are camped in a stable fourteen miles from home, and ploughing in two shifts from dawn to moonlight and they send you down a week's supply of bread, all of it rather poorly made—it makes a real difference in your life." The boys also complained that the girls destroyed their underwear through overly vigorous washing; hence they rarely had it washed. This last condition was not alleviated until Anna Louise received money from her father to buy one thousand meters of muslin.

Still, Anna Louise found cause for celebration. She gloried in the 200-odd children who passed through John Reed and moved into Soviet society as productive human beings. She rejoiced in her love for her new friend Yavorskaia, who gave up her summers to be a mother superior to the children.

To achieve self-sufficiency for the colony, adults skilled in cottage industries were needed. Anna Louise sought disciples where she could find them, but increasingly she tried to bring them from overseas. Only in that way could she retain some control over their competence and attitude. A French-Russian shoemaker came from New York, as did two "dental mechanics." Later she convinced a left-wing Genevan watchmaker named Prousse to open the first watchmaking establishment and school in the Soviet Union and proudly accepted one of the first watches made in the U.S.S.R. as her own. Like any good missionary recruiter, she did not disguise the difficulties at the commune, but she had a way of making any hesitation seem an unworthy weakness of will. When Lipp, the shoemaker, raised a question about his wife, she responded directly:

> . . . It is a common fact that most communes smash on account of the women, who seem unwilling to cook for other women's husbands, or to look after other women's babies. This is especially true of American women, . . . [who] . . . mostly expect to be supported.
> So my advice is this: if you are going to have to support your wife anyway, consider where you can do it most easily, America or here. . . . If she will support herself, . . . she will be an example to the other women . . . who may prove a serious problem to us. . . . If we have five intelligent women and *all* of them do nothing but look after her own youngsters all the Russian communists are going to say we are terribly bourgeois.

After a summer of organizing for the commune, she found herself pulled in three directions. She wanted to go back to America; lecture invitations were accumulating, and there would be no problem in paying for the trip. She also wanted to go to China, where Trotsky had persuaded her the "imperialistic entanglement" would soon lead to a revolution. Finally, there was good reason to stay at John Reed and write a book on the children's colony. Typically, she did all three.

She wrote the book first. Entitled *Children of Revolution*, it presented the most hopeful picture possible of the experience on the Volga: "The very first night they held a meeting. They had a supper of thin potato soup—just potatoes boiled in water, with a little sunflower-seed oil to supply fat—and then they gathered round the lamp to discuss the future. They decided to get up at six every morning." She justified her romanticization of the situation with the knowledge that the purpose of the book was to make money for the colony. But by the time she finished writing, the demand for human interest material on the U.S.S.R. was slight. Boni and Liveright rejected the manuscript. She finally had it privately printed in Seattle, where her father sold it at fifty cents a copy.

She left for the United States in time to stop in Geneva for Christmas and the first two weeks in January. The vacation enabled her to get to know her niece and nephews. The mild winter cold did not prevent her from hiking and climbing, and her favorite sports renewed her spirit. Conversations with Tracy reconfirmed her sense that they were both pursuing the same social ideal. Each was sad that their father's dream of a family united in Seattle had not worked out; both still accepted the central tasks of that dream.

The visit had its difficulties. As always, Anna Louise assumed that family was there to take care of her. She left it to Edith to wash her clothes, to make train reservations for a trip to Chamonix to climb, and to pick up after her. One day, while Anna Louise was on the way home from a ski trip with the whole family, Tracy spoke to her about her behavior. An argument ensued, and both of them lost their temper. Tracy stopped the car and said that if she would not apologize to him, he would not go on. Anna Louise stormed out of the car and started down the road. Tracy promptly drove home. When Anna Louise arrived at what she thought was the house, she burst in, sat down in the living-room and started removing her heavy hobnailed boots. It was not until twenty minutes later that she discovered that she had walked into the house of her brother's next-door neighbor and colleague, Basil Matthews.

In late January 1925 she returned to the United States to publicize the achievements of the Soviet Union and to make contact with her home audience. A number of her recent articles for *Hearst's* had been turned down by the new editor, Norman Hapgood, and she surmised it was because she was out of touch with Americans. "I want to swing clear to the coast," she wrote her father, "especially in those districts where recent farmer-labor developments have taken place. . . . I am inclined to stay away from the more recognized 'communist groups' such as the workers' party, etc. . . . Better consult Mr. Hapgood on this, for I do not want to do anything which might hinder future writing for the recognized periodicals of the country. . . . I can do Russia more good by telling facts in simple English, to the general public of America."

Her first lectures were in New York, then up and down the East Coast and across the Alleghenies. She met with more hostile responses than on any previous trip. The conservative press made certain that readers were informed of her political orientation. The DAR attacked her; a pamphlet called *The Woman Patriot*, subtitled "Dedicated to the Defense of the Family and the State against Feminism and Socialism," was passed out at all her speeches, identifying Anna Louise in exaggerated terms as the person "in charge" of all of Russia's children's colonies.

Nevertheless, the tour was a success. She was an impressive speaker and persuasive publicist, and she was particularly effective at women's colleges, where many of the students asked what they could do. To Anna Louise's distress, some even appeared the next year in Moscow, wanting to be set a revolutionary task.

During the visit to the United States, her friendship with Hal Ware and Jessica Smith waned, largely because Anna Louise thought Jessica scorned her continuing connections to bourgeois circles. But her bourgeois connections fell through, too. *Hearst's International* folded, ironically because its success cut into the potential readership of a new, more lucrative Hearst periodical, *Cosmopolitan*. Hearst decided to absorb the *International* into *Cosmopolitan*. Hapgood sent Anna Louise to the editor of *Cosmopolitan* with what she called a glowing recommendation, but her potential new employer wanted confessions, not news of life in Russia, and Anna Louise decided that her path did not lie with "the petty tradesman's world to whose tastes of sex and luxury Hearst catered."

Anna Louise arrived back in Moscow in May 1925, accredited only to the Federated Press. She thought of herself as a free-lancer. She spent the summer working in the apple orchards at the John Reed Children's Colony and trying to complete the colony's transformation into an American idea of a farm. Despite the thousands of dollars that had been poured into the colony, conditions were still very bad. The children were ill, several of them with trachoma; the kitchen was so disorganized that the girls who worked there were more exploited than ever; the school was practically nonexistent. Anna Louise blamed no individual but faulted the lack of organization. She did, however, serve notice on the officials in Saratov that unless genuine attention to organization was forthcoming, she would send no more funds to John Reed.

In fact Russia was not as exciting as it had been two years earlier. Stalin's efficiency continued to win skirmishes against the romantic personal style of Trotsky and others, and Anna Louise began to look elsewhere. That summer, as Trotsky had predicted, the most exciting revolutionary developments in the world were in China where the Soviet-supported Nationalist party (Kuomintang) had extended its control over the entire province of Kwangtung and its capital Canton. The lure and promise of China had been instilled in Anna Louise by both her family and Oberlin College, and she now decided to exploit her reputation as a foreign correspondent to chronicle the Chinese revolution.

Anna Louise requested an interview with Stalin but was turned down without explanation, and on October 8 she left Moscow for China. Clear about the shifts in the political wind, she submitted another article on Stalin's personality to *Survey* magazine. The last letter she received before her departure was a rejection slip.

> Dear Miss Strong:
>   Stalin, as you say, is an interesting figure. But I do not feel that you have got underneath the surface into the fiber and makeup of the man. After reading your article I know certain facts about him, but I do not feel that I have seen him vividly or that I know him.

The greater her distance from her subject, the less convincing she was to herself and to her readers. It was unlikely that Stalin would have granted an interview to someone so closely identified with his rival. But for Anna Louise, Stalin's rejection almost ensured weak journalism. It should have been an omen of her future struggles with the phenomenon of Stalin's rule.

7

Two China Trips

The Mongolian man was the most fascinating creature I ever
saw outside of a fairy tale book. . . . Good thing for you that I
didn't go along, or I might have applied for the job of second
wife. They say such things are done among the Mongols.

—Anna Louise to her father, October 1925, on board
the Trans-Siberian Express

Anna Louise boarded the Trans-Siberian Express for Vladivostok in a raw
relentless downpour that complemented her state of depression, and her
private, first-class compartment only contributed to her despondency.
The Soviet chief concessions committee refused to make her their representative in New York. She had no obligations until the beginning of
her American lecture tour in January and was headed for China on an
adventure she had wanted for years, but she was leaving Moscow with
neither personal nor institutional ties behind her. She had wanted to
become indispensable. If she had succeeded, she would not have been
on this train going east.

In her most bitter moments, she complained that all that her freedom
amounted to was that "there is nobody in all the world who cares." She
longed for attachments that would give her stability, reasons to choose
one direction over another. The men to whom she had been attracted
were now her good comrades, but she was not essential to any of them.
She could not understand why she was so different from the women to
whom they were attached. She was uncomfortably aware that in little
more than a month she would be forty years old.

The depression apparently passed. As the raw slopes of the Urals gave
way to the sunny plains of Siberia, she wrote to her father that she had
"changed to a summer dress . . . and thrilled with joy to know what a
great and vivid world lay open" before her. She boasted that the Trans-
Siberian Express was "steadier, faster and cheaper" than American trains,

and that while she had no lover or husband to give focus to her life, she had friends in every land who would be glad to see her. Ahead of her, after the month in China, was the heaviest schedule yet of lectures on the Soviet Union.

During the trip she struck up a conversation with a Russian woman on her way to meet her husband in Mongolia; the woman herself was a "high-up" advisor to the Mongols. By the time the train had arrived at her acquaintance's destination, Anna Louise had conceived a new plan for her own journey. At the stopover, she tried to persuade the woman's husband to help her cross the Mongolian mountains to Urga (Ulan Bator). From there she would continue "the fifteen-hundred-verst drive across the Gobi Desert, coming in by the back door. . . ." The trip itself would be an adventure, and she would get the opportunity to interview one of China's most important warlords, General Feng Yü-hsiang.

He refused her request. Without a Mongolian visa, he warned, he might be forced to abandon her at a frontier four hundred versts (265 miles) from any railroad station while he drove on to Urga. She continued on the "prosaic road" via Harbin with Danish and Swedish merchants and various diplomatic couriers. A week and a half later she was in Peking.

In the fall of 1925 Peking was still a city of old China. The seventeen-meter-thick walls of the inner city were intact, framed by square merlons pierced by loopholes. Moats surrounded the walls, rancid with green slime and overgrown with plant life. Vera Vishnyakova-Akimova, a Russian friend of Anna Louise's then living in Peking, described the oppressive poverty and ill-health: "Beggars stood, sat and lay along the sides of every street . . . dirty, half-naked, often blind or with red suppurating eyes. Trachoma gathered a bountiful harvest. With wild yells, they crawled or ran after the passerby, stretching out a small, saucer-shaped wicker basket or a tin begging cup."

Remarkably, Anna Louise wrote little of the horrors of Peking. Instead, she proclaimed that she had "fallen in love" with the city: "If I had any real work here, I would love to live here." She declared emphatically that it was *not* the "exotic culture of shrines and ancient palaces" or "the shopping for jade and silks in second-hand shops outside the walls" that attracted her, but the ferment in the city and its continuity with the Russia she had left behind. She delighted in Peking as a city of talk, public and private. Invitations appeared from a dozen organizations and schools to lecture on the Soviet Union. More than forty percent of China's college students were living in Peking and many were enthusiastic students of Western thought, particularly the works of Marx and Lenin. Only the previous May, an unarmed student protest in Shanghai had been violently suppressed. The students appeared at Anna Louise's lectures eager to ask questions. Among them was Chen Han-seng, a student and teacher at Peking University who would later work in America as an expert on Chinese foreign relations and international agrarian reforms. Chen never forgot his first glimpse of Anna Louise. Her unassailable composure and impassioned voice captured attention in the large, packed lecture hall in the YMCA. Everyone, Chen recalled, was impressed by her wide range of knowledge and her forceful presentation of the achievements in revolutionary Russia.

On business at the Soviet embassy soon after her arrival, Anna Louise suddenly found herself face to face with Fanny Borodin, about whom she had known nothing since Fanny and Mikhail had "vanished" from Moscow in the summer of 1923. Fanny immediately urged Anna Louise to revise her travel plans to include some time in Canton, where Mikhail was working with the leadership of the Chinese Nationalist party (KMT). "You must not miss our Canton," she insisted. "It is very different from the rest of China. Already, here in Peking, I grow homesick. Here in the North—medievalism, feudal armies, confusion. No one has any plan; everyone waits for the foreigners. A flabby country still; but our Canton is hard as nails, clear-cut as crystal. The Cantonese know what they want; they are begging nothing from foreigners. They are going to take what they want—and help all China." Anna Louise was easily persuaded, and Fanny set about making arrangements through Soong Ch'ing-ling, the recent widow of Dr. Sun Yat-sen, the founder of the KMT.

Anna Louise had originally planned to visit the warlords around Peking. Now she publicly refused to see General Chang Tso-lin because his lifestyle included "a dozen wives and concubines." Chang, she claimed, was "Japan's puppet," not worth a trip. In fact, she was anxious to get to another warlord, General Feng Yü-hsiang, the "Christian general." Fanny had given her documents from Mikhail to Feng, instructing the general to go immediately to Moscow. After freezing for two days on an unheated train that took her past the jagged, rocky mountains north of Peking and on toward the Mongolian deserts and plains, Anna Louise was less convinced of the value of her visit. In a small reception room with mud walls and a mud floor, Anna Louise found "a stolid man, tall and strong, who recited his program with a bored and courteous air." American missionaries had embraced Feng because he had declared himself to be a Christian and had sought their help in suppressing opium, liquor and tobacco, but Anna Louise was no more impressed by his program than she was by his facile manner. The "essential thing for Feng," she wrote, was "to finish communications across the great roadless spaces and thus build a self-subsistent domain." Anna Louise saw Feng as a skillful manipulator who would flatter whoever he thought would aid him in his egocentric drive for power. The "Puritan" environment on which he insisted seemed affected. "He goes in entirely too much for the Spartan life," the Swiss governess to Feng's children told Anna Louise bitterly. "All summer I taught his children in a mud hut in a Kalgan courtyard. The boys and girls swept the mud floor with their own hands." The doorless, windowless room that Anna Louise shared with her had no stove to fend off the bitter November cold, and Anna Louise was relieved to find that her roommate shared her displeasure.

Anna Louise's journey to Feng's headquarters did, however, prove to be important to her, for she met his wife, Li Teh-chuan, who had been a YWCA secretary before marrying Feng, and now spent her time organizing welfare work for her husband's soldiers. When Anna Louise met her, she was ill from exhaustion and the rough conditions of her environment, but the two women felt a bond between them. Thirty-three years later, Li Teh-chuan, by then minister of health for the People's Republic of China, welcomed Anna Louise back again to China with the memory of that first encounter.

Anna Louise's next trip was south to Hankow to interview the "literary general," Wu P'ei-fu. Wu's surroundings were as emblematic of his world as were those of Chang and Feng: "a large, barracks-like building, with many delegations coming and going, leaving behind them disorder of papers and cigarettes." Despite Wu's use of foreign sources to increase the industrialization of his territory, he was far from progressive; his clear loyalties were to his friends and to the maintenance of traditional social structure. His reputation as a classical scholar did not mean enlightenment but repression. With Wu, however, Anna Louise was more adept than she had been with Feng. At the end of their interview, Wu gave her a present of a fan on which he inscribed a poem "To Miss Strong from Wu P'ei-fu." The poem contrasted the political instability of Europe and Asia with the permanence of individual virtue and implied that Wu would triumph in the near future. Whatever she thought of the poem, Anna Louise kept the fan.

Abandoning the warlords, she eagerly boarded a boat to Shanghai, only to be appalled by China's most cosmopolitan city. Divided into international and French concessions, Shanghai relegated most of its Chinese inhabitants to a separate "Chinese city." In Peking the signs of imperialism had been more covert—or at least not constantly oppressive. In a letter to her father, Shanghai merited only one terse, cadenced sentence: "Tall Sikh policemen, brought from India, beat shrinking coolies openly in the streets." Gratefully, Anna Louise retreated to the French quarter, to the tranquil house of Soong Ch'ing-ling.

Like many before and after her, Anna Louise was first impressed by Soong Ch'ing-ling's serenity and beauty. "Soong Ch'ing-ling," she wrote later in *China's Millions*, "is the most gentle and exquisite creature I know anywhere in the world. Slight, clad in spotless linen cut in Chinese style, she has a gracious dignity which seems unsuited to the rough struggles of revolution."

Born in Shanghai, Ch'ing-ling had been sent in her early teens to Wesleyan College in Macon, Georgia. Her father had been educated in the United States and had raised his children as Christians. When he had returned to Shanghai to start a printing company that published Bibles, he had also joined with Dr. Sun Yat-sen to produce anti-Manchu propaganda. The Soongs had become one of the most important families in China. Many of Ch'ing-ling's siblings had intimate connections with the circles of high finance in Shanghai. Her older sister, Ai-ling, had married the business man H. H. Kung, whom Anna Louise had known at Oberlin; one of her brothers, T. V. Soong, had greatly extended the family business, especially into banking; and her younger sister, Mei-ling, was getting involved with KMT politics.

Like Anna Louise, Soong Ch'ing-Ling was the radical of the children. She had met Sun Yat-sen in Japan and had married him in 1914, against the wishes of her family. Even before her marriage, she had been known as a young woman of strong will and determination, as well as a person of remarkable dignity and grace. During the ten years of their marriage, she had shared her husband's visionary leadership of the nationalist movement in China and had adapted with extraordinary flexibility to his successes and defeats. After his death, she took seriously her responsibility to carry his commitments forward. When Anna Louise met her in the fall of 1925, Soong Ch'ing-ling was just thirty-three years old and a widow of six months.

At the time of Anna Louise's first meeting, Soong Ch'ing-ling's political separation from her sisters and brother was not yet firm, but she was already defining her own alliance with the Communist party and the left of the KMT. She carefully educated Anna Louise on the situation in Canton and directed the next steps in her journey. The traditional route from Shanghai to Canton was via Hong Kong, but after the beginning of the great Hong Kong-Canton Strike in June 1925, a special licensing system prohibited any ship that passed through Hong Kong from docking in Canton. The rule was strictly enforced, for it enabled the Nationalist government in Canton to continue its support for the striking Hong Kong workers while increasing its own revenues and access to foreign goods. Thousands of striking workers and their Cantonese supporters were lined up along the Pearl River to assure that the system was enforced.

"It would be easier for us," Soong Ch'ing-ling told Anna Louise, "if you went direct from Shanghai to Canton by one of those Chinese coast steamers or some German or Russian boat. These avoid the forbidden zone around the Hong Kong seaport." But when Anna Louise protested that the complexity of the situation required a visit to Hong Kong, Ch'ing-ling agreed to write to her brother, T. V. Soong, for help to enter Canton after a visit to Hong Kong.

Confident that nothing was beyond Soong Ch'ing-ling's powers, Anna Louise boarded a ship for Hong Kong. At first glimpse, Victoria, the port, "lay spacious and beautiful as ever. . . . Great cliffs of gaunt brown embroidered with tropical verdure ran up two thousand feet from the water's edge, crowned and crowded with costly dwellings." Behind its gorgeous facade, she found the once great port "like a ghost town in Nevada when a mining rush has passed." The elegant houses that loomed over the harbor were selling for less than a third their previous value; the city was losing more than a million dollars a day in revenues. Anna Louise attended public meetings where subscriptions were being taken to support "anti-Red troops" and found that most people had only a vague and nightmarish vision of a place called "Red Canton," haunted by violence and terror, somewhere beyond the fog of civil war.

Once a day a British steamer made its way up the river to the little island of Shameen, where a settlement of foreigners lived within shooting distance of Canton. It was from Shameen in June that British and French soldiers had fired across the river, killing or wounding more than five hundred Chinese demonstrators. Despite the well-publicized ruling that forbade any Chinese boat to approach the British steamer, Soong Ch'ing-ling fulfilled her promise. As the steamer made its way through a maze of sailing ships and sampans, one tiny motorboat suddenly darted toward the British ship. The boat flew a red flag with a blue corner and a golden sun, the flag of the new China. Its mission was to pick up Anna Louise.

In the stern of the boat sat two women—Fanny Borodin and "a dark, little flame-like girl" who was introduced to Anna Louise as Liao Meng-hsing, "Cynthia" Liao. No one but Cynthia would have been able to break the barricade. Respect for her father, Liao Chung-kai, a martyr of the Nationalist movement, was such that a request from his daughter was certain to be honored. Cynthia herself had been one of the demonstrators who was badly hurt in the assault from Shameen Island.

At the dock in Canton, the three women were met by Mrs. Liao's maroon car. This was the same car, Cynthia told Anna Louise, in which her father had been shot the previous August. On the way to the Liao house, Cynthia and Fanny briefed Anna Louise on the family's history and the present situation in Canton. Liao Chung-kai, the "ascetic monk" of the revolution, had been the one man able to unite the left of the KMT; after his assassination, there had been a "state of terror" in Canton. During the fall, however, under the military leadership of Chiang Kai-shek and the political supervision of Mikhail Borodin, the most menacing opium warlords had been liquidated, counterrevolutionary attacks had been repelled and the province of Kwangtung, in which Canton was located, had been unified. Strikers were now living in what had once been opium dens and houses of prostitution. Although threatening news of attempts from the right wing of the KMT to eliminate all leftist elements came from the conference at Western Hills near Peking, in Canton there was optimism.

A banner above the gates of the Liao house proclaimed the vigor and confidence of the women who had survived Liao Chung-kai. It read "Undying Spirit." In defiance of Chinese custom, Mrs. Liao had become more rather than less public since her husband's death. The women gathering at the Liao house were planning a mass meeting for the following day; the committee included young and old, peasants and millionaires, teachers, secret service agents and housewives. Most prominent among them was the stately, middle-aged first wife of Chiang Kai-shek, the new president of the Women's Red Cross. Anna Louise was impressed by the political astuteness and conviction apparent in all the heated conversation, but it was a little speech by Mrs. Liao that moved her most. "She says to tell you," translated her daughter, "that women, after everything, are more important than men. For if all the men in the world should at once be slain, there would still be the unborn in the bodies of women, and from these another world would grow. But if all the women should suddenly be slain, then life itself would cease forever over the whole earth."

The women at the meeting were also impressed by Anna Louise. Fifty years later, Cynthia Liao remembered how well Anna Louise had applied her knowledge of strikes and revolution to the situation in Canton. The next day Anna Louise spoke about the revolutionary role of Soviet women to the mass meeting of women. As always, she taught by means of stories of successes and failures, and not through theory, telling of "Dunia, a textile worker in Moscow and how she lived before and after the revolution . . . and of how the women of her factory organized a hospital and a factory dining room and took the manager's house for a day nursery." The women went away with new projects and plans.

Her two remaining days in Canton were spent with the Borodins. Although Mikhail's official role was that of advisor to the Nationalist government, because of the financial support of the U.S.S.R. and the absence of any single Chinese leader able to unite the various factions in the KMT, he had become the focal decision maker in Canton. His prestige on the left was drawn in part from his connections to Stalin, in part from his extensive knowledge of the situation in and around Canton, and mainly from his careful supervision of the economic initiatives of Liao Chung-kai and the military successes of Chiang Kai-shek.

Mikhail was glad to see Anna Louise. Not only was she a friendly face from the past, she was a reliable conduit to the outside. Few foreign correspondents had been enticed by the rumblings of revolution away from the relative comfort and cosmopolitan pleasures of Shanghai and Peking. Anna Louise was excited by the prospect of bringing real news direct from Borodin to the West. In his office, Mikhail discussed plans to expand the revolution toward the North and explained the efforts of foreign capitalists to prevent economic stability in China.

He also made the rare gesture of taking a holiday. On the day before her departure, Fanya and he arranged a picnic on White Cloud Mountain, the highest point in Canton. In addition to Anna Louise, the party included Cynthia Liao and her husband; Soong Ch'ing-ling (who had made her own separate way to Canton) and her brother, the financier T. V. Soong. It was a happy occasion and a respite for them all. Anna Louise, however, was not content just to sit and picnic; she urged the entire group to climb the mountain. She succeeded in persuading only Cynthia. As they descended, Soong Ch'ing-ling told them, "You moved like mountain goats."

The next day, Anna Louise boarded a steamer for Shanghai and Tokyo. To her annoyance she had months earlier agreed to her father's suggestion of a brief series of lectures and interviews in Japan. In less than two days she managed to deliver three speeches, attend a luncheon and two tea

Ruth Maria Strong with Anna Louise, Tracy and Ruth, about 1892

Sydney Dix Strong, about 1910

Anna Louise aged two

Anna Louise aged six

Anna Louise at Oberlin College,
1902

Anna Louise climbing Mount
Hood, 1915

Anna Louise at the time she was engaged to Roger Baldwin, about 1912

English-speaking delegates to the 1922 Comintern meeting in Moscow;
Anna Louise is second from the right in the second row

John Reed Children's Colony in Cherumsha, U.S.S.R., 1925

Anna Louise arriving in Moscow, probably in April 1934; her husband, Joel Shubin, is far left

Anna Louise with the Lithuanian delegation to Moscow, summer 1940

Mao Tse-tung's cave, Yenan, 1946

Anna Louise with General Chu Teh, Kang Ke-ching and Mao's daughter in Yenan, 1946

parties and interview three men who "typified three fields of progress in Japan—finance, diplomacy and labor."

Her interviews proved to be a remarkably efficient way of penetrating the politics of the country. Viscount Eiichi Shibusawa was eighty-five years old. For fifty years, he had been the shaping force of Japanese banking and big business. Sixty-nine-year-old Viscount Shimpei Goto was an aristocratic statesman who had served his country as minister of three different offices, as the mayor of Tokyo and as a diplomat on numerous missions abroad. The youngest of the three, Bunji Suzuki, was the founder and president of the General Federation of Japanese Labor. As Anna Louise saw it, each was "balancing, balancing, like the crowds in the station . . . trying to go forward fast enough yet not too fast, in order to keep always erect and fall neither forward nor backward." To each she posed the question "Do you think Japan is happier now than in feudal times?" Each equivocated in his response and thus revealed much about himself and his country. By the time she left Japan, she was ready to take on anyone anywhere, including the corporate magnates of the United States.

In December she had a brief visit with her father in Seattle, after which she departed for Winnipeg, Canada, to deliver the first of the eighty-four lectures she would give in the next two months. Incautious when addressing groups such as a local Communist central committee, she urged one such group to cooperate with the student movement in America, to support pacifist groups on American college campuses, to form workers' clubs and to create additional newsstands and bookstores for radical literature. At leftist gatherings she proudly revealed that in China she had conveyed orders from Borodin to General Feng. Many of her speeches mentioned her intention to seek equipment and financial support for Russia from leaders of American industry.

In Chicago in early February she discovered that there was a price to pay for such indiscretion. An old Oberlin friend, Frances Gordon, had arranged for her to speak at a local high school. When Anna Louise arrived, she found no one to greet her except the high school principal, who was obviously "scared stiff." Earlier that day, Anna Louise later wrote to her father, an ROTC officer posing as a government official had called the mayor and eleven other city luminaries to warn them that as an "agent of the Soviet Union" she should not be allowed to speak. Anna Louise did not change the contents of her subsequent talks, but she did conclude that in the future she would avoid well-meaning college friends.

Her public addresses had at least three effects. Unknown to Anna

Louise, the FBI forwarded quotations from her remarks, accompanied by their own warnings, to appropriate businessmen. Some, like Gerald Swope, the president of General Electric who had instituted extensive employee-benefit programs, received her nonetheless and left her with the sense that she had laid "important foundations"; others, like Henry Ford, refused to see her. A more sympathetic but burdensome response came from the workers and students in her audiences. By the time she arrived in New York, she had again accumulated a following of people who wanted to explore the new frontier in the Soviet Union. She renewed her plans for an American industrial school in Moscow, a place where well-trained Americans would teach their skills to orphans.

The most immediate effect was the rapid increase of sales of *Children of Revolution*. Printed fliers and order forms, distributed wherever she lectured, identified Anna Louise as the "guardian" of the John Reed Children's Colony and advertised that all profits from the book and any contributions would go to the colony. By March 1926 more than 7,000 copies had been sold. But her fund-raising success only exacerbated another dilemma. Throughout the entire tour, Anna Louise had been engaged in a frustrating correspondence with Yavorskaia and local officials associated with the colony. Funds previously gathered by Sydney and Anna Louise for food, fuel and teachers had been spent on various other local projects, and now Yavorskaia begged Anna Louise to send $3,000 more for emergency relief. At first she refused in no uncertain terms: "All they want is to use those nice kids as bait to get more money for the local officials to spend on incompetents. . . . This makes me hot!" A week later she had second thoughts and suggested a compromise in the form of a new, joint commune that would include ten Russian-American farmers and mechanics, "most of them Communists." Yavorskaia quickly rejected this proposal and further provoked Anna Louise's ire by revealing that rumors were being spread attributing to Anna Louise mismanagement of funds and false promises of salaried jobs for Americans. This, Anna Louise concluded, was pure blackmail. To send the money in this context would be a "criminal" act to save her name and "would prove me indeed the spasmodic philanthropist."

Once in New York, her fury increased at the Russian method of conducting business. Representatives of Amtorg, the Soviet overseas trade bureau, claimed to have no knowledge of her trade mission and acted as if the encouragement of trade was tantamount to committing "prostitution to save their country." Daunted but determined still to exploit the resources of American industry, she made contacts on her own. It was easier than she had imagined. For the next five weeks she spun through a whirl of luncheons and dinners with presidents of banks and chairmen of oil companies, spreading the word that Russia was a worthwhile investment. For most of the men she was a welcome window on a world to which they could not venture themselves for fear it would signal leftist tendencies to their conservative investors. Her role was to be "well-dressed and happy, as living proof that an American woman could emerge in health and confidence after four years in Soviet Russia." She played the part well and took pleasure in dressing up and being the center of attention at elegant dinner parties, but she recognized that at best she was a goodwill ambassador. She wanted contracts; friendly conversation was not enough.

Between engagements, she rushed to meet deadlines for a dozen promised articles. In addition to feature stories for newspapers, there were three articles due on China for *Asia* magazine, pieces on the Soviet Union for *Survey* and an assortment of contracts for single articles for *Outlook, Country Life, Current History, Christian Century,* the *Nation* and *New Masses*. Each piece was a small drama for which Anna Louise set the stage, laid out the design and history, and then let the warlords or the women of China or the leaders of Japan speak for themselves. The reader's experience was of an intimate but important meeting with some of the most interesting people in the world.

Two themes appeared in all that she wrote in the winter of 1926. The first was that progress required of human beings that they change the way they lived their lives. Behind this lay the conviction that such change was possible and desirable, no matter how limited the resources or how embedded the traditions. More clearly than ever before, Anna Louise accepted violence as an inevitable and acceptable component of such progress. To those who argued that the Russians or the Chinese were killing people or stealing property, she presented a peasant who contrasted the horror of conditions before the revolution to a new world of books, teachers, harvests five times greater than before, and a sense, for the first time, of personal dignity. Her second theme was the importance of women in the revolutions she was witnessing. The trip to China had convinced her not only that change was most dramatic for women but that much of the good happening in the world was due to the efficiency, tenacity and intelligence of women.

Having spent her energy finding the right words to applaud the boundless resources of the women of the world, Anna Louise fell apart. In the last week in March she turned in most of her manuscripts, canceled all her appointments and crawled into bed at the Women's University Club, where Ruth Standish Baldwin, Roger's aunt, had arranged for her to stay during her time in New York. She was weak and sick from the grippe but also confused, depressed and angry, and she wrote to her father that she had had it with lectures and fund-raising. For months she had played to perfection her role as publicist for the Soviet Union while concealing her anger at the inefficiency and lack of support from Russia itself. In America she was a success, but for what cause, what project, what action, she was not sure. Still perplexed, she finally pulled herself out of her sickbed, finished two more articles and spent the rest of April purchasing equipment for the John Reed Children's Colony and the American Industrial School.

After a happy visit with Tracy and Edith in Geneva and a brief stop in Berlin, Anna Louise arrived in Moscow in late May. A cryptic note from her father greeted her return. "Please tell me if you are a communist," he had scrawled on a small, narrow piece of paper. "I am sometimes asked and I say you are not, because you told me you were not and gave me good reasons why you weren't. Just write yes or no on this slip." On the bottom of the slip, Anna Louise wrote her response: "*Not* a *party member*. Will not deny much sympathy with Communist ideas, even agreement often. What *is* a communist? ALS."

Her question was genuine. She had thought her attempts to organize the Russian-American Club, the John Reed colony and the educational workshops were the kind of thing a good communist would do, but her failure indicated that she had been wrong. She also thought it perfectly logical that she embrace many of the ideas of communism without joining the party. She saw little to be gained by becoming a member of the "inefficient" American Communist party, and she had no intention of giving up her American citizenship to join the Soviet party, even if the latter would have her. What she told her friends in Moscow, but not her father, was that she had not ruled out joining the party some time in the future, but for the moment she was not ready.

Actually, she had little sense of where she would live or what she would do in Moscow that June, let alone how she might fit in the party structure. Her anxiety was increased when Paul Kellogg, the editor at *Survey*, wrote asking her to get a statement from Trotsky on communism versus fascism: "All of us are united in thinking that no one could manage it if you couldn't. Could you?" Anna Louise knew, as Kellogg did not, that Trotsky was in difficulty in Moscow, but agreed to try. She pursued the interview with less than her usual determination. She was "unable to see

Trotsky right away," she wrote back, because of her plan to go to the Volga, but "I have put through your request to him in writing." What would come out of it, she added, "depends partly on whether he has in mind certain things he wants to say to a selected audience of American liberals." A month later she informed Kellogg curtly that neither her letter to Trotsky nor a phone call to his secretary had produced any response, and she was too busy to make any further attempts. In fact the final contest between Trotsky and Stalin had started, and as she had foreseen, Stalin appeared to be winning.

Anna Louise found some relief in the discovery that things were going better at the colony than she had feared. An anxious trip to John Reed, now under the supervision of a woman named Ada Graves, persuaded her that the colony had thrived in recent months. Seventy-two out of eighty-seven malaria-ridden children were now well, and the financial turmoil had abated. There had been nasty rumors about Anna Louise: according to one story, before leaving for the United States she had taken pictures of naked boys in indecent postures as an act of subversion; word had also been passed that *Children of Revolution* was counterrevolutionary. But by the time of her arrival, Konovalof, the president of the provincial government, had issued an official statement that "any tales against Anna Louise Strong are entirely without foundation." Furthermore, he himself had read *Children of Revolution* and found no cause for the accusations against it.

The American Industrial School, now called American Industrial Workshops, was also doing better than she expected. She found a site fifteen miles outside of Moscow in Tarasovka with a run-down two-room cottage that she could rent for very little money. She took the house, telling herself it was only a mile from the train station and that after she fixed it up she could use it for guests and as a summer house once she found a suitable apartment in Moscow. One of its pleasures was that she could walk out the back door and swim three times a day. The exercise helped her take off the twenty pounds she had gained in New York. In her letters, she extolled the austerity of her new setting and the benefits of long walks and exercise.

She decided that she had made so much money from her articles for the North American Newspaper Alliance that she would have a Ford car shipped to her at the cost of $560. She immersed herself in research for an article on marriage and sex education in the Soviet Union. After attending a congress on motherhood and infancy she reported that Russian women considered abortion evil but believed it was better to legalize than to forbid it. "Soft absorption in family coziness which saps strength" was considered as irresponsible as "promiscuity which spreads disease." As soon as she finished the piece, she headed back to John Reed for three weeks.

There she became immediately caught up in the minutiae of daily life. She hired a "new and wonderful" teacher and made plans to spend at least six months at John Reed in the fall and winter. The teacher agreed to come, she reported proudly, only because Anna Louise was in charge. At the same time she informed both Soviet officials and her family that she had definitely decided to disengage herself from all responsibilities for the colony. She explained the apparent contradiction in her behavior by saying that she wanted to spend time at the commune in order to improve her fluency in Russian. She still cared about the children and would help them when she could, but she no longer wished to be the guardian on whom they depended.

In mid-August, when she was back in Moscow, she consulted a doctor about a cough that had lingered since her March grippe. She was ordered to stay in bed for at least a week, but two days later Tracy, Edith and their two younger children arrived for a combination vacation and business trip. The YMCA in Moscow had been closed down some years earlier, and Tracy had to make arrangements for the disposal of equipment. Anna Louise had repeatedly urged the family to visit her, and now they had come. Determined to be the perfect tour guide, she translated for Tracy and took Edith to the markets and the children to restaurants while complaining the whole time in letters to her father that she was exhausted.

Tracy and his family left on September 1. Feeling "sicker than I ever have," Anna Louise went back to the doctor, who spent more time denigrating communism than he did listening to her chest. After enduring an hour of his heated proclamations, Anna Louise mildly suggested that the same abuses occurred in the United States. "But of course," he replied, "America is a bourgeois land. One expects abuses there."

He finally diagnosed Anna Louise's condition as chronic pneumonia and prescribed a six-week stay in a sanatorium in the Crimea. "Between ourselves," she wrote her father, "I am also going to get away from a lot of things in Moscow." She meant in part the Trotsky-Stalin conflict, but more specifically the trouble caused by an American couple, the Babins, who had publically accused her of misusing $30,000 from California donors while simultaneously allowing them to starve in Moscow. There was no $30,000, and the Babins had been doing very little work for more than three times a Russian salary, but Anna Louise reflected quietly that "you can't blame Russians for believing these tales, since I am obviously richer than Russian writers, a foreigner, and not a communist."

The sanatorium had been the czar's summer palace on a cliff overlooking the Black Sea. For almost two months Anna Louise lay on a verandah twelve hours a day, eating bowls of sweet butter and an endless supply of caviar off plates from the czar's collection. Two pounds of grapes were brought to her each morning with the strict command that every grape must be finished by evening. Despite some anxiety that she was regaining the twenty pounds lost over the summer, Anna Louise did as she was told.

For the first time in years she had time to reflect on her future. A letter from Ellen Hayes, one of the major benefactors of the John Reed Children's Colony, relieved her of lingering hesitations. Ellen urged her to give up her other work for the writing she did so well. Anna Louise wrote back expressing agreement: "In a way this is a confession of failure. For five years I have wanted to take some actual part in Russian life, not merely to write about it. It has been a strong personal craving that has led to many excessive sacrifices for relatively little achievements. But I think I must face the fact that foreigners can't do it; they won't be allowed to and they haven't the command of the situation to do it. The other job is big enough and I must get back to it." She was convinced that she was almost "two years behind" on knowledge of Soviet affairs.

At the sanatorium she also found time to consider her father's situation. "I thought," she wrote Sydney, "that you had enough saved up to get a regular little income from it. Or do you—from the money Grandma left? If all you have is the house and the lot and $1,900, I think you must be rather up against it without any salary and I think it is time for your children to subsidize you. I am quite a rich person now! I didn't put in my years from twenty-five to forty bringing up children as you did, but saved my money. On the whole, your method was probably best, if one has the chance."

Then she confronted the main issue that had come between her and Sydney for the past fourteen years: "Regarding Roger Baldwin, I think you are right, it would have been better for me if I had never met him. Although you can never tell. If I had not been infatuated with him for several years, I might possibly have had an open mind to marry someone else, and that might, or might not, have been a good thing. Whatever, the past is so integral a part of the present that you can't wish it otherwise without wishing yourself some quite unknown existence. I don't myself think a lot of Roger's organization [the American Civil Liberties Union]; he has become institutionalized like everyone else who goes into relations with New York foundations." Her long letter closed with an invitation to her father to accompany her that winter on a trip to Mexico. She would pay their expenses, and they could explore together a country whose recent attempts at agrarian reform interested them both.

The luxury of the sanatorium did not entirely cure Anna Louise's lungs, but it greatly improved her sense of humor, especially about herself. She returned to Moscow in November and declared that she would become a "conservative—in *habits*." She would build herself a two-room apartment, hire a secretary, use her car and let the world think what it might. "Russia gets on better when I don't meddle with it," she admitted with no trace of dismay. Meddling by a foreigner, she had learned upon her return from the Crimea, was also now antithetical to the party line. She tried and failed to arrange interviews with both Stalin and Trotsky. On December 20, 1926, the day before she left Moscow, she wrote to Paul Kellogg to explain why: "A distinct anti-foreign trend is the order of the day, since it is now orthodox to believe that they can build socialism in one country alone, irrespective of world revolution." The new Stalinist orthodoxy did not dissuade her from her intention to pursue revolutions in Mexico and China; it confirmed her sense that she needed time away from Moscow to analyze the redirection of the party line. She discouraged her newly acquired American booking agent, Mildred Smith, from over-scheduling the coming winter's lecture tour.

Anna Louise kept to her promised slower pace for the next six months. She spent Christmas skiing with Tracy and Edith near Geneva, delivered a few lectures in New England in January, then headed for Mexico—alone, despite a repeated invitation to Sydney to join her. Impatient with his daughter's ever-shifting plans, Sydney had already made a trip to Mexico with a "goodwill commission" of Americans. Anna Louise offered to pay half his fare for a second trip with her as a belated Christmas present, but he refused.

She found Mexico in a state of romantic confusion. Under the rule of President Plutarco Calles, the country was both more and less "bolshevik" than the American government and press had been asserting. American oil men still had sufficient power to have Anna Louise's mail intercepted and, more importantly, to have retained most of the land that by law was to have been redistributed among the peasants. She considered the leaders of CROM, the largest Mexican trade union, "gangsters" who broke the strikes of smaller unions and were fervently anticommunist.

But when she went to CROM meetings, the workers themselves "cheered Russia" and were eager to hear about life in the Soviet Union. In Mexico, as in China, Anna Louise was asked to speak wherever she went and was greeted with unreserved enthusiasm and applause.

She was taken by the passion, "grace and joy" of the Mexican people but amused by the incoherence of their politics. She went one night in Mexico City to see a Russian film, and although the audience was as enthralled as was she, "they cheered everyone without distinction," just as, outside the theaters, workers spoke in one adulatory breath of Lenin, Trotsky, Bakunin, Kropotkin, Gorky and Tolstoy. She found most of the Mexicans she met as naive as she herself had been in 1919 during the Seattle strike.

She also made two important friendships. Russian friends had suggested to her that she might find a friend in Alexandra Kollontai, the Soviet ambassador to Mexico, and they were not mistaken. Slim, lithe and well dressed, possessed of energy and intelligence and a powerful orator in thirteen languages, Kollontai not only analyzed politics incisively but, as Anna Louise discovered, had "an emotional nature" much like her own. It was clear, when they parted, that they would see each other again.

The second friendship was a more surprising one. After spending a long afternoon entranced by the frescoes of Diego Rivera, Anna Louise sought out the artist, "the most famous revolutionist in Mexico." His person was as powerful and as attractive to her as his paintings. She happily spent most of the next two weeks with him. Rivera was, she concluded, "not the destined leader" of Mexico, but he became the "passionate revealer" from whom she learned about not only the struggles of the Mexican peasants and workers but also the vital embrace of art and revolution. Through his tutelage Anna Louise came to see genuine art not as something for museums but as something "serious; it gave rise to real struggles." When she departed from Mexico on March 13, 1927, with a sad but acutely rational analysis of Mexico's confusion in her head, she carried the gift of a painting under her arm.

As she left Mexico, she was making plans for another trip to China—this time for an indefinite stay and in the context of what the Western press was now nervously admitting to be an authentic revolution. Bored and hot, she impatiently waded through a dozen lectures in Texas and Florida, all the while following as best she could the northern advance of the Nationalist troops in China. In New York in early April she placed feature articles on Mexico in several newspapers and made the circuit of magazine editors to discuss projected pieces on the revolution in China. In contrast to what she had found eighteen months before, this time not only *Asia* and *Survey*, but *Harper's*, the *Atlantic*, the *New York Herald Tribune Magazine*, the *Nation* and *Christian Century* were all willing to make tentative commitments for China articles.

In one article she wrote while in New York, "Stalin, Boss of Russia, Breaks an Idol," she anticipated what awaited her on her return to the U.S.S.R. After repeating her 1924 characterization of Stalin as Mark Hanna, the all-powerful Republican party boss who had held no official government job, she expanded her claim that Stalin's source of strength lay in his lack of public presence. "Trotsky is a personality, he inspires millions. Stalin is a perfect secretary. Yet Stalin wins and Trotsky loses . . . [because] . . . personal allegiances are at a discount among the Communists." She concluded on a bittersweet note: "All revolutionary life is less enthusiastic for the loss of Trotsky. . . . No one would die for Stalin. But increasingly hundreds of thousands would die without enthusiasm for the organization of which he is secretary and accepted voice."

On this ambiguously safe note, she turned her mind back to China. She spent the week before her departure for Shanghai with her sister Ruth in Palo Alto, relishing the role of the sophisticated, adventurous aunt. The entire Niederhauser family saw her off; it was the first time that her nephew John and niece Bumpy (the name she had given Ruth Louise when she had the measles) had ever been on an ocean liner. Writing to her father the day after sailing, Anna Louise could find little to say about her visit except that "Charles and Ruth have a lovely home." The mild envy her sister's comfort and stability had provoked was more than assuaged when she was assigned a single cabin on deck with bath at no extra charge because she was a "famous writer."

The *China Courier*, an English-language newspaper in Shanghai, greeted her arrival in China with a feature article that began: "Anna Louise Strong, probably the most famous American woman engaged in newspaper correspondence and other journalist enterprises, arrived in China for an indefinite stay." The piece referred to Anna Louise as one of a "trio of newspaper workers"—the others being Arthur Ransome of the *Manchester Guardian* and Walter Duranty of the *New York Times*—"who have told the true story of new Russia to the English-speaking world."

Less than two months before, Shanghai had been the setting of both the greatest triumph and most appalling defeat of the Communist-dominated portion of the Chinese Nationalist party, or Kuomintang (KMT). Contrary to previous plans, Chiang Kai-shek, the general leading the center and right-wing factions of the KMT, had brought his armies to Shanghai and the coast rather than inland toward a northern meeting with General Feng. Hearing of his approach, students and workers led by the Communist party in Shanghai had risen up and taken the city themselves. In retaliation, Chiang had ordered the murder of thousands of Shanghai labor leaders and Communists. When Anna Louise arrived in Shanghai, the KMT was split into two factions, left and right. In Nanking, Chiang was in control of the army and now ruled enough of China to be the most powerful person in the country; only the "progressive" faction of the Nationalists, centered in the three cities of Wuhan in central China, stood in his way. Borodin and Madame Sun Yat-sen were in Wuhan, where the ineffectual majority of the central executive committee of the Kuomintang had remained and repudiated Chiang. The allegiance of General Feng in the north was still uncertain.

Anna Louise was ill at ease in Shanghai. At the missionary home where she was staying she was surrounded "by missionaries from up-country awaiting the turn of events" that would either send them back inland or home to America and England. On her first Sunday she made a tour of churches, where she found rifles in the pews and ministers who spoke from "lofty pulpits in sweeping black robes" of "God who made the British Empire and who still has a job in the world for that empire to do." Despite ardent efforts, she was unable to find the Shanghai labor leaders, who were in hiding in fear of their lives; Shanghai University, where she had lectured and made some contacts on her trip in 1925, was now closed down. From the YMCA secretary in the squalid town of P'u-tung across the river from Shanghai, she heard stories of the killings of hated foremen by workers and of executions of workers and labor leaders by Chiang's forces. And she watched workers wait for hours at the YMCA's well to get a swallow of pure water for their families.

From the "unspeakably small and filthy hovels" of P'u-tung, she went to visit T. V. Soong in the house where she had first met his sister, Soong Ch'ing-ling, a year and a half before. "Clad is an exquisite Chinese robe of dove-blue color, he seemed infinitely removed from the harsh squalor of war and revolution." But Soong also seemed significantly changed from the "joyous boy" she had met in Canton in 1925 to "a man torn by indecision and doubt." He had taken over the building of a new economic base for the Nationalist government, but by his own account "the militarists had destroyed his success and looted his treasure." He professed a desire to build the treasury again under the alternative government in Wuhan and assured Anna Louise that he had remained in Shanghai only out of terror for his life were he to make any moves to depart. Yet despite Soong's "scathing" denunciations of the Chiang regime, Anna Louise detected his strong attraction to Nanking and all that it represented economically and socially. When they parted, after a second visit, Soong revealed more than he may have intended. "Au revoir, until we meet in Peking," he told Anna Louise, and she understood that this meant he would not soon be on the river toward Wuhan.

Among his many mixed signals, Soong had been clear about one thing: Anna Louise should go quickly to Hankow, the industrial city that was the center of the Wuhan government. Bill Prohme, an American journalist working for the Nationalist News Agency, urged her to visit his wife, Rayna, who was editing the *People's Tribune* there. And a German correspondent, Von Salzman, who had just returned from Hankow, persuaded her not even to bother with a trip first to Nanking: "Nanking does not live. Hankow will live; if not the men, at least the idea that is alive there. If crushed, it will live in history and return again. What is this idea? Nothing so definite as communism. Nothing I can define in detail. All the same, it is that which is behind all revolutions—the sudden hope of long submerged masses." Finally, a telegram from Soong Ch'ing-ling pressed Anna Louise to join her in Hankow. Nothing she might learn in Nanking or Shanghai seemed as important as seeing firsthand what it was that filled Hankow with such intensity. She booked passage on a German boat which, unlike the British steamers, took women, and climbed aboard for the three-day trip upriver to the port of Hankow, which she found "thickly lined with foreign gunboats."

Soong Ch'ing-ling was living on the top floor of the central bank overlooking the bund and invited Anna Louise to stay in an apartment adjoining her own. After tea and a long conversation in which Soong Ch'ing-ling brought her up to date on the situation in Hankow, Anna Louise headed for an older stone building whose lower floor housed the *People's Tribune* and whose upper stories were now the home and offices of Mikhail Borodin.

In the one-room office of the *People's Tribune*, sixteen-year-old Jack Chen was at work on a cartoon for the next issue of the paper. His father, Eugene Chen, foreign minister for the Wuhan government, had set up the *People's Tribune* office in Wuhan, and when Rayna Prohme had mentioned her need for a cartoonist, he had volunteered his handsome, talented son. The remaining staff of the newspaper, a hard-working American named Millie Mitchell, was busy at her typewriter when the door flew open and Anna Louise sailed in. Without a word of greeting to

Chen or Mitchell, she swept to the rear of the office and began bombarding Rayna Prohme with questions.

Anna Louise had met her match—and her perfect opposite. Born in Chicago, Rayna Prohme had graduated from the University of Illinois in 1917, married and soon afterwards divorced the playwright Samson Raphaelson. After roaming the world for several years, Rayna had married her second husband, Bill Prohme. Together they had gone to Peking, where Rayna and her husband started writing for the *People's Tribune*. Small and delicately built, Rayna Prohme had fiery red hair and an explosive passion for the revolution, to which she had committed twenty hours a day for over four years.

When Anna Louise was finished getting the story she wanted from Rayna, she departed as abruptly as she had arrived, without even a polite word to Millie Mitchell or Jack Chen. "Do you believe that?" Millie asked Jack. He shook his head in amazement. Both he and Millie knew the identity of their sudden visitor; they had wanted to meet her, not watch her sail by. Chen was more surprised then hurt. He later recalled "a large, very good-looking woman, totally concentrated on what she was doing."

Anna Louise proceeded to the side entrance that led to Michael Borodin's apartments. Half a dozen automobiles were parked in front; Borodin was still the most sought-after person in the Wuhan government. She found him propped up in bed in his third floor apartment. She was shocked at how frail and troubled he looked. A broken arm and a persistent fever from a tropical disease contracted years before had sapped his strength at the very time when crucial decisions were demanded. The recent defection of an important general, Hsia Tao-yin, to Chiang Kaishek, followed by the success a few days later of counterrevolutionary forces in Hunan province had convinced Borodin that he must burn important documents and prepare for a quick departure. To increase his anxiety, his wife had been captured a few months before by enemy troops and continued to be held hostage in Peking by General Chang Tso-lin— if, indeed, she was still alive. Borodin said starkly to Anna Louise: "You thought, did you not, that we did a big thing in October, when we made the Revolution in Russia? Well, this revolution is many times bigger. It is one-fourth of all earth's people. It is the biggest thing in the world. It will take long. It will kill more than one Borodin before it is through."

For the next two weeks Anna Louise explored Hankow with relentless precision, trying to discover just how and why this was "the biggest thing in the world." She walked the dikes, talked to waterfront workers, visited metal and cotton factories, attended meetings of trade unions. Although workers continued to labor seventeen hours a day for a few dollars a month, and children of seven and eight were still in evidence in the factories, she was encouraged by the "fundamental questions" asked of her. And while she was learning about "Red Hankow," she could share her knowledge of the comparable experiences of Soviet workers.

Daily conversations with the government leaders were disheartening. From Eugene Chen she learned the "official program" of the government, which stressed radical changes for peasants and workers. But she soon realized that the threat of Chiang Kai-shek was a more present concern to him than his own vision of a united front of peasants, workers and small bourgeoisie. On one afternoon visit Anna Louise found Borodin talking with Ch'en Tu-hsiu, secretary of the Chinese Communist party, and explained that since she had gone to Russia too late for the Revolution, she had "come to China earlier, in order to be on the scene in time." With a grim smile at Ch'en Tu-hsiu, Borodin corrected her: "Miss Strong is unlucky in her revolutions. She came too late for the Russian Revolution and now she has come too soon for China."

Even without the revolution, these were the least lonely days Anna Louise had spent in years. Gatherings each evening at the Prohmes' brought together everyone from Russian advisors and American intelligence agents to the dancer Irma Duncan and correspondents like Arthur Ransome and Randall Gould. The only common denominator at the Prohme salon was the English language; beyond that, both the company and the conversations were unpredictable. People talked about movies as well as unions; they sang IWW songs and played music. Even without much of the drink in which others indulged, Anna Louise relaxed as she had not since her bohemian days in Greenwich Village. In this company, her bobbed hair, bright embroidered blouses and insistent voice were almost inconspicuous. If the spirit moved her, she would rise in the small room and dance with a grace that surprised her companions.

It took the stern voice of Joseph Stalin to end such camaraderie. On June 1, 1927, a secret radio message arrived for Borodin and M. N. Roy, an Indian aristocrat and Communist who had arrived in Wuhan from Moscow in early April. Roy, who had learned Marxist theory from Borodin eight years before in Mexico City, had spent most of the spring disputing his teacher's united-front policy. Having failed to convince Borodin to support a separate revolution of peasants and workers, Roy appealed to Stalin. To Roy, the message from the central committee was a radical order for substantial confiscation of land and the formation of a new army of peasants and workers; to Borodin, the message was deliberately unrealistic, self-contradictory and self-protective, a political gesture rather than a call to action. Roy gleefully flaunted the message and created havoc and terror among the more moderate Nationalist leaders still in Wuhan.

Borodin saw only one remote possibility of salvaging some of the gains of the revolutionary movement: an alliance with Feng Yü-hsiang, who had been steadily advancing toward central China from Inner Mongolia. Feng agreed to meet with representatives from Wuhan on June 10 in Chengchow, a junction of north-south and east-west rail lines three hundred miles to the north.

A huge crowd gathered at the station platform on the morning of June 7 to send their envoys off to Chengchow. Both Europeans and Chinese were dressed in their most elaborate outfits; Anna Louise reported the occasion as if she were a society editor. The wife of the influential KMT leader Wang Ching-wei was wearing a lilac Chinese gown, but Eugene Chen, who appeared "in a Chinese robe of classic style made of heavy, dull cream silk," outshone them all. Bands played intermittently, and at the arrival of the last traveler, a general, bugles blared a military fanfare.

Anna Louise had been given permission to accompany the leaders to their negotiations. Her sense of being special was further augmented by the graciousness of her friends at the train station. Eugene Chen brought her thoughtful, practical gifts: a large flashlight, a fan, a well-filled canteen with cups, and a bag of copper coins for small purchases. Mrs. Sun Fo, wife of Sun Yat-sen's son by his first wife, presented her with canned peaches and tea biscuits, and Soong Ch'ing-ling, knowing Anna Louise's great weakness, provided a box of Cailler chocolates, somehow spirited from Switzerland to Wuhan. With Rayna Prohme, Anna Louise was assigned to a four-berth compartment, identified by a sign reading "Western Women's Bedroom." Rayna's house servant, Li, accompanied the two women and made their beds, brought tea and hot water and took care of their baggage; he slept on suitcases in the aisle outside the compartment. Berthed next door to Rayna and Anna Louise was the Russian military advisor, and in the first and last cars of the train were 300 soldiers, responsible for the safety of their leaders. For political reasons Borodin, Soong Ch'ing-ling and Eugene Chen did not go.

For two days the trip was uneventful. The scars of war were few; soldiers leaning out of the train windows with bayonets in hand were the most vivid indication of violence in the land. Then the train came to a sudden stop. A bridge had been destroyed by northern troops and the travelers had to disembark and walk four miles to a station where they could find another train. Anna Louise dismounted in good spirits, glad to be relieved of the burden of her suitcases, camp-bed and typewriter by Li, who found three coolies to help him. After slipping and stumbling down a long, steep trail, her interest in the adventure diminished. She had become separated from Rayna and had no sense of where she was going; no one around spoke English. Hsu Chien, the minister of justice, passed her with his long legs dangling over a donkey, and the minister of communications, Sun Fo, rode by on a handcar. She arrived at the next station with no help from anyone and to her amazement was greeted by "dozens of utterly naked little boys peddling tea and hot water from great tin pots." A new train soon arrived, and the travelers proceeded without further mishap to their destination.

Everything politically important at the conference took place behind doors closed to Anna Louise, but she spoke with enough of the generals to ascertain that "on one point all were secretly agreed; they had decided that the workers and peasants and communists must be suppressed." Anxious to know more, she set out on her second night in Chengchow with Rayna and an interpreter to find Wang Ching-wei. It was a doomed and somewhat lunatic search. None of the three knew the old, walled city where they were wandering, and none of them had the faintest idea where Wang resided. They knocked at every door where there were soldiers in evidence—soldiers being a sign that there might be generals nearby—but saw only "great, wonderful trees springing raggedly out of the midst of the streets and yards; picturesque temples, shadowed pagodas" and countless local residents talking, cooking and sleeping under the walls of the city.

The next morning she and Rayna were abruptly awakened and told to pack for an immediate return to Wuhan. The meeting was over. It had, all the announcements declared, been a success; recognition of Wuhan had been achieved. Only gradually did Anna Louise learn that, pushed by Wang Ching-wei, the KMT had agreed to accept a military dictatorship under Feng, with a secret but clear understanding that peasants, workers and especially trade unions were to be suppressed. The Communist party was to be expelled from Wuhan and Borodin sent back to Moscow. In return for these gestures, Feng had agreed publicly to espouse the memory and program of Sun Yat-sen and to join Wuhan's troops against the hostile forces of General Chang Tso-lin.

On June 19, just six days after her return from Chengchow, the Fourth Congress of the All-China Labor Federation met in Wuhan. By the last day a daring manifesto had been hammered out, urging open struggle to maintain the unions and reaffirming unity with the peasants and the petty bourgeoisie against feudal militarists and imperialists. Particularly important to Anna Louise was the clear identification of the struggle of China's workers with that of workers in the Soviet Union. Then, hours before a planned celebration, hostile troops of General Tang Sheng-chi attacked and occupied the meeting hall. Waiting in Borodin's office for an interview, Anna Louise was one of the first to hear of the attack and of Borodin's quick decision to challenge this last insult. She took her scoop to the *People's Tribune* before she hurried to a previously scheduled meeting with Shou Cheu-ging, president of the Labor Federation. By the time she reached Shou, the conflict had been resolved. Public statements proclaimed that the assault was not a political gesture but the action of a few undisciplined, corrupt soldiers. But in Shou's bent and weary posture Anna Louise read the truth of the disaster. The congress had been a momentary respite, a brief space in the open air for those who knew their future was underground.

Looking for hope that the revolution might continue, Anna Louise went south to Hunan, which had been called the "reddest" area in China. Missionaries, foreign merchants and officials of the military government were glad to explain to her how order had been "restored" after the wild revolts of the peasants. They boasted of the executions of "communists and rioters" and assured her that the province was now quite safe. Y. Y. Lee, the reactionary head of the Commission for the Reorganization of the Kuomintang, admitted that the peasants' union had had ten million members in Hunan alone. When Anna Louise asked why it had been suppressed she was told that "the peasants had cut all the women's hair and killed all the chickens and cut down all the trees and generally behaved like crazy folk." Despite the ample evidence that many women still had long hair and many trees were still growing, all the officials she met persisted in repeating this line, while the peasants and workers were too terrified to speak. But through persistence and tact she gradually found informants who gave accounts very different from the official ones.

The theme that emerged most forcefully was that of the struggles of women. From a teacher in one town, a student in another, she learned of the rapid emergence of women's unions and their fights to free women from the bounds of overt slavery and enforced marriages. The tragedy that captured Anna Louise's imagination the most was the story of Wang Su-chun, a young Hunanese woman who had been killed shortly before Anna Louise's arrival. The daughter of a Christian farmer, Wang had been educated through senior middle school and was a rebel from a young age. Her feet had never been bound, she wore dresses rather than the conventional trousers, and she had bobbed her hair—a sign of female liberation all over the world in the twenties. None of these gestures compared, however, to the heresy of her own announcement of her engagement to a local young man, after which she proceeded to organize a successful women's union of which she was made president. By the time the reactionary soldiers drove the KMT out of the small town, Wang was hated by everyone except the women she had organized. Her own neighbors turned her over to the soldiers as an "agitator" and after a series of verbal assaults, the soldiers cut her "to pieces with knives and bayonets."

For Anna Louise, Wang was an exemplary martyr because she was *"chu feng t'ou,"* an expression that roughly translates as having a "head held like a pillar in the wind." Wang's head, Anna Louise proclaimed when she told her story for *Harper's Magazine,* was "a lofty head that stuck out above other heads like a cock on the steeple" and caught "all winds first. . . . The wind her head was high in and that blew her to destruction was clearing the path of history."

Back in Hankow in mid-July, Anna Louise sought to keep her own head high in that same wind. During her absence, the military dictatorship of Feng and Wang Ching-wei, now in alliance with Chiang Kai-shek, had taken full control of Wuhan. T. V. Soong was back in Hankow, negotiating for Chiang Kai-shek, but Soong Ch'ing-ling had fled for Moscow, as had many of the Russian advisors. Borodin had repeatedly delayed his own departure, in part at least because he did not want to leave the country where his wife remained a prisoner. But on July 12, to everyone's surprise, Fanya was declared innocent in her trial in Peking, and in moments she was swept away to safety in the Soviet embassy. Now he had only to decide which route might be safest out of China.

When Anna Louise heard that he had finally decided on the difficult route through the northwestern provinces and the Gobi Desert, she asked for permission to go along. Borodin's first response was vague. He told her he was about to make a temporary retreat to a protected resort in Kuling, just to get out of Hankow, and would see when he returned. On Saturday night, July 23, Borodin was back in Hankow, and Anna Louise was at his door. She asked again. "Hard trip," he said. "Think you can stand it?" She reminded him that she had climbed some of the more difficult mountains in the world. Then he demanded, "What do you want to go for? Going to write a book about it?" She nodded, although that had not been foremost in her mind. Borodin told her she could come, but she could take only two suitcases, and he would depend on her to keep a diary of the trip. She was to be ready to depart on Monday.

The party actually departed on Wednesday. A Buick and a Dodge sedan, three open passenger cars and three trucks along with tents, food, and baggage were loaded onto the special train that was to take them on the first leg of their journey. Among the twenty travelers, most of them Russians, were Eugene Chen's two sons, Percy and Jack. Percy was a good mechanic and driver; Jack was along for the adventure.

After a day and a half, they arrived at the first stop—General Feng's headquarters in Chengchow. Feng had guaranteed Borodin safe travel through his territory, and he wanted to consult with him before his departure. Feng gave a banquet the night of their arrival, and, aware of herself as the only woman in the party, Anna Louise dressed carefully in a white linen skirt and black and white blouse. But after being driven to the banquet in a "dust-encrusted truck" and seeing the other guests, she resolved to buy herself a khaki uniform for such occasions. To her dismay, when she dressed in her new outfit for the next night's banquet given by one of Feng's young commanders, she was again inappropriately attired. The elaborate European menu and attentive servants with fans clashed vividly with her new khaki uniform.

Suddenly, at six o'clock on the third day, Borodin ordered everyone to pack up: they were leaving that night. Once they were on their way, Anna Louise learned that the hasty departure had been occasioned by an order from Wang Ching-wei to Feng to arrest Borodin and return him to Hankow. Anxious to maintain good relations with both Nanking and Moscow, Feng sent "regrets that Borodin had gone."

The remaining hundred miles of train travel took more than four days. With a regularity that greatly irked Anna Louise, the train waited at station after station for enough coal to continue. When the train finally reached the end of the line, twenty miles west of Shan Hsien, late in the afternoon of August 4, the dusty passengers found a shallow spot to bathe in a creek near an orchard. A huge pot of noodle soup was brought from a local hotel, and the vice-governor of the province came to call. That night Borodin set up his tent for the first of many times, and the nineteen fellow travelers spread their mats and cots under the "checkered moonlight."

The next morning the group discovered their first major problem. Many of the Russians were attempting to transport all of their wordly belongings. Loaded with awesome efficiency, the Dodge sedan in which

Anna Louise was to ride resembled a traveling marketplace. Suitcases, bags and baskets were roped onto the back of the car and reached to the level of the roof. Gasoline, tires and Anna Louise's suitcases were strapped on each running board. Stuffed inside the car were three canvas beds, bedding, a water bucket, four thermos bottles, cans of food, tools, a teakettle, a primus stove and two watermelons. Five hats were pinned to the inside ceiling, coats were laid on the seats, mugs were hung on the window catches, and two revolvers swung from screws on the inside of the windshield.

Into the little remaining space squeezed the five passengers—all, that is, except Anna Louise, who settled obliviously into half the back seat. Percy Chen drove; his brother rode up front with him. Neither front door would open because of the baggage on the running boards; throughout the trip they had to exit through the windows. Anna Louise insisted on sitting next to the one door that did open. With her in the rear of the car was the wife of a Russian doctor and Chang Ke, a young Chinese Communist scholar traveling with the party as a translator. At Anna Louise's feet was her typewriter.

It took three hours to cover the first nine miles of the trip. In three days they had gone only 32 of the 1,900 miles between them and a safe train to Moscow. They walked and pushed the car as often as they rode, and Anna Louise began to think that just walking would have been more efficient. On the fourth night they found comfort for their aching limbs at the ancient hot-springs resort at Lin-t'ung, twenty-five miles from Sian. Once the retreat of the T'ang emperors, the intricately tiled pavilions floated in flower-encrusted ponds; inside one elegant building, the bathtub of a legendary courtesan awaited Anna Louise. She was hesitant at first to take her turn at the bath, but after being shown that the waters were truly from running springs and were not infested with the diseases of those who came for cures, she luxuriated in the tub. Somewhat intoxicated by the whole experience, she wandered outside after her bath and sank onto a stool near Borodin, who was resting in a chaise on the terrace of a pavilion. When Percy Chen blundered into the scene, Anna Louise was softly singing hymns. For weeks, Percy had been watching what he interpreted as Anna Louise's growing crush on Borodin. Now he stared openly despite the glare from Anna Louise when she caught his gaze. After two verses of "While Shepherds Watched Their Flocks by Night," Borodin slowly opened his eyes. "For God's sake, woman, at least sing the 'Internationale,'" he roared. Anna Louise burst into tears and hurried away. Borodin turned to Percy: "Did I hurt her? I did not mean to."

In Sian, while the cars were being repaired, Anna Louise interviewed an American missionary, the British head of the post office, a Catholic priest and several nuns, from all of whom she pieced together the recent history of the area. Borodin was busy exchanging visits with local officials, and Anna Louise kept out of his way. Back on the road, three days later, she earned the respect of her companions by helping them push when the car came to steep hills, wading knee-deep through green mud, and finding ingenious ways to filter muddy water so that it would be drinkable. The only task she avoided was cooking, and after a while it was silently agreed that Anna Louise was to be the "supervising" chef. Among the rules established early in the trip, to conserve traveling time as well as water, was that each person was allowed only one cup of coffee in the morning. When Voroshin, Borodin's bodyguard, appeared one morning with a mug the size of a saucepan, Anna Louise was horrified. "You don't do something like that," she cried, "you are supposed to be a good scout."

Her temper also flared whenever any harm threatened the sedan. One morning after breakfast, when they were staying in a small walled town north of Sian, Percy Chen and Borodin's driver decided to switch cars for the day. Anna Louise stood by with growing dismay as she watched the Russians pile additional baggage higher and higher on *her* car. When the stack reached three feet, she said, "No. It can't stand any more." For five minutes the men talked among themselves, then began to pile more objects on the car. Anna Louise stomped up to them, planting herself like a pillar between the loaders and the car. "This car will not move," she declared. "I say it will not move." There was a moment's silence, but nothing was removed from the car. Anna Louise turned, marched to the gate of the village and laid herself down across the entryway. Stretched out to her full five feet, nine inches, she filled the entire space. Nothing moved. Awestruck, the men unloaded the car. Jack Chen began to think that her infatuation with the car was almost as great as her attraction to Borodin.

Through the long evenings of talk and the difficult days of passage, Borodin and Anna Louise grew increasingly close. She was his best audience for his discourses on opera, theater, movies and literature, and with her he could begin to sort through the complexities of the last few years that had ended with this strange excursion. Like her, he had an explosive temper and was particularly incensed by the "inefficiencies" of others. After one tirade against his Russian aides, he "grew depressed" and confessed to her: "When I get angry it is not just at a few mechanics: it is at our Russian temperament. I say to them: 'Look at that American sedan. They have a flashlight and everyone can find it. They have a certain order in their car and everyone knows it. They do not say, "Yes, I put it in the car, but now, the devil!" This is no accident. It is a whole culture in action. When shall we Russians learn it?' "

By August 28, when they reached Ningsia (now Yin-ch'uan), the frontier town on the edge of Inner Mongolia, Borodin had fully recovered from his illness. Caked with mud from hair to shoes, the travelers had passionately awaited the joys of a good bath and a bar of new soap, but after eight days in the dull market city, they were willing to give up baths to be on their way. There was no gasoline in the town, so they were forced to wait for their own freight trucks, which had fallen far behind the sedans. Furthermore, the Buick badly needed repairs, and the blacksmith who could make them was constantly high on opium. Percy Chen and Chang Ke finally kidnapped him and kept him isolated for two days until he sobered up enough to confront the car.

Ahead lay the Gobi Desert and the most difficult part of the journey. After days of scouting and reflection, the group had chosen an ancient camel route that would take them over hundreds of miles of desert and mountains nine thousand feet high. The route had the advantage of relative safety from the troops of Chang Tso-lin and other enemy warlords, and there were wells and oases along the way, although the number and exact location of these were the subject of considerable local dispute. It was unclear if any automobile had ever before traversed this path. Some people in Ningsia predicted it would take six days to reach their destination at Urga (Ulan Bator); others said at least six weeks. It was agreed that much of the baggage should be sent by camel and three of the trucks and one open car abandoned in Ningsia.

At four-thirty in the morning on September 5, the caravan finally resumed its course. By twilight, they arrived in Wang Yeh-fu, "the ultimate outpost of life before the desert." Anna Louise was enchanted by this jewel of a town, which lay in a valley fed by little brooks and terraced with orchards and gardens. The town even had an inn with clean, comfortable accommodations; each traveler had his own *kang*, the Chinese-style clay bed heated from beneath by the fire that also served for cooking. After her best night's sleep in weeks, she rose early to explore the locale and soon came to the "edge of hills which looked over the desert." Hypnotized by the lonely beauty spread out before her, she was startled to hear the wailing of a child. On a narrow dirt path beneath where she stood was a small boy, twisting and turning as if utterly lost. Fearful that her "strange, white face" would terrify the child even more, Anna Louise was relieved when a man appeared and scooped the child away in his arms. A few minutes later she came upon two young Mongol shepherds with whom she carried on an hour's conversation; the only word they understood in common was *"hao,"* the Chinese word for "good," but hand gestures worked very well. In one short hour she felt she had encountered the extremes of isolation and companionship she knew so well.

Anna Louise rejoined Borodin and the Chens for a visit to a Mongol prince. To her disappointment the prince was quite ordinary, as was his house. Later in the day, however, the group was lingering in a courtyard outside the town baths when a prince and princess out of a fairy tale appeared before them. The man wore an emerald-green gown sashed with vermilion over which a flowing coat shimmered in the afternoon light. His long black boots with curled toes were vivid against the white coat of the graceful pony on which he rode.

That night, as Borodin, Percy, Jack and a few others were talking around the fire, Anna Louise began to describe her vision of true romance. She had, she told her listeners, always wanted to come to Mongolia: "I imagined that there I would be sitting outside the camp and suddenly a man would appear on horseback. He would pick me up, sweep me onto his pony, and ride away." Her words were spoken with such solemnity that no one dared laugh, but it took all of the assembled will not to giggle at the image of the huge Anna Louise riding off on a tiny Mongolian pony with an equally slight Mongolian prince.

Once out on the desert Anna Louise resumed her efficient, professional persona. In the freezing cold of the night air she would find a place near the little bit of fire and type away. During the mercilessly hot days, she had more stamina than most of her companions. The riders discovered that the best way to get the car moving when it was stalled in the sand was for all the passengers to get out, place their sleeping mats under the wheels and push. Once the car was accelerating, they would run with mats in hand and leap onto the running boards. The doctor's wife was now riding in another vehicle, which left Jack, Chang Ke and Anna Louise to reenter the car. Percy would call out "All aboard," and first Jack and then Chang Ke would climb on. "Anna Louise, hanging on to the car as it gathered speed," Percy recalled, "would spring like a ballet dancer onto the running board and propel herself through the door." Percy tried to get Anna Louise to get in second, but she would not hear of it.

Her journalistic compulsions were the source of repeated embarrassment. Trying their best to perform their bodily functions with discretion, but with no trees or bushes behind which to urinate, Jack and Percy got out of the car at one point and raised the hood to cover themselves from Anna Louise. She mistook their tact for secrecy. "What's the matter?" she asked and stumbled into their private space. "What are you boys doing?" she asked. "We are feeling the tires," Percy answered. "I want to feel the tires as well," she responded helpfully. As the men maneuvered around the car away from her, she became more disturbed: "Why are you boys walking away from me?" "We don't need your help," they replied. Hurt, she retreated inside the car. The scene, Jack Chen recollected wryly, could have gone right into a Chaplin film.

Near the end of the journey the nights became increasingly cold, and Anna Louise suffered more than the others because she had not bought the warm sheepskins in which everyone else bundled at night. Unwilling to complain but unable to sleep, she got up one night and began to walk to keep warm. In the morning, at breakfast, the others suddenly noticed that she was missing. They called as loudly as they could and finally spent an hour searching. The desert provided no footprints, and with no further clues they gravely decided to continue on without her. The cars had gone about six miles when to everyone's relief "a small speck showed up the horizon." When the Dodge pulled up at her side, she burst into tears. "I got cold, so I walked," was all she could say between her sobs.

Finally they started the descent of the last grassy mountain to Ulan Bator. The capital of Mongolia was only a few log cabins surrounded by hundreds of yurts, the tents in which the Mongols lived. But there was something like a hotel, and it was only a two-day car trip to the Trans-Siberian railway at Verkhneudinsk and thence easy riding to Moscow. Anna Louise was unwilling to accept the end of the adventure. The morning after their arrival she rode off on horseback to a Buddhist monastery fifty miles away. On her return three days later, she poured out stories of the reverence for learning she had found among the lamas and proudly reported that to cross an ice-cold stream she had removed all of her clothing and waded through. When Jack Chen went to her room at the hotel to see if she had recovered from her most recent excursion, he noticed a large stack of paper. "Yes," said Anna Louise, "I have finished the book."

8

Marking a Time
and Place

I stared in amazement suspecting irony; then seeing she was
quite serious, I replied that Russia might be the most interesting land, and supreme in many good qualities, but that she
had picked out precisely the things which Russia had none
of—freedom and good cooking. A hot argument ensued, convincing no one. When in the course of the discussion I mentioned the freedom of movement offered in America, Tatiana
Borisovna looked shocked. "What a very disorganized country
you have," she cried.

—Anna Louise Strong, *The Road to the Grey Pamir*

Borodin flew from Ulan Bator to Verkhneudinsk, where he took the
express train for Moscow to report to the central committee on the
disaster in China. Anna Louise and the others followed by car and a
slower post train.

As she reflected on the previous weeks' experience with Borodin, Anna
Louise found judgment difficult. Stalin's insistence that the Communists
not break with the Nationalists had clearly been responsible for the massacre in Shanghai. During the trip Borodin had cast aspersions on the
Nationalist leaders but had also indicated that he had had no alternative
other than to support the policies of the central committee against the
peasantry. Anna Louise had no place to turn. As she wrote the story in
her book *China's Millions*, she mentioned Borodin's doubts only in passing but nevertheless concluded the first volume with a prediction that
China's revolutionary future lay mainly with the peasants and not in an
anti-imperialist alliance of the bourgeoisie and the workers. Beyond these
passages she held her tongue in print and in public. There might be a
role for her in Moscow; there was none now in China.

She arrived in Moscow on October 8, 1927, and found the capital in a state of high apprehension. The tenth anniversary of the October Revolution was approaching, and the struggle between Stalin and Trotsky had reached its last round. By his alliance with Bukharin, Stalin had consolidated his position in the bureaucracy and the party against the "Left Opposition"; it was no longer a matter of if Trotsky would fall, but when. Anna Louise had seen little of Trotsky for some time. Political prudence had governed her, and she made no further effort.

She had hoped for a "grand show" during the festivities, but when Trotsky stepped from his car in Revolution Square and tried to address the crowd, he was set upon by the police and Stalin's supporters with cries of "Down with Trotsky, the Jew, the traitor." His car windshield was broken and some shots were fired. After all her happy anticipation, Anna Louise was utterly silent to her father about the actual events of the anniversary celebrations.

Once again she had no place to stay. Her apartment in the Lux Hotel had vanished with the end of her job in the children's commission. She finally took a room at the Hotel Metropol for "the shocking price" of four and a half dollars a day, almost what she paid two years before for an entire month. Moscow was much changed. All free and easy intercourse between Russians and sympathetic foreigners had vanished: the range of her contacts was reduced to her friends. In the Metropol with her were the Chen brothers and their father; the American journalist Vincent Sheean, who had followed Rayna Prohme from Wuhan to Moscow; the Borodins; her friend Alexandra Kollontai, now about to be appointed to the Soviet embassy in Stockholm; and most of the foreign correspondents, including Walter Duranty, Eugene Lyons and Albert Rhys Williams. Soong Ch'ing-ling arrived shortly from a rest in the Caucasus.

The company was extraordinary, but Anna Louise was ambivalent about her obvious isolation from Russian society: "I am here near an important source of the sort of material America likes—personalities," she wrote her father a bit ruefully on November 5. "I am on the ground floor as never before in my life, going to the theater with Kollontai, Eugene Chen, or to a party got up by Borodin, besides entertaining stray Americans like Harry Dana or Scott Nearing. . . . Just how I shall do all these, and still get out my book, when normally I would need a rest after the Gobi trip, I don't know. . . . [I] start work about seven in the morning and . . . everyone comes to me, instead of me going to them."

Not all the visits were happy ones. On Sunday, November 13, Chang Ke came worriedly to her door. Rayna Prohme had fainted in a room at the Hotel de l'Europe. The two hurried out. On the steps of the Metropol they met Vincent Sheean. At the Europe, Rayna lay unconscious on a couch in the room of the Chinese labor delegation. Sheean lifted her gently, and a bizarre cortege made its way through the wintery streets back to the Metropol, where they laid her in Anna Louise's bed. Fanny Borodin came upstairs, bustling with an annoyingly cheerful efficiency. "I knew something like this would happen," she said. "Mrs. Prohme works too hard and thinks too much. I never worry. Besides, she doesn't take good care of herself. Now, you take my advice and make her eat lots of lemons. There is nothing on earth so good for the system as to eat a lot of lemons."

Lemons proved of no avail. The doctor did not arrive until evening, then gave Rayna ether to make her sleep, despite specific warnings that she was allergic to it. Rayna spent the night alternating between delirium and violent vomiting. Anna Louise passed the night on her own couch, ministering as best she could to her friend. With the help of Walter Duranty, Sheean finally obtained the services of Dr. Linck at the Germany embassy.

Linck's visit helped to calm Rayna, but he suspected encephalitis. On Saturday evening, November 20, he told the others: "The process I have foreseen has begun. It must take its course." Rayna remained unconscious for most of the next day. Anna Louise was alone with her at her death early Monday morning.

Grieved and angry, Anna Louise wrote to her father that, while she had hoped to be home for Christmas,

> I shall be delayed here until the end of December. I have forgotten if I have written you about Rayna Prohme's death; I think I did. Anyway, she was ill in my room and then in the room adjoining, and I was the only person to look after her. This with the funeral cut some twenty days out of my work here and left me tired. . . . So I am waiting for two reasons, to finish the interrupted book, the second on the trip with Borodin, and to await Bill Prohme, Rayna's husband, who is coming here from Manila, and I fear if he gets here in the middle of a Russia concentrated on the fight of the Party Congress in December, with all of Rayna's Bolshevik friends unwilling to take time for him, and no one to tell lies or soften facts a little bit, he may go completely crazy. Bolsheviks are hard and impersonal; and except for a few Americans here, Rayna certainly had a rotten deal at the end, hunting rooms from place to place, fainting in the rooms of casual acquaintances, and not looked after by the people responsible for her coming here.

Rayna Prohme's funeral took place on Anna Louise's forty-second birthday. Despite the snowfall the night before, the mourners insisted on walking across Moscow behind the catafalque. The traditional band played funeral marches from Chopin and Beethoven as well as the more usual revolutionary airs.

Fanny Borodin walked with the mourners, but her husband did not. He was under orders to keep his public distance from the Wuhan group while the party decided what to do about him. He was removed from all responsible positions and spent most of the next year awaiting the verdict. Though he was eventually made the scapegoat for the failure in China, Stalin protected him, and he suffered a more gentle fate than other Soviet China hands. He was neither relieved of his party membership nor arrested, and in early 1929, after extensive criticism and self-criticism, he was appointed deputy director of Bumprom, the paper and lumber trust.

The happy group from Wuhan scattered. Eugene Chen went to Paris; Soong Ch'ing-ling lingered awhile in Moscow, shaken by the news that her sister Mei-ling had married her arch-enemy Chiang Kai-shek, then returned to China; Sheean went to Europe to forget. Anna Louise was left without a place to go until, lonely and without enthusiasm, she returned to the United States in January 1928 for another lecture tour.

She wanted to write and resented anything that took her away from it. But she had difficulty in finding new topics and knew she was in danger of going stale. In May she returned to Russia and visited the remnant of the John Reed colony in Cherumshan. Twenty of the girls, now overage for the colony, remained disconsolately in the children's home; the authorities in Saratov were unable to find jobs for them. In need of a vacation and in search of a topic, she set out on horseback over the edge of the Caucasus. She reported mechanically that there were signs of hope and much unrelieved poverty. Her letters were unhappy and terse.

In the midst of her depression she once again rediscovered her energy in nature:

> Swinging back toward Moscow along the Georgian military highway, I was seized by the sudden hunger for high peaks. In the early part of the trip, every morning had found me utterly exhausted; it was the first horseback trip I ever took. The month had hardened me; my new fitness looked at Mount Kazbek.

Kazbek was 16,544 feet high. "I must climb it," she cried. And paused: "But I have no mountain gear, not even bloomers."

Undaunted, she found herself a local guide, who outfitted her with "slippers of soft leather lattice work filled with hay." Lacking dark glasses or grease against the glare of the ice and snow, she put on a dark veil and bundled into a sheepskin. The whole enterprise was a victory; after her return she wrote to her father:

> Takes from three to five days from the last hotel stop; I took two days and four hours, stopping two nights on the mountain. No danger, good guide, porter to carry up bedding on the first night, but I carried it down the last morning. Slept (?) at the height of 13,990 feet, or nearly as high as Rainier; this was just the beginning to which I went in ordinary shoes. . . .
>
> By the end of the day, when the glaciers were thawing and the hay had got wet and worn through, these lattice slippers let the sole of one's feet right down on the hard pointed ice fields. . . . Got to about 16,300 feet, at which point we came out onto an exposed saddle where the storm was too bad to continue.

It was a rebirth. She returned to Moscow with her strength renewed "like the great land around me" and her weight down to 170 pounds.

With renewed vigor she searched and found an apartment with two rooms, hot running water, a fireplace and a small kitchen, by far the most comfortable and spacious home she had ever had in Moscow. She had been in less than a week when her friend Albert Coyle asked if she would share her rooms "with an American couple . . . who want to live and work in Russia always." Anna Louise gave them her bed and took the couch. The expectation was that the couple would find a place of their own. But they had little money and less Russian; after a week she had to ask for her bed back. She was angry: "I think it is plain imposition to come to Russia with nothing but high ideals and no money and expect everyone here to help them to get along. . . . In the future [I will] think twice of applauding enthusiasm with no funds. The way in which I have been guilty in the past of encouraging 'folks of goodwill' to come to Moscow comes back to me now as I see Coyle doing it." But her resolution was weak. Five years later her friend Seema Allan wrote to an acquaintance that "half the foreigners in Moscow had at one time or another lived in her house at her impulsive invitation and then been thrown out because she got mad at something. She is generous by fits and starts, and stingy at times as well."

Even with frequent "guests" Anna Louise completed her book on China. The translation into Russian proved difficult, but eventually it was published in two volumes in Russia, and as a single one in the United States. The few reviews it received in the United States were friendly, but the sales reflected American disinterest in China. In Russia and Germany, however, the book sold very well, and royalties poured in.

These were productive years. She was making a lot of money on her books, lectures and articles and was investing it well, buying American real estate and stocks. She wrote not only for big "capitalist houses" but also for small left-wing publishing firms and magazines. Most notable among these were the "blue books" published by E. Haldeman-Julius, an iconoclastic radical in Girard, Kansas. In 1927 alone, Anna Louise sent him at least half a dozen articles, all of which appeared as pamphlets selling for five cents apiece. Most of these were revisions of pieces previously published in the mainstream press, but now they were available to the poor and to the working class.

After the expulsion of Trotsky from Russia in early 1929, she found the political climate in Moscow unpleasant. Her past association with the fallen leader made her suspect to most Russians in positions of central authority, and she sought less threatening terrain in the outlying regions of the Soviet Union. Her road took her to Samarkand in south central Russia. She hoped to go from there to Kabul, the capital of Afghanistan, and thence to India.

She left Moscow on November 21, 1928, with a number of contracts, the most lucrative of which was for a book on the condition of women in Soviet Central Asia. She spent over two months in the capital, Tashkent, waiting for a visa to Kabul. Because of British Foreign Office anxieties about her radicalism, it never materialized, but she took advantage of the delay to explore the region thoroughly. It was, as she wrote fellow journalist Walter Duranty, "a glad succession of thrills." Even the weather was like "some remarkable new wine."

Uzbekistan was a difficult testing ground for the new Five-Year Plan, an audacious nationwide program calling for the final abolition of the NEP, the collectivization of agriculture, and the enforcement of equal rights, especially among national minorities and women. In a region still rural, with a population to a great degree illiterate and dominated by a patriarchal structure that recognized no social equality except that between dominant males, class conflict over the new laws had merged with sexual conflict. Serfdom had been the norm, and women were still bought and sold as slaves and household servants. The major organizing force in support of the central government was newly liberated women.

Anna Louise responded to the situation with a righteous enthusiasm:

> The fight for women's freedom in Soviet Central Asia is cruel and bloody, as are all wars between new laws and entrenched custom. The central government supports the women. . . . Yet hardly a month passes without the news that in some distant village a woman has been murdered. . . . "At the last

vacations," a Tashkent student told me, "our young folks organization selected from its members those who should go down and agitate in the villages. We sent one girl down to a village not far from the city. Next morning she was returned to us in a peasant cart, cut into small pieces. These words accompanied the body: 'This is your woman's freedom.' "

Despite these and other atrocities she found that progress was being made:

At the biggest meeting . . . [the women] . . . couldn't keep quiet even to hear the speakers from Moscow. They shouted, stamped, tore their veils off and threw them toward the platform. Everyone tore at the veils as they passed, and at that, the speakers on the platform tore their veils into strips amid great shouting of "Long live Women's Freedom." . . . [A few days later] there occurred a murder of a woman by her husband and local mullahs—it was followed by a demonstration trial and executions, to impress on the Uzbeks that women's lives are also human and not to be taken, as heretofore, with casual impunity. . . . I count myself favored of the gods in being allowed down here.

Only reluctantly did she return to Moscow and then to America for a lecture tour. Despite the fact that her book on China had just appeared, her most successful topic was "Women and Marriage in the Soviet Union." To an audience perplexed by the dislocations of the twenties, Anna Louise painted an inspiring picture of strong marriages, well-brought-up children, rational divorce and enlightened sexuality. "One of the reasons that marriages are so lasting," she told an audience in the Old South Meeting House in Boston on January 27, 1929, "is that everyone is so busy. The husband is not looking for excitement and allurements outside of his house. . . . In spite of the freedom you do not see anything of the flapper type and almost nothing of the practice known as 'necking.' The reasons are quite simple. In Russia, young people are not overfed, not overstimulated by automobiles and other luxuries, and their nerves are not kept at a high tension by the speed of living." The pattern in Boston was typical: after speaking for an hour, she answered almost fifty questions and finally retired to great applause.

Not everyone was pleased with Anna Louise and her work. Convinced of her subversiveness, the Daughters of the American Revolution picketed her speeches and tried to disrupt meetings with hostile questions. More and more frequently she was denied the use of public halls. Her file at the FBI rapidly grew longer.

Although she was aware that the FBI was keeping an eye on her, she showed no sign of distress. Her letters were as candidly detailed about political issues as they had always been, and she treated the attentions of security agencies almost as a game. After her return to Moscow she wrote to her father:

> Here's a Sherlock Holmes test for you. Note the enclosed envelope. You sent it to me and it was in my wastebasket. Rose Hanna [her literary agent] happened to quote someone to the effect that all mail coming to the country was opened, and I got this out to prove that steaming letters wouldn't work on this one. Then I examined the flap and wondered. The edges do not match!! Did you write on the outside of the envelope before opening it?

Before a response could arrive, she was off again, this time to the "roof of the world," the Pamir Mountains, five hundred miles east of Samarkand. Alexandra Kollontai, back in Moscow in preparation for her promotion to ambassador to Sweden, told her that her ex-husband, General Pavel Dubenko, was planning to make the first airplane trip from Tashkent to the Pamirs. Dubenko had been a leading general during the Revolution and was now commander of the Soviet Army in Central Asia; after considerable pressure from Anna Louise, he gave her one of the four seats on his airplane.

She left Moscow by rail on June 5 to meet Dubenko in Tashkent. By coincidence, her old friend Bill Shatoff was on the same train. He was a wonderful companion, equipped with hundreds of stories from his travels as a national organizer for the IWW in the United States. Shortly before his deportation to the Soviet Union in 1918, he had taken over the tsarist consulate in New York City and issued passports to overseas revolutionaries wishing to return to the new Russia, including one to Trotsky. Now he was directing the construction of the thousand-mile Turkestan-Siberia Railroad. To Anna Louise he was a true pioneer, bringing civilization to "the wild tribes of the Asian steppe, untamed since Genghis Khan."

She left Shatoff in Tashkent only to discover that the flight to the Pamirs had been canceled because the new landing strip had been built too short for takeoffs. Before she could adjust her plans, all movement was blocked: "Enormous swarms of locusts that once under Moses ate up Egypt come in clouds from Afghanistan and Persia, eating the country bare. As long as they are flying nothing can be done against them; they derail even trains with their masses." Anna Louise detailed the fight against the locusts with the enthusiasm and precision of a war correspondent, analyzing the most successful methods of dealing with the insects, noting the righteous religious hostility of the mullahs, welcoming the flocks of rosy starlings who proved the most effective enemy to the infestation.

She finally left Tashkent with a Colonel Lavaroff and a detachment of the Red Army going to Osh, a beautiful town reputed to have been Adam's residence after his expulsion from paradise. The name itself, Anna Louise reported straight-facedly, "was given to the town when King Solomon, weary from his long journey (and it must have been a long journey here from Jerusalem), said to his oxen 'Ush' or 'Osh,' which is central Asian for 'Whoa.'"

Impatient with still another delay, she joined up with a geological expedition under the guidance of Professor Nikitin from Leningrad University. Her goal was the pasture soviet at Sary Tash, a nomadic commune, complete with people's courts, schools, and women organizers. Nikitin's expedition was going within forty kilometers of Sary Tash, and he proposed that Anna Louise accompany them until their paths diverged at the Toldik Pass, where she could find a native guide and continue on alone. She could meet Lavaroff and his relief company when they came through Sary Tash later.

After extensive bargaining, she bought a horse for 350 rubles, a second-hand saddle and the supplies she would need. The first day of the trip was a horror. The horse, which she named Alai, shied at the slightest strange movement. By the next morning she had left the horse with the caravan and struck out on foot. Her independence proved a mistake. She was soon so footsore and hot that when a swarthy Uzbek appeared, her fatigue overtook her independence and her sense of shame.

> He offered me a seat on his horse behind him. He had neither saddle nor stirrups, but rode atop a mighty heap of baggage, and since there were no rocks nearby to serve as a mounting block, I did not see how I could possibly climb up. So I declined. . . . Seeing this, he dismounted and indicated that he would push me up on the horse. The process was most undignified. . . . The Uzbek was patient and apparently without a sense of humor. Quite soberly he got me up with head dangling on one side and feet on the other, and then with his aid I secured a seat.

The caravan caught up with her, and Anna Louise resumed riding her own horse. The oppressive heat gave way the next day to torrential rains. Alai threw her into a swamp; she was attacked by dogs, which she drove off with stones. After being thrown again, she once more walked on ahead. She forded a river, but by the time she reached Gul'cha, the next stop, her feet were covered with blisters.

At an altitude of over 11,000 feet on Toldik Pass, Anna Louise took leave of the geological party. For the "overly high" sum of six rubles, a guide took her to Sary Tash, where she found the pasture soviet. As Anna Louise arrived, the people's court was trying a case of underage marriage. Since the marriage had been consummated, the court decided to leave it intact but sentenced the fathers to eight months' labor without imprisonment. "This would disturb their souls, but not their household," Anna Louise noted with satisfaction, "since the women do all the work there anyhow."

Lavaroff and his detachment eventually reached Sary Tash, and she set off with them south toward Murgab. Her troubles with Alai continued. The horse spooked at some flapping sheepskins and Anna Louise fell. Her hip was so badly bruised that she fainted from the pain. The company stopped half a day to let her recover and then pushed on. In constant agony, she passed by beautiful Lake Karakul, dominated to the west by Mount Communism, highest peak in the U.S.S.R., and then, at over 13,000 feet, proceeded through a countryside as desolate as the moon. The weather was merciless, freezing by night and scorching by day. To make matters worse, she got badly sunburned, especially on her hands, for which she had neglected to bring gloves. Finally, on July 11, after a seventeen-day journey from Osh, the party arrived at Murgab, the "capital of the Pamirs."

There was almost nowhere to go from Murgab. Anna Louise rested, took a few side trips further south and resigned herself to returning along precisely the road on which she had come. Wishing to be rid of a rather difficult and out-of-place guest, Lavaroff proposed that she accompany a representative of the regional party headquarters named Mamashef back to Osh. Lured by the prospect of moonlit rides through high mountain passes, she accepted the idea.

The two were joined by a wealthy caravan man from Kashgar, who supposedly wanted the safety of official company. The second morning of the trip he ran off with all the horses, and it was two days before the local Kirghiz caught him. Anna Louise had to put up two-thirds of the reward that Mamashef had promised the posse. Since there was nothing else to do with the thief, he continued onward with them with a vague threat of retribution in Osh.

Three days later, Alai and the Kashgarlik's horse fled during the night. Mamashef, angered by the delays, which he attributed to Anna Louise, simply rode off, abandoning her and the merchant on the shores of Lake Karakul. Three hours later, Mamashef returned in a towering rage. He had come across the horses about five miles down the road. The horses had begun to follow him, and he had realized that it would be impossible to arrive in the Alai valley with the horse of his guest but not the guest. "Bad luck follows you!" he screamed. Anna Louise kept an unaccustomed quiet.

> Never before in my life had I been in the presence of an angry male upon whom I was dependent and to whom I dared therefore not reply. Yet this had been the traditional position of women of all ages, and though modern doctrines of equality had spared it in me, an age-old instinct arose at need.

As they approached Sary Tash, Anna Louise gladly left Mamashcf and the Kashgarlik for a group of European Russians from the Economic Institute. Her public conclusion was forgiving:

> In looking back at the three mad days I was driven by the once-hospitable Kirghiz, I cannot really blame him. He came of a race whose women work harder than men and rank lower; no western tradition of chivalry had marred that view. I had been handed to him by the post commander in a way that he could not refuse; and I, who might have refused to encumber him, had been singularly blind.

She was too weary to do anything but return to Moscow, where she at least had the consolation of discovering that she had lost thirty pounds.

Once again, however, she was drawn away from Moscow. With Stalin's consolidation of power, the collectivization of agriculture had begun. The aim was to create large-scale "agricultural production factories"—collective farms, or kolkhozes—in time for spring sowing. A large contingent of party faithful—the "twenty-five thousand"—were recruited and sent to the countryside to organize the new method of production. For Anna Louise it was an exciting moment, comparable in magnitude, as Alexandra Kollontai suggested to her, to the change between the Roman Empire and feudalism. She set out to report the whole experience and made at least three extended trips to the countryside between late November 1929 and the first week in May. The first was to familiar territory, Saratov. During the ten days of her visit, she witnessed both the impetus toward change and the depth of the resistance. The change was not merely in production techniques; a cultural revolution had been unleashed on the land and the tool-owning rural middle class known as the kulaks. "It is clear," she wrote, "that the kolkhoz has become something here quite different from a dispassionate economic experiment in better ways of growing grain. It is the atheist's flag against the church; it is youth's shout against the oppression of age; it is the struggle of new life against the patriarchal society."

From the Volga, she went on a thousand-mile journey to a newly collectivized area of the Ukraine. She took with her Lement Harris, a young, Harvard-educated American who had forsaken a comfortable life in the United States to help organize farm production in the Soviet Union. He was one of the few men in Russia at that time who had actually driven a combine and could explain the technical aspects of agriculture. Anna Louise and he spent the two weeks before Christmas exploring the successes and problems of the first tractor station in Shevchencko.

She was privately upset by what she found. Shevchenko had been a difficult area to collectivize. A century earlier many Germans had immigrated, and now their prosperous farms made up 25 percent of the region rather than the usual 4 to 5 percent. Such villages had much to lose by collectivization and had resisted it, often violently. When she returned to Moscow, she delayed writing about the experience until she could find the proper context. "Many chaotic things are happening," she wrote to her father, "in which one must get one's balance before putting them on paper. There have been weeks at a time when if I had written what I thought for America, I might have been chucked out of Russia. That indeed would have been the smash of my life."

Coming to grips with the harsh realities of collectivization produced a number of changes in Anna Louise. She protected her father from any direct confrontation with the violence. When the correspondent Eugene Lyons arrived in Moscow after seeing Sydney in the United States, she asked him "a favor and a promise" not to tell her father anything about the unpleasant sides of the revolution in agriculture. Lyons agreed and later commented: "Miss Strong is sensitive on these matters. She is not one-tenth part as cocksure and ruthless . . . as she seems to be in books and on the platform. . . . Again and again the impact of Soviet life has been hard on her nerves."

It took her a while to arrive at a position on collectivization acceptable to both her conscience and the censor. A pale, exhausted, but still determined party member told her, "We are like a man on skis coming down a swift slope. Our acceleration is terrific and grows constantly greater. . . . We cannot stop. . . . All we can do is guide our jumps and hope to land properly." She was clear about the stakes. "There is of course much cruelty and terrible injustices—what can you expect when the execution of drastic policies must be put through by twenty-year-old half-instructed

Young Communists who are anxious to make a record for loyalty, and who are far more extreme than intended. One could sum up the injustices even in one township and have enough for kind pacifist souls to damn Russia forever. But on the other hand, one hundred million people are being shaken, willy-nilly, through three centuries in a decade." She eventually came to see collectivization as a process let loose rather than imposed by Stalin: he "merely analyzed and authorized what farmhands were already instinctively doing." And in *The Soviets Conquer Wheat,* even though by her own admission at least a million kulak families had been displaced, expropriated, and/or killed, she wrote:

> It was impossible to know what was really happening across the land, except in snatches of unrelated triumph and horror. It was as impossible for soldiers in the trenches to estimate the chance of general victory. The commanding staff, in such situations, gives information carefully chosen to stimulate heroism, and ignorance is carefully maintained till the crises are past. . . . Even [the Bolsheviks] felt the strain of the struggle, as they had not felt any struggle since the civil war.

Eventually she reconciled herself to the cruel stage of violence and the suffering: both kulak and organizer, she concluded, were guilty of terror and murder, but world history exonerated collectivization. Alexandra Kollontai appears to have been particularly instrumental in helping her come to this conclusion. Anna Louise wrote her father that Alexandra had said "some unforgetable things about the divergence between the old leaders and the new ruthless generation now ruling—I shall use them. . . . She said: "To me the human soul is still the greatest thing in the world. But we shall not come back to it for another fifty years. This generation is building the mechanism for the future; they have no time for ultimates. We who think of justice and brotherhood and human happiness—we must step aside in time, lest we be thrown out roughly. . . . That lies behind all the tragedies of our leaders, from Trotsky to Bukharin. . . . Stalin is not a leader in the old sense; he is a symbol of unity pushed on by a thousand men. And he is very exhausted, very nervous from it."

Publicly she kept her peace. She wrote in Russian a pamphlet on the Ukraine tractor station that was issued in a first printing of 300,000 copies. Its success brought her a commission to do a text on the Russian Ford assembly plant for use in high school English classes. Her frenzy of writing and reporting ran so high during the spring of 1930 that she canceled her American lecture tour. In April she made another trip to the countryside, this time to Siberia and Central Asia, in part to attend the completion of the Turkestan-Siberia Railroad, a feat Bill Shatoff had accomplished almost two years ahead of schedule. She came back from that trip with tales of the industrial town New Siberia (Novosibirsk) that had grown in six months on the Siberian steppes. The broad land over-whelmed her and seemed to provide some justification for her public political statements:

> This country is so big and has so many sides that one can think whatever one likes. One can sink oneself in the news of collectivization and soon think that nothing in the land is going on except a desperate class struggle (though perhaps no more ruthlessly than our early land possessions were fought over, and certainly not more ruthlessly than we dispossessed the Indians). Then one can visit some of the giant modern factories going up . . . and think there is nothing more than a grand triumphal march towards socialism.
>
> [Or] one can hear . . . complaints . . . and decide that all that characterizes Russia is a lack of soap, sugar, butter and a standing in line for all sorts of commodities.
>
> There is one very good tale going the rounds. . . . It is the year after the five-year plan. The sky is black with airplanes. A man is riding in last year's model and is overtaken by a friend in the new model.
> —I see you have the new plane from our Super Factory.
> —Yes! In this model we have surpassed the Americans. Can't show it now. I'm in a rush.
> —What's your hurry?
> —I hear that they are selling eggs in Kiev.

At the same time that her subject was becoming more and more com-plex, the audience was growing steadily—in the United States, Russia and much of Europe. The same article would sometimes appear in both the *New York Times* and *Pravda*. She was, as Walter Duranty said to her, the best feature writer in the world on Soviet domestic policy. Her books were widely reviewed; through her pamphlets, she was even reaching the masses. To her delight, she was listed in *Who's Who*. Between the end of November 1929 and March 1930 she finished rewriting the *Pamir* book, condensed both volumes of *China's Millions* for textbooks, wrote the little book on the Ford plant, produced three forty-page pamphlets in Russian for peasants, and supervised the translation of her books on Samarkand and the John Reed colony. In addition she wrote, by her own conservative estimate, thirty-seven articles. She found herself getting fat, she complained, from sitting too much at a desk.

The book on the collective farms, *The Soviets Conquer Wheat*, was published in 1931 and, like its predecessors, was well received. It was especially seductive to an American audience caught in the slough of the Depression, with almost a year to go before the next presidential election. The persona of the book is a well-meaning, intelligent, moral American, slightly confused by the twists and turns of world history. By a judicious use of vivid and authentic detail, the book tries to lead its readers from a narrow, moralistic reaction to the fate of the kulaks to sympathy with the aims of collectivization. Like many of the peasants and troubled intellectuals, Anna Louise pictured Stalin as a man of revolutionary but cautious intelligence who had moderated the initial excesses of 1929 and 1930. There was some truth to this picture, but often now, in her zeal to instruct, her writing became propaganda.

Despite her successes, Anna Louise still felt the lack of a home. Tracy and Edith were in Geneva, focusing on the affairs of the World Alliance of YMCAs. Ruth and Charles had moved to Menlo Park, California, where Charles was again teaching high school. Each of the families had children; Robbins, Tracy's oldest son, was finishing Oberlin College. The Seattle house stood empty except for an occasional renter. Sydney, now seventy-one, lived most of the year in the Wolcott Hotel in New York City, continuing to publish anthologies like *We Believe in Prayer*. His age was beginning to show, and though he still helped to place his daughter's articles, he spent much of his time in reminiscences. Despite Anna Louise's repeated requests for a visit, he showed no sign of wanting to return to the Soviet Union.

Most of the people Anna Louise had known in the early days of the Soviet Union had returned to the United States. Some had also returned to political respectability; others carried on the fight for socialism at home. In Moscow, Anna Louise was neither a party member nor a visitor. Her identity lay in the continuous production of articles and books. It was proving not only physically tiring but psychically draining as well.

New hope came from a visit to her old friend Mikhail Borodin in the middle of June 1930. In 1929 and 1930 a large number of skilled laborers had come from the West to the U.S.S.R. for work, often explicitly recruited by Soviet labor agents. Borodin had been placed in charge of this group. When Anna Louise came to see him, Borodin asked her if she had not once had the idea of starting an "American type" newspaper in Moscow. "I've had the idea for years," she responded. "If you want to start it, I'll take the job of getting a staff and issuing the sheet. But I won't do any organizing in this country. I know my limitations." She assembled and circulated a prospectus. Her father was unenthusiastic, remembering the experience of the Russian-American Club, but in Russia the idea quickly grew, and on July 6 she approached Valery Meshlauk, vice-chairman of the Supreme Council of National Industry, for assistance.

The newspaper was intended as a forum for the problems of the Americans working in the U.S.S.R. and a source of information about developments in Russia and back home. It would carry baseball scores and be written in a "lively American manner." She took the idea all around Moscow. Prominent American engineers like Hugh Cooper and Bill Calder were enthusiastic; the chief American correspondents, Walter Duranty and Eugene Lyons, tentatively promised to contribute to it. She approached the press officer at the Foreign Office, Joel Shubin, with the idea. He intimated that they might like it as "their paper."

A core staff was soon formed of Anna Louise; Jack Chen, who had remained in Moscow to study art after his arrival from Wuhan; Ed Falkowski, a Kentucky miner turned writer; Maxwell Stewart, a former editor of *China Outlook;* and Herbert Marshall, the secretary of the London Film Guild. The men were all short, so the group became popularly known as "Anna Louise and the four dwarfs." Others soon joined them, including Millie Mitchell, back from Hankow, and Joshua Kunitz, a writer for the *New Masses* who was in Moscow studying the theater.

At first they had a wonderful, if chaotic, time. Anna Louise's nominal supervisor was a genial man named Vasutin who paid little attention to the development of the paper. Authorizations arrived just as Meshlauk had promised. Anna Louise personally typed most of the first issue of the *Moscow Daily News* and did the layout herself. The copy was hand-set by linotypists who did not know the Latin alphabet. Everyone read proof, and then Jack Chen took the forms over the cobblestone streets in a four-wheeled droshky to the print shop. American cigarettes proved a successful form of bribery, and printers took extra time to set the cartoons and heads in a language with which they were not familiar. Anna Louise made no intimate friends on the staff and rarely ate in the cafeteria with the others, but she threw herself into the enterprise, working twelve-hour days. This was her paper.

Then the first edition of the *News* came back from the Glav-Lit, the literary censorship bureau. A funny story by Falkowski on the difficulties of finding an apartment in Moscow was blue-penciled out, "a slander to the Soviet Union." In vain Anna Louise tried to explain the American sense of humor. The censor would not yield. She pounded the desk, kicked at the chairs, stormed about the room screaming and waving her fists. The censor was still not intimidated. Aghast, Vasutin advised Anna Louise to concede, which in desperation she did. Happily, the censor failed to pick up the fact that the caption mistakenly attributed to Lenin on a Chen cartoon was actually from Trotsky.

After the third week of publication, Anna Louise left for her lecture tour in the United States. It was as if she had dropped off the earth. Articles she sent back to the *News* were not printed; her furious cables went unanswered. When a copy of the paper reached America, she discovered that Vasutin had been replaced by a man named T. L. Axelrod. The paper was filled with badly translated articles from Russian papers and was so dull that Amtorg stopped carrying it for fear of alienating American businessmen.

Her lecture schedule was too hectic to permit her to do much more than worry. She saw all her relatives and lectured in cities from Boston to San Diego. The halls were packed, the audiences enthusiastic, although there was occasional trouble. When no one could be found to chair a meeting in Seattle, Anna Louise went on without an introduction. A number of hostile questioners threatened to produce chaos until Jimmy Duncan, who had been the head of the Seattle AFL in 1916, jumped up on the platform and took over the chair. He prefaced his action, however, with a series of derogatory remarks about some of the groups who had originally sponsored the meeting and who were paying Anna Louise's fees. Instead of being grateful, Anna Louise took him to task after the meeting for his comments.

The trip brought home to Anna Louise how far her mision had taken her from anyone on whom she might rely. She sat alone crying in her hotel room in Oakland, California, on Christmas Day 1930, listening to the carols from the floor beneath, answering a hundred letters about articles, lectures and politics. The next week she collapsed at the La Jolla home of her old friend from Kansas City, Ruth White Lowery. A doctor prescribed medicine for a supposed pituitary deficiency; she felt better but canceled a number of engagements and remained in Southern California to write. By the end of the month she was well enough to meet Valery Meshlauk, who happened to be visiting the United States. He assured her that she should return to Moscow and that she had full authority as editor.

The signs on her return were not auspicious. No one met her at the train station. At the *News* offices, almost the entire staff had been replaced by a new group of highly paid typists and translators who were busy turning dull Russian prose into bad English. The few Americans left from her original group waited in an inner office for her to make things the way they had been before.

This proved difficult. Even her desk had been appropriated by one of the new secretaries. Despite an explosion and rage and her status as managing editor, the desk was not returned, and she had to work at home. Worse, another English-language paper, "for workers," had been started in response to a claim that the *Moscow News* was "too bourgeois." The *Worker's News* was, if possible, even duller than the *Moscow News*. The only relief from the grayness of the two papers were the names they called each other.

If her paper had to look like a Russian paper, she decided, at least she could do a better job. She started attending all the party congresses and would rush home after an interminable speech to try to scoop *Pravda*. This led to constant conflict with Axelrod, who proved to be a dogmatic ideologue. He insisted on waiting for the official Tass News Agency transcript of each speech and then printing it verbatim. By April 1931 Anna Louise had realized that the real conflict was a double hierarchy. Unbeknownst to her she had a counterpart named Chunak who was *also* managing editor, but in Russian. She tried to resign "to go to China" for two years, but her resignation went unacknowledged.

In the course of trying to salvage something of her newspaper, she turned for advice to Joel Shubin, whom she had met several years before and encountered again at the Foreign Office the previous fall. He was now editor of the *Peasant's Gazette*, which impressed Anna Louise with its clear writing and respect for readers. With every conversation, her respect for Shubin's complex and penetrating intelligence increased. He intimidated her and was impatient with her criticisms of the Soviet Union, but he taught her to avoid explosions and instead to analyze her problems so that they could be solved. He confessed that he had been attracted to her for years but only now felt certain that they were "on the same side of the barricades."

The two offered a strange contrast. Five years younger than Anna Louise and Jewish by origin, Joel was short and wiry with thick glasses and thinning dark hair. A quiet, reflective man, he moved calmly and unobtrusively about the world. While Anna Louise wrote rapidly and furiously, he worked slowly and carefully. Joel was a party saint, a selflessly dedicated Communist. He had been married and widowed a few years earlier and had a teenage daughter, Ducia.

He and Anna Louise saw more and more of each other. It was a welcome relationship to her, relieving the loneliness of her solitary apartment and the fear of being an old maid. Soon Joel was spending nights with her, and the word spread in Moscow that the two were a couple. As speculation grew, the unkind story was passed around that Joel and Anna Louise would certainly marry, for "there were no fortresses impregnable to the Bolsheviks." The prediction proved true in fact though not in spirit. By late 1931, with neither fanfare nor ceremony, the two had decided they were married. As was the custom in the Soviet Union at that time, she later wrote, "since we were adult . . . we simply declared to his relatives that we were married and living together. From that time I was loyal to him as a wife." No letter survives by which Anna Louise announced her marriage to her father, nor is any comment of his on the subject preserved.

Like Anna Louise, Joel and Ducia had been living in a two-room apartment. The first formal gesture of the two as a couple was to exchange their two apartments for a larger three-room one on Kozitskaya Street near the Bolshoi Theater. For Anna Louise, the marriage marked the abandonment of her romantic dreams. She was a long way from the Gobi Desert: "We know companionship more free and friendly than the world elsewhere can show; but the mystic exaltations which at times we come on in the verses of the old poets seem rather alien. Shall I confess it? The great lovers of tradition, the Tristans and Iseults, Paolos and Francescas, Héloïses and Abélards—we wonder if they were quite sane and normal? . . . To give 'all' for love, whether in or out of marriage, would seem to us antisocial, immoral. We do not even give up our jobs."

Their marriage coincided with Anna Louise's leave of absence from the *Moscow News*. She had managed to get Axelrod fired but did not get the kind of authority she had wished as a result. The new editor, Vacsov, was worse. She continued to offer her resignation, but no one would accept it. During the summer of 1932, she stayed out of the office and worked for Borodin at the Labor Commissariat. The *News* kept her on salary and on the masthead. In desperation, she agreed to an unnecessary trip to Central Russia to explore production in the new tractor works of Stalingrad and visit the huge new dam at Dnieprostroy. She returned to Moscow and immediately left again, this time with Joel, for a trip to Kuznetsk to see the steel mills. Their friendship and marriage grew steadily, each reinforcing the other. In Joel, Anna Louise felt, she had found a "comrade . . . through whose presence one becomes steadily the person one desires to be."

At last, Anna Louise had a home in Russia, but she still needed a job that satisfied her. Difficulties with the *Moscow News* grew steadily. She worked hard summarizing an exceptionally long speech by Stalin for the first page and laid it out carefully next to one of Chen's cartoons. Vacsov withdrew the cartoon, replaced it with a picture of Stalin, and printed the entire speech verbatim. Anna Louise was furious. "Who is to say," asked Vacsov irritably, "what the gist of the great Stalin's speech is?" "But," she sputtered, "we look just like *Pravda*." There was no reply.

Outraged, she considered returning to the United States and writing and exposé of Soviet journalism. She was dissuaded by an "especially sensitive" Russian Communist (almost certainly Borodin), who suggested that she write to Stalin. Three days after sending off her letter, she received a call from Stalin's secretary that the matter was being investigated. The next day Vacsov told her that her name would be removed from the masthead, as she had requested. The following evening another phone call informed her that she was to meet with Stalin, Vacsov, and "some other comrades," two days hence.

Vacsov came to pick her up, bustling with importance and excitement. The two sped along by the Alexander Sunken Garden and turned in at the White Gate to the Kremlin. A sentry stopped them at the ancient drawbridge, checked their credentials, and sent them on their way. The auto passed Troitskaya Tower and turned left toward the government buildings. They were admitted to a conference room on the second floor.

As they walked in, Stalin, Lazar Kaganovich, and Kliment Voroshilov rose in greeting. Stalin was "stocky and strong, with bronzed face and graying hair . . . ; he seemed like a man who is neither tired nor rested, but who has worked very long and can go on working much longer. . . . Voroshilov was more vivaciously wasteful of energy; Kaganovich was tall, handsome and dark."

With no preliminaries, Stalin spoke to Vacsov. "How does it happen that the comrade here complains that you give her no authority, yet insist on retaining her name and call it an anti-Soviet act if she takes it off? Why is it necessary to use such violence?" Anna Louise thought this meant that Stalin would simply accept the removal of her name from the masthead. But Stalin pressed on: "Would the removal of her name not be a demotion?" Anna Louise was suddenly liberated: "The will that had been dead within me was alive, flaming and free." Quickly and precisely, she explained to him what she wanted. American efficiency could help Russia, but the Soviet Americans needed a newspaper to assist them in their difficult fight to integrate themselves into Russia. There was not a large enough audience to support two separate papers. Stalin interrupted: "Was there not a difference between engineers and workers?" She was momentarily taken aback, then resumed: "American workers and American engineers—all of them in Soviet Russia—are not different enough. They both have the same problems and need one paper to unite them, not two to separate them. We need one good daily."

Vacsov caught the direction of the conversation and quickly added his support for "one strong daily." Suddenly, all were agreed. Anna Louise added one final, all-important request, that Mikhail Borodin be named "responsible editor." She, Vacsov and Axelrod would be assistant editors. "How swiftly everything had happened. How suddenly it had come clear. . . . It began to explain my work; then it began to explain the Soviet Union. It solved new problems as they arose. It gave me a method. Other hours in my life marked by great emotion—when I have adored great men—have all died out; I cannot recapture their feeling. But that half hour grows with years. Even today I can feel the atmosphere of that meeting—its sympathetic but unemotional analysis, seeking fundamental lines and relations and acting to set them right."

For the first time Anna Louise felt she understood how the Soviet Union worked. It was not a dictatorial regime but rather a system of committee meetings that ultimately reached into every aspect of life. Some of the committees were elected; some seemed to arise spontaneously. As the committees met, at whatever level of power, they discussed, made demands, raised complaints, until finally they discovered the purpose in the entire group. Stalin was leader because he was better than anyone at this process, the "best committee man" she had ever met. He had made it possible for the collective idea of "one strong daily" to emerge. Once the purpose appeared from the group, she now saw, it became the party line that everyone was bound to follow because he or she had willed it originally. If you were on the outside of the process—a kulak or a capitalist—the results would appear dictatorial. If you were part of the process, it could appear to be what Stalin would claim it was in 1936, "the most democratic system in the world." The one thing the system did not provide for were sympathetic, passive spectators.

Upon her return, she poured out the events to Joel and concluded: "I'd like to take orders from those men anywhere in the world. I feel they wouldn't give an order until I knew myself it was the thing to do."

"I think," he replied, "you must be getting ready to join our party."

She could not in fact join the CPSU, since she was neither a citizen nor willing to give up her American passport, but with the marriage to Joel and the restructuring of *Moscow News* she had found a focus for her life and work.

Seema Allan, an American who worked as a reporter on the *News*, provided a vivid picture of her at this period in a letter to a friend in California:

> She's a great girl, that Anna Louise. She is . . . very good looking, despite the avoirdupois. Her hair is white, her cheeks are pink, her eyes a bright lively blue. She is as full of energy as a young girl—she is as full of temperament as a prima donna. She will raise hell with anyone from the telephone operator to the Central Committee of the Party in order to get what she wants. And she nearly always gets it. She goes around in a funny suit or a dress with Ukrainian embroidery—a figure one turns on streets to follow with one's eyes. . . . She's generous by fits and starts and stingy at times as well. Every person who comes over here from the States knows her or has a letter to her—she's known as the "oldest American resident" here—laughed at for her foibles, liked for her naturalness, and admired because she knows the country, because she'll go to any far corner of it with a pack on her back and then tell a story that makes one sit up at night to follow.

At home Joel taught her much about a life that knew no salvation outside the party. During the great famine of 1932 he spent forty-four days flying from farm to farm in the North Caucasus devising policies to save grain. He lost thirty pounds and came home covered with lice. Yet he took it as reward enough that a million bushels had been saved; he neither asked nor expected other recognition. Anna Louise saw that he did not take his orders unthinkingly from the party, as a kind of passive instrument, but that his will was one with that of the party. His party work was not an act of submission, but an affirmation of strength.

In November 1933 she took her new knowledge back with her to the United States. She was excited by the energy of the New Deal; many of her old friends were now in positions of influence in Washington as part of the left wing of the Roosevelt administration. She hoped to atone for her absence from the United States by now becoming a bridge between the New Deal and the American Communist party: "I had fled from their complexities to build in an alien country. . . . But American workers could have used all of me—my writing, my ability to organize, in instinctive reaction to my American background, my analyzing brain, which at twenty-three had conquered philosophy and thrown it aside as alien to life."

In Hartford for a lecture, she gave an extensive interview to a young reporter, Julia Older, who had just graduated from Wellesley College. Julia was fascinated that a descendant of Elder John Strong, who had founded the neighboring town of Windsor, could be running a newspaper in Communist Russia. She wrote an eight-column spread in the *Hartford Courant* that began: "Pioneer stock will out." Anna Louise was so delighted that she invited Julia to come to Russia.

She was preparing to return to her hotel after the Hartford lecture when a small, fiery woman stopped her. "That was great," the woman said. "You're coming home with me." Anna Louise found herself irresistibly swept toward a car and whisked off to the southern suburb of Cromwell. The woman was Emily Pierson. Five years younger than Anna Louise, she had been a leader of the Connecticut suffragette movement and had taken an M.D. at Yale in the early 1930s. She was unmarried but had adopted a daughter, Anne. The two older women were intensely drawn to each other—"like two friendly tornadoes," Emily's daughter remarked. From this first meeting until Anna Louise's death, two rooms were set aside on the second floor of Emily's large Victorian house for Anna Louise's use; she occupied them regularly for the next twenty years.

Two weeks later Anna Louise stopped to see Lincoln Steffens and Ella Winter in Carmel, California. Although Steffens was sick, she spent several days there, catching up and explaining some of her new thoughts. "The most important thing you can do," he advised her, "is to write your autobiography." As the idea took shape in their conversations, Anna Louise found it more and more appealing. The book would not be a self-indulgent "confession" but the portrait of an American attempting to change herself into a true communist. It would be written to recover for the reader the experiences and confusions of thirteen years of life in the U.S.S.R.

She returned to Moscow in April 1934, resumed her duties as assistant editor on the *Daily News* and began to write the autobiography. Except with Mikhail Borodin, she was silent about the tensions involved in the new project. Joel was oblivious to the enormity of the challenge she had taken on; like her father, he did not seem to know what it meant to be tempted by service to two worlds.

At first the writing was all wrong. She wanted to talk about Trotsky and the others who had been so important to her in the 1920s. Borodin patiently turned back preliminary drafts, explaining that Trotsky was not important because he could not be a part of the world and person her book would illuminate. Distressed, she sent drafts to Steffens. He encouraged her:

You have a big subject, you know. To make and cross a bridge from one age to another, from one whole, new united philosophy to another is something that was never done in any other transition in history; not that I know of. John Reed might have done what you are doing. You see, I say *doing*—for the first time. Max Eastman can't do it, not even personally. And you can't quite. Your difficulties with Trotsky is [*sic*] the sign of your failure. That great man . . . matters with both you and Max. Certainly you can see, can't you, that under our old culture justice must be done to him and that, under the new Soviet culture, justice is for the people. Don't answer that justice is for both. . . . In your case your concern is not with Trotsky. You get the sense of the mass moving along the "line" and that's what once you did not have and what your readers over here do not have, and ought to get, from your story. Well, hang on to that glimpse, strengthen it, and make us see it. That we *all* have to stick together on that until it is established in our habits. Then we can, and shall, differ on points and details.

It would be better for you if you would master the Trotsky thing; see what Borodin and the Party have to say, but if you can't, make a separate chapter or book of your experiences with that man. He was a hero to me once too, but when he put "right" above unity and broke our front to be right, I, from here, recognized that he was not of the New Day, but the old. He says to the world what is only for the Party. I have things I would like to say about the Party, but I can feel in my bones that I must not say them at this stage to the enemy. As against Labor or even against the millions in Russia, Trotsky does not matter. Get back on the line, Anna Louise, and go back knowingly; and tell that. It's one of the biggest lessons we "Christians," we capitalists, have to learn. The truth from now on is always dated; never absolute, never eternal.

Steffens' letter helped clear her path. She would not only write about her journey from one world to another but would make her book a map for those who might wish to follow her, a warning, from one who had almost reached the summit, of the hidden crevices and dead-end passages. The words began to come more easily, her fluid and efficient prose barely masking her attempt to convince herself and the American Communist party that she was now worthy of membership. As she wrote, she took care to have various sections checked for political reliability. The Russian-language manuscript of the chapter on Stalin was corrected in green pencil by Stalin himself.

She did not avoid the issues that had been and remained the most problematic: "I looked down into my soul, amazed at the depths I saw. I still had in me the remains of a regular Hearst correspondent. I held 'my picture' higher than the world." She went to Borodin to discuss her continuing desire to print matters as she saw them; every submission to the Glav-Lit still occasioned a small internal rebellion. "Isn't propaganda," she asked, "merely a question of deceiving our friends without quite deceiving our enemies?" "Not so," he retorted. "Our enemies suspect, but they do not know." "So telling the truth," she replied, "is a matter of strength?" Borodin paused a moment and smiled: "Not quite. One may tell the truth—meaning by truth a clear description of the general line of our struggle, the fact that it is a serious one, and the type of its problems. But one may not give away sensational unanalyzed 'facts' from which no good can come."

Steffens' letter took on clearer meaning. Here in Russia, truths were correctly analyzed facts. Correctly analyzed facts were ones that enhanced the movement toward peace and the progress of socialism. Borodin added: "We Bolsheviks think that in spite of the technical backwardness of Russia, it may devolve on this country to save world civilization." Hence "truth" could not be judged by each individual: a collective analysis had to be made, and the repository of that analysis was inevitably the party.

Anna Louise thought herself reconciled to the epistemology. Yet there is an uneasy tone in the chapter of the autobiography where she addresses the question of truth, a brittleness that suggests that she could not quite believe her own argument. But even that was, of course, confirmation of what Steffens and Borodin were telling her; she had not yet made the full transition to the new socialist viewpoint. But she continued to try and asserted: "I will not tell the 'whole truth,' for truth is never 'whole'; there are always at least two truths in conflict; the truth that is dying and the truth that is coming into existence. . . . History's greatest gift to victors is that not only they but their truths survive."

Her difficulty in writing about the transformations of her own soul was not eased by the changes occurring in the world around her. While she wrote, Moscow was in the throes of urban renewal. The old wooden houses and churches were torn down for sturdier, if less charming, twenty-story apartment buildings for the workers. A new subway was pushed through the central part of the city, causing tremendous disruption. The Second Five-Year Plan emphasized the production of surplus, and many party members responded by growing rich. The party itself was rapidly becoming stratified. Anna Louise went to Alexandra Kollontai: "Is not the situation now developing almost as bad as the NEP? Perhaps worse, since inequality seems to infect the party itself now?" Alexandra was again all reassurance: what problems there were, were the consequence of the admission of large numbers of new people to the party. For a while Anna Louise was mollified.

Then her closest Russian woman friend, Yavorskaia, contracted typhus. Yavorskaia had devoted her life to the homeless children of Russia with a self-abnegation that Anna Louise had envied. Once when she was infested with lice, Yavorskaia refused to visit Anna Louise because she knew her friend's horror of vermin. Yet she had denied herself all privileges, even that of a party membership. On Anna Louise's last visit, Yavorskaia clung to her hand. "You are one of the few I can talk to," she said. "One can't tell troubles to outsiders. Nor often to party members." As she died, she cried out: "There is no equality. There will never be equality. I am so worn out and disappointed by people that I want some place in the country where there are only trees." Back at the apartment, Anna Louise wept and railed at a party which had moved away from such selflessness.

Yavorskaia's last words sent a tremor through Anna Louise' newly erected morality. What was equality? It could not mean "everyone the same"; that would be awful. Yavorskaia, she compelled herself to conclude, should not have insisted on the false equality of equal suffering. Her abilities and her dedication entitled her to special meals that would have perhaps saved her life and permitted her to continue the struggle to build Soviet power. And slowly Anna Louise accepted the price of her convictions.

As she finished writing her autobiography, Anna Louise convinced herself that the collective struggle to build Soviet power reconciled her long conflict between free individuality and community. The conscious acceptance of the discipline of the party "meant that you chose a joint goal with such firmness that you didn't wait for others to boss you: with your own will and hand you cut off any lesser desires that conflicted. . . . It is more than freedom; it is an end forever to loneliness. Not to 'be chosen,' but to choose with others. Freedom and comradeship can grow wider always. Increased organization does not squeeze out freedom, but multiplies its vast variety of choices."

By the fall of 1934 the manuscript was almost completed. Julia Older, who had come to work on the *News*, helped condense the text to 430 tight pages. On November 24, her forty-ninth birthday, Anna Louise finished. Assertively and ambiguously she titled it *I Change Worlds: The Remaking of an American* and celebrated with Joel by going to the theater every other night for two weeks. The book, she noted in her preface, had done more for her than it would for any of her readers.

In January 1935 she was back in the United States to lecture and publicize *I Change Worlds*. It was acclaimed by reviewers and made the best-seller list. Knight Publishing Company capitalized on the success and reissued an updated version of *China's Millions*. It, too, sold well; John Cournos, in his introduction, even suggested that it be read alongside André Malraux's *Man's Fate* for a full understanding of the situation in China. Julia Lathrop took Anna Louise to lunch with Eleanor Roosevelt in New York, and a relationship began between the two that was to last for over a decade.

During the trip, Anna Louise discussed joining the American Communist party with Earl Browder, the general secretary. He thought she would be more useful outside the party, as a "non-party Bolshevik." But by this time Anna Louise was convinced that the fulfillment of her transformation could come only in party membership. Finally Browder yielded to her insistence and accepted a check. She thought of herself as a member thereafter, although Browder never sent her a membership card, nor was she ever assigned to a party unit. From then on, she sent a yearly "contribution" as dues through a neutral contact. It was not unusual to pay dues secretly, nor were all members of the American party assigned to cells. What ambiguity remained served all concerned.

Anna Louise went home to Moscow at the end of March and plunged into her work at the *News*. But even under Borodin's care, the paper had changed. Over the next year more "ideological" Russian articles appeared. Borodin took his time confronting her distress. "Our real trouble," he said, "is that we do not know our readers well enough. Our readers themselves are a mixed lot and inexpressive; they give us no clear policy." As Anna Louise sorted through what it meant for a paper to have policy dictated by the readership, Borodin continued: "I have been seeing our readers at factory meetings of 'Readers of *Moscow Daily News*.' I ask them what language I shall use, and they tell me Russian. Why do they need an English paper?" Borodin concluded that as *News* readers became more integrated into Soviet society, they needed better and more "Soviet-type" analyses.

Anna Louise tried to remedy the problem by providing the material that Borodin required. She collected stories from rural communes south of Moscow and reported her findings in a new analytic style. But it didn't work. The two books she wrote during this period, *This Soviet World* and *The New Soviet Constitution*, show her failure. Gone are the vivid personal stories that brought worlds to life; instead, there are citations from Marx, quotes from party congresses, excerpts from other reporters' interviews with important figures. Almost no new names appear; characters from old books return in the same roles they played earlier. Almost all her new subjects insisted on anonymity. She repeated party clichés. The result was boring.

Throughout the fall and winter, she vacillated between attempts to imitate Joel's self-abnegating discipline and explosions over the ruin of "her" paper. She stayed away from the office and tried to distract herself by extending her family life. On her invitation, Ruth and Charles' daughter Bumpy came for an indefinite visit. Anna Louise assumed that Bumpy would do secretarial work for the *News* or another agency and help with the household in return for learning Russian and expanding her education. But her niece found more attractions in the young men at the embassies and nights on the town than she did in Soviet offices. To Anna Louise's embarrassment, Bumpy was not reserved about her infatuations, and it was with relief that Anna Louise finally learned that Bumpy was to marry a young American diplomat. Her despair at her relatives was not relieved until the next year, when Bumpy's younger brother John came to study plant biology, and he proved to be the independent and supportive relative Anna Louise had hoped for.

Meanwhile the political climate was changing rapidly. Stalin now stood preeminent. Most of the remaining "Joint Opposition," including Zinoviev and Anna Louise's old friend Kamenev, had been arrested after the mysterious assassination on December 1, 1934, of Sergei Kirov, Stalin's close friend and probable successor. The assassin was apparently a deranged member of the Zinoviev opposition, and connections had supposedly been found not only to the secret police but to Latvia and Nazi Germany. For whatever reason, Stalin reacted crazily. Not content with sentencing Zinoviev and his colleagues to a prison term, in the name of Soviet security he commenced in 1936 what became known as the "purge trials." All those who had been held prisoner in relation to what were called "border terrorist" incidents, whether related to the Kirov case or not, were summarily tried by a special court. Shortly after Anna Louise returned to Moscow in 1936 from her annual American lecture tour, a large number of high party officials, including Zinoviev and Kamenev, were again indicted. On August 19, 1936, they went on trial, now for active treason. Anna Louise attended the trials and heard many of those whom she had hailed as heroes of Soviet power condemn themselves as traitors. Within the next eighteen months 98 out of the 139 members elected to the central committee in 1934 had been tried and shot.

She was not sure what to make of it, but she was certain that she should not be in Moscow. She stopped discussing the trials in letters to her father. Borodin suggested that she would be better as a kind of roving reporter, without editorial responsibilities. At the end of October 1936 she officially resigned from the editorial board of the *News*. Joel encouraged her to look elsewhere and repeated her own words back to her: "We do not even give up our jobs." Her real "job," they both knew, was revolution wherever it flamed.

She stayed in Moscow for the ten-day session of the Soviet constitutional convention on December 5 through 16 and heard Stalin slowly and quietly proclaim that the U.S.S.R. had for the first time become a socialist state. Behind him on a high platform were the thirty newly elected members of the Presidium, replacing those who had been shot. In front of him was a sea of delegates from all over the U.S.S.R., and in the first row of the balcony were the envoys from the People's Front in Spain. Four days later Anna Louise was in Toulouse, France, boarding a passenger plane for Madrid.

9

Old Frontiers
and New Deals

I found it harder and harder to write or lecture on the U.S.S.R.
. . . Nobody would accept a human picture: that the U.S.S.R.
is a state, with a state's organs and functions, and informed
with certain great aims and tasks in history. . . . The U.S.S.R.
had to be either the Devil or the Deity. . . . The one side
would not admit a single virtue; the other side would not admit
a single flaw. . . . The people I really cared for, on whose side
I felt myself to be fighting—they winced so if a single human
weakness in the U.S.S.R. were noticed. So I let my audiences
pressure me into giving what I knew was a partial picture. . . .
I told no lies, but I didn't tell all the truth. And I still think
this may be the correct procedure.

—Anna Louise Strong to Raymond Robins,
October 26, 1950

If Wall Street gets control again, under the present World War
conditions, they will never let the people express themselves
again. Already talk of disenfranchising people on relief is wide-
spread. We would move straight into fascism.

—Anna Louise Strong to Eleanor Roosevelt,
March 8, 1941

The longest night of the year was yielding to dawn as Anna Louise's plane
crossed the Pyrenees into Spain. She was acutely aware that this was the
beginning of a new pilgrimage as yet undefined. Spain was also the place
where the future of many nations was being determined.

She noticed the signs of change as she waited for a driver in the airport
customs shed: posters proclaimed that "the evil heritage of capitalism in

the habits of men requires a long and serious struggle," and in every ordinary conversation the word "revolution" appeared. What struck her most, however, was the absence of the signs of war. Driving south along the coast to Valencia, the temporary government capital, the car carrying Anna Louise, socialist Swedish lawyer Senator Georg Branting, and British geneticist and editor of the London *Daily Worker* J. B. Haldane passed a group of girls waving orange blossoms. Senator Branting turned to Anna Louise: "Don't you see the red terror?" It was the first time she had laughed in many weeks.

In Valencia, hotel rooms were at a premium. The press department of the Ministry of State could find her nothing. Near tears, she turned away from the desk at the Hotel Victoria and collided with "a tall military form in a long, black rainproof slicker." The man smiled down at her in recognition. "You don't know me," he said, removing his cap. As he did so, Anna Louise exclaimed, "André Malraux." Her concern about a room was quickly forgotten as the French writer, now serving as a pilot, led her away from the crowded lobby. Two hours later she had accepted an invitation to dinner later that week at the chateau where Malraux and his fellow flyers had their headquarters. With renewed energy, she found two American women who were willing to take her in for the night, and by the morning she had not only secured a room for herself but had offered to share it with still another American woman.

The next day she started by going to a bullfight where, to her delight, there was a woman matador. Instincts developed over years took her next not to the Republican leaders but to the small village of Borboto, an hour's bus ride away. Most of the 150 inhabitants were farmers; like many other small landowners in Spain, they had formed a consumers' cooperative a few months earlier in order to receive credits and seed from the government. When Anna Louise saw that the newly formed village committee's office was the village church minus its altar, she began to ask questions. Rumors abroad had emphasized the savage destruction of churches by the leftists throughout Spain. She was told that the village committee had confiscated the church property to protect it from gangs of hooligans. The identity of these hooligans was unclear; some said they were anarchists, others, that they were fascist provocateurs employed to discredit the government. Sentiments were mixed about the occupation of the church. What bound these people to the new government was that it provided credit and seed.

Thus informed, she went to talk to the government leaders about their visions of the future. Getting appointments with them was easy; interviewing them was more difficult. It took three trips to the office of Julio Alvarez del Vayo before she was able to see him, but when she finally did get her chance, she was flattered to find that the journalist turned foreign minister seemed as interested in suggestions from her as she was in the information he provided. At Communist party headquarters she met Dolores Ibarruri, "La Pasionaria," whose slogan, "Better to die standing than to live on your knees," had inspired thousands of Spaniards. Anna Louise gained a vivid sense of the intense commitment binding the heterogeneous groups who made up Loyalist Spain.

Five hard-working days later, she made her way to Malraux's headquarters. He greeted her warmly and pointed proudly to the others at the table: "French, Belgian, Czech, Italian," adding with a smile, "Communist, Socialist, Republican, anarchist." To their distress, Malraux was making daily flights to the front. He explained that it was important to break down class barriers between officers and combat soldiers in a war intended to break old traditions. "Besides," he added, "it is easier to fight than wait."

Anna Louise understood only too well. After a week in Valencia, she had spoken with almost all of the available leaders and was eager to get closer to the battlefront. Malraux again came to her aid. He maneuvered a place for her in one of his cars headed for Madrid.

Madrid was the precarious edge of the civil war. There was no coal that winter, and all of the better hotels had been turned into hospitals. By the time of Anna Louise's arrival in January 1937, aerial bombing by Franco's planes had been stopped, but the city continued to be shelled from the ground, and at night a dark, ominous silence shrouded the streets. After trying unsuccessfully to make telephone contacts, Anna Louise wrapped herself in a coat and crawled into bed to get warm.

The next day she moved to the American embassy, where an illustrious collection of journalists camped on mattresses on the floor and shared a hastily contrived cooperative dining room. Despite the intermittent shellings, reporting the war from Madrid was like witnessing a love affair through binoculars; there was no uncertainty about the event, but it was not the best setting for talking with the participants. Anna Louise's reputation as a Communist and as a journalist able to publish in the Western press eased her way to the front. Moments after she had marched into the office of the famous Fifth Regiment, she was welcomed by its political commissar, Vittorio Vidal, known in Spain as Carlos Contreras. For the next three days, Anna Louise was Contreras' shadow.

In snatches of talk in Contreras' car and in the field, he related the history of the Fifth Regiment—from a spontaneous gathering of comrades to a model unit of more than 15,000 men and women who were now being absorbed into the unified army. Walking along a muddy road in a ruined old village, Anna Louise was concentrating on Contreras' stories when a mortar shell suddenly whistled in and a nearby house burst into flames. She stood paralyzed until Contreras grabbed her arm and shoved her into the gutter. It was "uncomfortably wet," and Anna Louise did not understand how this was much protection, but she had little choice but to stay where she was until Contreras released her.

After this episode, Contreras took care to warn her of impending danger in unlikely places. In the Loyalist trenches she interviewed dozens of young men and occasional women, and, as always, she had some key questions: "What are you fighting for? What message should I take back to America?" The answer that she carried to the United States came from a Catalonian boy who immediately thanked her for the help given by her government—the *Mexican* government. When Contreras began to explain that Mexico and the United States were two very different countries, the boy interrupted. "Wherever you are, you'll have to fight fascism," he said. "You help us now; we'll help you then."

The boy's words, supported by similar statements from many others, confirmed Anna Louise's sense that the war in Spain was the center of an international struggle against fascism. Spain had become "a universal conscience." The question was not just "Whither Spain?" but "Whither Europe?" and "Whither the United States?" Here was a cause in which the United States and the Soviet Union could and should be united. It was a moment when Anna Louise could stand for what she felt was right without being torn between her loyalties to the two.

She returned to New York determined to rally her fellow Americans to raise their voices and arms against fascism. Her arrival was greeted warmly and publicly. *Newsweek* carried a photograph of her disembarkation and noted that "Dr. Anna Louise Strong, American-born editor of the *Moscow Daily News,* an English-language paper read by 40,000 Muscovites, arrived in New York from Spain, where she visited the front-line trenches." *Soviet Russia Today* and the American Friends of the Soviet Union gave a banquet in her honor the day after her arrival; the guest list included Pearl Buck, Paul Robeson, Corliss Lamont and sympathizers with Republican Spain.

But there was a somber side. Awaiting Anna Louise in New York was a letter from Ella Winters reporting the death of Lincoln Steffens. She next discovered that Ralph Fox, a brilliant young British writer to whom she had been briefly but intensely drawn during her last days in Spain, had died at the front shortly after her departure. A letter from Ruth warned that their father, who had recently returned to Seattle, was growing increasingly ill and crotchety.

Her lecture tour began almost immediately and was more hectic than it had been in years. Of the two subjects on which she spoke as she crisscrossed the country, "The New Soviet Democracy" and "Spain in Arms," the latter was decidedly more popular. Lectures on the Soviet Union provoked hostile questions about executions and the "dictatorial" activities of Stalin. She countered such suspicions by describing at length in an article for *The New Republic* her understanding of the development of policy in the Soviet Union. She admitted errors, defended the constructive nature of Soviet labor camps, referred to the public confessions of those executed in the Kirov case and those arrested for sabotage in other incidents. She understood the skepticism she met but also knew that it had taken her fifteen years and *I Change Worlds* to begin to explain the Soviet way of seeing the world. In addition, she now placed enough value on her own identity as a Communist and the wife of a Soviet Communist to be wary of saying anything in public that could do harm to either her family or her professed party. Spain was a safer topic and one that consistently drew large, sympathetic audiences.

Her most memorable lecture was in Toronto where an unknown Catholic priest who shared the platform received significantly more applause than she. Anna Louise was envious of his reception, and after the meeting protested to Tim Buck, the head of the Canadian Communist party, who had been the final speaker. "That priest told them nothing at all about Spain," she complained, "but he got more applause by his manner than I got for all my information." Buck agreed but gently added, "An audience likes to take part in a meeting." It was an excellent hint for speakers, she decided, and one she would remember often during subsequent lectures but fail to heed. "I always have too much to say" was her excuse.

Much of what she had to say about Spain went into a small book, *Spain in Arms*, which she wrote on trains and in hotel rooms during the tour. She finished the book by mid-March, Henry Holt and Company had it in print by May, and more than ten thousand copies were sold in the first three months. The hasty writing to which she confessed in the introduction was most evident in a lack of structural coherence; although *Spain in Arms* roughly follows the path of Anna Louise's own trip earlier in the year, her attempt to explain the historical background results in a confusing chronology of the war itself. Her introduction, "An American Parallel," makes no attempt to hide the strategy that had by now become her signature. Her aim was to encourage American support of the Spanish People's Front and a general struggle against fascism. To accomplish this, she reminded Americans that their own independence had been hard-won and not without the aid of other "democratic forces." Spain, she argued, had "a claim upon us because of our own past . . . and a greater claim because of our own future."

She made similar arguments to Eleanor Roosevelt, with whom she was now exchanging two to three letters a month. In January she had received a warm welcome-home letter from Mrs. Roosevelt that included a request to translate a letter from Russian into English. She complied, then took the opportunity to urge the importance of American support for the Spanish People's Front. Mrs. Roosevelt's response was appreciative but noncommittal. They had lunch in May, after which Anna Louise sent an even more determined plea for government aid to the Spanish troops. Mrs. Roosevelt immediately wrote back but said only that she would pass Anna Louise's letter on to the president.

Disappointed and tired, Anna Louise left New York in early June for a second trip to Spain. The only breaks in her lecture tour since her arrival in the United States had been brief stops at Emily Pierson's house in Connecticut and an even shorter stay with Ruth in Palo Alto. Both women devoted themselves to her during her visits. Ruth was taking on the tasks that had previously been handled by their father; Anna Louise, increasingly placing financial matters in her sister's hands, had solicited Ruth's help in setting up West Coast lectures. By letter and telephone as well as in person, Emily kept a sharp eye on Anna Louise's health as well as her writing. At the end of May, Ruth and Emily each received a copy of *Spain in Arms*. Ruth's was inscribed, "From her appreciative sister, Anna Louise Strong."

A second trip to Spain had not been part of Anna Louise's plans for the summer of 1937. She was eager to get back to Moscow, where Joel had succeeded in making arrangements for the two of them to take a vacation in the Crimea. It was to be their first genuine vacation together. During her lecture tour, however, Anna Louise had met with the head of the American Communist party, Earl Browder, who had asked her to do another book on Spain, focusing on the Abraham Lincoln Brigade of Americans fighting there. Anna Louise interpreted this as an order from the party—and an acknowledgment of her membership. With a sense of mission, she returned first to Albacete and then to Madrid, concentrating on American soldiers, especially those who had been wounded in battle. The soldiers were eager to tell her their stories, and listening to their accounts, she began to devise what she saw as a unique format for the new book: she would describe a battle not only through the experiences of wounded soldiers but also by arranging the material so that each piece took up the story from the moment when a comrade fell. She was so taken with the idea and with the receipt of "orders" from Browder that she further delayed her return to Moscow and went to Paris, where she spent the entire summer writing the book. Only after she finally reached Moscow in September was she informed that "for reasons of internal friction in the American party" *Yanks in Spain* would not be published in the United States. (It was eventually published in Russian in the Moscow periodical *Roman-Gazeta*.) Years later she could still revive her fury that the delay in Paris had "cost me the only chance I had ever had to take a joint vacation with my husband."

Moscow offered little consolation. Joel had taken his vacation in her absence and was now engrossed in his work; between trips to examine provincial agricultural projects and party activities related to the upcoming elections, he had little time for family life. She had also missed the visit of her nephew Robbins, who had come through Moscow during the summer on his way back from three years teaching in Shansi, China. Robbins had arrived in Moscow to find not only his aunt out of the country, but his cousin Bumpy and her husband Glenn about to take permanent leave of Russia. He had, however, managed to find Joel, who invited him to dinner with Ducia at the apartment. Ducia spoke English well, and the two oddly related young people had a long conversation comparing China, the United States and the Soviet Union. At one point Robbins asked Ducia about her own interest in joining the party; she replied that she was not yet sufficiently in control of herself to become a member. "A member of the party," she told Robbins, "must be something and have something I haven't yet; he must be more than I am."

Robbins glimpsed some of his aunt's sources of difficulty in her Moscow home. Although Ducia spent much of her time at the university in Leningrad, when she was home she was a reminder of Anna Louise's inadequacies. Bright, vivacious, forthright, she seemed the model young Soviet woman. Her pride in the Soviet Union and her scorn for the United States were unbounded. Even in 1937 she seemed to have little doubt that her country was on the right road and ahead of everyone else. Anna Louise admired her stepdaughter but found small comfort in her presence. Neither of them had the patience or the temperament to break the barriers that separated them.

When Anna Louise returned in August, she was once again without an office or an institutional affiliation. Gatherings of young people eager to discuss electoral canvassing, the most recent nomination to the Supreme Soviet, or yesterday's arrests were seductive to Anna Louise but always seemed to occur just when she had sat down to write. Joel sometimes worked at home, too, and his slow, methodical style clashed with Anna Louise's intense, frenetic work habits. Moreover, her sources for new material had vanished entirely; much of what she learned about daily life in the Soviet Union now came from her husband or stepdaughter. She made increased efforts to follow a straight party line and wrote a vitriolic review of Trotsky's latest book, *The Revolution Betrayed,* with some hope of removing any taint of Trotskyism still on record. In a series of sarcastic jabs uncharacteristic of her other writing, the review proclaimed Trotsky the true betrayer of the revolution and concluded that he was engaged in a "conscious alliance with fascism." It was as if she had never known him, and she had not refrained earlier in March 1937 from adding her name to eighty-seven others in protest of John Dewey's Commission of Inquiry into the Soviet accusations against Trotsky.

In public, she continued to celebrate the achievements of the Soviet Union and her good fortune in being part of the country's astonishing progress. In a retrospective piece published in *Soviet Russia Today* in November 1937 she counted herself "one of the luckiest" among the "lucky folk now living" because she had "seen the new life take form" during her last sixteen years in the Soviet Union. Her only public acknowledgment that there was something else going on was a paragraph in which she admitted that there had been "plenty of rude shocks to the idealisms of my youth." But she reduced the causes of these "rude shocks" to "irritating hangovers of old regime inefficiencies, brutalities," a few rotten trees in an otherwise thriving forest.

Omitted from her published work in the mid-thirties was what she would later describe as "the great mental distress" of those years, and especially of 1937. It was not an easy time personally. Her close friend, Valentina Ivashova, with whom she had lived in Moscow in the twenties, was arrested and exiled with a ten-year sentence because she had bothered the offices of the GPU about the arrest of her husband. Three people from the *Moscow Daily News* staff whom Anna Louise characterized as both party members and "the most useful, energetic workers" were suddenly arrested, and the remaining staff were commanded to attend a

trade union meeting to express appreciation for "removing the wreckers."
Anna Louise refused to attend the meeting and protested to Borodin,
who told her that those erroneously arrested could fight and win their
cases through proper channels. She knew, however, that the innocent did
not always come back. She may not have known what she later admitted
in *The Stalin Era,* that hundreds of thousands of people were being
arrested, many of whom would be executed or die in exile, but she was
aware that the number of people who disappeared during the night and
were not seen again was increasing drastically.

Both ignorance and knowledge contributed to her own paralysis. No
longer able to travel widely or to gain access to a variety of party officials,
she had little sense in 1937 of the extraordinary extent of the purges. But
she knew that neither party membership nor a reputation as a good
worker was insulation against arrest. Indeed, a 1935 law had made it a
crime to be a member of the family of a person convicted of crimes
against the state. If Valentina's husband had been arrested, Joel too could
be taken at any time. And if Valentina could be exiled "as the wife of an
enemy of the people," Anna Louise could suffer the same fate. It was the
absence of a clear pattern or rationale that frightened her and hindered
action. "The terror," she later recalled, "was due not so much to knowledge as to lack of knowledge of the fate of friends." To speak out against
the arrests and "high tide of repression" was not only to endanger oneself
but possibly to make the situation worse for those who had already been
taken.

The reactions of those closest to her only made her more desolate and
confused. In uncontrollable bursts of tears, she told Joel of Valentina's
arrest, hoping against reason that he could at least save her best friend.
Instead of meeting her rage with his own, he replied quietly, "It was too
bad that she had to get entangled with that husband." Mikhail Borodin
was similarly unmoved when she stamped around the *Daily News* offices
insisting that he do something about the arrests of their fellow workers.
He not only could do nothing, he chastised Anna Louise for her narrow
view of these events. The leaders of the Soviet Union, he declared, were
preparing for "the greatest struggle mankind has known." To ensure the
strength of the country that would eventually "save civilization," it was
necessary to purge anyone who doubted or interfered with the stability
of the Soviet Union.

Just when Anna Louise thought she had achieved the kind of political
understanding that her husband and stepdaughter would approve of, she
was once again being told that her perspective was too narrow. What

should she do? She could make her annual winter lecture tour in the United States, but it was not clear that she had anything new to say. The solution, she decided, was to head out for new territory, and the place to go was China. Robbins had been urging her in letters throughout the year to return to China, "where nationalism and patriotism are coming much to the fore and where people are very anti-Japanese and wish with all of their hearts to get back the four northeastern provinces." She had not been back during the last ten years, she declared, because "China's had not been history that I could readily visit and report." Now she must return because "the Chinese people have at last united to resist Japan, and this is the most important revolutionary struggle for the future of mankind."

To her surprise, even after asking the American Communist party for support, she had trouble obtaining a transit visa through the Soviet Union. In early December she boarded a liner sailing from Venice for Hong Kong and Hankow. She was embarrassed to be taking passage on a ship owned by Fascist Italians, but it was the fastest means available. On board she swam daily, basked in the sun and ignored the pro-Japanese news broadcast over the ship's radio. She relaxed for the first time in a year and took secret pleasure in the knowledge that in the wintry hills of Shansi Province, the Communist troops had won their first victory over Japan.

In 1927, 80 percent—approximately 40,000 people—of the Chinese Communists had been killed by the Nationalists under Chiang Kai-shek. While she and Borodin were crossing the Gobi Desert, Mao Tse-tung was fleeing to the southwestern mountains after an unsuccessful attempt to lead a peasant uprising in Hunan. By 1928, Chiang Kai-shek had become dicatator of a nominal Republic of China, and no one identified with or as a Communist could feel safe in any of the accessible regions of the country. Despite repeated assaults, the Chinese Communists under Mao and the extraordinary general Chu Teh managed to establish a soviet government and rebuild the army in the rural province of Kiangsi during the next several years. In 1931 the Japanese had begun their conquest of northern China in Manchuria, but Chiang had continued to concentrate his military efforts against the Chinese Red Army. After a series of internal disputes and significant losses to the Nationalists, the Red Army troops set out in 1934 on the six-thousand-mile "retreat" to Northwest China that was to become known as the Long March.

In December 1936, in what has come to be called the Sian Incident, Chiang Kai-shek was taken prisoner by his deputies, Chang Hsueh-liang and Yang Hu-ch'eng, and forced to accept a united front with the Communist troops. The site of Chiang's capture was a place vivid in Anna Louise's memory—the hot springs resort where she had stopped with Borodin on their departure from China. Seven months after the events in Sian, Japan had significantly accelerated its invasion of China, beginning in Peking and moving quickly southward; by November 1937 the Japanese occupation of Shanghai had been completed, and while Anna Louise was sailing East, Nanking was falling to the invaders.

During the fall of 1937 the first extensive account of the activities of the Chinese Communists after 1927 was published in England by a little-known American journalist named Edgar Snow. As a young reporter in Peking during the thirties, Snow had made excellent contacts with the Chinese left and had learned some Chinese; in June 1936 he was quietly invited to be the first Westerner admitted to the Communist territories in the Northwest. Snow successfully made his way to Pao An, then the Communist capital, and spent four months interviewing Mao and other leaders about the history of the past nine years and the Communist vision of the future. Anna Louise had purchased a copy of his book, *Red Star over China,* for her trip; it was a scoop of which she would be envious for the rest of her life. She knew that Snow and his wife, Nym Wales, were in Shanghai and telegraphed ahead to meet them. Her visa would not allow her to disembark before Hong Kong, but the Snows came on board and briefed her on the situation of the Red Army.

Confident of good contacts and determined to pick up where Snow had left off, Anna Louise made her way rapidly by German plane from Hong Kong to Hankow, now the temporary capital. Nothing she had witnessed ten years earlier compared to the present "chaos of human misery." Tens of millions of people fleeing westward from the Japanese jammed the roads, waterways and railroads; refugees swarmed over every inch of the city, seeking food, shelter and lost relatives.

She found lodging at the home of Logan Roots, the "pink bishop" of Hankow, whom she had met in 1927, and promptly set about making arrangements to visit the Eighth Route Army in Shansi. Staying with Roots was Ilona Ralf Sues, who had left her work on the Anti-Opium Information Bureau in Geneva two years before to come to China "in search of a place where something constructive was going on." Sues had ended up as a publicity agent for the Kuomintang but had just been fired from her position and was making preparations to leave China. Anna Louise's arrival opened new horizons. According to Sues, although everyone in the household, including the bishop, "trembled" when Anna Louise "paced angrily up and down her room overhead and made the candelabra tingle in the parlor," they also all listened, "fascinated by that harsh, matter-of-fact voice . . . which went right to the heart of the most complex problems with merciless logic, amazing clarity, and remarkable vision." Determined to accompany Anna Louise to Shansi, Sues volunteered to go as her secretary and suggested her own guide, Francis Yao, as interpreter. Yao received permission for the trip, but Sues did not until after Anna Louise's departure.

At the railroad station in Hankow, thousands of Chinese were being turned away from the station, but as Yao proudly told her, "We go by Old Man Yen's special." Marshal Yen Hsi-shan, dictator of Shansi Province for twenty-seven years, was heading to his military headquarters in Lin-fen, a village a day's travel from the headquarters of the Eighth Route Army. Ten years earlier, Rayna Prohme had been Anna Louise's companion on a similar train; now she shared her journey with Professor Li Kung-po, one of the "seven patriots" who had recently been released from prison, where he had been sent for protesting Chiang's appeasement of Japan. A cheerful, energetic man who had studied at Reed College in Oregon, he was headed for Shansi—along with 600 students riding in freight cars at the rear of the train—to establish a new university in the Communist-held territories. With the Japanese occupying Peiping (as Peking was now called), as well as Nanking and Shanghai, many of the major universities of China had been abandoned, but the united-front policy was to reestablish these institutions in the western provinces as quickly as possible.

Marshal Yen was pleased to talk with Anna Louise but found discussion of the war "unpleasant" and much preferred expounding his theory of social reform through the replacement of currency by "production certificates." She spent most of her time with Professor Li, and the only discomfort on the trip was the increasing cold as they moved northward. Anna Louise had equipped herself with three thicknesses of woolen underwear and sweaters which she wore unabashedly under a silk-padded Chinese gown, but she still ached from the cold. To reassure herself that her suffering was provoked by external causes, she tested the temperature by putting water in her soap dish on the dining-room table. It satisfied her to see that it froze in fifty minutes.

In Lin-fen, Marshal Yen vanished with a classical bow after arranging for his guests to spend the night in the offices of an old flour mill. At dawn Anna Louise was greeted by a rickety structure on an old Ford truck, euphemistically announced as the "autobus." Up rocky hillsides, over a bridge of straw and boughs attached precariously to swinging posts, "through canyons so narrow that the dirt walls scraped our roof," the bus made its way north to a village unmarked on any map. Even before she descended from the truck she knew that she was in luck. "A dusty, gray-blue figure, like a homely farmer" leaned across the driver to shake her hand and greet her in broken German. It was Chu Teh, commander-in-chief of the Red Army, who according to legend could scatter his enemies with the mild wave of a fan and see a hundred *li* in all directions. Joining Chu Teh to greet her were the generals of the Eighth Route Army: Ho Lung, Liu Peh-cheng, Lin Piao, P'eng Teh-huai, all young men who in ten years had become the military leaders of the Communist revolution.

For the next ten days Anna Louise shared the meals and talk of the commanders and their men. She slept on a clay *kang* in the house of a local peasant and happily made the transition from the wine-flavored dishes provided by Marshal Yen to the bowls of rice and greens shared equally by everyone at the Eighth Route Army headquarters. She was impressed by the leaders' lack of pretension and candor, and especially by the "depth of their comradeship." They treated one another with respect and appeared never to boss or condescend to their troops. With an avidity she had not experienced since adolescence, she became their student and "took lessons in guerrilla tactics, heard stories of famous exploits and learned methods of keeping an army close to the people for whom it fights."

The premise of their strategy, Chu Teh told her, was to prolong the war in order to win. To achieve this, the military felt it necessary to educate and organize not only their own troops but the people in the territories they occupied. Soldiers had classes every day, even when they were on the move, and every regiment had political officers who spent most of their time instructing the local peasants in how to deal with the Japanese and organizing the masses to improve their own living conditions.

The army also educated through entertainment; theater companies, improvising on past and contemporary events, were creating a new drama all over China. To Anna Louise's astonishment, there were two theater companies in residence in this remote village, and despite crude performance conditions, the productions were so powerful that soldiers stood watching until ten o'clock in the evening. The head of one of them was the writer Ting Ling, whom many had presumed to be dead after her disappearance a few years before. After watching Ting Ling's group perform, Anna Louise inquired about the "latest tendencies in Chinese literature." It was an irrelevant question, Ting Ling responded: "I don't know a thing about literary tendencies; I've been six months at the front. But I have a clear opinion about the duty of the writer. He has only one task today: to help save the country. We put on dramas, make public speeches, draw cartoons on the village walls and teach the peasants to sing. We must teach at least two songs to every village." Two days after this conversation, Ting Ling was back on the road with her "Front Service Dramatic Group," and Anna Louise was reluctantly making arrangements to return to Hankow.

She arrived in Hankow in a foul humor from a bad cold and the desertion of her translator, Francis Yao, who had vanished in Chengchow on the return trip. When Yao finally got there, he was equally angry. "She treated me like a yellow dog of a Chink," he told Ilona Sues, "yelling, stamping her foot." Sues' defense, that Anna Louise "drew no color line, but treated us all like yellow dogs," was little consolation. (Nor was it to Anna Louise, who never forgave her when she read Sues' story in print some years later.)

But despite her ill health and bad spirits Anna Louise immediately called on Chou En-lai, who had just been appointed assistant chief of the Political Department of the Central Headquarters of the National Army. She had met him briefly before her trip; now she could ask him better-informed political questions. In a series of meetings he confirmed the commitment of the Communists to a united front policy and expressed his anxiety about "Trotskyists" and other subversives in positions of power in the government army. She was drawn to this serene, handsome man as she had been to only a few others in her life. He seemed to understand and respect her questions instantly.

In reply to a question about the present status of women in China, he suggested that Anna Louise meet his wife. Teng Ying-chao was a living library of stories of China's women. Ill with tuberculosis at the beginning of the Long March, she had been carried for four months in a litter before she was well enough to walk with the others. From her Anna Louise learned of the organizing and teaching the women had done on the Long March, of newborn babies, including a daughter of Mao Tse-tung, who had been left to grow up in peasant households, and of women like Kang Ke-ch'ing, wife of Chu Teh, who was illiterate when the march began and now taught political science in the Yenan Red Army schools. Toward the end of a long afternoon of talk, Anna Louise brought the conversation back to Ying-chao's personal history. How, on such a difficult journey, did she manage to overcome her tuberculosis? "I think that it was happiness that cured me" was the careful response. The journalist in Anna Louise retorted skeptically, "But the hardships?" "What hardships?" was the answer.

Back at Bishop Logan Root's, she found the American writer Agnes Smedley waiting for her. Each had known of the other before, but this was their first real meeting. Although people who knew them both always remarked on their differences, there were striking similarities. Both had been born in rural, midwestern America in the last period of the nine-teenth century, a period that produced many strong and independent women, and both had been inspired by an overly industrious mother who died young. Both had become writers early in life, but neither viewed writing as a sufficient career. Perhaps most important of all, both had experienced repeated periods of loneliness and despair provoked by the rejections of others.

On January 10, just a few days after Anna Louise's departure for Shansi, Agnes Smedley had returned from several months with the Eighth Route Army. Before coming to China she had been deeply involved in the Indian Nationalist movement and in the establishment of birth-control clinics in Germany and India. In Shanghai, in the early thirties, she and Harold Isaacs had started the radical journal *China Forum;* in 1936 she had reported the capture of Chiang Kai-shek in Sian and then moved to Communist territory at Yenan. But her mercurial moods and lack of sexual decorum had not served her well in Yenan, and late in 1937 she was asked to leave. She had wept and protested, but Chu Teh and P'eng Teh-huai had insisted with increasing gentleness that there was pressing work in Hankow.

Anna Louise was envious of Agnes' experiences and contacts in China, although she did her best to conceal her jealousy. She was grateful for Smedley's introductions to other correspondents and Chinese leaders, but her delight when the opportunity arose to return these gestures was unduly triumphant. A few days after her return, Anna Louise received an invitation to celebrate the Chinese New Year at the home of H. H. Kung, then the president of the Executive Yuan, a position equivalent to that of titular head of the government. Kung had been Anna Louise's classmate at Oberlin in 1905 and had met her again in the twenties. When he extended the invitation, he explained that "This is by custom a family festival, but my family is in Hong Kong, so I shall make it a classmates dinner." He included Agnes in the party, Anna Louise made clear, because of her association with Anna Louise.

Agnes, it turned out, was not as polite as their host. In the midst of an elegant banquet and innocuous conversation, she suddenly interrupted

Dr. Kung and asked for a large donation for the peasant guerrillas who were fighting the Japanese in Shansi, Kung's home province. Anna Louise froze with embarrassment, knowing, as Agnes certainly also did, that Kung was a bitter enemy of the Communists. As Anna Louise expected, Kung exploded angrily that he disapproved of people collecting extra money for the Communist Eighth Route Army, which, he said, should be content with its regular wages and not ask for special gifts. All three of them knew the injustice of Kung's response; the Eighth Route Army was twice as large as the number of troops for which Chiang Kai-shek was paying. Agnes did not attempt that argument. "Oh, Dr. Kung," she protested, "I am not asking for anything for the Eighth Route Army. Of course they are satisfied with their wages. I am asking you for the peasant guerrillas of Shansi who are protecting your property, Dr. Kung, against the Japanese." Agnes left the party with a large check for her peasant guerrillas, and Anna Louise retired to their quarters with a new sense of the difference between her and her housemate. Her good middle-class upbringing, she concluded, would never have allowed her to dare such a request. "But Agnes never recognized impossibilities."

One interview led to another during Anna Louise's remaining days in Hankow. Her conversations with Chou En-lai and Teng Ying-chao persuaded her of the importance of speaking with non-communists in positions of authority. She therefore called on Soong Mei-ling, the wife of Chiang Kai-shek and younger sister of Soong Ch'ing-ling. Anna Louise found Madame Chiang to be more "chic and sophisticated" than her older sister and far more Western than most Chinese women. She was, Anna Louise mused, something like Eleanor Roosevelt—a woman who could not only handle diplomats for her husband but who played her own active role in social movements and world affairs. At the end of one long conversation, Soong Mei-ling opened the door to her husband's study, and Chiang Kai-shek came out to greet Anna Louise. She was struck by how happy the general appeared, the result, she later concluded, of all the compliments he was receiving for his newfound resistance to the Japanese.

Anna Louise also interviewed a women's dance troupe, a conference of women in the YWCA, women students, textile workers and writers, and a group of "sing-song girls" and former "taxi-dancers from Shanghai's renowned nightclubs." From all of them she got much the same story: the greatest change over the past ten years was in the number of women working outside the home. But this did not mean liberation; all too often the enslavement of the marketplace replaced the older bondage of the home. Only in the last several months, under the pressure of the war against the Japanese, had things begun to improve. When Anna Louise began to write about these experiences, for the first time she referred to herself as a feminist.

In early March 1938 she was back in California, eager to convey her "messages" from the Chinese. Her first disappointment was the letters that awaited her from Eleanor Roosevelt. She had written to Mrs. Roosevelt from China, urging that the American government ally itself formally with the Chinese and expressing her desire to meet with Mrs. Roosevelt and the president to discuss what she had seen. Mrs. Roosevelt replied that she had shown Anna Louise's letter to the president, but "he says there is nothing, he feels, that can be done at the present time. The feeling in this country is decidedly pro-Chinese, but not to the extent of going to war with Japan, and, as long as we are not at war with Japan, there is nothing to be done but to remain neutral."

"You are a most wonderful person," Mrs. Roosevelt concluded, "in the way you get to all the trouble spots in the world. Unofficially you can go, of course, and say whatever you choose, whereas those of us who are officials have not that privilege." Such compliments and reminders of constraints did not appease Anna Louise. She immediately wrote back: "You know, America really could do it. We really could organize the whole peace focus."

That hope inspired Anna Louise for the next six months. It distracted her from her ailing father, whose senility had progressed to the point where, if he was left alone, he might wander naked down the street. After a short visit she left him to the care of others and hurried across the country, stopping only in Los Angeles and a few other major cities to lecture on her China trip. FBI agents eagerly took notes on her detailed descriptions of the Communist territories in China and remarked to their superiors that she "unvariably" (sic) referred to Communists in the first-person plural. In Washington at the end of March, she and Congressman Byron Scott urged aid to Loyalist Spain at a mass meeting sponsored by a "broad united front." She reported to Eleanor and Franklin Roosevelt at lunch the next week that the Washington audience enthusiastically supported her views, and she discussed with them her plan to organize large-scale financing of industrial development in China. She felt sufficiently supported in her scheme to write Mrs. Roosevelt periodically throughout the spring for advice on the project.

In part because of these fund-raising attempts, she decided to settle in New York City for at least a few months. Philip Jaffe offered her a place to stay in his apartment where she could write a book on her last trip to China, and she eagerly moved in—typewriter, temper and all. Jaffe put her in touch with his cousin-in-law, Dr. Chi Ch'ao-ting, an expert on Chinese history and economics. Under Chi's editorial guidance, the book became more historical and less autobiographical than her earlier writings. At times, Jaffe recalled, his cousin would dictate and Anna Louise would sit at the typewriter turning the facts into prose. By the end of June the book was completed and went to press with a letter of introduction by Madame Chiang Kai-shek, who pleaded for an end to assistance to Japan and wished success to Anna Louise's work.

In July, Anna Louise attended the Tenth National Convention of the American Communist party; then she left for the Soviet Union. In Moscow she found that the repressive atmosphere now penetrated every aspect of daily life. The entire membership of the Communist party was being subjected to a purge in which each individual had to relate his or her life history before others who were in positions to check on it. Anna Louise observed that suspicion of others had become a virtue: "Appeals to the 'watchfulness of the people' against spies and saboteurs filled the press and became the theme of motion pictures. Pamphlets told 'how the spy acts.'" Thirty years later she recalled her distress: "I could not approve of the excessive purges . . . . They seemed to be killing far too many people whom I felt might be innocent. They also seemed to shift suddenly from one extreme to another. People I knew might get the Order of Lenin one day and the next week be exiled as an 'enemy of the People,' and the following year be brought back 'rehabilitated' and given new honors, and then suddenly exiled again. I forced myself to accept such things, telling myself that revolutions always had excesses, and that I could not really tell who was innocent. Then gradually I began to feel an increase of bureaucratic pressures which made me doubt even the value of the revolution itself."

Ducia had recently married and moved to Leningrad, but the congestion at home was increased when Joel's sister Frieda, her husband and their two children moved in. Frieda's husband had lost his job for political reasons. Joel was away from Moscow less frequently than he had been, but his trips left him tired and less clean than Anna Louise could bear. After she once detected lice in his clothing, she insisted that he strip in the hallway every night before entering the apartment. Soon she wanted nothing more than to be out of Moscow, and by mid-September she had left for a vacation at a health resort in the North Caucasus.

It was at the resort, surrounded by vacationing officials, factory managers, and workers, that she first heard the news of the Munich Pact by which England and France effectively delivered Czechoslovakia to Nazi Germany. For a month after her return to Moscow, she dawdled, looking for enough material to write a few articles and have something to say in lectures in the United States. She then declared that she must leave Russia.

She was so eager to get out of the Soviet Union that when her visa was rejected by Polish border guards in Stolp she threw a tantrum that surpassed even her own previous legendary explosions. She had, she insisted in increasingly shrill tones, a visa "made in New York at the Polish consulate, warranted for ten months' wear and tear." But the chief border official had a "complex theory" that once it had been used, as hers was coming into the Soviet Union, the visa expired after three months. "Call the Polish consul in Moscow," she shouted. "He told me the visa was perfectly good." Faced with tears now as well as anger, the official offered to pass her through to Berlin. "But I'm going first to Prague," she retorted. With that, the official "went right up in the air" and "shoved her bodily" into the returning train to Minsk. She almost hit him.

She eventually made her way out of Minsk to Prague and thence to Berlin and on to Paris, each city increasing her presentiment of the coming war. In London the news reached her that her father had died on December 30, 1938. She hurried back to Seattle, arriving too late for the funeral but in time to take on the task of sorting through innumerable years of his and her belongings. She stored them in the house on Garfield Street and rented it out.

When she began her lecture tour shortly thereafter, she found that she was no longer reaching her audiences; she also had trouble placing newspaper articles, a problem she attributed to the bankruptcy of a number of papers and the merging of others. She turned to Eleanor Roosevelt, this time seeking rather than giving advice. After an encouraging lunch, she agreed in a letter to Mrs. Roosevelt's suggestion that she bring her energy home: "In strengthening the New Deal forces between now and 1940, by adding information, by writing and otherwise, I am ready to give any time and energy needed. For I consider these two years in America decisive for the future, not only of America but of the world."

Her task was to "rediscover America" by slowly touring the country, asking wherever she went "What has the New Deal done for you?" There was no better place to begin than California. "Life boils in California," she wrote. "It is a hot soup of many ingredients, each highly flavored, as in a good Mexican dish." She headed first for Altadena, the home of her old friend Kate Crane Gartz, who had been a key promoter of Anna Louise's lectures in Southern California. When Kate learned of Anna Louise's plan, she offered to lend her one of the many cars that sat in the garage on her estate.

Anna Louise drove off in a two-door 1935 Ford "singing and shouting with a sense of freedom and power." "Who are the fools," she asked herself as she headed north toward her sister's house in Palo Alto, "who say that the machine has enslaved man? If you command the machine, it is freedom, power, joy." The car, she decided, was the basis for a new form of community, "an odd new comradeship, knit by the complex pattern of autos meeting and passing." The roads of America not only connected the country physically but were the terrain for a vast and subtle cooperative endeavor.

In this spirit, she picked up as many hitchhikers as she could. All three of her first riders were men out of work; two of them got out in San Luis Obispo to spend the night in jail, the poor man's hotel. "Are the jails clean?" Anna Louise asked in concern. "Not as lousy as they used to be," came the answer. "There's a better class of transients since the Depression."

Her first stop was Santa Clara County, fifty miles south of San Francisco. Her headquarters was at her sister's house in Menlo Park, where she ensconced herself with the bland expectation that Ruth would be the Martha to her Mary, taking care of everything while Anna Louise received commendations for talking and listening. Ruth grumbled quietly to her husband but concealed from her sister whatever annoyance she felt.

It proved to be more difficult to learn what the government was doing than Anna Louise had imagined, "even though nobody tried to interfere." There were no lists of federal agencies, and none of the county officials appeared to have ever given the slightest thought to the social and political changes wrought by the New Deal. Gradually she discovered the organs of government scattered all over the county. She had intended to spend three days listing and annotating the New Deal agencies; after ten days with hardly a dent made, she turned the project over to the Young Democrats, who were "short of a program."

California was inexhaustible, but time was not. Joel had been appointed co-director of the Soviet Pavilion at the New York World's Fair and was already in the United States. Anna Louise had promised to meet him in New York by the end of summer. She spent a day with John Steinbeck, sharing with him her anguish for the "new pioneers," the

Oklahomans, Texans and migrants from Mississippi who came "humbly" to the fruitful California valleys "asking only to work and eat." They did not know, she said, that they had come "to challenge the lords" of those valleys. Nor had they expected to be denigrated as "Okies," a name she found an ugly "tactic for making them into a peon class." Immediately after seeing Steinbeck, she wrote to Mrs. Roosevelt urging her to read *The Grapes of Wrath*. Disappointed that President Roosevelt's plan to spend a day with her and Steinbeck had been canceled supposedly because of threats to his safety, she warned his wife that America was creating a new underclass whose lives were spent in barren misery. One woman she met had had a baby a few nights before on a rug on the ground. "Fortunately for her own chances of eating," Anna Louise commented tersely, "the baby was born dead."

Her anger remained as she drove north through the "wilderness of mountains" she had always loved. Traveling with her was one of her oldest friends, Ruth White Lowry. Ruth was a stockholder in one of the now-struggling mills of the Oregon woods and had used the excuse of visiting the mill for a reunion with Anna Louise. Together the women encountered scenes of even greater violence than Anna Louise had discovered on the coast. The passing of the Wagner Act in 1935 had made unions legal but exacerbated the conflict between workers and owners. In Grass Valley and even more dramatically in Westwood, the two women heard stories of murdered CIO organizers and the forced exile of hundreds of families who had tried to join the union. By the time she left Ruth in Oregon, Anna Louise was desperate for something familiar and unthreatening. "Long into the night" she drove toward Seattle, determined not to rest until she could do so in the frame house that her father had built thirty years before.

She arrived in the early morning and stood alone on the steep hillside on which the house was perched. "At last I opened the door to the bare rooms and entered. They were empty of the life that once surged through them, the life of an American family scattered now to the ends of the earth. One is in California, one in Switzerland, one wandering the world reporting wars and revolutions. The father and mother have gone back as ashes to a graveyard in the Ohio town which to them first was home. We are all of us migrants, we Americans."

After Seattle she was eager to reach Joel, and she moved with increasing speed across the "open spaces" of her native land. The endless stretches of flat earth and unrelenting heat diminished her energy but renewed her pleasure in the people and the country. Her sense of humor, lost weeks before in the migrant camps of California, returned. "I am traveling," she wrote in her journal, "on the bottom of a frying pan on a red-hot stove." A few miles later she shook with laughter as she passed a sign reading "Heated cabins just ahead." There was amusement in the names of towns: Rosebud, where "no rosebuds ever flourished," and Zero, which was "only a gas station and a woman waiting for a train." It took until North Dakota, where grasshoppers clogged her radiator, for her high spirits to falter.

She was in Minneapolis in mid-July visiting Lem Harris, who was organizing farmers' cooperatives, when Works Projects Administration employees struck to protest the Woodrum Act, which terminated all WPA cultural projects, reduced wages and increased hours for other WPA workers. Each night of her stay in the city, a group of women gathered in her room with stories of the police assaults on the picketers and the tear-gassing and shootings of men, women and children involved in the strike. In Flint, Michigan, people told her that for them Charlie Chaplin's *Modern Times* was not "an amusing exaggeration; it was our daily existence."

On Eleanor Roosevelt's specific request, Anna Louise stopped at the Tennessee River basin, site of the conflict-ridden Tennessee Valley Authority. The TVA was not, she knew, the experiment in socialism that some had claimed, but was "perhaps the clearest example of the whole New Deal attempt to make capitalism profitable even if you have to fight the capitalists first." More than fifty interviews later, she concluded that the TVA was the most "powerful" weapon created by the New Deal. Poor farmers in rural areas could for the first time afford lights, radios and electric fans; new schools had opened up; farms had been saved by the inexpensive electricity that powered water pumps, feed grinders and milking equipment. In addition, "the whole theory of the New Deal began to come to consciousness—the view that the federal government can no longer be merely a police power and clearing house for information between the states but must intervene actively in economic life." She also saw that in the hands of a reactionary government, the New Deal could be turned around "to undermine trade unionism" and excuse cuts in workers' wages.

Satisfied that she had more than enough to report to Mrs. Roosevelt, she "came back to the lands that are heavy with history," and finally reached New York, "the greatest city of earth." She found Joel keeping house in an apartment in Flushing, under the doting eye of an ebullient Hungarian landlady who had prepared everything for Anna Louise's arrival. There was barely time to repack her suitcase, however, before she departed for Hyde Park, where Mrs. Roosevelt had invited her to spend the second weekend in August.

The holiday at Hyde Park confirmed Anna Louise's hopes for her new role in American politics. The comfort of the Roosevelt estate was a welcome contrast to the motor parks and spare hotel rooms of the previous four months, and Mrs. Roosevelt was an appreciative audience for Anna Louise's as-yet-unshaped report on what the New Deal had meant to the people of the United States. She elicited a promise from Mrs. Roosevelt to visit the Soviet Pavilion at the fair and have dinner with Joel.

Aware after the weekend that her story of America had many contradictions and unspoken criticisms, Anna Louise returned to the Flushing apartment eager but not quite ready to begin work on *My Native Land*. The next weekend she drove with Joel through the Connecticut Valley to the old house in Windsor, Connecticut, that had once belonged to Elder John Strong. The sentimental excursion "over the hills and into the valleys" soon became a political journey past "the homes of the upper class, of their satellites and servitors . . . without a glimpse of the great social and technical efforts by which they were built." It had been over ten years since Joel's first visit to the United States, and he was struck by the new skyline in New York City and "new speedways through the heart of old regions," but even more by the changes in the people: "They are politically much wider awake than when I was here last."

The evening was spent at Emily Pierson's house in Cromwell. Emily and her daughter, Anne, were as anxious as Anna Louise to hear Joel's impressions of the United States. "I see it first," he said, "as a land of great spaces, where the human being has room to stretch out his arms and accomplish his desires. It is a land for the brave! I see it next as a land that is living and that has great capacity for change." Somewhat surprised by such a positive response, they talked long into the night about how world politics were bringing their two countries closer together.

Barely a week later the Nazi-Soviet nonaggression pact was announced, throwing Anna Louise into confusion. She had spent the previous years denouncing the dangers of fascism. Now her role as a publicist for the Soviet Union required of her a public defense of the Soviet action. She soon found out that there was a price to be paid for her loyalty, and the toll increased sharply on September 17 when the Red Army marched into eastern Poland. There were a few prominent voices in harmony with Anna Louise—she repeatedly cited George Bernard Shaw's claim that the Soviet entrance into East Poland was "Hitler's first setback"—but her impassioned proclamations that the Polish people welcomed the Russian troops were given little credence among her non-Communist American friends and readers. Particularly distressed by acquaintances who withdrew from the American Communist party, she pleaded with Granville Hicks, the literary editor of *New Masses,* to stay in the party and defend the Soviet Union, "with what intellect God gave us and what knowledge we have acquired." In his heart, she argued, he knew that the U.S.S.R. was right. Hicks responded angrily that "in his heart" he knew no such thing and that the revolutionary movement was "bigger than the Communist party." Unlike some, however, Hicks was willing to continue the dialogue from outside the party. "There is no one," he concluded one letter, "whose opinion I appreciate so much as I do yours and whose fallacies I would like so much to explore."

Her defense of the pact not only cost her some friendships but the support of most editors who did not follow the party line. The few who continued to use her articles did so on the ground that hers was a view "at variance with those commonly held." In contrast to her response to the purges of the previous years, Anna Louise was consistent in both her private and public statements about the nonaggression pact. The Soviets, she argued, had made every attempt to work out an alliance with Great Britain and France but had been rebuffed or denigrated repeatedly. The pact, she claimed to Eleanor Roosevelt among many others, was in the interest of peace; it was not an alliance with Germany but an agreement that would constrain Nazi aggression.

Mrs. Roosevelt wrote back immediately that she could not agree with Anna Louise on this issue. She admitted that in theory communism was closer to democracy than Nazism, but she could not accept the pact as a peace-making gesture because "it just lets Germany do its will." At the end of the letter, she pulled back slightly, as if suddenly realizing the personal difficulty of Anna Louise's role: "Let us hope you are right, however, and I am glad you feel as you do. Otherwise you might be feeling very unhappy about Russia."

There could not have been a worse time for Joel to be with her in the United States. The envisioned period of domesticity on Anna Louise's own terrain was soured by events over which they had no control and by Anna Louise's adherence to the requirements of her public stance. She tried to conceal her hurt at Mrs. Roosevelt's repeated cancellations of dates to visit the Soviet Pavilion and meet Joel. Mrs. Roosevelt finally yielded and invited them both to a private supper at her Greenwich Village apartment, but the meeting did not lead to the increased interaction for which Anna Louise had hoped.

Two who remained supportive were her sister Ruth and Emily Pierson, and Anna Louise leaned increasingly on both of them. She saw Emily frequently during the fall, either in New York or in Cromwell; and for the first time in years she maintained an active correspondence with Ruth, who replied with affectionate letters carefully balancing political commentary and family news. In one paragraph, Ruth troubled over the "coming world class struggle;" in the next, she shared her anxiety about her son, Sydney, who had been born a "blue baby" and later developed cerebral palsy.

Deciding that family could be some solace, Anna Louise arranged to visit her nephew Robbins, who was studying for his divinity degree at Yale. Kitty, Robbins' wife of three months, prepared anxiously for their special guest, but when Anna Louise arrived, she swept past her new relative, plopped herself down at a table near the kitchen and pinned Robbins in conversation about recent world events. As they talked, she dipped her fingers indelicately into the perfectly fluffed lemon meringue pie that had been set to cool in the center of the table. Oblivious to Kitty's distressed glances, Anna Louise devoured half the pie before she completed her explanation of the positive effects of the Russian invasion of Poland. There was no dessert for supper, nor was there any apology from Anna Louise.

On December 2, 1939, the Soviet Pavilion was abruptly withdrawn from the World's Fair, and Joel was called back to Moscow. Since *My Native Land* was still unfinished, Anna Louise stayed on in the United States. She spent Christmas and most of January in Florida with Ruth, finishing the book and straightening out real estate and insurance problems that Ruth was now handling. When Anna Louise was in California, she had raised the possibility of going into the real estate business with her sister; earlier that fall Ruth had advised Anna Louise against investments in stocks and toward investments in first-trust deeds on houses. In Florida the sisters agreed on this joint venture, which in fact meant that Ruth would invest and oversee Anna Louise's money. It was a rare respite for them. Ruth's husband had distrusted Anna Louise ever since the Seattle years, and on most of Anna Louise's visits she had paid little attention to him or her sister. It was also the first real chance for Anna Louise and Ruth to talk about the death of their father. By the time they parted at the end of January, Anna Louise had unhesitatingly concluded that she was closer to Ruth than to anyone else in the world except Joel.

Routes between New York and Moscow were rapidly closing when she decided in mid-May to leave for her Soviet home. Because of a circuitous route, she was in Berlin at the end of June when France surrendered and "saw at first hand how the victors control the writing of history. . . . Each press conference gave information that a correspondent had to send if he wanted to make good on his job." She was impressed by the efficiency of the German methods and equally horrified by their arrogance. At the time of her visit, the German Press Department was offering to take correspondents "in a few weeks to visit captured London." But she warned in her notes that "our past picture of a starving Germany, ripe for revolution, was propaganda and wishful thinking. . . . A billion small savings, a billion tiny sacrifices—enforced or voluntary—were combined with that infinite German attention to detail to win this war."

No matter what the line of the Nazi-Soviet pact, her intense discomfort over the misery of the remaining German Jews, coupled with fear for her own safety, led her to head abruptly for the border—on the other side of which lay Lithuania. The border guards were hostile but let her through when she fabricated contacts with high German officials whose names she had heard at press conferences. Only after she was safe did she allow herself to acknowledge the depth of her fear and her danger, since "it was an open secret that my writings did not favor Hitler."

She had had no particular desire to visit Lithuania, but once in Kaunas, she wanted to stay. Without much foreknowledge she had landed in a situation that epitomized the changes she had sought throughout her life: "Lithuania had become important, even epoch-making. A sovereign state was changing from capitalism to socialism quite constitutionally, without destruction of life or property. The thing had never happened before." From Anna Louise's perspective, the arrival of the Red Army in Lithuania just two weeks before had not meant conquest but "the release of forces among workers, peasants and progressive intellectuals that had been suppressed for fourteen years."

It was in this state of euphoria that she unexpectedly ran into her brother Tracy at the offices of the American Legation. He was in Kaunas as world director of the YMCA's War Prisoners' Aid Committee. Somewhat taken aback by the unexpected encounter, the two immediately plunged into an argument about the Soviet presence in Lithuania. She regaled him with anecdotes illustrating that a new world was being built

and that a barrier against the progress of fascism was being erected; all
he could see was the disappearance of his friends to Siberia. If his friends
were associated with the repressive Smetona government that had been
overthrown, perhaps they belonged in Siberia, she argued. She was blind
to anything she did not want to see, he retorted. They parted with no
resolution to their differences; neither was able to make a conciliatory
gesture.

A few weeks later, the special train carrying the Lithuanian delegation
to the Supreme Soviet of the U.S.S.R. departed, and Anna Louise was
on board. In Moscow "the bureaucracy and protocol that had been so
happily absent in Kaunas" made themselves immediately known. She
had arrived too late, she was told, to receive a press pass to the session
of the Supreme Soviet. Undaunted and no longer concerned about propriety, she accepted the invitation of President Paletskis and her "new
Lithuanian friends" to sit with their delegation. For a single session she
was on the floor of the Supreme Soviet and went with the Lithuanians to
lunch with the Soviet deputies. The Soviet Press Department was horrified. A press pass suddenly materialized and along with it a severe warning that she "would not again be admitted to the floor with the Lithuanians."

The excitement over, she settled into daily life with Joel. The apartment had become even more crowded. In addition to Joel's sister and
brother-in-law and two children, Ducia was visiting with her new baby.
The housekeeper had a baby too, as did the secretary Anna Louise had
hired on her arrival. At times the flat looked like a nursery. But to Anna
Louise's surprise, the moments of bedlam were few, and she concluded
that Russian babies were better behaved than American ones. Her contacts in Moscow were suddenly better than they had been in years. A
number of her Soviet friends who had been sent to Poland and the
Ukraine "to help organize the new territories" were willing to share the
stories they brought back, and she was welcomed into a circle of writers
and filmmakers whose company and talk she found freer than that in
political circles.

It was Joel who told her, late one October evening, that he thought
she should be in her own country when the war that was rapidly approaching finally came to Russia and the United States. She took his
remark fairly casually; she had assumed she would return as usual in
January for her annual lecture tour. It was already impossible to go to
America via Europe, so she had planned to take the Trans-Siberian Railroad and leave from Japan. The Japanese, however, had labeled her "a

dangerous security risk," and a friendly official warned her secretly that they would not let her through. Spurred by Joel's concern, she haunted various Moscow offices in search of an exit route until Sir Stafford Cripps, recently appointed British ambassador to Moscow, suggested a solution. He had come to Moscow in May via a new air route from Chungking, Chiang Kai-shek's most recent capital in China. Anna Louise received permission to take a train to Alma-Ata and fly from there to Chungking. That evening she danced around the family dining room gleefully announcing that she not only would get to both China and the United States but would be the first foreigner to leave the Soviet Union by this particular route.

In early December Joel took her to the train. "I do not expect you back in 1941," he told her, "but I hope you may return by 1942."

10

Lands Revisited

> Only when you know what you want of life can you rightly choose the mate with whom to share life.
>
> —Anya, in Anna Louise's novel *Wild River*

> No, we're not back where we started. We're two hundred million lifetimes ahead. We not only built the Red Dawn Farm and the Dnieper Dam. We built the people that burned the farm and blew up the dam in the war to save the world from the Nazis.
>
> —Stepan, in *Wild River*

The plane from Alma-ata stopped the first night at Ha-mi, in eastern Sinkiang, where Marco Polo had stayed centuries earlier on his way to China. The only place that accepted transients looked as if it had been there since Marco Polo's time. Two young boys were assigned to the guests to make certain they made their flight the next morning. Unfortunately, the boys had no clock, so they awoke Anna Louise every hour from midnight on to check the time. She was more amused than angry: "Future travelers by this route will doubtless find more modern lodging at the airport, supplied with clocks. They will never even see where Marco Polo stopped."

The next morning she discovered that the plane had been loaded with Ha-mi melons, famous for their excellent flavor. It was "positively dangerous," she insisted, to carry so many. The pilots, who were making extra money carrying Western canned goods into the desert and melons out, turned a deaf ear. Throughout the two-day flight, the huge melons rolled around at the passengers' feet, accompanied by a continuous chorus of protest from Anna Louise. Both the pilots and Anna Louise breathed sighs of relief when the melons were unloaded in northern Szechwan for a local warlord.

In Chungking, Anna Louise was taken to an unheated hillside house that had been set up as a hostel for the foreign press. To her outspoken dismay, Chungking was under the control of reactionary bankers and officials, many of whom had fled Shanghai two years before. The American ambassador, Nelson Johnson, seemed more interested in "the relics of antiquity" than in the war raging around him, and insisted that "Chiang was a true democrat worthy of a full commitment" from the American government. A "deadly jest" was circulating in the city: "Japanese are only lice on the body of China, but Communism is a disease of the heart."

At the house of the British ambassador, Sir Archibald Clark-Kerr, she met Rewi Alley and Evans Carlson, who had just returned from a six-month trip through eight southern provinces of China to investigate conditions in the industrial cooperatives that Alley had been instrumental in organizing. Carlson, a former American marine major, was known to Anna Louise as a supporter of the Chinese Communists and a friend of both Franklin Roosevelt and Agnes Smedley. Rewi Alley was a New Zealander with a volcanic passion that surged forth when he described the sixty Communist prisoners who had been forsaken in a South Kiangsi prison since 1934. Anna Louise immediately began to bombard him with questions about his trip.

She also sought out Israel Epstein, a United Press correspondent who had been helpful to her in Hankow in 1938. He filled her in on the background of the New Fourth Army, the much-hailed Communist force that had been organized along the lower Yangtze. In another fortuitous encounter, she ran into Li Kung-po, her compartment mate two years before on Marshal Yen's special train to Shansi. Li had failed to establish his university because of conditions imposed by General Yen, but he had remained behind Japanese lines promoting education among the peasants for the last two years. At the end of a long talk, Li presented her with a collection of brightly colored hand-blocked posters and invited her to a conference of leading intellectuals. The conference itself was a disappointment; the participants, almost all eminent scholars, artists and business leaders, seemed to her politically naive. But Li made the occasion memorable by using his introduction of Anna Louise to give her her Chinese name, Shih Teh-lang, "one who is especially brilliant about history." Six years later she discovered that out of that meeting had come not only her Chinese name but the Democratic League, a key political movement in the forging of the new China.

Each of the Chungking days had its rewards, but it was the nights that proved to be most important. Living quietly in the city was Chou En-lai, who remained relatively safe only because he had been responsible for saving the life of Chiang Kai-shek during the Sian Incident. Chou sent word to Anna Louise that he would like to meet with her for a series of late-evening interviews. On the first evening he revealed that he wanted to give her a detailed account of the armed clashes between Chiang's generals and the Communist-led forces, which had been accelerating over the past two years. "Do not publish this material unless I send you word to do so," Chou said. "We do not want to increase friction by prematurely revealing these clashes. But we want this material to be in trustworthy hands abroad to release if Chiang, as we fear, attacks more seriously."

Chou's story was lengthy and complex. In addition to repeated attempts to take areas within the Communist-held Special Border District, the KMT had set up an armed blockade against all Eighth Route and New Fourth Army territory. Students attempting to reach the Communist capital in Yenan were detained in Sian; neither medical supplies nor doctors nor payrolls for the Communist-led troops reached their destinations. By the summer of 1940, clashes between Communist-led armies and other forces of the central government had occurred in Hopei, Shantung, North Kiangsi, East and South Anhwei and on the northern edge of Chekiang. Chou had demanded an investigation commission, but none was sent. Pamphlets and KMT army staff denounced the Communists as "the most dangerous element in the nation." Organizers of Rewi Alley's industrial cooperatives were kidnapped and assassinated as "Reds."

Chou also presented evidence that KMT generals were actively cooperating with the Japanese. The climax of these events had come on December 10, when Chiang Kai-shek had signed an order for the New Fourth Army to leave the Yangtze valley and move north of the Yellow River to be amalgamated with the Eighth Route Army. This order meant virtual suicide for much of the New Fourth Army, since it had operated for the preceding two years in small detachments stretching from Shanghai, and there was no way to protect the troops as they withdrew. Most of these troops were dependent on local support for survival; Chiang was offering no food or funds to aid in the transfer.

The implications of these moves, Chou explained, were not "merely" military, but political. If Chiang's orders were followed and all of the Communist troops were concentrated in northern China, the country would be split in two, leaving the Communist-held territory as an excellent target for the Japanese and setting up a situation in which Chiang could negotiate control of central and southern China. The next step would be an alliance between Chiang Kai-shek and Japan, Germany and

Italy. Before the end of their last session, Chou gave Anna Louise a twenty-six-page essay and other documents to support what he had told her. He also asked her to "tell Borodin that despite the many things that had happened, his name would be remembered by the Chinese people for the help he gave in establishing the revolutionary interpretation of Sun Yat-sen's Three People's Principles in his reorganization of the Kuomintang."

Just before leaving Chungking, Anna Louise was granted an interview with Chiang Kai-shek. He indignantly denied any intention of making peace with Japan or of splitting China in two. She did not believe him and was bored by the interview. Her attention was now focused on getting through Chinese customs in Chungking without having her notebooks confiscated.

The customs search was fortunately casual, and she made her way easily to Hong Kong, where she contacted an old friend, Liao Cheng-chih, whom she had first met in Canton in 1925; he was now handling foreign relations for the Communist-led armies. Liao told her it was he who would contact her if and when it was time to publish what Chou had told her. After a brief stop in Japan, she boarded a steamer for San Francisco. En route, she caught a fragment of a radio message from Chungking announcing that General Yeh Ting, commander of the New Fourth Army, had been court-martialed because of the "revolt" of his troops. She knew something was terribly wrong but learned no further details because all subsequent broadcasts were cut off. Only in New York, where she hastily went after landing in San Francisco, did she discover that on January 6, 1941, 80,000 KMT troops had attacked the retreating rear guard of the New Fourth Army as they moved through a narrow mountain pass. More than half of the 10,000 New Fourth Army troops were unarmed; the casualties were numbered at more than 4,000.

Official reports from Chungking that reached New York in January claimed that the Chinese Communists had accepted the disbanding of the New Fourth Army and that "there would be no more trouble." From Hong Kong, Edgar Snow sent more accurate details of the attack but had no further information as to the Communists' plans for the New Fourth. Anna Louise was not surprised, therefore, when in early February she received an unsigned letter airmailed from Manila stating simply, "The time has come to publish what you know." The envelope also contained the text of the Chinese Communists' official order reorganizing the New Fourth Army and another official statement by the "spokesman of the Revolutionary Military Committee" listing fifteen steps of a plot by pro-

Japanese elements in Chungking to take China into the Nazi-Fascist Axis. By the time she received the envelope, which had been mailed on January 26, some of the steps in the "plot" had already been taken.

Chou had clearly outlined her task to her. She was to attempt to reach not just the Western left but Chiang's American backers, hoping to persuade them to withdraw their support when they learned that Chiang was using American aid to fight a civil war rather than a war against Japan. She went at once to the North American Newspaper Alliance, which specialized in scoops that had not been secured by the regular news agencies. The managing editor indicated that he could place her material in the New York Times and ordered two articles, which she immediately wrote. She next went to Washington where, over lunch, Mrs. Roosevelt tried to arrange an appointment for her with Henry Morgenthau, Jr., secretary of the treasury, who was responsible for financial assistance to China. He was away on a week's vacation. Disappointed because, as she subsequently wrote to the secretary, Chou had specifically said that he respected Morgenthau, she conveyed the essence of her information to John P. Davies in the State Department and Harry Dexter White in the Treasury Department. After rushing to dinner with T. V. Soong, now Chiang's personal envoy to Washington, she returned to New York.

The news in New York was distressing. A friend on the staff of the New York Times informed her that the Times was not planning to publish her articles, "preferring to support the tales from Chungking that the attack on the New Fourth Army had merely been the suppression of unruly rebels." Furious, but more concerned about getting the news out accurately than about her own success or failure, she went to her friend Joseph Barnes at the New York Herald Tribune and suggested that she give him the most important basic material, which she did not consider her "personal property" to sell or not sell. Barnes told her that rumors were already reaching the Tribune that there were serious clashes between Chiang Kai-shek and the Communists, but he had not had enough facts to publish anything. With her data in hand, he would be very glad to publish a story under his own by-line. The story came out immediately, and Barnes scored a personal scoop. Two American Communist friends, who guessed that the material came from Anna Louise, chastized her for giving the material to the capitalist press instead of to the Daily Worker. Anna Louise later remarked that Barnes' article was the only "real scoop" she had ever had. She subsequently published her own account in Amerasia.

With the information from Chou duly disseminated, the hectic pace of her first few weeks back in the United States slackened, and she faced for the first time in twenty years the need for a home in America. She had been using the Hotel Wolcott in New York as a mailing address and temporary residence, but it had both deteriorated and become more expensive. To her dismay she discovered that she had gradually accumulated thirteen suitcases of clothing and other possessions in the storage basement at the hotel.

She most liked living, she realized, in a place like Hull House or the Henry Street Settlement where "there was no need of doing personal housework and intelligent conversation was available at meals." But such places were disappearing. Returning from a long walk on the Palisades in New Jersey in late February, she noticed a very old "For Sale" sign on a piece of property that included an eighteenth-century house and a view of the New York skyline. She was entranced. She bought the house at once and moved in with her thirteen suitcases and a typist-companion whom she had hired in New York.

For the next few months, Anna Louise divided her time between writing and remodeling. She was convinced that the Palisades house was the answer to a long-held dream of a place where she and friends could live together cooperatively. When she was away, the other residents would look after the property. The house was easily divided into four apartments, each with its own fireplace and view of the river; she could either rent the other apartments or share ownership at very little cost to anyone. She could not imagine why anyone would want to continue living in a "dingy Greenwich Village two-room flat" when they could live cheaper and better in her house; ferries and cars gave easy access to the city and a phone call from New Jersey "cost the same as from one part of New York to another." The location would be particularly good for writers who "needed easy contact with New York editors" but did not need the noise of Manhattan. Her greatest anxiety was that there might be more people who wanted to move in than the house could hold; the solution, she decided, would to be to build small cottages on the terraces that were contained within the one-acre property.

To her dismay, she was unable persuade even one person to try out the arrangement, except for those she paid as typists or housekeepers. By fall she sadly relinquished the fantasy, although she harbored no regrets about the purchase. She had learned how to remodel a house, and she had grasped "how the dead hand of the past binds the future generations through what is called 'real property.' "

Across the Atlantic, Joel was also busy. "All the family," he wrote, "is building a house in Fizsanvoka. So next year we'll stay in our own dacha." He had just received copies of her book on Lithuania and urged her to write another on her impressions of the world in 1940–41. The affectionate letter, signed "With lots of kisses," did not reach Anna Louise until May. By then she had written to him repeatedly, complaining about the mail; all she had received was a dictionary. She complained to him that she was wasting too much time with good friends. The same people who refused to move into the Palisades house were constantly making demands, and "I have not yet learned to protect myself."

On the first of May, Joel wrote again; he had been writing constantly but had received only two letters from her since December. Three weeks later, she wrote to him from Ruth's house in Menlo Park. She was angry because she had sent him two addresses and had received only the one letter. She discussed at length her ambivalence about her next writing subject, then confessed that "all this is academic, for actually I've done no work for three weeks. The California sun makes me lazy." She recalled that her father had chosen Seattle over California because he was convinced that life in California would be "too soft." Mostly she was lonely. A weekend at the beach with Ruth's family accentuated her distance from Joel. She closed her letter begging him to write again and often.

By the end of May, she had moved to a cottage by the sea at Half Moon Bay, and again her letters to Joel were dotted with expressions of loneliness. Ruth and Charles had spent the weekend with her, helping her to build a guest room so that she could have her own California house with a place for more permanent guests. She enclosed plans and photographs of the cottage and acknowledged that Ruth was "very efficient in all such matters." She launched into a comparison of American and Russian floor plans: "You know," she wrote, "in the U.S.S.R., they always isolate the kitchen from the rest of the house. That makes it impossible for the housewife to join in the interesting conversation of her guests. Our kitchen here—of nicely polished wooden shelves and cupboards—is in the alcove of the big living room. . . . As Ruth moves about getting meals or washing dishes, she can talk freely with people seated in front of the fireplace." Still, she would have preferred to have been in the Fizsanvoka dacha. She continued to have difficulty getting her writing going and instead was keeping busy buying presents for Joel and Ducia. She had bought Ducia a sweater with a zipper and Joel a wool army shirt, "which I hope to bring you when I come."

At dawn on June 22, Hitler's armies began their surprise attack on the

Soviet Union. Anna Louise cabled Joel immediately: "Everyone here urges seek press connection and hasten Moscow even if only for federpress [Federated Press] stop remembering last autumn discussions want your views Hotel Wolcott." Joel cabled back, in Russian, that she should not come to Moscow unless she had a better newspaper connection than the Federated Press. In the meantime she and her friends were madly pulling the strings that would get her quickly to Moscow. Both Jessica Smith and the news editor of the Federated Press requested a rush passport for her from Secretary of State Cordell Hull. Jessica also raised $1,500 to pay Anna Louise's way back through Chungking and Alma-Ata. Convinced it would all work out, Anna Louise checked into St. Luke's Hospital in San Francisco, on the advice of Emily Pierson, to have a small lump removed from her breast before starting the long trip. The medical operation went smoothly, and on July 8 a farewell dinner for her was held at the American Russian Institute.

The passport, however, was not forthcoming. Unknown to Anna Louise, the FBI had been following her even more closely than in previous years. Agents' reports mixed absurdities with accurate accounts of her lectures. One agent, identifying Anna Louise as "the former wife of John Reed," claimed that she had given a speech in Moscow denouncing the United States and calling the United States flag "nothing but a rag." An FBI informant stated that "she and her husband went to Russia in the early days of the Stalin regime, where her husband edited the first English-language newspaper in Russia; that she was educated in the Russian language and became an international Soviet agent; that she was in China during the early stages of the Chinese-Japanese war but was deported for her activities." Someone in the bureau surely knew that much of this was ridiculous, but there was sufficient "anti-American" material in her file to make her a candidate for the "custodial detention" program that the FBI had proposed. There was also the matter of her *Amerasia* piece that attacked Chiang Kai-shek for his anti-United Front policies. The article had caused a small sensation, especially in Chungking, and it was unlikely that Chiang would have welcomed her passage through his capital.

Nor was there any further word from Joel. Throughout August she continued to write to him with the expectation of seeing him soon, but by the end of the month, her letters were full of contradictory plans and moved erratically from the mundane to the monumental. "Do we still have our apartment?" she asked. "If you are taking things out, the only things I care about are the letter files, which contain the only copies of many of my articles. Not all of the drawers are important, of course, and none are really important in comparison with your time and energy." She anxiously queried him about conditions in Moscow and told him her plan to write a book on the Soviet Union's preparations for the war. She had accepted a lecture tour in Canada for the fall; with the invasion of the Soviet Union she was suddenly in more demand as an expert than she had ever been before.

She finished the book, *The Soviets Expected It,* before the lecture tour began in mid-October; Dial Press rushed it into print, and it was an instant success. She gave answers to many of the questions Americans were asking: Why had the Soviet Union not collapsed under Hitler's assault? What lay behind the surprising strength of the Russian forces? Could the Soviet Union in fact defeat Hitler? Her answers reassured her fellow Americans: they had nothing to fear because "the Soviet people have no doubt of the future." The Nazi-Soviet pact of 1939, she averred, had in fact been a measure taken to ensure the victory of freedom-loving peoples over fascism. "If our own progressive forces rise to this opportunity and take full share in the worldwide struggle," she concluded, "we are on the threshold of a great expansion of freedom in our own land."

She carried the message of hope from west to east across Canada in the most whirlwind tour she had ever conducted. Unlike previous tours, this one was organized not by "some radical leadership" but by mayors of cities and lieutenant-governors of provinces. The physical price for her new recognition was high. She arrived at each city exhausted from uncomfortable sleeping compartments and was immediately whisked away to a formal breakfast, followed by a public appearance at a university or radio station. Then there would be a formal lunch, a committee meeting, a public dinner and finally her major lecture. A select delegation would escort her to the train late in the evening, and she would be on her way to the next engagement.

Another kind of exhaustion awaited her back on the Pacific Coast, where she had reserved a few days to go again to Seattle and prepare the house there for sale. All but the two basement rooms were now rented. Ruth had taken most of the furniture and some books to her own home in Menlo Park. Yet to Anna Louise the house still contained "memories and dreams, long ago realized or thwarted." Crossing the threshold, she was struck by the fact that her mother had never seen this house on which her father had based his unfulfilled vision of a family "great work."

For several days she cloistered herself in the two rooms that had been her father's bedroom and study. Much of the time she was in tears. "As I went through the files of old letters, it seemed that a life passed under my hands, a life of great integrity, and I must decide what to save of it. It was the life of my father, who was the best and perhaps the only real Christian I have ever known." Among the files she discovered an album in which her father had pasted his daughter's writings; never again, she thought, would such a full collection of her work be so carefully kept, even by herself: "I knew with a pang that a parent's love for his child is always greater than the love of the child for his parent, and that this is one of the conditions by which our human race survives."

All of the usable furniture and some books she shipped to Ruth to hold for her. From the papers, she saved everything she thought she might wish to read again and "everything that any grandson, who might be interested someday in ancestors, would care to see." She burned the rest.

She resumed her lecture tour but was so distracted by the rekindling of memories in Seattle that even the attack on Pearl Harbor had little impact on her. She was "thinking too hard about other things." She continued to write frequent letters to Joel despite the total absence of word from him. Her letters said little about the war but detailed her attempts to renew old acquaintances and make new ones.

Christmas was spent at Ruth's house, followed by a hurried trip to lecture in Los Angeles before heading east. After the lecture, a man named George Willner, who had once worked for the *Masses* and was now a Hollywood agent, approached her about writing a screenplay that drew on her knowledge of Russia. Willner was particularly interested in a filmscript that would tell the story of how the Russians built the Dnieper Dam, then destroyed it themselves to prevent its use by Hitler. Anna Louise was so taken with the idea that she wrote a nine-page scenario before departing for New York.

A week later, returning to the house in the Palisades, she was searching for something in the damp basement when she suddenly found herself unable to walk. Her housekeeper finally heard her cries and with considerable effort dragged her up the stairs. She was taken by car to New York, where Emily Pierson, who had rushed to the city from Cromwell, mistakenly diagnosed the problem as acute arthritis. It was actually the first sign of Paget's disease, a bone disorder producing great pain at the joints, brittleness of bone structure and progressive deformation of the lower skeleton.

Still in severe pain a week later, Anna Louise sent word to Canada to cancel the second part of her scheduled tour. An urgent reply came back, saying that most of the lectures were in places where there had never been a talk on the Soviet Union and it would be a serious loss if Anna Louise withdrew. She decided that she would cancel any dates that were not of political importance and conduct the rest from a wheelchair.

At the last stop on her schedule, a small town in Nova Scotia, she was greeted by a telephone call from George Willner in Hollywood. MGM wanted her to work as a technical consultant on a film they were about to make about Russia. They would pay her $300 a week for a six-week contract. "That's wonderful," she exclaimed. "Wait a moment," George cautioned. "We want you to wire a reply refusing the offer and asking for better terms." "Are you crazy?" Anna Louise protested. "I would come to Hollywood without any salary just for the railway fare." She nonetheless acceded to Willner's advice and a contract for eleven weeks instead of six was negotiated.

The job was the most luxurious employment she ever had. The assistant producer picked her up each morning and escorted her to a large office thoughtfully located on the ground floor because of Anna Louise's continued difficulty in walking. A stenographer appeared whenever she wanted one. As soon as the young woman entered her office, Anna Louise would ask her to lock the door and roll her chair to the window. Once located to her satisfaction, she would raise her skirts, expose her legs to the sunlight that came streaming in, and dictate for hours. Her amused friends told her that she was the only person they ever knew of who had taken a cure for arthritis while getting $300 a week from MGM. Still another benefit from the job was that at the age of fifty-seven, after working for more than thirty years, she finally acquired a social security number.

She found herself so taken by the enterprise of script-writing that she got together with Edgar Snow to write a script called "Judgment Seat" about a young nurse, Anna, who finds herself torn between political commitment and humanitarianism in China. The script was sent to Orson Welles, who first appeared to be interested; nothing ever came of it.

Well before the end of the eleven weeks, Anna Louise had recovered enough to visit Yosemite Park and write to Joel that there was "no other spot on earth quite so well adapted for seeing much beauty without undue effort as in California." She felt so well after her time in Hollywood that she decided to move her residence to California. In early spring, just after the end of her job at MGM, she bought a house two blocks away from where her sister lived.

It was a house with possibilities. Four large rooms provided enough space for a secretary or live-in companion. There was a well-kept backyard full of fruit trees and a fine rose garden. In the high-roofed garage Anna Louise constructed a kind of cupola, which became the place to which she could escape to write and where she could leave all her private possessions and papers. She moved the bedstead that had belonged to her father into her bedroom, put his filing cabinets and desk in the study, and settled back to wait out the war years.

By July it had been a full year since she had heard from Joel. During the spring she had cabled him several times. None of the cables had been answered. Unable to ignore the silence any longer, despite the logical explanation that no letters or telegrams were getting through because of the war, she wired Kamenov, head of VOKS, the Association for Cultural Relations. Would he please, she asked, trace her husband, Joel Shubin. Two weeks later, on August 4, she received a cable saying that Joel Shubin had died of lingering lung disease on March 4, 1942, in Krasny-Ufinsk in the Urals.

At first she refused to believe it. She sent off dozens of letters to Moscow, to Joel's brother Boris and sister Frieda; to Ducia; to her friend Maxim Litvinov, the chief of the Foreign Affairs bureau; and to everyone else she could think of. To all of her Moscow acquaintances she made the same request: would they go to or call the Shubin apartment and try to locate relatives. From everyone she begged for details: "If they run into things they think would hurt me, such as that Joel married again or lived with somebody else, don't be afraid to say so. I don't think that he did; he wouldn't take time to. But I should be very glad to know that he had somebody looking after him who cared about him, in that black Krasny-Ufinsk."

Slowly she accepted the knowledge that he was dead. "I feel rather knocked to pieces," she admitted in one letter. "But," she continued, "there are so many worse things happening now than one person's death." The next day, however, she sent off another letter to Litvinov: "It is the absence of all detailed news that is hardest. Somehow I don't even yet believe that Joel is dead. They have so often mixed him up with other Shubins. But Krasny-Ufinsk sounds authentic because that is where he might well have been. On the other hand, lingering lung disease does not sound so authentic." She asked the Litvinovs to find out everything they could of his life in the last year: what was he working on, when and how he fell ill, who was with him when he died. Most especially, she pleaded, would they find out if he had left any messages for her.

On August 7 Anna Louise received a telegram of condolence from Jessica Smith, who more than most understood the ties and the pain of distance from Moscow to the United States. Anna Louise wrote back that she now felt that the news about Joel was true, but that her anguish was unrelieved because of the absence of specific information. "Death," she told Jessica, "is so much more than death when there are no living details or any words or acts. One of the worst things is that death can happen in March and one cannot know until August; cables went into the void and nothing returned."

"This means, I think," she ended the letter to Jessica, "that Moscow will never again be even a part-time home for me. . . . I must try, very swiftly, to build some sort of home in this country, with some small circle of friends to take the edge off loneliness as age draws on. . . . I must consider very seriously what work and what contacts and what localities the future shall hold."

As she neared her fifty-seventh birthday, Anna Louise found herself world-famous, marooned in America without husband, children or a regular job, with a bone disease that made walking difficult and painful. At least the U.S.S.R. had been redeemed from the opprobrium of the pact with the Nazis: her two countries were at last on the same side. All America thrilled to the heroic defense of Moscow and cheered when the troops of Marshal G. K. Zhukov turned the tide of battle at Stalingrad. When German Field Marshal Friedrich Paulus surrendered at Stalingrad in early 1943, it became evident that the war was eventually going to be won by the Allies. Anna Louise could only wait.

Despite people to see and lectures to give, she was at such loose ends that she happily lectured on China to the Palo Alto classes of Commander Stuart Bryant, who had been stationed in the Philippines and China and held a negative view of the leadership of the Chinese Nationalists. Out of these classes came a casual friendship with a twenty-two-year-old named Sidney Rittenberg, who had worked as a CIO organizer for textile workers in Roanoke, Virginia, until he was drafted, and who was now taking Chinese language and culture courses for eventual assignment overseas. Sidney was married to a young woman named Violet. Anna Louise promptly recruited her as a typist for two or three afternoons a week. Somewhat later, when the Rittenbergs had housing problems, they moved into Anna Louise's spare rooms for a few weeks. Three years later she would meet Sidney again in Kalgan, North China, and ten years after that, in Peking.

On George Willner's urging she expanded the brief outline she had made for a film on the Dnieper dam to a nineteen-page treatment. MGM found the story too pro-socialist, but Willner was still sure that it had movie possibilities. He offered Anna Louise $900 against 50 percent of the rights if she would turn it into a novel. Novels, he assured her, were easier to sell as movies.

Anna Louise took the challenge and spent the late fall of 1942 writing. To her delight, Angus Cameron, an editor at Little, Brown, accepted the manuscript and even encouraged her to write more fiction. The book, entitled *Wild River,* is dedicated "To Joel, my husband, who in living and dying showed me the Soviet way of life." Through the story of two young Russians who struggle both to become good comrades and lovers to each other and to build the new Soviet Union, Anna Louise assembled the hopes and fears generated by her twenty years in Russia. The novel's most striking portrait is not of the new society, but of its heroine, Anya, who seeks a man who does not see her as an object to be possessed.

Anna Louise spent the ten months after finishing *Wild River* lecturing and seeing Ruth and Charles. In the early months of 1944 Macmillan approached her for a secondary-school textbook. The wartime friendship between the U.S.S.R. and the United States had produced a demand for information about "Russians as people." Within three months she had produced a draft of *Peoples of the U.S.S.R.* A hundred dreary official Sovfoto photographs accompanied the text, which dealt exclusively with heroic, smiling characters from every republic of Russia, all busy resisting oppression. There was probably not a new thought in the book; a sad parody of her earlier work, it signaled the practical end of Anna Louise's writing about the U.S.S.R.

The most dramatic words in *Peoples of the U.S.S.R.* were the dateline to the preface: "June 13, 1944, Airport in Montana." The Department of State had resumed issuing passports for travel to Russia, and Anna Louise was planning to leave on "one more historic trip." From a Polish priest, Father Orlemanski, who had made the trip six months earlier, she had learned of a little-known air route from Fairbanks, Alaska, to the far eastern part of Siberia, over which the lend-lease planes flew, and with the help of Jakob Lomakin, the Soviet consul in San Francisco, she secured passage to Fairbanks from a secret military base in Great Falls, Montana.

It was a dangerous trip, and for the first time Anna Louise made a will. It was short and direct: "I give and bequeath all my property both of real estate and of money and of all other values to my sister Ruth Strong Niederhauser." In an attached document, she estimated that her estate came to around $50,000; she appointed Ruth as executor, asking her to use the money "to execute the desires that I have discussed with her." These desires were that the money be used to "carry on the general purpose" of her life. Since both Tracy and Ruth lived "as comfortably as is good for anyone, and at least as comfortably as I myself have lived, merely to spread this additional money around among them would seem . . . a fruitless dissipation." These were, she concluded, uncertain times in which "many things may happen."

When her friends at the American Russian Institute found out that Anna Louise had passage back to Moscow, they gave a formal party at which presents were collected from left-wing associations all over the West Coast. The material was packed under the supervision of the Russian consulate and forwarded to Great Falls under Anna Louise's name, c/o Colonel Kotikov, the Russian purchasing agent. Convinced by this that she was a Soviet courier transporting valuable secrets back to the U.S.S.R., J. Edgar Hoover, then head of the FBI, authorized a complete search of her luggage, including that which the Soviet embassy had packed. In the meantime, Anna Louise arrived by train in Great Falls at midnight on June 12. No one was there to meet her, and she angrily called up Kotikov's office. When she reached the night secretary, who knew nothing, Anna Louise blew up. Cowed, the secretary awoke Kotikov, who told her to take a room at the Rainbow Hotel and that he would meet her the next morning at ten.

Morning came, but Kotikov did not. Anna Louise called his office and was told that he was on the way; she called two hours later and was informed that he had been called to another airport for a conference. She took this as a sign of the importance of her trip. "I am betting," she wrote to Rose Isaac, "that it is a conference with Gromyko, the ambassador from Washington and Lomakin, the consul from S.F., who intimated that this might occur." Actually, American authorities were trying to delay her at the base until they could make a thorough search of her effects.

Kotikov finally arrived around four o'clock and told her to come to the airport the next morning for her flight. The next day the Americans informed her that as a civilian she would not be allowed to ride in a military plane across Canada, but that she could pick up the flight in Alaska. Anna Louise yelled at everyone in sight and stomped around the airport, but there was nothing to be done. All of her luggage except one suitcase and a handbag was allowed on the lend-lease flight, and she flew to Seattle to catch a Pan American flight to Fairbanks. The FBI sent a disappointed letter to the Washington bureau chief, E. M. Ladd, reporting that her luggage contained "books, a blood pressure gauge, architectural materials, watches, paintbrushes, steel tape, candy, tea, tobacco, and letters addressed to Soviet architects and artists and doctors from various Hollywood organizations, but no microfilm or microfilm equipment." They neglected to mention that she was also carrying large quantities of greasepaint from Hollywood actors to their Moscow counterparts.

In Fairbanks, Anna Louise brushed aside airline inquiries about "return flights" with the assertion that the "Russian military mission is making arrangements." She departed two days later on a converted DC-3 cargo plane. Furnishings for passengers were limited to a few benches and a large central table. She bundled up in all her furs and lay on the table. It took two very uncomfortable, cold days for the plane to reach Krasnoyarsk, the town nearest to the Trans-Siberian Railroad. From there Anna Louise had expected to take the train to Moscow, but when she encountered a small delegation of important Moscow party officials she requested and received a seat on their plane. This ride proved even more uncomfortable than the previous one. The plane had no toilet facilities. To make the situation worse, the pilot was trying to set a record for minimum gasoline consumption and held the quaint notion that low-altitude flying would reduce wind resistance. Most of his passengers spent the trip sharing a large bucket in the middle of the aisle. Three days later a dozen miserable and exhausted travelers arrived in Moscow; Anna Louise never found out if they indeed set a record. With some difficulty, she managed to get her immense load of baggage to VOKS, where it became the object of a general celebration.

She tried immediately to find out the circumstances of Joel's death. Her sister-in-law Frieda confirmed that Joel had died of pneumonia, which he caught while awaiting evacuation from Moscow. The rest of the family had successfully reached eastern Russia; Ducia had had a second child there. Frieda had survived the war by growing potatoes on the plot of Anna Louise's and Joel's dacha—the house itself had been destroyed by the Germans. After Frieda returned to Moscow, she took care of the serious repairs needed in the flat and the Shubins collectively had paid the rent, even during the period of evacuation.

Anna Louise turned the flat over to them, keeping one room for her occasional use, and moved into the Hotel Metropol, partly because of its central heating, partly for the company of the other foreign correspondents. She was anxious to get to the front, but the Russians were proving extremely uncooperative to all foreign journalists, no matter what their political reputation.

Her opportunity finally came not from the Russians but from the Poles. In late 1944 two groups contended for recognition as the Polish "government." The government in London was fiercely anti-Russian; the other, based in Lublin, had evolved from a secret Warsaw council. Both groups were in Moscow in late 1944.

Anna Louise approached the Lublin delegation and was promptly invited to visit the provisional government and take a trip to the front. She was so pleased that for the first time in her life she missed a flight; she had been partying too hard the night before in celebration of Polish independence. The train she ended up taking went the long route through Kiev, crossing a land more devastated than anything she had ever seen. The retreating German armies had systematically blown up all structures, deporting or killing the inhabitants. As the train crossed the border during a sleet storm, glasses were lifted. "How beautiful is our Poland," a voice said in the dark of the compartment. "My breath stopped," Anna Louise remembered. "What was there to say? The edge between earth and sky had vanished. Outside a merciful night was veiling the desolation. The conductress came in with a single candle. The faces were those of Pilgrims to the Holy City."

Anna Louise pressed on toward Warsaw. The river Vistula that divided the city had apparently stalled the advance of the Russian army, which remained in Praga on the east bank, waiting for the winter freeze. Civilians had begun to return, and on the day of her arrival in Praga, Anna Louise attended a concert by the "New Warsaw Symphony" Orchestra under the baton of the grand old man of prewar Polish music, Vincente Rzmowski. The first piece was an orchestral rendition of Chopin's "Polonaise Militaire."

She remained in Praga, occasionally visiting the front. Then, on January 12, 1945, the Vistula finally froze hard enough to permit the passage of heavy weaponry. Warsaw proper was taken, and Anna Louise entered the city with a group of correspondents early in February. The Germans had spent the preceding four months efficiently destroying the city. There was no water or gas or electricity. The sewers were clogged with tens of thousands of corpses of those gassed by the Germans. Anna Louise had no adequate words for the desolation of five years of occupation.

On her return to Moscow, she found the Russians even more hostile than before. They had no interest in helping her publish the story of the heroic Poles; they had no intention of assisting her in getting any more stories about the Soviet Union; Anna Louise's enthusiasm that the Poles were developing "their own form of socialism" met with no response. When Jessica Smith wrote to ask her for some articles on developments in Russia for *Soviet Russia Today,* she revealed the depths of her angry anxiety.

Dear Jessica:

This is . . . to let you know why you've not heard from me. . . . I've gone
sour. The suggestions in yours of December 8 sound good but impossible.
Trade unions: Gibbons tried for an interview with Kuznetsov, a personal
acquaintance, and the latter said: "With pleasure, but with the permission of
the press department." Interview was unreceived. Foreign trade: Ed Snow
came fresh from Roosevelt and tried two years to get anything at all from the
Foreign Trade Commissariat. He never got past the door. Interest in Americans? When 5,000 American doughboys, ex-prisoners, are spreading the news
how they wandered across Poland avoiding the Red Army because the Poles
were so much more hospitable. I see no hope of changing the quarantine on
intercourse, which the Soviets establish. The Russians want it. Now that many
press services close down disgruntled, the Russians who handle them are
merely relieved. Maybe they're right and any attempt at understanding is
really futile and the only final language is that of guns. Anyway, I've wasted
twenty years trying to spread common understanding, and . . . it doesn't
really seem to matter whether I live or die.

She was even more shaken by her trip to Yugoslavia that summer.
Yugoslavia alone among the East European countries had had a domestic
Communist resistance to the Nazis. Marshal Tito was a native hero *and* a
Communist. But the first night she was there, at the banquet in honor of
the newly arrived guests, the Soviet correspondent jumped to his feet
before the Yugoslav host could take his chair and proposed a toast to
"Stalin for the liberation of Europe." The more Anna Louise talked with
Yugoslavs, the more she discovered that they all thoroughly disliked the
Russians.

On August 6, just before her departure, she heard at a banquet given
by Marshal Tito that the United States had defeated Japan by exploding
an atom bomb over Hiroshima. She immediately expressed the fear that
the United States now seemed to hold an overwhelming military advantage in the postwar world and was not convinced by Tito's assurance that
the Americans would never use the bomb again. When she returned to
Moscow, there was a new mood of sullen anxiety among Russians. She
explained the hostility by looking toward America. On April 12, Franklin
Roosevelt had died. She thought Harry Truman "a man of far less wide
vision." With the declaration of the victory in Europe, Truman, to the
consternation of much of his staff, had put an immediate end to the lend-
lease program, even to the point of recalling ships already on their way
to Soviet ports. This was a severe blow to the U.S.S.R., whose economy
had been severely hit by the war. And, with a monopoly on atomic
bombs, some American advisors were openly talking about war between
the Soviet Union and the United States. Anna Louise's Russian friends

explained it to her and to themselves: "The (Russian) people feel cheated. They know that they suffered far greater losses than any other country in the joint war against Hitler, and they believed that they would get in return a long period of alliance and friendship with the West. Stalin also believed this and told us this."

Anna Louise again needed to get some distance from the Soviet Union, but regular routes between the U.S.S.R. and the United States had not yet opened up. While she waited, she wrote *I Saw the New Poland,* carefully skirting her misgivings about Russia, and with the help of Harry Hopkins, sent the manuscript off by diplomatic pouch in the late fall. She had a lecture tour scheduled for January and February 1946, but no way to get back to America.

Jessica Smith, who had arrived in Moscow in June, had also been trying to return to the States, and the two old acquaintances joined forces and managed to secure passage on the Soviet freighter *Minsk,* sailing on Christmas Eve from Poti on the Black Sea for Philadelphia. The two women were the only passengers and would be the first Americans to arrive in the United States by a Soviet vessel after the war. At first it was a pleasant trip, but as they approached the Straits of Gibraltar a fierce storm struck. Jessica had retired to the saloon when to her amazement she saw Anna Louise outside, slithering around the deck. Suddenly the boat was lifted on the crest of a wave, and as it plunged down into the next, a mountain of water broke over it. Captain Sariev managed to turn the boat into the wind and the *Minsk* rode more comfortably into the storm. Anna Louise came in from the deck, her eyes shining with excitement and pleasure. Jessica and the crew were aghast. The weather remained bad during the rest of the crossing, and the crew blamed it on "Poseidon's displeasure" at the presence of women aboard.

They were met at the docks by Stanley Salmen, Anna Louise's publisher at Little, Brown, by Jessica's husband, John Abt, and less visibly, by a host of anxious FBI agents. The bureau had found the name of Beria, head of the Soviet secret police, in Anna Louise's effects when she had left from Montana and were more convinced than ever that she was returning as an agent and courier of the NKVD. Since it was no longer wartime, restrictions on search procedures were stricter, and the FBI had to disguise its agents as customs officials who pretended that they thought Anna Louise and Jessica were carrying overly large amounts of American currency. Once more, nothing incriminating was found.

Anna Louise spent some time in New York getting her effects together, writing several articles and preparing for a nationwide tour. Before leaving, she spent an evening with Philip Jaffe and his wife, discussing what she should do next. Jaffe was still the editor of *Amerasia,* the most consistently informed and interesting periodical on China. The previous fall he had been indicted before a grand jury with the China Foreign Service officer John S. Service and four others for conspiring to publish confidential government documents. The case had been a political sensation. The grand jury refused indictments in three cases (including Service's); Jaffe had pleaded guilty with extenuating circumstances and received a fine of $2,500. Now he gave Anna Louise the details of the recent disastrous mission of U.S. Ambassador Patrick Hurley to Yenan, the Communist party headquarters, and suggested that after her lectures she return to China and send back articles to *Amerasia.*

The lecture tour was awful. Circulars from the American Legion and the Veterans of Foreign Wars preceded her, suggesting to her hosts that "you and other civic organizations get busy on this in an effort to defeat this Bolshevik who . . . has no business in this country. She and other underminers should be given a one-way ticket to Moscow and escorted by the FBI to the first boat." In some towns her opponents were successful in getting the lectures canceled; in others she was heckled. She insisted that Russia had no desire to dominate anyone else. "The Russians are tired, they are so tired. They care nothing for having other countries copy their government." She freely admitted problems in food, clothing and housing, but she responded with fiery hostility to any attacks on the motives of the U.S.S.R. At one talk, according to the FBI informants, she "became very excited and used strong language. She denounced [William Randolph] Hearst, congresswoman [Jeannette] Rankin, and made an inferential remark that the Bureau [of Investigation] helped to create misunderstanding of the Soviet Union through some of its investigations." She found herself so incensed at her treatment that on one occasion she barely stopped herself from proclaiming that Russia was her country.

Anna Louise was in a hurry to get out of America and back to China. Every delay increased her imperiousness, and she was even more insensitive than usual. Just before the end of her stay in New York, she ordered the American Russian Institute to send some one over to type. The young woman, Rose Lavoot, remembers:

"I timidly rang the bell . . . and stood trembling in the hallway. Suddenly the door opened and there stood this tall, imperious figure with the rattiest, tattiest fur coat I ever saw in my life in her hands. Are you the girl Bernie sent to type? Yes, I am. She thrust the coat into my hands and I thought she was going to tell me to throw it into an ashcan or give it to the first ill-clad mendicant I came upon. Again, that commanding voice: 'Take this out and have it cleaned and tell the man to be careful, as it is going on a long journey.' I swear the coat looked as if it had done the Long March standing up on its own. I must have approached a dozen furriers on 4th Avenue, all of whom looked at me with apprehension, expecting to see guards behind me coming to fetch me back to the state asylum, before I found one who accepted it. . . . She was so difficult to work with that I ran back to the Institute."

When Anna Louise reached the West Coast, she found that the only planes flying the Pacific were from the Naval Air Transport Service (NATS), and they took only military and diplomatic personnel. She made preliminary plans to take a train back to New York on June 13 and sail from there on a freighter to Leningrad, but she also approached some contacts in the State Department, filing a "statement of urgency" and announcing her intention to proceed to China to write articles dealing with the United Nations Relief and Rehabilitation Administration (UNRRA), the Red Cross, and American business. Her application asserted that her proposed trip was "in the national interest of the United States." The application was granted; on June 29, 1946, she boarded a NATS flight, and she arrived in Shanghai on July 6.

11

Yenan:
The City in the Hill

They were giants in Yenan.
Already they are shaking the land.
On hard earth at sundown
Mao pushed the tea cups on a table,
Moving nations into place.
On Saturday at the dance
Peanut shells were dropped under chairs,
Water drops froze on the floor
While everything danced:
Actors exulting in leaps.
Little devils kicking with youth,
The Russian doctor like a Cossack,
Chou with consummate grace,
Liu with sharp precision
And dialectical flings,
Chu Teh like man's long march,
Easy, rhythmic, tireless
Down the long hall of history.
But when Mao took the floor,
It gave time to the band,
And the same was not the same,
For we tuned to the stars in march,
And we whirled the earth like a spindle.

—Anna Louise Strong, Yenan, 1946

From Shanghai Anna Louise pressed on to Peiping, where her nephew
Robbins had returned the previous October with one of the first contin-
gents of missionaries. She stayed with him in the American Board Mission Compound at 28 Deng Shi K'ou street and immediately set up not
only a residence but also the headquarters of the Federated Press. The
more conservative members of the mission were quietly scandalized, but
charity prevailed, since few missionaries had yet returned and Anna

Louise was, after all, both the daughter and the aunt of Congregational ministers. While she was in Peiping, she went regularly to the Union Church on Sundays and sang all the verses of the hymns from memory.

The United States was the only foreign power playing an active role in China at this time, and both the Communists and the Nationalists found it important to keep on the good side of the Americans. In 1944 an American military observer mission, known as the Dixie Mission, had been established in the Communist-held territories, and provision made for frequent "observation" flights from Peiping to Communist headquarters in Yenan and thirty-seven other points in Communist-controlled territories. Transport for reporters was provided on a space-available basis. Since the American group had an official policy of neutrality, they could not deny passage to an accredited correspondent regardless of political affiliation. Anna Louise went quickly to Soong Ch'ing-ling, who made the necessary arrangements with the Communist party, and got passage on a flight to Yenan on July 31.

Almost all the buildings of Yenan, except miraculously the tall pagoda at the intersection of the Yen and South rivers, had been destroyed by Japanese bombing. Permanent residents had taken to caves, the traditional lodgings of Shensi peasants. When Anna Louise arrived at Whittelsey Hall, headquarters of the Dixie Mission, she was assigned her own cave, hollowed into the loess of the mountain side. A most comfortable residence, it was twelve feet wide, twenty feet deep and arched like a Quonset hut. The inner walls were neatly whitewashed, and rough homemade bricks covered the floor. The front wall, which was the entrance, was made of wooden lattice work held together by pegs. It was closed in the winter with paper and in the summer by mosquito netting. She loved its simplicity, cleanliness and efficiency.

Anna Louise realized that her access to American air transport gave her a singular opportunity. During the war against the Japanese, even the most intrepid reporters such as Edgar Snow had been able to penetrate only to Yenan. Now the Communists controlled twenty times the area and one hundred times the population that they had ten years before. But most Western reporters went only to one city. As long as she was able to avail herself of American airplanes, she could visit all the regions under Communist administration and provide a picture of the overall success of the Communist effort.

She spoke about her project to General Chu Teh immediately after her arrival and found him receptive. The military situation, he explained, was misleading to outsiders. Chiang appeared to be taking many previously liberated towns. But it was Communist strategy to give up these towns and exact a price in casualties and captured resources. "I have just exchanged seventeen towns for 60,000 men," he explained. "The KMT army is like a big ship, but we are like the sea. When the ship comes, it troubles the sea, but after, the sea flows back."

Chu Teh took her proposal to the central committee, which rapidly approved the project. They suggested that she stay in Yenan until the end of August, interviewing as many people as she could and getting a sense of the achievements in that area. Arrangements were made for an interview with an important member of the central committee whom she had not previously met. It was scheduled for August 5, but had to be postponed a day when a flash flood made the river impassable. In the late morning of August 6, Anna Louise boarded an auto-truck at the observers' compound. The vehicle slid down the muddy riverbank, picked its way between the boulders, and ascended the ravine on the other side to the "Yang Family Hill," Yang Jia Ling. Accompanied by two special interpreters, Lu Ting-yi, the chief of information at Yenan, and Dr. Ma Hai-teh (George Hatem), the Lebanese-American doctor who had worked with the Communists for almost fifteen years, she ascended a steep path between the corn stalks and tomato plants to find herself in front of the four caves of Mao Tse-tung, chairman of the Chinese Communist party.

Mao was waiting to meet the group, his small daughter clinging to his pant leg. He wore a dark-blue cotton suit with large patches on the knees. Anna Louise's first impressions were of "a large man, with the slow, massive but easy movements of a midwestern farmer" and an "elemental vitality directed by a deep but mobile intellectuality." He greeted his guests in such an unpretentious manner that Anna Louise overcame most of her nervousness. The group sat down on four low wooden stools around a table under an apple tree on the flat clay terrace. A hill rose up sharply behind the caves to the east and dropped just as sharply down to the valley that held the small plot in which Mao raised tobacco for his cigarettes.

Anna Louise began by asking about the prospects for a political settlement between the KMT and the Communists. "The American government will decide that," responded Mao. "If they give no more aid, Chiang will have to settle in six months to a year. By ourselves, we would not want to fight for even one day more, but if we have to, we can fight for as long as fighting goes on. Others want to kill us, so we defend. Anyone can understand that." She moved to the source of Communist success, their policies of land reform in agricultural areas. "The peasants want to realize the slogan of Sun Yat-sen," Mao told her, "that the tiller should have the land. Our demand to partition the landlords' land is proper. We make a difference between traitors, bad gentry, and middle and small landlords. We are more severe to the first, gentle to the others. We do leave all landlords with a livelihood and are considering an agrarian bond issue to buy out landlords over the years. The peasant could then buy the land with government aid and guarantee."

From land reform the talk shifted back to international relations. Mao emphasized that it was a mistake to see the hostility between the United States and the U.S.S.R. as the most important aspect of world politics. "The mood of American reactionaries is very like that of Hitler and Japan [before World War II]. They use anti-Soviet talk as a pretext, but only a pretext. Their claims about the danger of war with the Soviet Union are just a smoke screen under which America hopes to control all the rest of the capitalist world. America can do nothing harmful now to the Soviet Union, but only to the other capitalist nations." Mao illustrated his point on the table: "Here are the American reactionaries." He placed a large teacup at one side of the table. "Around them are first the American people." A ring of little wine cups was set into place. "Now here is the U.S.S.R." A cup at the other side of the table. "Between the U.S.S.R. and the American imperialists are all the other capitalist nations." Mao laughed with pleasure at his conceit as he lined up cups of all sizes and surrounded them with matches and cigarettes. "Now, how could the American imperialists fight with the Soviet Union? First of all, they have to attack the American people. The people do not want war. Already the American reactionaries attack the American people, breaking the price controls and dumping American goods in foreign markets when the American people could use these goods themselves. To make war on the U.S.S.R., the reactionaries would have to attack the American people very much harder. They would have to introduce fascism in America. Without a fascist system holding down the American people, a third world war is impossible."

Conscious that this was the first anniversary of the dropping of the atomic bomb on Hiroshima, Anna Louise asked: "Can't the Americans attack Russia directly from their bases in England, Okinawa and China with the atom bomb?" Mao replied: "It is quite true that these bases can be used against the U.S.S.R. But the first people oppressed by America are not the Russians, but the people of all other capitalist countries. The broad masses of these countries do not like this and will resist." Mao sat back and concluded with a large grin: "American reactionaries are merely a"—he searched for a word—"*chih lao-hu*." "Straw man," translated Lu, looking for an equivalent. Anna Louise was perplexed: "Scarecrow?" Dr. Ma caught the difference. "No," he interjected, "not a *tao ts'ao jen*, but *chih lao-hu*, a paper tiger."

"Quite right," said Mao. "A paper tiger is not something dead stuck in a field. It scares children; it is made to look like a dangerous beast." Mao chuckled, perhaps because the only use for paper tigers in Chinese culture is to send prayers to heaven. "All reactionaries are paper tigers. Terrible to look at, but melting when the rains come. In the long view, the power is with the people. Chiang Kai-shek—paper tiger." He said the last words in English and laughed at his terrible pronunciation. "How do you like my theory?"

The evening was approaching. A noise on the hill startled Anna Louise. Neighboring children had gathered to see the tall foreign woman. Mao suggested that she switch places with him so that the children might have a better view of her. She complied and remarked to Dr. Ma the irony that in Yenan a western reporter was a more interesting attraction than the chairman himself. As they started to resume their talk, Chiang Ch'ing, Mao's young wife, came out with more tea and an invitation to dinner. The meal was to be served at the Date Garden, some five kilometers up the river, near where Chu Teh lived. Mao suggested they continue their talk there.

Supper was mainly tomatoes and other vegetables, followed by a special dessert, "eight treasures rice." Because of the paucity of treasure in Yenan, however, only four ingredients had been added: plums, walnuts, dates and peanuts. The dessert was a gesture of respect to Anna Louise, for all rice had to be imported to Yenan from the liberated areas along the Yangtze River. "We southerners found the millet diet of this northern region difficult when we came here twelve years ago," Mao remarked as they talked of the history of Yenan in recent years.

Anna Louise returned to the question of the atomic bomb: "The Americans can bomb any city in Russia." Mao laughed: "The U.S.S.R. is a large country; at Bikini they did not even kill all the pigs. Communists really have power. We are millet plus rifle. Millet plus rifle is stronger than cannon or airplane bombs." Anna Louise understood that Mao was not being naive about the power of the new weapons. He knew that many Communists and other progressives were convinced that the power of the bomb in American hands had totally changed the course of history and given the reactionaries an invincible strength. Stalin himself was urging the Chinese Communists to reduce the level of hostilities between them and the KMT for fear America might use the bomb against China or even the Soviet Union. Mao wanted to stamp out such defeatism in China, and even more important, indicate to Stalin that the Chinese party not only disagreed but would not comply with his suggestion that they stop any possible advances at the Yangtze.

The conversation continued late into the night. Finally Mao and Anna Louise agreed to meet again in a few weeks. Bright stars shone over the wild hills as Mao escorted Anna Louise to a horse that was led over the rocky path to the waiting truck.

In Yenan, Anna Louise was happier than she could ever remember being. There was constant work but without the tyranny of deadlines. Except for an occasional bombing mission by KMT planes, which Anna Louise would rush out to see, there was little to distract her. She settled into relaxed concentration: "There was no sense of hurry in Yenan. There was a sense of the ages, of time and space. There was a sense of the earth and the slow rhythm of the seasons, of the wide difficult expanse of the Chinese land and the wheeling of the sun above it, bringing seedtime and harvest. . . . So Yenan, despite the war, . . . [was] . . . a haven of peace."

Anna Louise traveled around the county, talking with agricultural workers at Nan Ni-wan, the farm that had been carved out of barren hillside; with doctors and nurses; with teachers at the Academy of Marxism-Leninism; with actors and actresses at the Yenan School of the Performing Arts. There were orchestra concerts, plays by Ts'ao Yü, Lu Shun, and other major playwrights, lectures, and constant discussions. A daily newspaper in Chinese and a weekly one in English kept everyone informed about local and international news. The Communists not only lived in Yenan but had transformed a backward Chinese town into a complex, thriving culture. All her life Anna Louise had wanted to live in a place like this one.

When she was not investigating the institutions of Yenan, she interviewed party leaders about Chinese Communism. Over three days, Lu Ting-yi gave her a long and complex history of the Chinese Communist party, emphasizing its peculiarly Chinese nature and ending with the claim that "Mao applies the universal truth of Marxism-Leninism to the special conflict in China. None of his policies is either copied from certain books or based on personal experiences. . . . Mao's method of thinking opposes both dogmatism and empiricism. He advocates a study of theory as well as the dictum 'There is no right to speak without fact finding.' " The emphasis on the Chinese nature of the revolution was further developed by Liu Shao-ch'i, whom Anna Louise saw as "the most brilliant party theoretician after Mao." He told her that by bringing peasants into the revolution Mao had changed Marxism "from a European to an Asiatic form." To illustrate, Liu pointed to the "little devil," as young messenger boys were called, who brought them peanuts. "He knows that peanuts are only for guests and for birthday parties. It never occurs to him to ask for them, or for any wages. . . . And he is happy because he is a comrade among comrades and is fighting for a better China. We have no industrial workers in China to create communism, but we have some millions of kids like this, and their discipline and devotion are perhaps better than that of industrial workers. . . . Class consciousness is very strong in them. Such people were never known by Marx."

The Chinese were advancing bold theses challenging the right of the Soviet party to dictate policy to Communist parties in other countries, and they hoped that Anna Louise would take these to the outside world and perhaps convince the United States to differentiate between various forms of communism. Liu concluded by citing to her Mao's judgment on unthinking adherence to theory drawn from other circumstances: "We ought to tell them that their dogmas are absolutely useless, more useless than cow dung. For dung can be used, while dogmas cannot."

Anna Louise was gleeful. The Chinese approach to agrarian reform seemed to avoid the excesses in Russia about which she had had to keep her peace in the 1930s. Pragmatism had attracted her since her college days. Trotsky had taught her the value of the concept of separate paths to socialism. Here in China was precisely what she had felt lacking in American Communism, the justification for building an authentically *American* movement. She wrote an ebullient five-page letter to Angus Cameron at Little, Brown:

> I'm thinking of staying [in Yenan] all winter. . . . This crowd is Asia's unbeatable bunch! They will be here when Chiang is ashes. . . . To me the chief attraction that makes me want to . . . face a winter here in my cave is the "love for the people" that emanates from most of the people you interview. . . . To talk with them is to feel warm and caressed.

Shortly before leaving Yenan to explore other liberated areas, she had another long talk with Mao. Since their first conversation, the United States had given close to a billion dollars in new war supplies to Chiang. Mao was openly angry and disappointed. Anna Louise asked him if the party was worried. "Not really," he answered. "We have liquidated fourteen brigades of the Kuomintang during the month of your stay in Yenan.

. . . There is a sort of blood transfusion from the United States to Chiang. But then this is again transfused from Chiang to us. Chiang gets supplies from America, and we must depend on acquiring these supplies. We lose some men, but then the soldiers of Chiang take their places." Mao spoke now with heavy irony and occasional biting laughter. "A soldier of Chiang is today captured and disarmed. Tomorrow he is fighting on our side. This is the dialectic." Mao continued sadly: "It is very strange, this war. . . . For twenty years all things have come from the enemy."

Fully expecting the answer to be no, Anna Louise asked if it were now possible for the Communists to be beaten. "This depends on how well we solve the agrarian question," Mao answered to her surprise. "If millions of peasants get land and are eager to defend their land . . ." He trailed off, then resumed. "We may loose Ch'eng-te, Harbin, the seaports in Shantung province, even Kalgan. But the agrarian question will be decisive."

Mao then returned to the focus of their first interview. The decision by America to fortify Chiang was a sign that "the imperialists have made their own decision. It is to make us a colony by means of Chiang." Mao foresaw a possibility that if Chiang were unable to deliver what the Americans wanted, they might intervene directly. But that would be "a heavy burden for American imperialism, since they were increasingly obliged to maintain all the reactionaries of the world. The skyscraper is higher, but the foundation is smaller," Mao argued. "The day of the atom bomb's birth is the day on which the end of American imperialism begins . . . because imperialism depends on the bomb and not on the people. . . . Whoever depends on the people wants to make peace." He continued with an analysis of the treacherous instrumentality of technology: "Who depends on the bomb, wants war. Thus grows the antagonism between imperialism and the people. The bomb will not annihilate the people. The only end will be that the people annihilate the bomb."

Anna Louise wrote up her notes from the two interviews and left a copy with Lu Ting-yi, "to have it checked for political accuracy," asking that the corrected version be in Peiping on the September 21st plane. On September 11 she left for a tour through Northeastern China. Her daily dispatches made their way back to more than a dozen American newspapers, ranging from the *People's World* to the *St. Louis Post Dispatch*. Everywhere she went, she found the people unworried about Nationalist attacks, and she noted surprisingly little disruption of Communist communication lines. She amassed a large amount of information on land redistribution, on the successes and failures of agrarian policies, and the changing status of peasants, especially women. In Han-tan, she suggested to the local administrators that KMT officials were so notoriously corrupt because their salaries were too low. This produced a heavy laugh. "No, no. Any official in the KMT who does his work correctly and is honest would be called a Communist."

In Kalgan, one of the first major cities to come under Communist control, she reencountered two old acquaintances, the writer and director Ting Ling, whom she had not seen since 1938, and Sidney Rittenberg, who had been working for UNRRA. Sidney told her that UNRRA was in such chaos that he had quit and come to Kalgan with Mildred Price, the director of the China Aid Council and a fellow North Carolinian. He was hoping to get to Yenan. Anna Louise saw a solution to some of her problems. Rittenberg's politics appeared good and "he speaks and reads Chinese like Confucius." He could be her collaborator. She sent a letter to Chu Teh asking if she might bring Rittenberg back to help her. Permission was granted. Rittenberg, however, was not a correspondent and would have to travel as the Chinese did, across the land. Furnished with a paper that proclaimed him a "friend of the Chinese people," he set out on the four-week trek.

Anna Louise had to leave Kalgan hurriedly because of a sudden attack by Nationalist troops. She made two stops in Inner Mongolia, at Harbin and Tsitsihar, where all those she spoke with confirmed, sometimes bitterly, that the Rusians had provided the People's Army with no assistance, "not even one bullet," and went on to Tsingtao in Shantung Province, where most American troops were concentrated. In the hope of finding out "what the Americans think they are doing," she attended a ball at the navy base. She found that the Americans' expectations paralleled her own: a number of young officers connected with intelligence operations persistently sought her out and punctuated their dancing with pointed questions about Communist plans. Finally Anna Louise stopped in the middle of one dance and with good humor said: "Young man, do you know whom you are talking with?" "Of course," her partner assured her. "Well," she responded, "let me tell you, I do too."

She stopped for a few days in Peiping during the last week of October to visit Robbins and to do some shopping: a dress for Mao's daughter, cigarettes and Oh Henry! bars for Lu Ting-yi and Huang Hua, and candies for all the children. Just before she left, she met with a Catholic priest and some American high military officials. They were much concerned about the fate of the missionaries in liberated areas. Anna Louise knew of some cases where missionaries had been imprisoned and admitted hearing of much worse; she suggested that it might be useful to station a representative of the National Christian Council in Yenan. Robbins volunteered to take up the project with the council, and Anna Louise said that she would raise it with Huang Hua.

She did so as soon as she got back, and Huang Hua promised to investigate. She then turned to her own plans. Two projects occupied her time now. She was determined to maintain communications between Yenan and America. She had arranged with Evans Carlson and Congressman Hugh De Lacey for the distribution of news in the United States, but since she would not remain in Yenan for too much longer, she required a dependable English-speaking person who would assure regular radio contact. She turned to Sidney Rittenberg, who had arrived just before her and was now working with the information bureau and the radio service. She explained to him that the recent appointment of John Leighton Stuart as U.S. ambassador to China was likely to cause difficulties not only for those Americans who were trying to maintain some balance between the CCP and the KMT but also for the free flow of news. "They may withdraw . . . privileges from correspondents or from anyone in Yenan," Anna Louise told Sidney. "They may even stop the Yenan plane." She elicited his promise to continue transmitting news from Yenan over assigned frequencies to the United States, no matter where she was.

Rittenberg was somewhat surprised at what Anna Louise expected of him and was even more taken aback when she informed him of the second project with which he was to help her. The central committee had already approved her writing a biography of Mao, to be issued together with a companion book of excerpts from Mao's writings. Sidney demurred a bit, wary of getting in above his head. Anna Louise was annoyed. "If you work with me, I will list you as a collaborator; if you don't, I won't mention you. Furthermore," she said, half smiling, "you will never get another Oh Henry!" Anna Louise showed him the case of candy bars she had brought back with her. As the sole source of chocolate in Yenan, she was very convincing.

She was determined to be left out of nothing. When she found out that a gathering had been scheduled for the night of October 30 to which she had not been invited, she confronted her guide Ling Ch'ing and insisted she be included, in what she was not sure. Ling looked embarrassed and finally told her that the occasion was the sixtieth birthday party of the commander in chief, Chu Teh. "Well, I want to come," retorted Anna Louise. Ling, who had endured much from Anna Louise, said he would do what he could. The following day a crimson invitation card beautifully engraved with gold lettering appeared, addressed to Anna Louise.

The party was an unusually merry affair, enhanced by many toasts to the quality of life in Yenan. During the course of the party, Anna Louise expressed to Mao her joy at "how restful" it was in Yenan. "Indeed," Mao agreed. "Look at Chu Teh. He has spent many winters here. He is the same age as Chiang Kai-shek, but Chiang's hair is all white, and Chu Teh has only a few gray hairs." Anna Louise rose to the bait. "But Chiang sits easily in Nanking, while Chu Teh lives in a cave." "I do not think that Chiang sits so easily," Mao retorted smiling.

The gaiety of the party was short-lived. KMT attacks increased, and the Nationalists retook towns of symbolic importance. It was apparent that Yenan would soon become a target. On November 16 word came that Chou En-lai had informed General George C. Marshall in Nanking that he saw no point in continuing the peace talks and asked to go back to Yenan. To Anna Louise's distress, Chou had little time for her on his return. Finally, knowing his love for cards, she sent an invitation for bridge. It was turned down with "soon." A subsequent invitation received the same answer. Anna Louise took matters into her own hands.

Shortly after dark, she set out to walk to the Date Garden, some three miles up the Yen River. Ling Ch'ing, who had remained assigned to her as translator and guide, watched aghast as she made her way up the rocky riverbed. He had been given strict orders never to let her go anywhere by herself, especially on foot. But he was also prudent enough not to risk trying to stop her.

Determined to find out what was keeping Chou away, Anna Louise arrived at the large meeting hall in the Date Garden, brushed past a set of astonished guards and entered the main room. The eyes of the entire central committee of the Chinese Communist party turned toward the intruder. Anna Louise stopped, suddenly realizing where she was, and blurted out something about wanting to see Chou En-lai. With a smile Chou stepped down from the dais on which the group was gathered and escorted her back out into the night. "Anna Louise," he said, speaking as one might to a bright child who had overstepped her bounds, "you are right that there are important matters going on. But I have spoken with you three times since I have been back. We must settle these questions now, in the party. When they are over, I will speak with you. Until then, leave me alone." And he proceeded, as Anna Louise later told Sidney with proud tears in her eyes, "to scold me. He actually scolded me."

Chou kept his promise. A few days later, he met with her, Dr. Ma and

Sidney over supper and informed them of the central committee's decision. Yenan would be abandoned if the attack came. The party believed that Chiang's attacks would dangerously overextend the Nationalists. The Red Army would not return to guerrilla warfare; all that was necessary was to wait until the Nationalists made themselves an indefensible target. Liu Shao-ch'i had remarked, Chou reported, that if Chiang attacked, Yenan would become his Stalingrad. Now, Anna Louise suggested, it was time to play bridge. To her disappointment, Chou and Dr. Ma took two out of three rubbers from her and Sidney. For the second time in a week she pouted all the way back to her cave.

As the winter came on, almost all other foreigners departed; the only new arrival was Jack Chen. Life settled into a comfortable routine. Anna Louise moved to a cave high on Radio Hill where she had "a view down three valleys that was breathtaking at night when there was a full moon." Her requests for interviews and even assistance in typing were met quickly. Walking one day with Chou and Sidney, Chou marveled to her: "Look at us! Chiang can't go outdoors without an army. Can Truman?" Anna Louise was not sure if he could, but knew that he didn't. The question pushed her to reflect on the difference between China and the U.S.S.R. "That is what really worries me about Moscow. It is more and more undemocratic and bureaucratic," she confided, "not the direction they ought to be going in. I never feel as free in Moscow as I do in Yenan. As long as I have been in the U.S.S.R.—they don't talk with me at all." "Who doesn't?" Chou asked. "No one in the leadership. I never see them, but I see all of you," answered Anna Louise.

She did see them all, and not just for interviews. On Saturday nights almost everyone gathered in either the Date Garden or Yang Jia Ling for a dance. Only the Liaison group was never told about the occasions. The orchestra was mainly brass and percussion, played by musicians from the academy, augmented by classical Chinese instruments such as the pipa. As she danced with Chou, Mao and the others, Anna Louise spun an extended conceit about the similarities between the dancing styles of the leaders and their approaches to policy. Chou danced the waltz with elegant perfection in black slippers brought back from Nanking. Liu Shao-ch'i had a mathematical precision which, just when it threatened to become "too arithmetically exact," would swing into higher mathematics with "a few exciting flings." Chu Teh danced as if he were on the Long March and could keep his partner going even if she were too tired to stand. Mao spent much time discussing dances with the drummer, as if to set the beat; he would then dance to a rhythm all his own, which nevertheless usually came out right. Eventually, however, the percussion player rebelled and said that Mao was interfering with his work.

As the winter wore on, Anna Louise wrote up the "paper tiger" interview and "The Thought of Mao Tse-tung" and turned the articles over to Lu Ting-yi for political editing. The article on Mao's thought caused special excitement: it was the first serious attention a foreigner had paid to Mao's theoretical contribution to Marxism. It was translated into Chinese and extensively worked over by a number of high party officials, then translated back into a text Anna Louise could publish after she left Yenan. Her Chinese friends found her a quick and sympathetic pupil and continued to emphasize to her the differences between Mao and Russian theorists.

Toward the end of January 1947, Anna Louise had another long formal interview with Mao. The KMT push on Yenan had materialized, and plans were being made to evacuate the city. Mao spent most of the session giving Anna Louise statistics about the situation of the Red Army and assurances of ultimate victory. "Chiang gets impatient now," Mao told her. "That's why he occupied Kalgan and Chefoo and now prepares to attack Yenan. He has to send troops into no-man's-land. This [Yenan] is no strategic or economic center. He wants to occupy the place where the central committee is so he can tell the nation that 'the Communists are finished.' That way they will feel reassured. But even if we leave Yenan, the fight will go on the same way. If you ask which is better, to keep or to leave Yenan, it is better to keep it. But if we leave it, we are still all right." "When will the attack come?" Anna Louise asked anxiously. Mao told her that it depended on how long it took the KMT to complete their troop movements and bring up grain and ammunition. "How long?" she persisted. "Between ten days and two weeks," said Mao.

Over the next week the evacuation of Yenan began in earnest. First to go were the sick and the children. The road from the hospital was filled with a pack train of donkeys carrying on each side cribs lined with sheepskin. The seriously ill were carried on stretchers borne by four men: the hospital caves that had contained 180 patients stood empty by the end of the first week. The people of the region also moved out; peasants took grain stocks farther into the hills. It was, Anna Louise told George Ma, "the most orderly evacuation" she had ever seen or heard of. "Everyone seemed sure that they would return one day."

As Anna Louise saw the inhabitants of Yenan move into the sea of the countryside, she knew that she wanted to go with them. She spoke to Lu

Ting-yi, who told her the journey would involve too much strenuous walking. It was generally known that Dr. Ma had to massage Anna Louise's swollen legs after the Saturday nights of strenuous dancing. Unwilling to accept Lu's verdict, on each of the next three days she walked the five miles from Radio Hill to the Date Garden to show that she could do it. Then she went back to tell Lu of her stamina. He reminded her that Mao wanted her to carry important information to the world. Anna Louise demurred; she was not that important. "I want to go with the troops," she pleaded. "I'll ride a mule, walk, crawl—anything, but don't send me away." The next day she saw Chu Teh and Chou En-lai. They told her again of the arduousness of the journey ahead, and Chou, knowing her weaknesses, added that there would be vermin and no baths. She was still determined to go with the troops.

That evening Chou invited her to his cave for dinner with the other foreigners in Yenan—George Ma, Sidney Rittenberg, and Sid Engst. Chu Teh and then Mao arrived; they all sat down to eat around the large table. Mao and Anna Louise did most of the talking during dinner, discoursing on the international situation and the sins of the KMT. After dinner, Mao excused himself and Chu Teh turned to the subject on everyone's mind. "You have all asked to stay; we have decided that all of you may, except Anna Louise. George has business for us in Peiping and will escort her there." The tears trembled in Anna Louise's eyes. Chu turned sympathetically to her. "I am a soldier," he said. "Rittenberg and Engst are young. You are older even than George. But more importantly, your job is to be a writer. The troops will be constantly on the move with no place to settle into. You will not be able to write under those conditions, nor get anything published."

Anna Louise started to cry. Both Chu and Chou tried to comfort her. Chou assured her that Mao would give her important material that only she could publicize successfully. Tearfully she said that she understood: "It is better for all if I go?" Obviously affected by the strength of her emotion, they reassured her once again.

It was not until the next afternoon, when Engst came over to say hello, that she was her buoyant self again. "What would an old lady like me do out in the country," she said pointing at her swollen legs. "Besides, Chou told me there would be bedbugs and lice out there, and if there is anything I can't stand, it's being filthy."

On the evening before she was to leave Yenan, she was invited to a farewell interview with Chairman Mao after a performance of opera theater in Yang Jia Ling, a sentimental farewell in a spot which had been a source of much happiness. Anna Louise was given a seat in the front row beside the leading members of the party. It was bitter cold, and the crowd shivered despite padded clothing and the charcoal braziers set between the front row and the stage. After the performance, Anna Louise went with Chou and Mao to one of the caves—one was as good as another since almost everyone had moved out. Chou gave her a pamphlet called "A Decision on Some Problems in the History of the Party"; it detailed Mao's arguments for national Communist parties. Mao then gave her the "Economic and Financial Report of the Border Regions," which recounted the successful policies employed, and asked her to take both documents to the world Communist parties. He was especially concerned that she show them to party leaders in the United States and Eastern Europe. Mao added that he did not think that it was necessary for her to take them to Moscow. She could return to China "when we again have contact with the world, in about two years."

And then, suddenly, it was no longer an interview. Mao began to give her orders as how best to convey the situation of the Communists. If the question of "so-called atrocities is raised," he said, "try to convince them that our army is one of the most disciplined in the world. Of course there are cases, but that is often because of the bias of those reporting them." Should Anna Louise speak with Communists, "tell them that the CCP *must* win and that American imperialism and Chiang *can be beaten*." Mao reemphasized the point: "This is important. Many people think that we can't win. They say that the war will be protracted and that nobody can win. This is not true. If you talk with Communist parties, say that Mao says this. If you speak to others, say it for yourself."

"Tell the Americans," he said, "that the strength of the democratic groups is not too small. . . . They can beat the reactionaries. Tell the British not to overestimate the strength of American imperialism. Americans and British have a psychological weakness about their opponents. In Europe there is not this psychological weakness." He concluded with a discussion of the atomic bomb again. "It is finished. Foolish people still talk of it, but it will never be used. Its bursting in Japan destroyed it, for the whole world turned against it. Atomic energy will be handed over to the people, but the atomic bomb has finished its life."

Anna Louise left Yenan on February 14, 1947, and went immediately from Peiping to Shanghai. She took a room at the Broadway Mansions and started to try to implement Mao's directives. She cabled the Committee for a Democratic Far Eastern Policy (CDFEP) in New York with the news that she had the latest information from Yenan and other liber-

ated areas and asked them to set up at least three big lectures in San
Francisco, Chicago and New York to cover the price of her plane fare
home. The committee was an group of progressives, including some
Communists, and was sympathetic to the Chinese Communists rather
than to the KMT. Her old friend Israel Epstein was a major force in the
committee; the executive secretary was Maud Russell. Both had had
extensive experience in the Far East. During the next few days no telegraph response came, so Anna Louise settled into the life of Shanghai
and started to write her book on Yenan.

In early 1947 American troops constituted a de facto army of occupation in Shanghai. Automobiles full of American soldiers sped down the
crowded streets with little regard for the safety of rickshaw boys and cart
pullers. Those few Chinese students who came to visit Anna Louise were
immediately picked up by Chiang's police, even though only KMT true
believers still thought that the Nationalists were ultimately going to win.
Anna Louise became a center of attention, especially for the foreign
journalists, because her recent travels and contacts provided more interesting news than anyone else had. She would come down to the correspondents' bar in an extravagant Chinese silk gown and take over one
side of the room with a knowledgeable discourse on the development of
Communist military strategy. At moments during the night, if music was
playing, she would announce that she "wanted to do a dance," and would
then, without a partner, command a central portion of the floor.

Until the Communists finally left Yenan, around the fourteenth of
March, occasional news came through. Chou En-lai sent her the transcript of an interview he had with W. H. Newton from the Scripps-
Howard papers, asking her to be on the lookout for its publication and to
check it against the transcript he had agreed on with Howard. Huang
Hua, to whom she had expressed anxieties about Communist treatment
of missionaries in liberated areas, wrote assuring her that the problems
were related to "old disputes between the missionary (in question) and
the local people over numerous matters." Ma Hai-teh informed her that
"just the other morning Mrs. Mao was talking about you with fondness.
She says as soon as things quiet down you must come here again and stay
permanently. All the comrades here have you always in mind and constantly mention you."

Shanghai was the center of UNRRA, and representatives from many
countries were curious about the Chinese Communists. Soon they were
coming to Anna Louise. Her writing and what she had to say was sent
back to India, Southeast Asia, the Philippines and Japan as well as into

Europe. Anna Louise talked to anyone who came by about her experiences in Yenan; among those most interested was John Leighton Stuart, the American ambassador to China and the past president of Yenching University.

Anna Louise agreed to his request for a meeting because she still believed that a considerable body of American opinion, both inside and outside the government, had respect for the quality of the Chinese Communists. Stuart, however, had not the slightest interest in anything about Yenan but only wanted to reach the Communist leaders in order to "negotiate peace." He was especially disturbed that the Communists had vanished into the hills, leaving him no way to contact them. Anna Louise suggested to him that he announce in the press that he wanted to negotiate; they would surely hear of it. This seemed not to be what was in his mind. Then she asked: "What kind of negotiation? Does the fighting continue or does it stop while you talk?" He seemed not to have thought about this. Finally he told her that he would insist on an armistice during negotiations. Anna Louise told him that this would not be possible. "Look at the situation," she said. "All over North China and into the Northeast, Chiang's troops are holding the fortified cities. The American airlift carried them there and installed them there. All around them in the countryside the peasants are on the side of the Communists; they are fighting Chiang's troops when these come out to loot. Now you want a cease-fire. Are Chiang's troops expected to eat during the cease-fire or to go without food? If they want food, is the American air force going to take it to them by airlift, or will they go out to get it from the peasants? If they go get it from the peasants, will the peasants give it or resist? You can't stop fighting in a situation like that."

Stuart refused to see the force of Anna Louise's logic. She found it strange and sad that a man who had lived in China all his life should be unable to comprehend what seemed to her simple facts. But he had at least expressed an interest in the problem. Thus she was surprised and distressed by the airmail letter that came back from Epstein at the CDFEP. No one cared about China, he said; she had better return through Moscow and set up a winter lecture tour about the U.S.S.R. at more moderate fees. She decided instead to remain in Shanghai and complete her work on the liberated areas; she had found a first publisher for it in India through the efforts of M. N. Roy, who had not forgotten her since their first meeting in Hankow in 1927.

She expressed but one note of caution in her enthusiasm for her experience in Yenan. When her nephew Robbins came through Shanghai on his way back to the United States, she conveyed to him Huang Hua's assurance that the Christian churches in the liberated areas were not being oppressed. Robbins put her in touch with Plummer Mills, a secretary of the North China Council of Churches who was close to Leighton Stuart and General Marshall. After some talk in a hotel overlooking the bund, the three agreed that their hopes and dreams for China were similar. Mills began to share with Anna Louise more of the information he had from Stuart and Marshall on the difficulties churches were having in the liberated areas. It was not very pretty, and Anna Louise admitted the truth in these reports. Then she began to tell of the atmosphere that existed in Yenan, of the down-to-earth camaraderie and simplicity. Mills in turn acknowledged the truth of what she was saying about the mood and hopes of the Communists. After he left, Anna Louise and her nephew sat in silence for a long while. Finally she remarked: "He is an honest man, and what he says about the conditions in the Communist-controlled rural areas is true. But when I am in Yenan, it is so wonderful and so beautiful, and that also is true. You know, I don't know what I believe."

No sign of these hesitations appeared in *Dawn over China*. After she finished it in May she made reservations for a flight back to the United States, but shortly before her planned departure, word came from the Soviet consul that a casual request a month before to visit North Korea had been approved, and she might return via that route. After a further delay until the middle of July, she boarded the Soviet freighter *Ilytch*, bound from Shanghai to Vladivostok.

12

Arrest in Russia

Was it in *Pilgrim's Progress* or where, that it was seen that
from the gates of paradise, the descent is very straight and
direct to hell?

—Anna Louise to Madame Maurette, May 17, 1949

Free-lancing doesn't work any more in a rapidly integrating
world. Because I liked shortcuts, I didn't see to it that I had a
firm base in my land and deep roots. . . . I cut over the world's
frontiers armed solely in my self-righteousness.

—Anna Louise to Emily Pierson, September 9, 1949

The journey did not start well. Instead of proceeding directly to Vladivostok, the ship went due north to Dairen to pick up a group of Russians
leaving Mongolia, then retraced its steps southward, circumnavigating
Korea. When Anna Louise reached Vladivostok, she had to be hospital-
ized for recurrent dysentery.

During the month she spent exploring North Korea and lecturing to
Korean cadres on Mao's vision of Communism, her anxiety to publicize
the achievements of Chinese Communism rose sharply. In *Red Star*, the
Soviet army newspaper, she read an article entitled "Two Years of China's
Civil War." The final sentence sounded a knell for the "unhappy evacuation" of Yenan and the defeat of the Chinese Communists. The writer
had not the slightest understanding of the elaborate strategy that Mao
and the others had detailed to Anna Louise. "They are still caught in the
Stalingrad mentality," she concluded. "Sacrifice thousands to save every
inch of territory." Despite Mao's suggestion that she stay away from the
Soviets, she vowed to tell them the reality of the situation in China.

In Moscow she moved back into the room Joel's sisters kept for her in
the apartment. Publicizing the achievements of the Chinese Communists
did not prove easy. A letter to Foreign Minister Maxim Litvinov, the old

friend who had helped her after she had learned of Joel's death, went unanswered. The foreign editors of both *Pravda* and *Izvestia* were very much interested in her material about Chinese military strategy and economics—until they talked with their editors-in-chief. She finally placed a few articles in the *Literaturnaya gazeta,* a literary newspaper that often served as a kind of *salon des refusés* for newsworthy items that were on a tangent to official policy. Three weeks later she found out that her articles were the first mention the Soviet press had made in months of Mao Tse-tung.

She discovered the official Soviet view when a student from a diplomatic school called on her stepdaughter. He spoke slightingly of the Chinese as "having failed." Anna Louise hastened to assure him that this was not the case. "Oh no?" he replied. "They have lost all their capitals." Anna Louise retorted that they had done it on purpose. "They can't win," the young man reiterated, "they have no industry and no proletariat."

Anna Louise took her manuscript to Borodin. Still the head of the *Moscow Daily News,* he was also an associate editor at the Soviet Information Bureau, which sent out propaganda to central Europe. As surviving dean of Soviet China hands, he was eager to see her material and pleased with what she reported. He suggested that she rearrange the account about to be published in India as *Dawn over China* so as to make the international element more prominent. In directing her to a publisher, Mikhail mentioned casually that "some editing" was needed, "to save your reputation in Russia."

Anna Louise rewrote the book quickly, but the publishing house was slow to commit itself. By late October she was so frustrated that she decided to explore possibilities in Eastern Europe. In Poland and Czechoslovakia top party leaders eagerly attended her seminar on the "creativity" of Chinese Communist theory. Presses in Prague, Warsaw, Budapest, Belgrade and Berlin as well as publishers in Paris and Rome accepted her book. She returned to Moscow "with a sense of triumph," ready for a showdown with the Soviet publisher.

The editor continued to express interest but would not sign a contract. Again, he wanted a "few more changes." Anna Louise blew up. "I'm leaving for America," she screamed. "I haven't time to keep rewriting. If there is anything you don't want to publish in my book, I give you permission to cut it out. I do not permit you to change anything or add anything I haven't said. Publish the part you like, if you like any of it." He inquired if she would make the same changes in the other editions. "Certainly not," she shot back. "You may tell them what changes you make; but I will not impose your changes on other publishers whose editions may already be in type." The editor was silent.

She left Russia the third week of November 1947 and proceeded directly to Paris, where she located the chief representatives of the Chinese Communists—Liu Ning-yi, delegate to the trade unions; Ch'en Chia-k'ang, the delegate from the youth organizations; and Lu Ts'ui from the women's organization. They met for dinner on New Year's Eve in a Chinese restaurant and reminisced happily about the heady days in Yenan. As the meal drew to an end, Liu switched to his official voice; Chou En-lai had told him just before his departure for Paris that events were "moving faster than expected" and all the party leadership agreed that Anna Louise could make plans to return to China in the near future. Anna Louise was overjoyed; the conversation immediately turned to the most appropriate route. Two possibilities existed: through Hong Kong and Nationalist China, or overland, through Russia to Manchuria. Liu thought that she should go through Moscow because there was much to report on in liberated Manchuria. She could move south with the armies of Lin Piao as the Communists came closer to victory. Furthermore, Liu added, once she arrived she could take charge of an English edition of Mao's works.

This was more than she had hoped for. Anna Louise's hesitant reply that she would be limited by her lack of facility in Chinese was dismissed. Liu assured her that she could discuss the text with excellent translators and that it had been noticed in Yenan that she had improved some of the existing translations of Mao; furthermore, her prose style had been judged a suitable English equivalent of the chairman's.

Anna Louise's enthusiasm was constrained only by her desire to be in the United States for the presidential election the coming fall. Henry Wallace was building the Progressive party with the support of disaffected New Dealers, left-wing liberals and Communists, and Anna Louise wanted to be part of it. Liu saw no problem in the delay and indicated that they would be in touch with her in the United States, either through Chen Han-seng, a director of the Institute for Pacific Relations, or through Tang Ming-chao, a Chinese member of the Communist Party of the United States.

After dinner, conversation turned to establishing radio contact between the headquarters of the Chinese Communists in North Shensi and America. Anna Louise told her Chinese friends that she had been in contact with a friendly ham radio operator in Palo Alto, as well as with the *Allied Labor News* and the *CIO News*, about sending and receiving broadcasts.

They discussed the technical details of transmission frequencies and broadcast times and adopted the cloak-and-dagger scheme of code words Anna Louise had sent by letter to Liu a few days earlier. These were to be used so as not to break the regulations against broadcasting to an enemy. The letter to Liu had been intercepted by American intelligence and added to Anna Louise's FBI file; it generated an expensive nine-month radio intercept program by the Federal Communications Commission and a bureaucratic war between the FCC and the FBI as to who had the right to monitor the transmissions. Nothing incriminating was taken down.

Elizabeth Gurley Flynn, a prominent lifelong member of the American Communist party, greeted Anna Louise's arrival in New York in early January with an entire column in the *Daily Worker* entitled "Welcome Home, Anise." After a brief visit to Emily Pierson, Anna Louise delivered a major address in Carnegie Hall organized by the National Conference on American Policy in China. On the platform with her were Rexford Tugwell, the New Deal brain-truster who had become co-chairman of the Wallace for President Committee; Hugh De Lacey, who had been defeated in his bid for reelection to Congress; and W. E. B. Du Bois, the distinguished founder of the National Association for the Advancement of Colored People.

Anna Louise was the star. Her central message was that U.S. policy was turning the next government of China irrevocably against America. "The basic reality in China," she proclaimed, "as seen today by several hundred million people, is that American planes, bombs, and bullets are killing hundreds of thousands of civilian Chinese." On the other hand, the Russians were providing no help to Mao, Chu Teh and their forces, for "they are so afraid of being involved in the Chinese war that they went home and pulled their borders behind them, and maintain an iron blockade against the Chinese Communists. They do not even allow trade in food or cotton goods or medicines with Manchuria, for fear of being involved in that civil war."

This lecture and the ones that followed it reduced the temptation to return immediately to China. She wanted to publicize the successes of Chinese Communist strategy, and she hoped to apply what she had learned to the reorganization of the American Communist party. Her first disappointment was finding left-wing American publishers as unreceptive to her material as the one in Moscow. Progressive presses were "interested" but unwilling to commit themselves. She therefore went on tour and in lecture halls at least reached a large audience. In Oberlin, when asked why "the Russians were trying to take China from the United States," she retorted that "the Chinese were taking it, and not from us," and that "the Russians would like to have it for their own as much as America would," but that both sides were going to be disappointed. In the Midwest, however, her lectures were more often on Russia than on China, and she was often defensive and ill at ease about her text. On March 14, she found herself in a debate with William Henry Chamberlain, a noted foreign correspondent hostile to the U.S.S.R. Anna Louise declared that she found an "hysterical talk of war" in the United States for which there was no parallel in the Soviet Union. But she stumbled over questions about the Communist coup that had just taken place in Czechoslovakia, and according to the FBI agent in attendance, she was "short and cryptic in her answer, and it was evident to everyone that she was emotionally upset."

Her house in Palo Alto had been completely bugged by the FBI. As soon as she got there, she threw herself into the Wallace campaign. After some internal debate, the American Communist party had decided to support Wallace. Anna Louise hoped to be a bridge on matters of foreign policy between the Progressive party and the American far left. She wrote offering her services to Senator Glenn Taylor, the Idaho Democrat who would be Wallace's running mate, and made her presence felt in West Coast politics: Harry Steinmetz, the Progressive party delegate from San Diego, thought of her as "the sharpest political mind in the country." On April 10 she was elected delegate from the Palo Alto area to the Progressive Party Congress.

The purpose of the Congress was to set up the organization and platform of the Independent Progressive party. She hoped to help shape Far Eastern policy planks and spoke a few times on the floor about China. A gratifying applause greeted the announcement of her name, but it quickly became apparent that most of the delegates were more concerned with the relation of the Communists to the new party than with developments in China. The diverse factions in the Wallace movement were united only on the nomination. Wallace was trying hard to downplay Communist involvement while various representatives of the American Communist party were trying to take over control of the movement. Communist party members especially were openly suspicious of both Anna Louise's arguments and the elegance of her room in the hotel.

Disappointed, she made plans to return to California, but first she met with Chen Han-seng, whom Liu Ning-yi had identified as a contact. Chen confirmed what he had written to her at the end of March under the pseudonym "Hans." It was "best to go back to China"; she should immediately apply for a new passport before her identification with the Wallace campaign became more prominent. She would be of most service to Chinese leaders if she stayed in the United States only long enough to get a good picture of potential political developments before returning to China.

When Anna Louise returned to Palo Alto, to her shock her sister would no longer receive her in her house. Anna Louise had relied increasingly on Ruth and had even used her in her attempts to establish a radio link between Yenan and the United States. But as Ruth and Charles' involvement in Anna Louise's life grew, so also did the interest of the FBI in the principal of Las Palomas High School and his wife. To the Niederhausers, it has begun to feel too much like 1920, when they had been forced to leave Seattle largely because of their connection with Anna Louise. There had been attempts to remove Charles as high school principal. Charles had always maintained his distance from his wife's sister; now he asked her to forbid Anna Louise's presence in their home. The ban severed Anna Louise's one nonpolitical tie to America and was a particularly painful articulation of her isolated position: "I neglected to realize that to [Ruth] I was by no means the closest person; she had a husband, three children and some grandchildren, any of whom meant more to her than I did. She told me she was afraid my radical reputation would injure her husband in his job. This was clearly only part of the reason, for the husband was almost due to retire in any case on pension from his post. . . . I surmised that the political climate was changing, that my sister, who had previously felt considerable pride in introducing me to her friends as a well-known traveler and writer, was herself worried lest my reputation was no longer a benefit but a liability to her."

Anna Louise made desperate attempts to maintain the bond. The sisters met a few times in other people's houses. On one such occasion Anna Louise gave Ruth a diamond ring. "It was the one that she had always coveted," she wrote later to their brother, "the one that came to me when grandmother died: Ruth felt cheated, because you got Mother's ring for Edith and Uncle Russell judged that Grandma's diamond should go to me as the oldest. Anyway, it was worth well over $1,000, and I handed it over . . . in the hope that it would prove a tie. It didn't."

In the midst of her distress, she received another letter from Chen urging her to apply for her passport. To her relief, despite a bill proposed by Congressman Karl Mundt that would make illegal the granting of passports to Communists or those who consorted with Communists, she received her papers the first week in May. She immediately wrote to C. B. Baldwin, the executive secretary of the Progressive party, asking what use she might be over the next few months, as she expected to leave the country early in the fall. As a delegate she was duty-bound to remain for the convention, and she wanted to make one last attempt to overcome the American Communist party attitudes that were keeping her book from being published and that were dragging the Progressive movement toward defeat.

To get away from her sister's tormenting proximity, she moved to Los Angeles, bought a house in La Crescenta and turned her attention to the crisis in the American Communist party. During the New Deal years, Earl Browder, the general secretary, had sought to cast the party as the "loyal opposition." Not surprisingly, a number of important members of the central committee, most prominently Eugene Dennis and William Z. Foster, had attacked Browder as a "revisionist" and a "capitulationist." The dispute had remained internal until Jacques Duclos, a leading French Communist theoretician, had published under his name a blistering attack on "Browderism," almost certainly written in Moscow by the party theoretician Andrei Zhdanov. This had led to a bitter and often personal conflict inside the American party and had brought an end to any hope that it might be integrated into the mainstream of American politics. In February 1946 Browder had been expelled and replaced by Eugene Dennis, and during the next two years, there had been a thoroughgoing purge of Browderites at all levels of the party.

Anna Louise's experiences in Yugoslavia and especially China had shown her the wisdom of adjusting policies to particular national conditions: the automatic submission to Moscow's line following the Duclos letter seemed disastrous. Even though Chen Han-seng shared her low opinion of the American party leadership and Browder had publicly associated his ideas with those of Mao, Anna Louise did not support the Browderites. Indeed, Foster had sought and received from Mao himself a telegram of congratulations on Browder's expulsion. But Anna Louise had grave worries about the achievements of the new leadership and drew up a "Memorandum Concerning Factionalism in the Communist Party" which made the following points: first, that the leadership struggle after the Duclos letter had not resulted in a "reconstitution of the party along correct lines," as Duclos had demanded, but in the effective disintegration of the party structure. Second, that not only did the American working class find itself without a class-based leadership, but that present Communist party theory could give no account that was not personal of the failure of the

American party. It did no real good, she observed, to blame everything on the fact that the last three general secretaries had turned out to be revisionists or that the ex-editor of the *Daily Worker* was now a professional informer for the government. The question was why. Third, that the expulsion of the "right capitulationists"—i.e., Browder and his allies—had been undertaken without any consultation with the rank and file. Consequently, she concluded, the American Communist party found itself with neither a program for America nor an analysis of its own situation. The only cure for this quandary lay in the party pursuing "an independent course at all times."

She circulated her letter to friends on the West Coast and through the efforts of friends to progressives and party members on the East Coast as well. It did nothing to enhance her relations with the new Soviet-oriented leadership group, who, like the Russians, maintained a silence on China. Chen Han-seng called her attention to the fact that for over a year not a single editorial on China had appeared in the pages of the *Daily Worker*, and she became even more determined to have her book published. But her political situation changed radically on July 24 when, two days before the Progressive party convention opened in Philadelphia, eleven of the top leaders of the American Communist party were indicted and charged under the Alien Registration Act of 1940 with conspiring and advocating the overthrow of the U.S. government by force. Intraparty disputes now took a back seat to the reality of repression. A letter from Ch'en Chia-k'ang in Paris again urging her to return to China was delivered by Fred Field, the rich American who had long helped left-wing causes. All that kept her in the United States was her book. Finally, she went to see Israel Epstein at the CDFEP, determined to force them into a corner. "I am about to return to China," she told him. "When I left Yenan, Mao Tse-tung himself told me to take the news of China's revolution especially to the United States. Must I go back and report that I have already placed my book on China in seven or eight countries but could not get a publisher in the United States?"

Epstein was sufficiently sympathetic to the Chinese cause to agree that the CDFEP would publish her book, though he asked that she condense it to half its length. Anna Louise reluctantly agreed; the result was published in December 1948 under the title *Tomorrow's China*. Noticeably not included was the material Liu Shao-ch'i had given her on an "Asiatic form of Marxism."

As she rewrote, Anna Louise prepared for her return to China. Tang Ming-chao told her that Liu Ning-yi was again in Paris and would assure

Anna Louise arriving at LaGuardia Airport, New York City, after her expulsion from the U.S.S.R., February 1949

Anna Louise with Mao Tse-tung on National Day, October 1958

Anna Louise with Chairman Mao, W. E. B. Du Bois, Shirley Graham, March 1959

Anna Louise and Chao Feng-feng in a village in Zhejiang Province during the "three lean years" of famine, May 1962

Anna Louise and Chou En-lai at her seventy-seventh birthday party, 1962

Anna Louise's seventy-ninth birthday party with Chen Yi

Anna Louise writing, 1965-6

The meeting with Chairman Mao in January 1964; left to right: Sidney Rittenberg, Israel Epstein, Chairman Mao, Anna Louise, unknown, Frank Coe, Sol Adler

Anna Louise with Ho Von Brot, a South Vietnamese school-
boy victim of napalm bombing, Hanoi, 1964

Ho Chi Minh, Anna Louise and Chao Feng-feng, Hanoi, 1964

Woodcut of Anna Louise receiving *Quotations from Chairman Mao Tse-tung* from the Chairman, 1966. Anna Louise is wearing a Red Guard arm-band.

Anna Louise greets the Red Guard, May Day 1967. Behind her is Sidney Rittenberg

Anna Louise on her hundred-yard swim at Pei-tai-ho, age eighty years, nine months

The funeral service, Peking, April 2, 1970

安娜・路易斯・斯特朗永垂不朽
MAY ANNA LOUISE STRONG LIVE FOREVER IN OUR MEMORY

her passage to China. The Soviet consul in New York, however, would give her a visa only to Moscow and refused her request for a transit visa to Harbin in Manchuria. Anna Louise was surprised but assumed that it was simply the usual Russian preoccupation with bureaucratic righteousness; after all, the U.S.S.R. still recognized the government of Chiang Kai-shek. After another month of delays, she left New York on September 17.

In Paris, Liu Ning-yi had just returned overland from Harbin and assured Anna Louise that the route was open, although there was no direct train. She mentioned that she had as yet received no transit visa and asked Liu for a formal letter of invitation to enter the Communist-controlled areas of North China. He wrote out a letter in Chinese and English to Chang Yan-ch'ing, then commander of the area around Harbin, indicating that Anna Louise was traveling at the express invitation of Chou En-lai and requesting him to convey her to the present headquarters of the central committee. There could be no formal visa, Liu explained, since the Communists were not yet officially a government. "As soon as you have been checked out by the Soviet customs at the Manchurian border," he said, "present these letters and ask them to phone to the customs on the other side. They will see you through. You may show these to any Soviet official whose duty may be to ask. The sooner you go, the better. Events are near."

Anna Louise left Paris the first week in October. Her journey took her through Warsaw, where she gave an interview to *Glos Ludu*, the official organ of the Polish Communist party, on the impending victory of the Chinese Communists. This was picked up by the Soviet news agency Tass and reported in all the Soviet papers.

In Moscow she made little attempt to acquaint her friends and relatives with the past year of her life. Instead, she went promptly to the Press Department of the Foreign Office, explaining that as a journalist she wanted not a new residence permit but a transit visa to Manchuria. Vasilenko, the Press Department chief, seemed taken aback and urged that she stay for the anniversary celebration of the Revolution in early November. She would be invited to Foreign Affairs Minister Molotov's reception, he assured her. "Then your transit visa can be quickly arranged."

Anna Louise refused the bait and inquired further about the transit visa. Did she have her Chinese entry visa yet? Vasilenko asked. Recognizing the game, she smilingly retorted, "Do you mean from the embassy of Chiang Kai-shek? Do you think that will help me in Manchuria? I have credentials for Harbin." And she opened her purse to show him the documents Liu had given her.

"Please not," Vasilenko demurred, and Anna Louise understood that it would not be proper for him to look at credentials from a group the Soviet government had not yet recognized. She said she would apply to Nanking's embassy if the U.S.S.R. required it. Vasilenko thought for a minute and then said: "I don't see why we can't give you a permit out, and you be responsible for what happens to you next. . . . We might even give you an out-and-in visa for two months so that you could return if you ran into unexpected trouble." He promised her a visa in a couple of days. When she went back to claim it, Vasilenko was reported to be ill. Anna Louise never saw him again; all of her future dealings at the Foreign Office were with Simonov, a "lesser and cruder underling."

A ritual of demand and evasion ensued. Anna Louise kept her temper with Simonov for a while, then exploded. "Give me a reason!" she shouted angrily. Simonov told her that "bandits" were disrupting the railroad lines in Manchuria. This was too much. "Are you alluding to the fact that the Chinese Communists are running the railroad?" she taunted. Simonov was openly incensed, the more so because she had hit upon the truth. Anna Louise was out of control by the time she left. She spat out: "Let the first atom bomb fall on this office. Then I won't mind if the next one falls on me."

Shortly thereafter she received a letter from a "progressive American group" asking her to attend and report on the International Women's Congress in Budapest. The Press Department immediately granted her request for a visa, "with some relief," she felt. In Budapest she met a large group of Chinese women, many of whom she had known in Yenan or the liberated areas. They were delighted to see her and promptly invited her to join them on a special train from Moscow to Harbin on November 22.

Exultant and incautious, Anna Louise rushed to a public telephone and called the Foreign Office in Moscow to tell them to hurry up with her visa. She returned immediately to Moscow to make final preparations, but it was useless. The Chinese women came, and Anna Louise wished them farewell in the dining room of the National Hotel. The Foreign Office was more and more openly annoyed at Anna Louise's repeated visits; nor were they any happier when Anna Louise attended U.S. embassy functions clad in her most outrageous Chinese gowns, proclaiming the imminent victory of Chu Teh's forces.

During those receptions at the embassy Anna Louise spoke with American officials of the difficulty she was having in obtaining her visa and in operating as a foreign correspondent in the Soviet Union. She also told anyone who would listen that the Soviets did not control Mao, that their information on Chinese affairs was poor, and that the Russians were afraid the Chinese forces were becoming too powerful too quickly. It was possible, she thought, that Mao, while publicly supporting Soviet primacy, might "pull a Tito." It is not clear how much of these conversations reached Soviet ears, but Anna Louise said much the same sort of thing to close Russian friends. On occasion, members of the American embassy staff would even give her a ride home.

All she learned of the progress of the Chinese People's Liberation Army came from BBC shortwave broadcasts and foreign correspondents who had access to the Paris edition of the *New York Herald Tribune*. Nothing appeared in the Soviet press until in early December a four-line notice on the last page of *Pravda* announced the capture of Shen-yang, 350 miles northeast of Peiping. This meant that the entire northeast of China was under the control of the Communists. On December 6 Anna Louise read an announcement that Süchow, 300 miles south of Peiping and the last KMT bastion north of the Yangtze River, had also fallen to the Communists.

She became increasingly desperate to get to China. A letter came from Fred Field telling her it was "a misfortune that you are stuck so long in Moscow." "We are," he wrote, "trying to break the blockade at this end but do not know with what success." Anna Louise redoubled her efforts. She called Elsie Cholmeley, the wife of Israel Epstein, long distance in New York, told her the story of the Chinese women and asked her to persuade the American party to pressure the Russians for her visa. She got Czech and Polish press agencies and Reuters in London to send requests for a series on the China front. But all demands to the Foreign Office were answered by silence.

Anna Louise went to Borodin and demanded to know why Soviet newspapers carried neither news nor analysis of the situation in China. Initially Borodin referred her to problems in the "line": "The analysis of the Chinese situation is being reconsidered at high levels; meantime, the papers keep still." Besides, he insisted, "*this* is Rome; I mean, *this* is the center of the world." Anna Louise pressed him, as an old friend and a China hand, to explain to her why Moscow would not publish her book, which had already appeared in India and was about to come out in the United States and several European countries. He looked at her silently, picked up the telephone and called the publishing house. As he argued with the editor, Anna Louise heard him say: "But they are winning, aren't they? Doesn't that prove their theory is right?" For the first time she recognized that the difference between the Russians and the Chinese might force her to a major choice.

As the People's Liberation Army surrounded Tientsin and Peiping, rumors circulated in Moscow that the U.S.S.R. was trying to arrange a peace settlement between Chiang and the Communists on a basis satisfactory to Chiang. The North Korean ambassador at first welcomed Anna Louise when she approached him for a visa to North Korea, then refused to return her calls.

In her desperation she became increasingly vocal about her anger at what she took to be Russian bureaucratic stupidity. She proclaimed to various correspondents that she would give Stalin an earful about her delays and reminded all who would listen that she was on a mission for Mao Tse-tung himself. Aghast at the risks she was running, several of her friends tried to get her to keep her anger to herself. Even after her old friend Arthur Adams urged her to keep quiet about the whole visa issue, she turned in any direction she could find for help. When she ran into Harry Eisman, a political exile from the United States who had fought with the Red Army in World War II, she immediately invited him to her hotel room to talk about her situation. Eisman spent the afternoon trying to reassure her. Much later she learned that the security police had picked him up as he left her hotel and sent him, war medals and all, to Siberia for five years for "acts hostile to the Soviet people."

Finally, a foreign correspondent took her aside and told her bluntly that her difficulties came from the fact that she was considered a Titoist: "Suppose you had to choose between Yugoslavia and Russia?" This presented no problem. "No, I don't think I could be called a Titoist," she replied. "I am not very good on theory and I have thought that both sides have made mistakes. But as I look at it, from the standpoint of the world revolution, the Yugoslavs are expendable." The other continued: "Suppose, however, you had to choose between China and Russia?" Anna Louise was startled; it was, she later remembered, the first time that she had come up against the reality of the differences between Mao and Stalin. "I don't know. If it should come to a choice between the Russians and the Chinese, the answer might be different." It was possible, she recollected later, that the room they were in had been bugged.

In early February, as news leaked out that KMT troops were defecting in massive proportions and a final Communist victory was assured, Borodin mentioned to Anna Louise that the World Federation of Trade Unions had set its next meeting for sometime in May in Peiping. Anna Louise immediately realized that arrangements for the delegates could be made only in Moscow, and that Liu Ning-yi, as head of the trade unions, would certainly be coming there to supervise visa and transportation problems. A request from Liu that she be granted a visa could not be directly refused.

Anna Louise began careful detective work. From newspaper reports of a labor conference in Paris that Liu had been attending, she determined his probable arrival date and went to the National Hotel, where Chinese delegations always stayed. With as much casualness as she could muster, she asked the room clerk if Comrade Liu Ning-yi had arrived from Paris yet. "We expected him last night" was the answer, "but the plane from Prague did not arrive. He will probably be here this evening."

Exultant, Anna Louise returned to her hotel. She spent most of the evening composing a letter detailing her troubles and asking Liu to get her a visa in connection with the trade union conference. If this proved impossible, she wrote, she would return to either London or the United States.

The next morning she went to the National Hotel, asked for Liu's room number and walked boldly to his door. It was opened by one of his associates; she saw Liu himself in the room talking with a Russian. Liu smiled a welcome, then gestured that he did not want to be interrupted. Anna Louise left the letter with the man who had opened the door. She saw Liu beam approval as she turned to go. A few hours later the telephone rang in Anna Louise's room. It was the interpreter asking her to a meeting the following evening.

This time Liu himself opened the door. She poured out her troubles, incuding her most recent anxiety that for the last few days she had been unable to contact Borodin. Liu had "no knowledge" of Borodin's situation but assured her that there was no problem with the route. "Perhaps," said Anna Louise, "the Russians don't want to accept that the Chinese are going to win." Liu admitted the possibility: "The U.S.S.R. does not even know that there are works of Mao on people's revolution that detail what we have done." But, he hastened to assure her, nothing had been said to him about restrictions on departure. His close friend, the Russian general in charge of the border region, was now in Moscow and had made no mention of any problem with Anna Louise. He promised to do what he could and made another appointment for the following day.

Greatly relieved, Anna Louise avoided her hotel and went directly to her room in the Shubins' apartment to make preparations to leave Moscow. The next morning, February 13, 1949, in a mood of self-righteous triumph, she called the Foreign Office and informed them that they no longer needed to bother about her request. "The Chinese comrade who had invited me to return to China is now in Moscow," she told them loftily. "I will leave it up to him to help get my visa, or return to the United States."

She went to bed shortly after supper. At about ten-thirty she was awakened by loud knocks at the door. She first assumed that it was Boris or another of her brothers-in-law banging in friendly protest at the early hour of her retiring. Putting on a kimono, she opened the door to her room, which led directly into the bedroom of her stepdaughter Ducia. Two men in uniform carrying sidearms stalked in: "Come at once. You are under arrest."

Still half asleep, she began to protest that they had come to the wrong house. The men told her to hurry. Anna Louise glimpsed Ducia cowering in her bed, the covers pulled over her head. She mumbled that she needed to get dressed; the two agents nodded acquiescence but continued to stare at her. Anna Louise finally recovered enough of her self-possession to insist that they turn their backs while she put her clothes on. With the reflexes of a seasoned traveler, she collected her purse, passport, extra clothes, all her foreign currency, and the vitamin pills she took regularly for the Paget's disease. At the last minute she grabbed her padded Chinese gown. As the group moved through the kitchen, she saw Frieda covering her face with her apron and a third policeman standing guard over the telephone.

Anna Louise was escorted into a large black car. She consoled herself with the fact that she had not been handcuffed and pushed around like friends of hers who had been jailed in America. But the threat of force was very present. The car sped off to a large building that she instantly recognized as Lubyanka, the infamous central prison of the secret security police.

In Lubyanka, the routine of jail procedure closed around her, strangely familiar, she thought, "because of all the detective stories" that she had read. Her belongings were confiscated, and she was led to a small cell and told to strip naked. As she sat on a stool with her head against the wall, still dazed from shock, a woman doctor entered and listened to her heart. The rest of the physical examination had no reference to the state of her health but only to the possibility of her carrying "concealed documents, weapons, or possibly some lethal capsule to commit suicide." The soles of her shoes were ripped out, the seams of her stockings inspected, and her shoelaces removed. Finally, as she stood shivering from the cold, she was told to get dressed. The doctor looked at her carefully and returned the shoelaces, saying: "You will feel more decent with your shoes laced." Anna Louise thanked her and noted she did indeed feel better with her shoes tied. She asked the doctor why she was there; the woman responded that she didn't know.

She was next marched into a room where a portly man with two rows of war ribbons across his chest sat behind a desk. "Why am I here?" she asked. "That's not my affair," came the answer. "I am the warden." Was there anything she needed? Anna Louise requested a diet high in milk and vegetables and low in meat. She also needed vitamins, especially B-1, which she took regularly for nerves, and D for Paget's. The warden gave her vitamin C, which made her even more nervous, for she knew it was the vitamin of choice for those about to be sent to Siberia. As she was taken to her cell, up stairways sheathed with heavy wire netting to prevent suicides, the clock on the wall showed three in the morning.

The night was difficult, punctuated by frequent bouts of diarrhea. There was no toilet in the cell, and she had to knock on the door each time for an escort to the bathroom. She lay awake trying to figure out what might have landed her there, still assuming that it was a bureaucratic mistake. Outside, the morning edition of *Pravda* carried the news of her arrest; against all protocol, the request to see her by Foy Kohler, the American chargé d'affaires, was turned down. In New York the *Daily Worker* abruptly discontinued its campaign to have her awarded a Pulitzer Prize and ceased the serial publication of *Tomorrow's China*.

An attendant brought breakfast of weak coffee, rice-milk soup, sour milk, and bread. When the woman returned for the barely touched tray, she seemed disappointed: "Do you not feel well?" "How could I?" Anna Louise snapped. The morning passed, lunch came. In desperation, Anna Louise took advantage of the information on her door that she had a right to daily exercise, weather permitting. She summoned the guard and was taken for a walk on the remarkably spacious roof that had been divided by high walls into separate areas. Only one prisoner at a time was allowed in each section. At no time during her sojourn in Lubyanka did Anna Louise see another inmate.

It was not until late at night that a guard informed her that "the commissar awaits you." She was taken upstairs through a large double office into a room with a long conference table covered in green felt. The guard directed her to sit at one end of the table; at the other sat the commissar; halfway down the table a secretary was poised to take notes.

Anna Louise demanded at once: "What am I here for?" "I'm asking the questions" was the brusque reply.

The first few questions intensified her fear. The commissar had evidently never heard of her, despite that fact that, as she informed him, not five years before a book of hers had sold 300,000 copies in Russia. He was suspicious of her nationality and refused to accept her statement that her profession was that of a writer. "What am I then?" she asked indignantly. "You are a correspondent," he asserted and directed the secretary to write it down. The implication was not reassuring. Anna Louise knew that Russians thought of writers as "engineers of the human spirit," but that correspondents were little better than second-class spies.

"How many times have you entered the Soviet Union? When?" were the next questions. The commissar was visibly shaken by the long narration he received in response. He could not accept that the Soviet authorities had been so lax as knowingly to have granted Anna Louise permission to come and go as she wished for almost thirty years. Every trip she described confirmed her dangerous status.

At the end of her story, her inquisitor slowly rose to his feet and "thundered" the judgment in a tone so stentorian that Anna Louise understood only the last three words: "for spying activities." She asked him to repeat what he had said. The sentence came back with only one additional comprehensible word, "frontier." Slowly she grasped that she was to be "chucked out" to a country of her choice. She faltered a final request: "I don't suppose I could choose Manchuria?" "That is excluded—a Western country," he retorted. "Then put me on a boat for London." This offended him even more: "A boat is not a frontier. We must put you on dry land." The only sense that Anna Louise could make of these restrictions was that the deportation must take place in secret. She wearily indicated that either Poland or Czechoslovakia would be acceptable, a choice that obviously perplexed the commissar, for the accepted escape route for spies was through Finland.

Anna Louise spent the next two days painstakingly authenticating the contents of her files. Each evening she was taken upstairs and shown a large pile of material that she was to acknowledge as hers by her signature. Knowing that some material, such as her notebooks on the steel center of Kuznetsk, might be considered subversive now but would not have been twenty years earlier, she made attempts to date the documents. The commissar would have none of it. Finally the task was completed. Anna Louise gave the secretary a list of the personal items and clothing that she would like to take with her. The detailing of the clothes brought home to her that she was going to be dropped over the Polish border in the dead of winter. Nevertheless, she took comfort in the knowledge that she was well acquainted with Gottschalk and other top Polish leaders, whom she assumed would help her initiate a process of redress as soon as she arrived in Warsaw.

On the evening of her fifth day in Lubyanka, she was told to prepare for departure. She protested that she was too exhausted and ill, but the same doctor who had first examined her rapidly declared her "fit to travel." As she left, in a last gesture of innocence and defiance, she asked the prison secretary to telegraph the Hotel Bristol in Warsaw for a reservation. He said that he would "take it up."

The commissar confronted her once more. "You are guilty of spying against the interests of the Soviet state. We might have a trial, but this would take a long time and mean a long confinement for you. In view of your age, we think it better to expel you to Poland." Although certain that she was being treated unjustly, Anna Louise was silently relieved. She knew that in the present international climate, materials in her files would be interpreted as incriminating. It was better to seek other routes to prove her innocence.

It was almost dawn on the sixth day when her luggage was brought to her, "expertly packed by men," she noted: "a pile of dresses, no belts, no accessories, a pile of bedding, and forty pounds of canned food, the Russian male's idea of what you need on a trip." On the drive from Lubyanka to the airport, she saw the sun glint on the towers of the Kremlin. "If I live long enough, I'll see you again and with honor," she said to herself, "but never again for long. You are no more 'my affair.' "
At the airport she was led into a ten-seater plane; some hours later they landed in a muddy field, where she was transferred to a jeep and taken to a footbridge over the river separating Russia from Poland: "Alighting here by a sentry post, the guards carried my very heavy suitcases to the center of the bridge and placed them there. I followed. They handed me my passport and pocketbook with my American currency ($613) and left me. From the opposite shore a rather puzzled sentry was advancing toward me. I hastily opened my passport and found that it contained a Polish visa and showed this to him when he came." She was asked where she wanted to go. Warsaw, she said. There was a train in a few hours. As she was driven off in a coal truck, she asked the border post to send a telegram to the Hotel Bristol requesting a room. It was ten P.M. when she arrived at the Bristol. Two reservations had been made, she never found out how.

All she wanted was sleep, but even that had to be limited, as the room clerk officiously noted, because her visa expired the next day. This was bad news. The next day was Sunday, when all government offices were closed. Wondering where to turn for help, she remembered Rhoda Miller, an Englishwoman married to a Polish Communist; Rhoda was the head of the new Telepress agency.

She appeared on Rhoda's doorstep the next morning, but the look of surprise and fear that spread over Rhoda's face was not reassuring. Moscow had obviously made its charges public. Inside the house where Rhoda hurriedly ushered her, Anna Louise asked for help in fighting the charges. That, Rhoda said, was impossible. "Your whole reputation in East Europe," she pointed out, "is entirely derived from your previous reputation in Moscow. No one in Poland or any other East European country can or will do a single thing for your case. Only the American party, which has known you for thirty years since before you went to Moscow, has the right and duty to take up your case. But the American party is so servile that you haven't a chance."

Despite her experiences the previous year, Anna Louise protested Rhoda's condemnation of the American party. She argued that if Dennis and the others knew that the "evidence" against her was derived from the same material that the American party had praised, they "would take it up with Stalin." Unconvinced, Rhoda warned Anna Louise to stay in an inner room and went out to seek the advice of friends. On her return, she reported that everyone with whom she had spoken had confirmed her judgment. Anna Louise was not to call again, or to approach any other member of Telepress, which as a news agency could be seriously compromised by any further contact.

Completely exhausted and with no place to rest, Anna Louise faced the fact that her visa was about to expire. There was no plane going west until the following day. A series of phone calls finally produced an official willing to extend her visa for one day, and on Monday she took a plane to Paris, rested for a few hours in a hotel near the city and wrote a letter to Lu Ts'ui, who had remained in Paris after Liu's departure:

Will you please tell Chairman Mao and Lu Ting-yi and Chou En-lai and especially Liu Ning-yi . . . that, so far as I could learn, it was my too persistent search into the road to China that the Russians finally attacked as "spying." . . . I assume it will be impossible for me to be any use to my Chinese friends for a considerable period of time to come. . . . If I am mistaken in this, and if there is any use they can make of me, however obscure and without name, and in whatever isolation and under whatever control, be assured that I would wish to come. For it has been and still is my wish that the last ten years of my working life—I think I still have ten more—be spent in the midst of the great Chinese revolution which will remake half the world.

Meanwhile, I must go to New York at once to report to my American comrades how catastrophically I have failed. I would have stopped in Paris a day to see you, but I thought you would not wish this. However, I still believe that before I die, I shall see my Chinese comrades and you among them, with honor once again.

Misfortune dogged her even on the transatlantic flight. The plane was driven so far off course by a storm that it had to land in the Azores; the flight took two full days to reach Gander. Ill from fatigue, she asked the stewardess to arrange an overnight rest in Newfoundland before the ordeal that awaited her at home. When the stewardess asked what had happened, Anna Louise replied, "I had a little trouble with the Russian government." In Gander there were messages from two news services asking her to call collect. She carefully composed a telegram: "Do not use my arrest as material for the cold war. I do not know why I was arrested or why they unjustly called me a spy, but the police of any country can make mistakes."

As she was reading the telegram into a telephone, the door of the booth was jerked open by a "very obtrusive man," Jack Lotto, from Hearst's International Newservice, bearing a letter from Barry Faris, the editor-in-chief. The letter reminded her of the "very fine job" she had done as their Moscow correspondent and offered a "deal." Anna Louise refused to say anything beyond the contents of her cable, but the prospect of spending a night in Gander with this obnoxious man at her side seemed worse than continuing the flight. It was clear he would pursue her even to her bedroom. She dragged herself back to the plane. Lotto commandeered the seat beside her. She still refused all comment, but when she asked for another seat, he followed her there, leaning over the aisle with a barrage of questions.

The flight arrived in New York at twelve-fifty in the morning on February 24, 1949. Anna Louise was asked to remain on board until the other passengers disembarked. No sooner was the aisle empty than two FBI agents entered and pushed a summons into her hands, demanding her presence for a grand jury hearing that same morning. She was next advised that the FBI wanted to speak with her immediately. "Of course," she replied, "I've just been interviewed by your counterpart in Russia." One of the special agents told her there was no counterpart to the FBI in Russia. Wearily Anna Louise said she would not withhold any information from an American government agency as long as it was not for publication. The interrogation concluded at 2:35, and Anna Louise was led to the immigration authorities, who tried unsuccessfully to prove that she was not an American citizen. During the course of their inquiry, she staunchly defended her current citizenship and her Puritan ancestry. The immigration interrogation broke up shortly after four A.M., at which point she was brought before a group of over a hundred reporters and photographers. The Associated Press captured the sad drama as well as it could:

> Protesting against "being forced" by pressure of newsmen to do so, the sixty-four-year-old repatriate turned a haggard face towards a battery of cameras, lights and microphones and said: "I have not done anything against the security of the Soviet State or any other state, either by espionage or sabotage." She continued: "I was very energetically searching for information which I considered to be part of my journalistic task, and if the Soviet government chose to consider this espionage, there is nothing I can do about it."
> But Miss Strong hastened to add that she considered her expulsion was caused by the "war hysteria which the American Press has done so much to stir up." As a result, she predicted that she "would not be the last, because any American journalist asking questions comes under suspicion and people in certain countries are afraid to talk with them."

A reporter shouted, "Did they treat you bad in jail?" It was the Hearst reporter from Gander. Exasperated, Anna Louise snapped, "Nobody in Russia has mistreated me the way you reporters have tonight." She heard a low woman's voice behind her, "Not all of us, please, not all of us," and was startled into the recognition that she should not indiscriminately indict the whole American press corps. She corrected her remark to refer only to Jack Lotto and turned again to the group with a repetition of her plea that she not be used to inflame the cold war: "I know that I have become something of a sensation. So, while I am news today, this is something like an atomic bomb. It can sit peacefully or go off and wreck worlds."

No friends had appeared, and there seemed to be no logical end to the reporters' barrage. Then she turned and saw Cedric Belfrage, an editor of the *National Guardian*, pushing through the crowd. She had met him a few times the previous year during the Wallace campaign; his vaguely familiar voice pierced the rumble: "I am taking you to a private house where nobody can bother you." A final question from the crowd of reporters drew the answer, "Official stupidity is not the monopoly of any country," and Anna Louise left with Belfrage and his friend Jacob Turner, a liberal businessman who supported the *Guardian*.

Anna Louise had a subpoena commanding her appearance at ten o'clock that morning before a grand jury. Belfrage suggested that she retain O. John Rogge, who was also representing Agnes Smedley in her libel suit against General Douglas MacArthur. Rogge, a former assistant U.S. attorney general, had been fired two years earlier for claiming that the Truman administration was planning another series of "Palmer Raids" on American leftists. He had been a leading organizer of the Progressive party.

The group arrived at Turner's house. At eight-thirty, before going to see Rogge, Anna Louise went to a phone booth for an untapped phone and called Fred Field. She did not give her name but said, "I think you will recognize my voice. May I come down and see you at once?" Field promptly said no, that he would come and see her. Anna Louise told him where she was and reminded him that she had an "important appointment at ten." Field promised to be there at nine-thirty. No one appeared. While Anna Louise waited, Belfrage contacted Rogge, who after the assurance of a $1,000 retainer arranged a postponement of the grand jury appearance until the next day. At eleven a young woman arrived who said that she would convey a message to Fred Field and Lem Harris. Upset that no direct access to the American Communists was forthcoming, Anna Louise explained that, while she had retained Rogge, it was far more important to her to get advice from the party. The woman said that Lem Harris would meet Anna Louise in Rogge's office to help advise her.

Around noon Anna Louise went to Rogge's office and, too sick even to sit, lay down on a sofa for the conference. Lem Harris arrived; he was in a great hurry, he said, to catch a plane. After learning that Anna Louise did not blame the Soviet Union but rather the exigencies of toughness in a modern state, he suggested that she could make speeches about her experience and should "let us advise you." These were the first encouraging words she had heard from a Communist in two weeks, and she grabbed at them: "I insist on direction," she said. "It's all too complicated for me." Harris started to leave with another kind word: "We need you." Then he caught himself, "I can promise nothing. I have only been asked to report."

Rogge found a doctor who certified that Anna Louise was unfit to testify at length. After calling Emily Pierson to tell her that she was coming to Connecticut, Anna Louise fell asleep at last. The next morning she appeared with Rogge in the courthouse at Foley Square. The grand jury was the immediate successor to the one that had indicted the lead-

ership of the American Communist party and Alger Hiss. In deference
to her condition, they asked her few questions and mostly listened to a
brief account of her life. At the end of the hearing the district attorney
read a list of names and asked her to identify any she knew. "I monoto-
nously denied knowing them one by one," she recalled. But when he
inserted the name of Lem Harris, "I knew in a flash that he expected me
to keep on denying, and that if I did so, he would be able to prove
perjury." She admitted to having known Harris for some years. The
district attorney asked her a question about Marxism, observing that after
her long sojourn in the U.S.S.R. she must be an expert. Anna Louise
merely replied, "As a correspondent I consider myself something of an
expert on events, but I have never been very good on theory." After forty
minutes the session was adjourned until the following Tuesday.

A group of reporters attended her exit from the court. Again Anna
Louise took the line that her arrest was to be blamed on mistakes by low-
level officials. She labeled as "poppycock" the claim advanced in many
columns that she was expelled for pro-Chinese sympathies. "Are you a
Communist?" came the inevitable question. "That's the $64 question. I'll
answer it if the grand jury asks it, but not for you. I never in my life
knowingly have done espionage against any country. There is nothing I
inherited from my parents I so prize as my American citizenship." Asked
at the end if she was glad to be back in the United States, Anna Louise
replied, "I'm glad to be anywhere I can get some sleep. I think that this
country is the most comfortable I have stayed in, but not the most exciting. After I've had some rest and possibly written awhile, I think I'll go
to some country where there is a war on." Did that mean China, a voice
demanded. She smiled sardonically and said, "Why, China is the most
peaceful country in the world."

Rogge whisked her away, and she took the train from Grand Central
Station to Cromwell where Emily was waiting. Aghast at Anna Louise's
state, Emily put her to bed with the prescription that due to "nervous
and physical exhaustion with cardiac complications," she would not be
allowed to go anywhere for at least three weeks. But simple rest was
unthinkable. A phone was installed in Anna Louise's bedroom, and she
set to work trying to convince the Communist party to reopen her case
with Moscow.

She knew that if the American party rejected her plea, her career as
she had known it was over and her thirty-year attempt to build bridges
between the "old" world of most Americans and the new worlds of the
American Communist party, the Soviet Union and China would collapse.

She also knew that she would eventually have to testify again before the grand jury and that news of her testimony would certainly leak out. She was determined, she told Cedric Belfrage, to resist all temptations to "play the Judas." As very lucrative offers to "tell all" started to pour in, on Belfrage's urging she retained the services of a literary agent, Maxim Lieber. By reflex and as much to collect her own thoughts as for any public purpose, she started to write an account of her recent experiences.

At first few people knew where she was, but the press was enterprising and soon the Cromwell household was deluged with phone calls. Emily heroically protected her friend against all demands, yet even she could not prevent another industrious Hearst reporter from climbing up the drainpipe to the second story. Anna Louise said nothing to any reporter after her first talk with Belfrage, but Belfrage now urged her to publish an account "to allay the great tension caused by your arrest." She tried to behave like a good party member and awaited word from others about publication. Lem Harris had agreed to contact her on Tuesday, March 1. No word came. On Friday she called him in Chappaqua, New York. The FBI took it down:

LEM HARRIS: Hello.
ANNA LOUISE STRONG: This is Mrs. Joel Shubin.
LH: *(After a significant pause)* Glad to hear your voice.
ALS: Look here. Were you planning to come and see me at all? It is very necessary. . . .
LH: You know, I just got back from the west and I . . .
ALS: I thought you were supposed to get back Tuesday.
LH: Well, I did get back on Wednesday.
ALS: I thought probably the weather . . . I really have to advise with you [*sic*]. I have been lying here in bed . . . and I think a good series of articles, properly done, will be my only defense against what is going to happen in the next ten days . . . Anyway, I've given tentative agreement to the *Chicago Sun Times* . . . In that very short conversation I had with you, you seemed to indicate that something of that kind would be good. . . . Would it be possible for you to come Sunday or Saturday?
LH: I've got to think about that . . . For me to come without seeing anyone first wouldn't serve any purpose.

Lem was close to central committee members; he probably called others in the leadership, but they were apparently unable to agree on a policy. On the eighth, with pressure to publish coming from her agent and with no word from Lem or anyone else in the party, she called back. This time she got a baby-sitter.

With each passing day the question of publication loomed larger. She was enticed by Belfrage's hope that her articles would repair the damage done by her arrest to relations between the Communist party and the left wing of the Progressive movement; the latter had taken her arrest as further confirmation of the repressive character of the Soviet Union. It was therefore essential, she thought, that prior to publication her articles be "shown around to progressives with a thought to editing and revision." Belfrage suggested that she replace Lieber with Roy Blumenthal, who had been a public relations man in the Wallace campaign and retained excellent contacts with that group. Rogge vouched for Blumenthal, and Anna Louise gave Belfrage a copy of the pieces she had been writing to take to him.

That evening Blumenthal called Anna Louise and said that he saw the central problem as "scare headlines," not the texts themselves. He would go ahead and show the articles to "prominent progressives" and call her the next morning with their opinion. At eleven the next day the telephone rang; it was not Blumenthal but a man who would not identify himself for fear of the FBI. She recognized the voice of Fred Field. He was very disturbed when she told him that she was about to release the articles, but he did not tell her to cancel publication; he asked only that she delay. Field closed the conversation with a plea that she talk to Rogge and a promise to come see her the next day. Anna Louise was unhappy—she had been waiting for definitive word from the party for ten days—but she acquiesced.

That evening Emily Pierson read over the first draft and suggested that she "tone it down a little." But she did not think that the story should be suppressed. Anna Louise also called Agnes Smedley, who advised against publication on the ground of general distrust of the mainstream press but told her to contact Chen Han-seng. Chen was away from Philadelphia; Anna Louise sent him a letter. Blumenthal called and said that the *New York Herald Tribune* had offered $5,000 for the series. He had shown it to them, he said, after Henry Wallace and John Abt had agreed that the articles would not inflate the cold war. Wallace had even said that they "were light in a dark room."

Anna Louise spent the next few days modifying the more histrionic passages and incorporating various changes suggested by Eslanda Robeson, the wife of Paul Robeson, the prominent singer and actor. Anna Louise had become friendly with the Robesons during the Wallace campaign; she accepted Eslanda's advice as representative of the Progressive perspective.

There was still no word from the Communist party. Fred Field did not come as promised. At the end of the week two women who would not identify themselves arrived in Cromwell. They told Anna Louise that she should not publish anything; they would not say if they were or were not from the party. Anna Louise asked them to read the articles to see what should be changed. The women took the hard line: they refused to look at the articles and urged that Anna Louise say nothing to the grand jury even at the risk of a contempt citation. They did not think the Civil Rights Congress that was defending the Communists indicted under the Smith Act would defend her, since hers was not a civil rights case. They held out no promise of a useful future, only the intimation that if she kept silent and obscure she might once again after some years "be received." By whom they would not say.

The argument raged for over two hours, with Anna Louise disputing them from her sickbed. Finally Emily stormed in, berated the two visitors for high-pressuring a sick person and reminded them that Anna Louise had for some time sought help from the party. If Anna Louise yielded to them, Emily continued, she would tell her that she "was on her own now" and throw her out. "I'm standing a lot for Anna Louise Strong," she snapped. "All the Middletown wires are buzzing. Am I doing this for a spy who takes mysterious orders from unknown people? Or for a good progressive who deals with Wallace and tells what occurred?"

Anna Louise was shaken and released by Emily's explosion. She asked her to leave the room for five minutes and turned to her two advisors with the terms she would accept. "I will sign nothing until I come to town on Monday next. Any changes that a responsible member of the party, competent to pass on these articles, wants to make, I will accept. If responsible friends want them suppressed completely, this too can be done. But then these friends must be prepared with me to face what will happen and guide me through the trap the grand jury sets for me. . . . Then I appear before the grand jury as a woman of mystery who wrote and then suppressed her story. That is something I cannot face alone and without advice."

The two women took their leave. The next day the morning *Worker* published an article hinting that Anna Louise had sold out to the *Tribune* for $10,000. With no real evidence, Anna Louise thought bitterly that John Abt had tipped them off.

Rogge had advised Anna Louise that if she published the articles the grand jury would treat her as a journalist rather than as a spy, and this seemed reasonable to Anna Louise. She spent much of the evening in a four-way conversation with Rogge, Blumenthal and the editor from the *Tribune*, negotiating turns of phrase and emphasis. The overeager attitude of the editor and his assumption that most readers would see the writing as an exposé of the methods of a police state worried her all night. The next morning she called Blumenthal back: "Unless I can use this as a bomb against the cold war and spy scare, I'm pulling it back. I don't get excited by all these thousands of dollars that you're mentioning [Blumenthal had indicated that she might clear as much as $15,000 on reprint rights]. They seem to me . . . like fairy gold. I've got enough to pay my lawyer. . . . And I would rather pull it back and just release it gradually and dignified through a little thing like the *National Guardian*, than have them pull out all these things that I wanted to print. I knew they wouldn't do it . . . but I would have wanted to say the cold war and the spy scare, we started ourselves in the United States. Because that's the way I feel about it."

Blumenthal hastily dissuaded Anna Louise from coming to New York that afternoon and suggested he come to Cromwell the next day. He agreed to insist on whatever changes she wanted. Anna Louise was immediately mollified: "I'm willing to blast all these illusions of a lot of people who think that the Soviet Union is just perfect. I'm quite willing to blast that, it should have been blasted long ago. But I'm not willing to say that the Soviet state is worse than other states; it does just like them."

The *Tribune* meantime was insisting on changes in Anna Louise's stories. When Blumenthal arrived the next day, he faced the *Tribune's* refusal to publish the statement that Anna Louise did not "blame the Soviet Union." Anna Louise irrationally told him to return $4,000 for the four words she wished to keep. A compromise was eventually worked out: she did not "accuse the Soviet state as such." After hours of deliberation Blumenthal took back to New York a set of articles that he thought were in final form.

The next day Anna Louise made one final attempt to reach the Communist party before signing with the *Tribune*. After arriving at Grand Central Station, she painfully made her way along 42nd Street to the offices of the Committee for a Democratic Far Eastern Policy and with difficulty climbed the four flights of stairs to their offices. She approached the executive director, Maud Russell, and asked her to take a message "downtown," to party headquarters. Maud explained why she could not and offered to call a messenger, but this was unacceptable to Anna Louise, who exploded in frustration. Then she said, "I'm on my way to sign a contract with the *Tribune*; they have offered me a lot of money and will probably publish the articles whether I sign or not. What advice do you have?" According to Anna Louise, Maud offered no advice.

Anna Louise went on to Roy Blumenthal's offices. Blumenthal was not yet in. Still full of doubt, she called John Abt and asked if he had said that her articles should be published. "I did not," he replied. "I said that you should use your judgment as a journalist." "John, I'm not just a journalist," she protested. "This is a political act with political consequences. I've just arrived back in America and have been sick in bed. I can't judge the political atmosphere." "I can't advise you" was her memory of Abt's response.

Blumenthal arrived, and Anna Louise turned upon him with the wrath of the betrayed. He defended himself by calling Jack McManus, an editor of the *Guardian* who had been present at the Wallace-Abt readings of the articles. MacManus confirmed that Wallace wanted the articles published and indicated that Abt had tried to keep Wallace from saying anything. Wallace would not, however, publicly endorse the articles.

Anna Louise and Blumenthal battled for four more hours over fifteen small changes until they finally arrived at a text that Anna Louise let go to the *Tribune* despite her continuing ambivalence. She went back to Rogge's house. He too was nervous about the *Tribune* editors and recognized that she would be happier if more people were in on the decision. She asked him to call Blumenthal and tell him to hold off the final submission. When the call reached Blumenthal, the *Tribune* had accepted all of Anna Louise's changes, and Blumenthal had signed the contract. Tired and confused, she demanded to see the proof sheets.

When they came, they were accompanied by a note asking Anna Louise either to accept publication or to cancel the deal and instruct Blumenthal to return the $5,000 and let the *Tribune* decide on penalties. Anna Louise was "surprised to find how well the stories read; the good that I thought the stories contained was really there." She insisted on one final change, failing which she said she would "mortgage her home" to fight the contract. Trying to establish a parallel between her case and the prosecution of the eleven American Communist leaders, she had asked in her final article, "But was it justice? Chucked out, branded, not a word of defense. Sure it wasn't justice. Justice isn't anywhere today. Maybe justice will be, after my time. Maybe! Maybe not! Certainly not if we don't stop this war frenzy and the atom bomb. That, as the commissar would say, that's my affair." The *Tribune* wanted to present her as the victim of a police state and had concluded the series with only the first four words. Anna Louise insisted on the entire text and the removal of the headline "Police State." The *Tribune* agreed but reserved the right to print any editorial it chose on the subject.

Anna Louise made two attempts to educate her left-wing audience before the appearance of the *Tribune* articles. In a long article for the *National Guardian* on "What do I still think of the U.S.S.R.?" she wrote: "The U.S.S.R. carries the great hope of mankind . . . as a mother carries a child toward birth." The emphasis on potential rather than achievement was accompanied by another note that she had not previously sounded in public. It was silly and wrong, she stated, to speak of the Soviet Union in tones so reverent as to make criticism impossible, for the U.S.S.R. "as it is today is [not] a model I would like America to copy." The articles, in fact, carried a stronger if more subtle anti-Soviet tone than the *Tribune* articles.

In addition to the *National Guardian* article, Anna Louise sent $1,000 of the money from the *Tribune* to the defense fund of the eleven Communists charged under the Smith Act. She asked Rogge to include a note reading: "For the American Communists who are getting as raw a deal from American justice as I got from the U.S.S.R., from a fellow victim of the cold war." The check went out through Rogge's office, and whether or not out of intentional provocation, the last clause was typed on the back.

All these efforts backfired. Eugene Dennis denounced the inscribed check in ringing terms as "tainted money . . . for a shabby promotion scheme," and refused what he called a "bribe." The news was published around the world and confirmed Anna Louise's perfidy in the eyes of many leftists. In Nanking, her nephew Robbins read of the affair and promptly dashed off a tongue-in-cheek letter saying that if she had extra money she couldn't get rid of, to send it to the YMCA. After the uproar subsided, Anna Louise donated the money to the defense of six Trenton blacks accused of criminal action (they were probably framed) in civil rights activity.

The *Tribune* was infuriated by the article in the *Guardian*, which violated at least the spirit of her contract granting the *Tribune* exclusive rights until April 15. It ran an editorial entitled "The Police State" directly over Anna Louise's first article on March 27 and referred to the series as "one of the most vivid, the most convincing and the most damning documentations of the processes of the Soviet police state." While this did not violate the letter of the contract with Anna Louise, it certainly encouraged the view that she thought herself the victim of a ruthless Communist state.

Despite her fury with the *Tribune's* editorializing, Anna Louise concluded that more political good than harm came out of the publication of the articles. "Reactionaries," she wrote, "all hate me worse than they did a year ago" because they had not been able to make use of her. (Though Anna Louise could not know it, J. Edgar Hoover irritatedly scrawled across a telegram that it was a "waste of time" to continue interviews and constant surveillance: "She is still pro-Russian.") "Progressives of the Wallace type" could now, she hoped, perceive her arrest as a matter of "the cold war and spy scare."

The articles did reestablish her credentials as a journalist. In her final hearing by the grand jury, she was treated more as a reporter than as a Communist, and the jury pushed less than it might have on naming names and organizations. When asked if she were a member of the Communist party, she responded, "I don't know." It was both a hedge and the truth.

Her main unfulfilled hope for the articles—that they would redeem her in the eyes of the party—was foolish, and she knew it. The American party could not agree to her claim that Soviet policy was being made by a few overzealous bureaucrats, and lurid details in her writing such as her fear of being "eaten by wolves" on the Polish border appeared to confirm a vision of the Soviet state as fundamentally inhuman and vicious. Anna Louise's claims that she had been sent on a "mission" and had received insufficient support from her American Communist friends were exaggerations of the fact that it was she who wanted to go to China. Lem Harris eventually wrote her that the articles made him sick. "Do you realize that you have added weight to the great lie that humans count for nothing in 'soulless Russia'?" Anna Louise answered: "Thank you for your estimates. Give my love to Kay."

There was for Anna Louise a bitter reward in the new understanding she had gained:

> We all have to learn something about the essence of the state. . . . The building of socialism in one state was and remains an essential tactic for a certain period of the world revolution. Such building, in a single state surrounded by hostile states, involves certain costs that should be recognized and not denied. It means that the state, instead of withering away, must become tougher, with a tough machinery of diplomats, police, army. Cops are cops, even in a state sheltering socialism; their function is not balanced judgment of individuals, but protection of the state organism against en-

croachment. For a state sheltering socialism, it is safer to make a lot of
mistakes against good individuals than to let through one bad individual who
might injure. . . . If they commit excess, the remedy lies with organizations
that know the individuals in question. It was the Committee for a Democratic
Far Eastern Policy and the American Communist party that should have
explained me to Moscow.

She now acknowledged what Mikhail Borodin and Joel had tried to tell
her for twenty years.

A recompense came in the offer of a contract from Ken McCormick,
editor-in-chief at Doubleday. He wanted to publish the book about China
she had tried to place with left-wing presses in Europe and the United
States and asked for rewriting only to answer basic questions about the
Chinese Communists. It was the perfect moment. On April 21, 1949,
the People's Liberation Army swept across the Yangtze in a myriad of
small boats. Within four days the occupation of Nanking was complete.
Chiang moved the capital to Canton, but the only embassy that even
bothered to accompany him was the Russian. By the early fall Mao
proclaimed from the top of T'ien-an Men ("Gate of Heavenly Peace") in
Peking that "the Chinese people have stood up."

Anna Louise spent much of the late spring and early summer at the
house of Raymond Robins in Florida, revising her manuscript and incorporating political advice from Chen Han-seng. Chen had disapproved of
the articles in the *Tribune,* and he spoke severely to Anna Louise about
her headstrong tendencies. She had continued to use the word "farmer"
in *Tomorrow's China* rather than "peasant," inattentive to the different
class implications each carried for the Chinese. "You do not seem to keep
in mind what we have said and explained," he told her, "for you are
always so hot for personal debate." Since this was serious and substantive
criticism, Anna Louise controlled her temper and changed the term. The
book appeared under the title *The Chinese Conquer China,* with a dedication "To Emily Pierson and Raymond Robins, who helped pick up the
pieces of a shattered work." It was well reviewed by Edgar Snow and
John K. Fairbank.

After completing the manuscript, she again tried to reach friends in
and around the party. It was not easy. The Dennis denunciation had cast
her as an enemy. A number of speaking dates for Progressive party
organizations were canceled because of CP pressure. A few people like
Edgar Snow resigned from groups that had followed the party line, but
the only significant organization to proclaim publicly that she had been
done an injustice was the Fellowship for Social Justice of the First Unitar-

ian Church of Los Angeles. The pastor of the church was Stephen Fritchman, a well-known progressive minister married to the daughter of a prominent Boston family. The church's letter requesting that the file be reopened was a thin reed in a strong wind, but it was signed by a number of non-Communists such as Corliss Lamont, I. F. Stone, and Joseph Barnes.

The attacks were particularly painful when they came from old friends. In an editorial in *Soviet Russia Today,* Jessica Smith wrote that with the Soviet "determination to avoid war and their persistent efforts to find a way for American-Soviet understanding, it is hardly credible that they would at this moment make a move of this kind without serious cause and without taking into consideration all its effects." Besides, the editorial went on, "when Miss Strong feels that she is being thwarted in any way, as is well known to anyone closely acquainted with her, she is apt to lose all restraint and stop at nothing to get her own way." Maud Russell wrote her that her *Tribune* articles had damaged "the cause for which we struggle," and the CDFEP denied Anna Louise access to their files and library on China.

These rejections deeply wounded Anna Louise. "Whether or not you agreed with my interpretation [in the articles], do you really think," she wrote back to Maud, "that it is decent to attack with such venom a person who was knocked down while honestly carrying out the mission which you among others gave her, and who has not for one moment since ceased the effort to act correctly for the cause of peace?" Worse even than the loss of friends was the reality of having no one to work with. When names of contributors were read at meetings of progressives, the announcer would look embarrassed when her check came up and say, "$25 from . . . a friend." During the summer she lived for some weeks at John Rogge's. She spent an evening there alone in a room so as not to break up a party given in honor of the author Howard Fast.

Once she arranged matters so that a contact was inevitable. During the middle of April, while she was living at Rogge's apartment, she asked to see William Patterson, the executive secretary of the Civil Rights Council, whom she had known in Moscow. Patterson cheerfully accepted a dinner invitation; when he arrived, he was horrified to see Anna Louise. There were only six for dinner. A debate developed between Patterson and Rogge on the relative merits of collective thinking and individual thinking. Patterson defended the former against Rogge; Anna Louise took his side, but he acted as if she were not there. As the party left the dinner table, Anna Louise asked Rogge to give her ten minutes alone with

Patterson. When she rapidly explained her version of events and repeated her desire to talk with the party, Patterson answered, "I will tell them. Tonight." Anna Louise was taken aback. "It is already eleven o'clock. It is not necessary tonight." "Yes," he replied, "it is necessary." The full weight of being a party member hit home. "You mean," she asked, "that since you have been forced into contact with me, you must report about it before you go to bed?" Patterson nodded stiffly. "I will let you know if anybody wants to speak with you." He left the room. Anna Louise made no further attempts to contact the higher echelons of the American Communist party.

Her mood was often low and self-punishing. She wrote Chen Hanseng, defending her publication of the *Tribune* articles and closed by saying:

> I am not sure what lies ahead of me, or whenever I shall ever again be allowed to associate with the people I love, or do with them any useful work. But when you see your Chinese friends, especially those to whom nearly three years ago I offered myself for as long as they should want me, will you tell them that if they have any use for my talent in writing, or in teaching English, and if the cloud of my name prevents using me in the old way, I would be glad to work in China, even in a prison, or in the isolation of some Peiping compound under detention, where I might edit other peoples' English, or write articles and pamphlets without my name.

At times her depression reached a dangerous depth. Shortly after Agnes Smedley died trying to reach China, Anna Louise replied to a letter from Cedric Belfrage: "You see, Cedric, how very very much better it would be to be dead. When you comment on Agnes' hard luck, I fear I laugh unsympathetically, for I have such an envy of Agnes and of the Eleven Communists [condemned to long jail sentences] and of all those privileged to be kicked in the face and stamped to bits by the enemy, and not by our own side." That her work was now proscribed by those for whom she had labored a lifetime was the heaviest blow. "It would have been better," she wrote in a dark moment, "if they had just killed me by auto accident in Moscow. Then something of what I was would remain."

What did remain were her hopes for America. "I owe the Soviet state neither allegiance, nor praise, nor even understanding," she wrote her old friend and editor Angus Cameron. "For many things will be done there that I cannot praise or understand without twisting my soul. . . . How can I, from a different past, pretend to follow their thinking. . . . I owe this state one thing only: to keep the peace so that they may build.

But this is also what I owe to my own people and to all the future of mankind. My allegiance is then to the American people and through them and beyond them to the people of today's and tomorrow's world. . . . It is they I was always serving, even when people said I was serving the U.S.S.R."

13

Putting Down Roots:
Salvation or a Church

There is a small devil in me which refuses the absolute and
when I saw . . . "Truth Is One," I replied quietly, "Quite so,
and truth is MANY."

—Anna Louise to Grace Nelson, November 2, 1959

In the accounts she herself gave of the arrest, Anna Louise maintained a
righteous anger at the bureaucratic stupidity of the Russian state and a
deep resentment at the "cowardice" and "infantile wish" of the American
Communist party for an omniscient Moscow. She was especially angry at
what she took to be the refusal of the group she felt had sent her to
China. "WHOSE job was it," she wrote to Raymond Robins, "to inform
Moscow what I was there for . . . ? It was the job . . . of . . . the
Committee for a Democratic Far Eastern Policy—also the American
Communists, who have ties with it, and who knew and blessed my China
trip. When Ed Snow told the committee: 'Wire Moscow; she's there on
your assignment' he was dead right." Snow had resigned in protest from
the CDFEP, but it had made no difference.

Most of all she was afraid of the change she detected in herself, "a
gradual hardening against things that so far I have loved beyond my own
life." And so she clung to her belief that the Communist party was
educable, that after a period of working with the Progressives, she would
prove her political reliability, and the party would reopen its doors. The
Chinese party provided her model: revolutionary yet pragmatic, based
on popular support, responsive to local and national problems, without
"the dictatorial tendencies of the Russians, the individualist tendencies

of the Americans, the independence and assertiveness of Tito, but [with] due place to international values."

At first it looked as if the process might work. Although West Coast Communists boycotted her, the Palo Alto chapter of the Progressive party, which included some Communists, was welcoming and suggested that she conduct a series of seminars on China. Tensions surfaced rapidly, however. She encountered Joe Starobin, the foreign editor of the *Daily Worker,* at a meeting in San Francisco and he, alone of all Communists, heard her story out. But he saw no reason to pursue her case further. She sent off a "contribution" to the party, which she still wishfully considered a membership fee. It was returned. On September 27, 1949, the *Daily People's World* in San Francisco carried a notice "Communist Warning on Anna Louise Strong": "It has come to our attention that Anna Louise Strong is attempting to ingratiate herself in progressive circles and organizations by giving them the impression that she has friendly relations with the Communist party. We wish to state emphatically that this is a deliberate misrepresentation . . . Whatever her purposes, they are not in the interest of the Communist party or the working classes." Anna Louise observed sardonically that the easiest way for the FBI to identify Communists would be to see who avoided her.

Communist hostility succeeded in dividing the Progressives. The state committee of the Communist party informed Palo Alto that "a nest of Titoists is getting started . . . ; it must be stamped out." The seminar on China, which had initially been a success, fell apart, and the woman at whose house the meetings were held was expelled from the party.

Perhaps, Anna Louise thought, Los Angeles would be more receptive. She had less personal history there, and there had been indications of support from the First Unitarian Church. She arranged a meeting with the Reverend Stephen Fritchman, the pastor of the church, a man with a long history of support of left-wing causes. His church served as a focal point for the discussion of progressive issues in Los Angeles.

Anna Louise had met him the year before at the home of a friend. Now she explained to him what had happened in Santa Clara County. "Would I be useful or a cause of friction if I applied to join your church?" she asked. Fritchman questioned her for over an hour, focusing especially on her attitude to the Soviet Union and American Communists. At the end he told her that they would be pleased to receive her and assured her that any Communists there might be in the church would "be polite to you inside the church even though they may not speak to you outside."

Anna Louise rented her Palo Alto house to her nephew, Tracy Jr., on the condition that she might use a room whenever she returned. She sold her other property around San Francisco, disposed of most of her furniture and bought a new house in La Crescenta next door to Hugh and Susan Hardiman, whose home was a social center for political progressives. There and at the church she slowly returned to a social life. Even a few members of the Communist party broke discipline to meet with her. Barbara Nestor, who had been in the party since its foundation in 1919, and LaRue McCormick, an important member of the Labor Defense group, decided that Anna Louise had too much integrity for the charges to be true. The party objected strenuously to these deviations, but it did not expel Nestor and McCormick, perhaps because they were so prominent.

Warwick and Helen Tompkins, who had written Anna Louise supportively after the publication of the *Herald Tribune* articles, became her good friends. Warwick was a film producer who had been blacklisted; his wife was a psychotherapist. Both had been expelled from the party for their efforts to reopen Anna Louise's case. Over the next few years they were sympathetic listeners and advisors.

It was her isolation from the broader world community in which she had spent most of her working life that she found hardest to bear. When her passport expired in June 1950, the State Department refused to renew it. Her address books, laboriously compiled across the whole world, had been taken from her in Moscow; she did not know how to get in touch with many people she had known. Sporadic attacks from the American Communist party continued to nag her. In January 1950 she had gone east on a speaking tour to a number of colleges and visited Philip Jaffe in New York. In 1948 he had stopped publication of *Amerasia* after two of his articles were severely criticized by the central committee of the party. When he had announced his intention to vote for Truman over Wallace, all progressives, including Anna Louise, had shunned him. Now she came to apologize and ask if she might use the files of *Amerasia*, probably the best source of material on China available to her after being barred from the CDFEP. Jaffe was glad to see her, and their parallel fates renewed the old bonds.

After talking with him, Anna Louise had a burst of self-confidence. It suddenly seemed obvious that she should simply walk down the street to Communist party headquarters and tell them her side of the story. She picked up the telephone and dialed the number; before the call went through Jaffe put his hand on the receiver. "Don't think that I want to interfere with you," he said, "but before you call that office you should look at this morning's *Worker*."

Under the headline "Anna Louise Strong Convicts Herself," the *Worker* carried a long letter from a California Communist, Hazel Grossman. Originally published in San Francisco, it had been reprinted in the New York paper because of its "exceptional interest." The core of the letter was an exposé of the supposed "anti-Soviet nature" of the article Anna Louise had written in 1927 for the *New York Times* about the differences between Stalin and Trotsky as leaders. Anna Louise had remarked that after Trotsky's fall, "all revolutionary life is less enthusiastic": out of context, the statement was damning. Grossman went on to deny the truth of Anna Louise's report on Liu Shao-ch'i's analysis of Mao's "new inventions in Marxism."

Anna Louise was outraged. The *Times* article had been seen by a CPUSA member before publication; the American party had ordered 40,000 copies of her pamphlet on Liu. She sent off an irate rebuttal to Starobin, "not for publication so as not further to harm the United Front." She knew that they would not have printed it anyway.

The illusions she had sustained for over a year finally vanished with this episode. She later wrote Pauline Schindler in Los Angeles: "I beg no more. I have finished kneeling. That [*Daily Worker*] box kicked me at long last to my feet and erect. . . . The more I kneel, the harder they kick me. They love to hammer a suppliant. The more I show love, the more vicious they get." She decided that her secret contributions were "useless and histrionic," and sent no more money to the party.

She did, however, pursue other paths to vindication. As the first anniversary of her arrest approached, she drafted a lengthy account of her thirty years of work in the Soviet Union and went to New York to deliver it to O. John Rogge. Rogge had become legal counsel for Yugoslavia in the United States and was making a trip to the U.S.S.R. in which he was scheduled to meet Stalin. She appended an eight-page brief to use in oral argument. Nothing came of it. Other contacts in New York proved equally futile. Ken McCormick at Doubleday was so eager for her to write a biography of Mao that he cabled the Chinese to that effect, and she sent a plaintive letter to Chou En-lai asking if there were any possibility of returning to China, even if this meant "accepting house arrest" and "pseudonymity." No response came to either request.

She still had enough notoriety to command occasional lecture dates, especially at colleges, and these kept her in the East for several months. At Oberlin, a thousand people flocked into the First Congregational Church to hear her proclaim that Mao was likely to be Stalin's successor. On her second day there, she gave a broadcast interview at the college radio station with Paul Willen, the head of the college forum board, and John Barnett, the editor of the college newpaper. The two students were supposed to stick to prepared questions to which Anna Louise rattled off answers with her customary vigor and confidence. In the midst of this smooth process, Willen asked an unrehearsed question: "Miss Strong, you have told us that your expulsion from the U.S.S.R. was due to a 'boneheaded blunder' of the Russian secret police, and you have told us that as a result of your expulsion Communist parties have broken off relations with you, and so forth. Do you mean to suggest that a 'bone-headed blunder' . . . determines world Communist policy?" Anna Louise started to explain, then stopped, tried again and failed once more. The group lapsed into embarrassed silence.

In the midst of some desultory conversation over dinner that evening, Anna Louise suddenly looked Willen in the eye and said earnestly, "Mr. Willen, that was a very interesting question you asked me this afternoon. Do you know why I didn't answer it? I couldn't." A floodgate had been opened. Anna Louise told Willen that the only time she could see a Communist was in a clandestine meeting that was always dangerous to the other's political life. She complained with some bitterness that the CDFEP would not allow her access to their files: "It is perfectly true what these congressional committees say about these organizations; they are nothing but fronts." Only a few Communist friends, she told Willen, had tried even privately to tell her that they did not believe the party line. Willen was astonished that Anna Louise could feel so personally betrayed and remain publicly so loyal. "You know," she responded, "I am no longer young. At my age it is not easy to give up something to which one has devoted one's entire lifetime. . . . I have had doubts, of course. . . . But when one believes deeply in something, one must accept certain doubts."

Willen apparently did not understand Anna Louise's "I believe, help thou mine unbelief," and widely publicized her revelations. This so incensed Morton Schrag, the chairman of the Oberlin Young Progressives Association, that he wrote a letter to Cedric Belfrage at the *National Guardian* denouncing Willen as a provocateur and urging the *Guardian* and the Progressive party to make use of Anna Louise's ability to inspire large crowds. Belfrage circulated a sympathetic memorandum to his fellow editors pointing out that Anna Louise was in no way critical of Russia and sent a copy of the Schrag letter to the executive secretary of the

Progressive party, to John Abt, and to Joe Starobin at the *Daily Worker*. Starobin's reply was firm: "The question is closed."

Belfrage scrawled "Tecumseh has spoken!" in the margin before sending the note on to Aronson. Aronson added "Ugh!" and they sent a copy of Schrag's letter (though not Starobin's reply) to Anna Louise, who hastened to assure Schrag that she had said nothing in private that contradicted what she had said in public: "I think it permissible in private talk between people of good intention and intelligence to discuss such matters. For only so does one clarify one's own thought. But I think in public talk one should be very careful about saying things which, distorted by the press, might help to inflame war. For *if* the U.S.S.R. has shortcomings to be corrected, this cannot be done by American criticism. . . . I shall give in public whatever truths I have tested and found worth handing on."

Under the prodding of Corliss Lamont, a small group of progressives wrote a joint letter to the Russian ambassador, asking him to reopen her case. The letter was sent on June 6 with twelve names attached. None of the signees had ever found a comfortable political home: in addition to Emily Pierson and Raymond Robins, these included the Union Theological Seminary professor Henry F. Ward, Edgar Snow, Albert Rhys Williams, and I. F. Stone. No answer was forthcoming.

Meanwhile, after thirty years of earning her living as a writer, Anna Louise was no longer bringing in enough to make ends meet. Upon her return to the West Coast, she drove over the mountains to Bakersfield and Fresno to research articles on migrant workers. In the past she would have approached the organizers for contacts. Now most of them would have nothing to do with her. She learned nothing that she wished to write about. In search of income, she turned to real estate. In the inflationary market of Southern California it was possible to buy old houses, fix them up and sell them at a considerable profit. In previous years, when she had not needed the funds, she had been amused at the profits from her speculations. She now exploited that experience, although she was careful not to allow herself to spend more than a dozen hours a week on real estate.

She was on a retreat in the San Bernardino mountains above Los Angeles with a group from the Unitarian church when the news of the outbreak of the Korean War came over the radio. Fritchman asked her to make a short presentation to the group, and her remarks were so impressive that she was asked to amplify her comments for the entire church membership. The speech she gave to a packed church was vintage Anna

Louise. She carefully reminded her listeners that she had been the only American correspondent in North Korea since the end of World War II, and in a combination of portraits and statistics sketched a picture of firm and clearheaded North Koreans, minimal Soviet presence, corrupt South Koreans, and a vastly unpopular American army. She stressed that the conflict was a civil war and the Russians were not militarily involved. Americans should follow the Russian example and stay out. The most obvious solution, Anna Louise told her audience, lay in Nehru's plan to bring the Communist Chinese in on the whole question: "otherwise China may be forced to speak through war."

The speech was a resounding success, and a mimeographed version sold out rapidly. A network of friends spread the word across the country and more than 5,000 copies were mailed out. A few more Communist party members broke the ban on relations with her, including Dorothy Healey, the head of the California Communist party. Anna Louise basked in the recognition and took the opportunity to send a copy of her talk to Soviet Ambassador Vishinsky, again pointing out her political reliability. Letters began to reach her asking for more information about Korea and the issues raised by the American conduct of the war. There were so many that Anna Louise began to mimeograph her replies. The first went out in September; it was followed by another in October, and a third in November.

Thus, in January 1951, *Today* was born, a monthly newsletter on "how it seems to me." Part column, part confession, part a plea for friends old and new to pay attention, *Today* analyzed Chinese, Russian and American politics. Anna Louise's old fire returned; she did her research carefully, selecting from both the American and the foreign press, rarely using left-wing sources, and delighting in hoisting the American government on the petard of an uncomfortable fact from *Wall Street Journal*. She also reprinted some of her old poetry, offered progressive Christmas cards for sale, took note of important books. An acquaintance from the church, Betty Rottger, volunteered to help with the editing and production. Betty was bright and as sharp-tongued as Anna Louise. There were periodic explosions between the two, but Anna Louise could not fault Betty's demonic devotion to the enterprise. Before long there were 3,000 subscribers, and enough voluntary contributions came in to cover the costs of production.

As Anna Louise saw it, the world around her had gone mad. In Russia, Mikhail Borodin, as well as almost all the other Soviet China hands, had joined the ever-increasing list of those deported to Siberia or shot. In early 1950 Mao had finally visited Stalin in Moscow; after several weeks of what Anna Louise quietly recognized as difficult negotiations, he acknowledged Stalin's sole leadership of the world Communist movement and received substantial Soviet industrial and military aid. In Korea, after an initial apparent stabilization of the situation by the intervention of American air power, American forces under General MacArthur dramatically escalated the war by landing troops at Inchon, far behind enemy lines. When MacArthur's troops pushed north to the Yalu River, which marked the border with China, Chinese forces swept across, pushing the Americans back to the original line of demarcation at the thirty-eighth parallel. Losses were great on both sides; many civilians died in the extensive napalm bombing. In the United States, confusion over the difficulties in Korea exacerbated the already fierce reaction to the cold war and the "loss of China." Senator Joseph McCarthy undertook to destroy American China experts. Congressional committees relentlessly pursued those suspected of Communist affiliations past or present. The First Unitarian Church's tax-exempt status was called into question. In New York, eighty-three-year-old Dr. W. E. B. Du Bois was arrested as a dangerous subversive. The Supreme Court upheld the conviction of Eugene Dennis and the other top Communist leaders for planning seditious acts, and they started long jail terms. Anna Louise noted that even the *Wall Street Journal* had commented that "an old mansion seems to be decaying around us."

Anna Louise was conscious of a slow evolution of her political position and felt obliged to apprise her readers of her stance:

> My views on the world situation have developed   through forty years in the progressive movement and are not basically changed by a personal catastrophe, even though it destroyed a worldwide work. These views are, briefly:
>
> 1. that capitalism has ceased to answer man's growing needs and will be replaced by what we call, roughly, socialism;
>
> 2. that the U.S.S.R. is the world's first socialist state, by no means a perfect example of what men want, but nonetheless one from which persons who want socialism can learn;
>
> 3. that the best use anyone can make of a life is to spread friendly understanding of the new socialist lands among people in America, so that whatever changes may lie ahead can be made with the maximum of knowledge and a minimum of blind strife. This is the use I have made of my life; I am not sorry;
>
> 4. that the immediate job today—for an American—is not the promotion of revolutionary change, but the promotion of world peace, so that those lands that already have made revolutionary change can show the world what they can do with it.

Her statement passed unnoticed in the public realm. Only two readers were irritated that Anna Louise seemed "to have given up the class struggle." Somewhat pathetically, *Today* now included announcements of an "open house, Sundays, 4 to 7 P.M. . . . And if Sunday isn't a good day for you, phone for another time."

Inevitably she accumulated a number of hangers-on. Adherents of the Hardimans' La Crescenta Ashram and an odd assortment of Southern California vegetarians found their way to her door. Her relatives remained scattered, and she was ambivalent about her need for them. Tracy was in Geneva as general secretary of the World YMCA. She had no contact with Ruth. Her nephew Tracy, Jr., and his wife were going to the Middle East. Her oldest nephew, Robbins, had moved from China to Korea and been caught with his family in Seoul at the outbreak of the war. When they finally returned to the United States, they stopped for a few months on the East Coast and then moved to Paris.

Her isolation made her often rude and insensitive, even to those who tried to help her. It was not that she was cruel, but she was accustomed to channeling her anxieties into her writing, and in near desperation without important work, she was sometimes not in control of her behavior. When a friend drove her to Long Beach for a speaking engagement and on the way back the car ran out of gas, Anna Louise berated her for being so "inefficient." "My time is worth money," she screamed. The woman broke into tears, and her three-year-old niece, who had accompanied them, leaned forward from the jump seat, begging, "Don't cry, Auntie." With a shock, Anna Louise came back to herself and apologized profusely, but she would have missed the other's anguish if it had not been for the child. As often happened, she was rude to her friends but concerned about those who had no resources. She proposed to LaRue McCormick that they mutually adopt the illegitimate child of an acquaintance of theirs and bring it up together. LaRue finally talked her out of it by pointing out how much energy her children had taken from her.

In July 1952 Anna Louise wrote to Emily Pierson about "a very simple event that I think is going to make a kind of inner transition in me. I shall preface it by saying that ever since my return from the U.S.S.R. I have not been fully living in the U.S.A. . . . I have had very hard crises every time I did *Today* and my psychotherapist friend, Helen Tompkins, said it was because I had not accepted living in America and was fighting my work. She was right, and I didn't know what to do about it. It got to where I was planning to consult a psychiatrist and got from Fritchman some names. Then last Sunday, a young secretary of the Ventura Longshoreman's Union drove over from Ventura, well over 100 miles round-trip—more like 150—to have a talk with me. He never once asked me about Moscow; he wanted my opinion about lots of local things. . . . And in talking I suddenly saw that a lot of things I have learned in other lands fitted his situation and were eagerly taken in by him. . . . Ever since then I have been suddenly at home on this Pacific Coast as if returned after thirty years of wars and wanderings, . . . as if a third section of life were beginning."

She asked Emily to send her twenty-five rosebushes, and when they were held up by California agricultural inspection procedures she bought her own; she put in a field of poppies and added some ground pine and ivy geranium. But the cultivating of her own garden was not enough. In the past, travel and adventure had substituted for intimacy; now she had neither. She had gathered about her a number of people who admired her for her brilliance and respected her past accomplishments. She *needed* them; they gave her succor and sustenance, but not excitement or anything new. She was living off emotional and intellectual capital.

In December 1952 Hugh Hardiman visited China with a "peace delegation." "Never," exulted Anna Louise in *Today*, "have I heard more joyous words than those of my friend . . . speaking on Peking Radio, reporting how the crowds embraced the Americans." But when Hardiman returned, he would tell her nothing, and Anna Louise feared that he had encountered people who had warned him against talking with her. Hardiman tried later to impress on her how greatly China had changed since she had been there, and gave her a copy of Liu Shao-ch'i's pamphlet "How to be a Good Communist" as an indication. He was annoyed when she retorted that the translation had been improved since she had last seen it in Yenan. "It must be a situation which occurs very often," she wrote to Emily, "Moses not reaching Canaan while Aaron gets through. John the Baptist saying 'He must increase and I must decrease.' I was prepared to hail Hugh as the new authority on China, from whom I, like all, must now learn. I was not prepared to have him act as if nothing I ever saw was important."

She began to despair about America. "We have not made gains on the problems that trouble the American people," she wrote on the day of Eisenhower's inauguration. "We have lost ground in civil rights. We have seen the witch hunt expand from Hollywood writers through doctors, lawyers, until it engulfs the United Nations. . . . We have seen the Smith Act devour wider categories of victims. . . . One quarter of the crew of the French steamer *Liberté*—good name—were kept on board in New

York Harbor for refusing to be screened by American inquisitors. We have seen our public housing system broken. . . . Our public schools are attacked by the purging of texts and teachers. . . . This is A HERITAGE TO BE RID OF AS WE ENTER 1953!"

On March 5, 1953, Joseph Stalin died. The last years of his rule had been marked by an increasing paranoia, but if Anna Louise acknowledged this, she hid it in public. For her, Stalin's death was a moment of historic importance, the end of the first epoch of modern socialism. And she dropped a hint as to where she thought leadership of the Communist bloc should now pass: "Whoever devises the theoretical base and the practical forms for the future socialist '*International*' . . .—and so far Liu Shao-ch'i has done more analysis than anyone else I know—will become Stalin's heir in the world movement, greater in world history than any mere ruler of the U.S.S.R. More than that, he will have laid the foundation for the world government which must one day be."

The public hint concealed a stronger private anxiety. When she wrote in *Today* of the purges then being held in Eastern Europe, she noted only that they were evidence that problems were being worked out. In private she wrote to Emily Pierson: "I don't think these people were guilty, any more than the Rosenbergs. . . . Not as much as the Rosenbergs, for nobody denies that the Rosenbergs' loyalty was and is to Russia. (Not that I consider that to be a crime.) But I think that the two persons I knew of, those Czech condemned men who were hanged, were devoted Communists. I think that if they confessed guilt in a court, they probably did it because they thought it best for the movement that they should call themselves guilty." Anna Louise went on to say that "the method of the trial and the savage sentences are a blot on the Czechs and the Soviet bloc." She closed with a new reflection, "Perhaps the time has come to say this. Has it? What do you think?" and then delayed sending her letter for a week, during which time she crossed out the entire paragraph of doubts and added a postscript, "I don't know what I believe. Comments wanted."

The issues of *Today* published during this period are as chaotic as the events Anna Louise sought to narrate. She was often unable to find a coherent thread; the time between issues grew longer; the pleasure in telling the world "how it seems to me" grew less. "Events move so fast," she complained, "with such powerful contradictions and such smashing drama, that those of us who are tied to the news grow exhausted from the shock of daily change. For two months I have sat at my desk, made fifty pages of news notes, single spaced, yet failed to assemble *Today*. My starter doesn't work; the motor is flooded. . . . I am spoiled by a lifelong stimulus of reporting exciting events in hopeful lands; now I must dig through tons of American newspapers in hard research and careful analysis."

Other elements conspired to depress her about *Today.* The successful launching of the *Monthly Review,* a Marxist, non-Communist journal of analysis and commentary, cut into her circulation and reduced the political need for *Today.* At the same time, publication costs were mounting. "I am sure your New England conscience would be horrified," Anna Louise wrote to Emily, "as mine is, by the hours and weeks and days on end that I spend just doing jigsaw puzzles and solitaire to KEEP FROM DOING *TODAY.*" She was sufficiently troubled about her behavior to consult both a physician and a psychiatrist.

The doctor gave her a complete physical exam and except for her weight and the Paget's disease pronounced her in fine health. The psychiatrist, a left-wing progressive named Milton Lester, told her she had no certifiable condition. "It might help you to have a good secretary who came for instructions and dictation." Neither diagnosis really helped.

Two people kept her on the West Coast. In July she received a letter from a woman named Marta Miller, who lived in the small town of Rim Forest, high in the San Bernardino Mountains. The letter was barely literate but carried a strong and direct appeal. One hot day Anna Louise drove up to Rim Forest for a visit. Marta proved to be a seventy-four-year-old Swede who lived with her invalid husband in a small cabin with a leaky roof and a clogged cesspool in a section of the national forest that had been set aside for development before the Depression.

Anna Louise was attracted to Marta's gruff honesty and strong, if unanalyzed commitment to left-wing causes. Marta saw in Anna Louise not only a much-admired progressive but the chance to resolve the central obsession of her life. Across the lot from Marta's house stood a large house that had been built originally as a communal center, it had a country kitchen, a huge living room and three bedrooms. The house stood on the highest knoll and commanded a stunning 360-degree view. Marta loved the clubhouse and had for many years dreamed of turning it back into a center for progressive-minded people. She had managed to buy up six of the surrounding lots to protect the view; now Anna Louise might buy the house itself. Anna Louise liked the idea and made the purchase. Rim Forest was an escape from the smog, both physical and political, of the lower valley.

The second person was Grace Nelson, a woman in her early thirties, married with two children, who ran a printer's shop that produced left-wing publications. A broken mimeograph machine led Anna Louise to approach her about printing *Today*. Grace had been awed on the half-dozen occasions in the 1940s when she had heard Anna Louise speak and now was overwhelmed by her first talk with her. She agreed to take on *Today*. The party did not take kindly to this breach of discipline. Shortly after their meeting, party members followed Anna Louise to Grace's house in Long Beach and hovered about, spying on the two women. Grace resigned from the party just as she was expelled.

Grace became a combination daughter, companion and girl Friday to Anna Louise. She took her shopping, drove her to lectures and doctor's appointments, and tried to relieve her loneliness on holidays and weekends. At other times the Nelsons would drive Marta out to the house that Anna Louise had bought in Desert Hot Springs and find Anna Louise waiting with a tureen of hot soup. The four adults would divide a bottle of wine and spend the evening playing slightly tipsy bridge. For Anna Louise, Grace and Tom Nelson were more like family than anyone else she knew; she even became fond of their five-year-old, Blair. It was, not however, always easy for the Nelsons. One weekend, when the Nelson family and Anna Louise were at Rim Forest, Anna Louise insisted that she must have the Sunday *Los Angeles Times*. After considerable effort, Grace located a copy and brought it to Anna Louise in her study. Anna Louise went into a tantrum at having her work interrupted.

She still longed for new places. Her nephew John Niederhauser was now an agronomist working on potato stocks for the Rockefeller Foundation in Mexico; when he invited her to come for Christmas, she happily accepted. She sent him a list of people she hoped to see and asked him to make arrangements. John, who at that time knew more about potatoes than he did about Mexican politics, casually set up a dinner party that included Vicente Lombardo Toledano, the head of the Popular Socialist party, and David Alfaro Siqueiros, the well-known left-wing painter. In high spirits after the dinner, she asked John the next day to drive her out to visit Diego Rivera in his studio at San Angel. The two old friends had a joyful reunion and spent most of the day discussing world affairs.

Encouraged at her reception in Mexico, Anna Louise boarded a plane for Guatemala City on January 1, 1954. Guatemala was probably the most interesting country she could visit. Like Mexico, it required only a tourist card at the border. In 1944 a revolution led by Juan José Arévalo had thrown out Jorge Ubico, a dictator who ruled as much in his own interests as in those of the United Fruit Company. In 1951 Arévalo had been succeeded in a democratic election by Jacobo Arbenz Guzmán, a progressive land-reform-oriented president.

Anna Louise spent almost a month in Guatemala interviewing leaders and peasants, sharpening her old tools. The only sour note was the publication of an item in the Communist *Tribuna Popular* on January 13, informing their readers that "Anna Louise Strong is a Yankee spy." She returned to La Crescenta to write a passionately clear account of her trip for *Today* and to plan a major pamphlet on the Guatemalan revolution. But all her enthusiasm left her in June when a CIA-engineered coup toppled Arbenz and his policies.

With her fire again damped, Anna Louise sold the La Crescenta property and bought a large old house in downtown Los Angeles called the Tower. She clung to her ancient hope of estabishing a community center for progressive causes but found herself instead renting out floors and rooms to strangers to cover her mortgage and living expenses. Plans for the next issue of *Today* lay untouched in her study, and she spent most of her time trying unsuccessfully to convince friends from the East to visit her.

One event raised her spirits temporarily. She attended a speech by Josef Winiewicz, the Polish ambassador to the United States, who had been a journalist before entering politics. During the question period, she rose from the floor with a query; Winiewicz recognized her and took special care to name her and recall her achievements to the audience. A few weeks later he had dinner with Cedric Belfrage and Jim Aronson and told them the story of the lecture. The two editors mentioned that the *Guardian* was about to raise the issue of Anna Louise's case again. He asked them to delay a while longer: he would shortly be in Moscow and would make inquiries. Aronson immediately wrote Anna Louise a guarded letter observing that "there is reason to believe that . . . mistakes will be admitted."

The new year prodded her into publishing another issue of *Today,* and a minor crisis over Taiwan produced one more. But she had turned her attention increasingly to real estate and was making so much profit on some deals that she begged Emily not to tell Cedric Belfrage, lest he think poorly of her. She read Adele Davis' *Let's Eat Right to Keep Fit,* became a convert to Davis' way of eating, and brought her weight down to 160 pounds. On New Year's Day, 1955, she was driving her Austin when it suddenly went into a skid; the car rolled down an embankment, turning over twice; its front end was severely damaged. By some miracle, she was only bruised, but she took the accident as a warning that she needed to be more cautious in her everyday life.

Meanwhile, Winiewicz had taken her case to the proper authorities in Moscow. "Anna Louise Strong?" was the answer. "That case was closed long ago; everyone knew that it was a mistake." As Winiewicz later told Aronson, he almost screamed, "Say so publicly!"

On the morning of March 4, 1955, Anna Louise was sitting in the study of her house in Los Angeles, trying to work on *Today*. The phone rang, and the caller said he was a reporter from the Hearst afternoon paper. After making sure that he was indeed speaking to Anna Louise Strong, he asked if she was aware that an announcement by Tass had cleared her of all charges and blamed the whole affair on Beria and Abakumov, the heads of the Soviet security police who had since been executed. "What have you to say about that?" "Very good, if true," Anna Louise replied flatly, still suspicious of Hearst. She hung up, and the phone rang again. This time it was Harry Schwartz from the *New York Times*. She immediately became cautious of her growing enthusiasm. "Are you satisfied?" Schwartz asked. "I am tremendously pleased," answered Anna Louise. "No, no," he insisted, "are you satisfied that Beria was to blame?" "I don't know," she replied. "I never met Beria, but he was head of the department that ran the jail. I suppose he had responsibility."

It was two days before the *Daily Worker* carried the news. In the meantime, Anna Louise was deluged with calls, congratulations, telegrams, and requests for appearances on radio and television. She went to hear Edgar Snow speak at her church, and the meeting had to be held up for forty-five minutes as everyone "shook my wrist off." In the midst of all the excitement, Anna Louise suddenly realized that she had heard nothing official from any representative of the Soviet Union. She wrote to the ambassador, Georgi Zarubin, requesting formal confirmation. Zarubin had been co-director with Joel of the Soviet exhibit at the 1939 World's Fair and an occasional dinner guest at the Shubins' in Moscow. An answer came back from the embassy counselor, indicating that Zarubin had given instructions to send Anna Louise a copy of the announcement by Tass. It read:

> In February 1949 the American journalist A. L. Strong, who was at that time in the U.S.S.R., was arrested by the organs of the State Security of the U.S.S.R. on a suspicion of espionage and sabotage against the Soviet Union and deported from the U.S.S.R.

As a result of an investigation conducted by the procurator's office of the U.S.S.R., it has been established that the former leader of the Ministry of State Security, Beria, presented the above charges against Miss Strong without grounds. In view of this, she is now exonerated from these charges.

There was no indication of why the charges had been dropped, or any suggestion of why Beria had arrested her.

Nor were the actual sources of her rehabilitation clear. Many files of those condemned under Stalin were being reviewed at that time, and most of the blame was put on Beria. Winiewicz's request probably merely hurried along what was already in process, especially since the Soviets were now seeking to improve relations with the United States. Three months later Eisenhower and Khrushchev inaugurated the "spirit of Geneva" with a summit conference. Equally important, shortly before the announcement, Molotov made a speech recognizing that China was henceforth to be considered a co-leader of the socialist camp.

The exoneration freed Anna Louise to speak more candidly than she had felt she could for the previous six years. She had no intention of rejoining the party and wrote to Belfrage that she no longer needed "to be bound—as I was, as you are—in expressing my comments and criticisms by the views of other people, even our friends." "Our friends" referred to party members. She abandoned her claim that her arrest had been a "blunder" and criticized the structural position of the secret police. "No human beings are wise enough and sane enough to arrest, try, and enforce sentence on other humans without open and public control. . . . From now on I expect to say this frankly, just as frankly as I say that the growing power of the FBI is a threat to the liberties of Americans." She pointed out that the Soviet Union had developed a method for clearing past charges that "works pretty well." Then she added as an afterthought in pen, "unless the people are already dead."

With her renewed sense of self-worth, she was able to turn again to the world. She wrote to Emily:

We must remember that every Jimmy Jones in Podunk has a field of knowledge in which he knows more than Lenin, or Stalin, or Mao. . . . And this is the field of life around him. And if Lenin or Mao could be transferred to Podunk, they would first have to learn what Jimmy Jones knows before they could effectively act. *This* is the basis for both the Christian emphasis on the value of every man, and for Stalin's statement that the "people" are of first importance; it is the basis of the old American initiative and originality which has been lost in recent years. And somehow we must again arouse the initiative and courage of the Jimmy Joneses in Podunk, to do the job they uniquely are fit to do.

And, as Christian, communist and pioneer, the first move she made was to apply for a passport.

Even Anna Louise was not surprised when the Passport Division gave her a "tentative refusal" and told her that her case was to be "taken under advisement." Her lawyers, Leonard Boudin and Joseph Forer, both Washington liberals, advised her to join her case to those of Paul Robeson, Rockwell Kent and others, in order to reduce expenses and profit from whatever decisions might favor them. She agreed and began the lengthy appeals process.

Once again speaking invitations flooded in. In May, Anna Louise set off for the Northeast, lecturing mainly on "China, the United States, and the World Crisis." Foremost in her thoughts was the Bandung Conference, at which a group of nations led by China, India and Yugoslavia constituted itself formally as a "third bloc" in world politics. Neither Russia nor the United States had been invited.

In June Ambassador Zarubin invited her to lunch and extended an official invitation to visit the U.S.S.R. Zarubin told her that "as soon as you bring us your American passport, we will give you a Soviet visa in five minutes." At a news conference immediately afterwards, she was asked to explain the behavior of her former friends who had once praised her writings and then for six years vilified them as treacherous, anti-Soviet sentiments. She stumbled over her honesty. "I haven't formulated an answer yet—none that I can express." Then she picked her way carefully forward: "Naturally I was shocked. To find the same human failings among my friends as elsewhere, to find that people don't stand by their friends. . . . But these matters of individual personality are of little importance."

The invitation from Zarubin was pleasing, but returning to Russia, except for a visit, was not the central item on Anna Louise's agenda. She wrote to Chen Han-seng, now in Peking on the staff of *China Reconstructs*. "Long ago," she reminded him, "in Yenan I received an invitation to return to China. Is that invitation still valid?" A cordial response assured her that she was welcome to return to China for as long as she wished as the guest of the Writers' Union and the Association for Cultural Relations.

Triumphant, she stopped at Oberlin on her return west to attend her fiftieth reunion before covering the United Nations' tenth-anniversary celebration in San Francisco for the *Guardian*. The summer and fall were spent trying to keep up with the renewed demands for lectures and talks. In November her seventieth birthday was celebrated in a gala at the First Unitarian Church, and on Thanksgiving night as she drove with the Nelsons up the long road to Rim Forest, she happily burst into a song called "Highway 69" that she had written to her native land.

With her return to public life, she had little time for *Today*. She resolved to write a book about Stalin and his times. In February, while working on the book at Rim Forest, she heard on the radio that Soviet Premier Nikita Khrushchev had made a secret speech at the Twentieth Party Congress in Moscow, denouncing the excesses of Stalin's personality cult and admitting "grave mistakes" had taken place. Feeling betrayed, she called her friend Dorothy Healey, the head of the California Communist party: "We knew all these things for twenty-five years, and I kept silent for the cause of socialism. What am I supposed to say?" She asked Dorothy to spend a few days with her at Desert Hot Springs to talk before she continued writing, and Dorothy, equally distressed, agreed. Anna Louise was even more distraught by the time they reached her desert trailer. Weeping uncontrollably, she awoke Dorothy at two A.M. and again at three and four. Dorothy was afraid that Anna Louise was losing her mind and grasped for some solid reassurance. She found it in an epigram from Stalin: "The logic of events is stronger than the logic of intentions." It convinced Anna Louise that if her work had in fact furthered the cause of socialism, it did not matter what she had known or believed. The Stalin quote became the epigraph to her book, and she slept.

She flew to New York to finish the book, staying at the home of Philip Jaffe to use his library and files. It was a difficult task; Jaffe would sometimes find her weeping over a chapter—whether from regret or nostalgia was never clear. But slowly the book was written and called *The Stalin Era*. It raised all of the important questions, but the answers were often ambivalent. Anna Louise detailed the reasons for accepting the legitimacy of the purge trials and then announced that the rationale had been given her by Mikhail Borodin, "who was arrested about the same time I was and died in a Siberian labor camp." She argued that a "great madness" had come down on the Soviet Union after the assassination of Kirov in 1934 and admitted publicly for the first time that, especially after the 1937–38 trials of Marshal M. N. Tukhachevsky and G. G. Yagoda, head of the secret police, "doubts were spread about the investigating arm of the government. . . . A sense of insecurity spread about the Soviet people." Anna Louise rejected both the totalitarianism theory that was becoming fashionable in the West and Khrushchev's reduction of the horrors to the acts of one person. She found the source for the terrors of the thirties and forties in the unleashing of the political police that had annihilated the "active horror of an informed people against injustice."

As a political leader, Stalin came off rather well. Anna Louise attributed to him most of the structures she thought had remedied the problems he later caused. He was still cast as she had experienced him in 1927, as the "greatest committee man, a man who could bring diverse views into harmony with a speed that amounted to genius." At his best Stalin embodied the advantages of "collective thinking," and this characteristic separated him from the "despots of history, despite many despotic acts."

The book was finished and the "new freedoms" were already being tested in Hungary when Anna Louise presented herself for a lengthy interview with the authorities of the Passport Division. Her two interrogators were intent on testing her willingness to speak harshly of the U.S.S.R. or favorably of the United States. It was an exercise in frustration for all sides.

> Q. Are there any constitutional safeguards afforded citizens of the United States?
> A. Lots of them.
> Q. Are there constitutional safeguards that we enjoy here that are afforded citizens of the U.S.S.R.?
> A. Lots of them. Their constitution has more safeguards in it than ours does, but it was not observed. The police violated it all the time. Some of ours get violated too. But I will admit that we have more safeguards over here than they have over there, and I have told them that over there, too.

The interview reminded Anna Louise of her sessions with the commissar eight years previously and became another lesson in the importance of context to interpretation. The questioners went to great lengths to establish that Anna Louise had returned to the U.S.S.R. in a "Soviet plane" in 1944; Anna Louise protested that her flight from Alaska had been in a lend-lease plane that had at least started its journey as an American plane. On a "Soviet plane," she was a courier; on an American flight, a journalist. She was, she reminded them, a registered voter in the Democratic party.

The session had predictable results. John Foster Dulles turned down her application, citing her many memberships in "subversive" organizations and her "consistent espousal of the Soviet line." There was nothing left but to await the outcome of the Supreme Court decisions.

Anna Louise desperately wanted to make "one more long trip" before she died. Her health was declining; she walked with difficulty and required the assistance of a cane. *Today* had finally ceased publication in mid-1956. She found herself sinking once again into despair; her depressions and tantrums were recurring with frightening frequency. Aware that she was being irrational and disturbed that she had been missing deadlines for the *National Guardian,* she went back to psychiatrist Milton Lester. As she wrote to Jim Aronson later: "Basically what seemed to come out of the session . . . is that I have a dickens of a conscience from my preacher father upbringing, and why the hell *should* I write if I don't want to. . . . What makes me, if I feel like quitting. . . . Well, promises are really an obligation of sorts, but from now on perhaps I should not make binding ones." But this, she knew, would not solve her problems: "I think I have been sitting on a certain amount of disillusion that was caused by events you know of . . . and that I did not even let this disillusion reach my consciousness but kept myself on the task of justifying the ways of God to man, and that this explains a hidden conflict. Think that this is the trouble, but that some thought will have to be given before I know just what comes next."

Only China, where the "ways of God" might be more apparent, really attracted her, and most of her time was spent fighting the State Department Passport Division. Passport cases dragged on through the courts until they were at last accepted for review by the Supreme Court in late 1957. Anna Louise made up her mind that, no matter what the outcome, she would leave for China during the summer. Early in 1958 she again approached Ambassador Zarubin and showed him the invitation from Chen Han-seng. "That is a very fine invitation," said Zarubin, impressed despite himself. He referred the matter to Moscow, and when Anna Louise had lunch with him again ten days later, he told her, "Whenever you decide to go, whether or not you have a passport, we will send you through to Moscow."

Thus assured, she made plans for departure. Zarubin was a little annoyed that she did not leave immediately, but Anna Louise had learned that departure without a passport was a crime, whereas entry to China, once she had a passport, was only a violation of passport statutes. She wished to avoid committing an act for which she might have to go to jail should she return to the United States.

On June 16, 1958, by a five-to-four margin, the Supreme Court decided the case of *Rockwell Kent* v. *John Foster Dulles* in favor of Kent. The painter, now seventy-six, had long been affiliated with various radical groups. The decision voided any grounds for denying passports on the basis of "belief or association."

In the mail a few weeks later Anna Louise received a passport and a Soviet visa from her lawyer, Joseph Forer. On hearing the news, Holland Roberts phoned her from Palo Alto. "You should leave at once for the peace conference in Stockholm," he told her. "Why Stockholm?" she asked. "Because that will be the best place to see all the people you have wanted to see all these years." "All the people" were her Chinese friends. Anna Louise called the airlines for a reservation. Then she called Emily Pierson. Emily had long wanted to return to China, which she had visited only once, in 1937. During the 1950s she had been denied a number of chances to visit the People's Republic because of her friendship with Anna Louise. Anna Louise gleefully announced: "I am flying to Stockholm in a few days and plan to go much farther. You had better come with me." Emily had not yet realized the implications of the Kent decision for her own passport. She immediately made arrangements to meet Anna Louise in Stockholm.

As Grace Nelson drove her to the airport, Anna Louise confided to her that she expected they would have to deal with a crowd of reporters. Grace nodded and concealed her chagrin; she had purposefully told no one of Anna Louise's departure, assuming that if she had wanted people there, she would have publicized the event herself. This time the news had not leaked and no one except the Nelsons and LaRue McCormick was at the gates. Crestfallen, Anna Louise left, almost alone at her own long-awaited exodus.

Anna Louise was not well when she arrived at the conference. The excitement and confusion of the departure had taken a mental and physical toll. She appeared to others as old and tired and dazed, "as if she was coming out of retirement and couldn't quite handle it." Paget's disease had opened up cracks in her legbones that made walking without crutches impossible. When late in the day she limped up to the hotel registration desk, the man assigning rooms looked up and asked if she would mind sharing a room with the South African woman who had accompanied her since Paris, as accommodations were running out. The South African looked toward Anna Louise and began to reply: "Well, of course not, I would be honored . . ." But Anna Louise would have none of it and in a voice that cut across the lobby proclaimed: "After the trip I've had, I wouldn't share a room with anyone, not even Jesus Christ himself."

During the conference, the inside talk was of the divergence between the Russians and the Chinese. It was obvious to those with whom she spoke where her preferences lay. She spent much of her time with Rewi Alley, who was now living and working in Peking. Liao Cheng-chih told her that she had long been expected back in China and that there would be no problem taking Emily with her. Tang Ming-chao, now the editor of *China Reconstructs*, told her he would meet her in Peking. Anna Louise replied that she needed a month's rest in Sweden before proceeding. But she had not figured on the Russian delegation. Nina Popova, head of cultural relations for the U.S.S.R., insisted that they were expecting Anna Louise in Moscow. Somewhat flattered, Anna Louise agreed to spend a month in Russia.

She and Emily left Stockholm on July 24 and arrived in Moscow after midnight. Only one piece of Anna Louise's baggage came through on the flight, and that one had broken open. Anna Louise arrived at her room in the Metropol at 3:15 A.M. The windows of the room were nailed shut because of the construction going on next door. It was hot and stuffy, but she was so tired that she dropped down on the bed without even undressing. She awoke two hours later with a bad headache from the closeness of the room. When she turned on the faucet in the bathroom, she was greeted by a gust of sewer gas. She wrote Grace Nelson the next day: "I swore to myself. *This* was Moscow's swankiest hotel ten years ago. Won't the Russians ever be civilized?" In a fury she stormed out into the hall and had her room changed, only to discover the next morning that the rooms on that side of the hotel not only did not have their windows boarded up but greeted the morning sun at four without curtains. "So you either sleep without air or with the sun on your bed. Russians are a great people. They stand anything."

Anna Louise was expected to give a speech that night. At nine-thirty the secretary of the meeting called and asked to have a copy by noon, so that it could be checked. Anna Louise demanded a typewriter and an interpreter. Forty-five minutes later the interpreter was in her room. By this time Anna Louise was so enraged that any speech she made "would have been so full of swear words that it would not have passed the censor." Luckily, her old friend from the 1930s, Valentina Ivashova, arrived at that moment and whisked Anna Louise away, explaining to the protesting secretary that the speech would be ready by five. They went to Valentina's apartment some ten miles away and by four had written out a short speech that they read over the phone to the interpreter. The interpreter demanded a Russian copy by five. Anna Louise and Valentina worked feverishly and delivered the speech to the interpreter in the taxi on the way to the meeting, only to be told that Anna Louise would read the first five sentences and the rest would be read in Russian. "By this time," Anna Louise wrote to Grace, "I looked upon this damsel as my torturer-in-chief and felt that I only existed to give her a chance to talk."

Miraculously, the meeting went off very well. Anna Louise's speech was a great success. She had become the official voice of the American delegation: "Friends," she began, "I bring you greetings from those Americans, and they are many, who do not agree with Mr. Dulles' foreign policy, and who fight for peaceful coexistence with the U.S.S.R." As she left the hall, Anna Louise was mobbed by a crowd of people pleased to see her "on the job" at the age of seventy-two.

The next day invitations poured in. She saw Alexei Surkov, the head of the Writers Union, who assured her that she would receive all royalties due her as well as restitution for any damages or losses suffered because of her arrest. He also offered her an apartment of her choice and the return of the files that had been confiscated in 1949. She promised to return to his office in a few weeks to decide these matters. "Thus ends the scenario of Virtue Triumphant," she wrote to Grace. "P.S. When I pass my bathroom, I can hear that the plumbing still leaks."

On August 8 Anna Louise and Emily left Moscow for Maleyevka, the comfortable rest home of the Writers' Union not far from Moscow. Except for the weather, it was a very enjoyable month, though the lavish meals prevented Anna Louise from losing the ten pounds she had planned to take off. The only uneasy moment came when a woman writer staying there accused Anna Louise of being pro-Stalinist. It was a new experience for her in the U.S.S.R.

She returned to Moscow toward the beginning of September and visited her old apartment. The room that had been reserved for her had long since been assigned to a stranger, but Frieda, now a widow, still lived in the rest of the flat with Boris and his wife. Ducia came to visit from Leningrad. At dinner Anna Louise learned that her arrest had been the beginning of hard times for other members of the family as well. Ducia's husband had lost his job as professor in the naval academy, supposedly for dereliction of duty, but possibly because of Anna Louise. Along with the job, he had lost his apartment, and the family had been reduced to living in a barracks until they had found a small apartment a few hours' commute from his new position. Ducia, unable to travel because of the children, had been teaching grade school, a position she despised.

Despite the misfortune that Anna Louise had inadvertently brought on the family, the Shubins were distressed to hear that she had been living alone in the United States. "Better come to Moscow," said Boris. "Here you have plenty of relatives. Here the widow of our brother Joel will never be without a family or home." Anna Louise was much moved by this expression of family solidarity, but she knew that she did not want to live with the Shubins, and she was not at all sure she wanted to live in Moscow.

Much about the city now distressed her. Taxi drivers and hotel servants were brazen in their demands for tips, which even ten years before would have been a stigma of dishonor in a socialist society. Most of her old friends were dead or gone. The few old hands from the *News* who were still around seemed to be unhappy. Valentina's easy criticism had hardened into cynicism. She had made substantial money writing textbooks but had been forced to "share" it with a number of people in the publishing business in order to assure further publications. Anna Louise was more disturbed by Valentina's acceptance of this than by the fact that she did it.

During the last few days before her departure, she wrote a series of articles for the *Guardian*. She saw Surkov again and asked him if he could learn why she had been arrested. He told her that those who could say were "no longer around. . . . Beria was to blame for most of the insanity of the time. He was really a devil. Stalin trusted Beria as a fellow Georgian, but Beria kept Stalin from knowing what the conditions in the country really were." Anna Louise did not dispute Surkov's explanations, but it did not make her want to live in Moscow. She told Surkov that she would wait to choose an apartment "until I come back from China" and asked him to hold on to her files until her return. On September 20 she and Emily Pierson boarded the plane for Peking.

14

The Spirit of Yenan

Said the governor of South Carolina to the governor of North
Carolina, it's been a long time between drinks.

—Sidney Rittenberg to Anna Louise, Peking, 1958

The flight from Moscow stopped for customs in Irkutsk in southern Siberia, and to Anna Louise's considerable annoyance, the Russians stamped
both her and Emily's passport "flew off from Irkutsk." No one "flew off
from Irkutsk" to anywhere except China; Anna Louise had thought that
if nothing official appeared on their passports the State Department could
not hold the China trip against them. Tired and anxious, they arrived at
the Peking airport on September 22 and were immediately escorted to
the Peking Hotel by Chu Po-shen, the deputy secretary general of the
Chinese People's Association for Friendship with Foreign Nations and, as
promised, by Tang Ming-chao.

Anna Louise "gasped" on entering what was to be her drawing room:
thirty by thirty feet, it was furnished with blue rugs, four overstuffed
armchairs, a mahogany desk and a couch. Beyond was an old-fashioned
bathroom with an enormous tub and a bedroom with twin beds, a dressing table and a huge wardrobe. The bay window faced south on to Chang-
an Chieh, the massive ten-lane boulevard that swept west to T'ien-an
Men, the ceremonial center of Peking.

The first days passed quickly. The only sour note came when Emily,
frightened by the experience in Irkutsk, refused to give up her passport
for inspection by the Chinese authorities. She insisted on taking it herself,
and while she was gone, Anna Louise lay on her bed, working herself up
into a nervous rage. The Chinese were going to throw them both out
because of this, she thought. Emily returned triumphantly: "I have just
had a fight with a tough cop." Anna Louise exploded. "You have just met
the politest and the most considerate security officer you'll ever have the
luck to meet. Do you realize the situation we are in? Our government is

practically at war with this government, shooting at them in Quemoy. And here you refuse to obey their simplest regulations. . . . Do you think that the American FBI would let a Chinese visitor act this way? Do you think the Russian passport authority would? But the Chinese let you get away with it because you are an old woman and they know that old women are unreasonable." Emily wilted under the barrage: "I guess you're right."

The next morning the phone rang. A familiar North Carolina drawl came over the line. "Sid Rittenberg," Anna Louise exclaimed, "how did you get here? Everyone thought you were dead." Rittenberg was in the hotel lobby. In Anna Louise's room a moment later, he explained that he had never left China but had been arrested by the Chinese on suspicion of being a spy shortly after Anna Louise's expulsion from the U.S.S.R. He had been exonerated in 1957 and was now working with the English-language radio. Other old friends, he told her, including Israel Epstein and Elsie Cholmeley, had also made their way to China and were living in Peking.

Two days later, Chou En-lai gave a reception for Anna Louise. Always a gracious host, he had drawn up a thoughtful guest list that included old friends and those he knew were friends-to-be. Defense Minister P'eng Teh-huai, whom she had known since 1938, briefed her on the situation on Quemoy and Matsu, and Lu Ting-yi, now minister of propaganda, promised to come by the following afternoon to explain recent political developments. Chou smiled at her. "You didn't expect all this when you were in Yenan." "I always expected you to win, but not so fast," she replied. "But now, is there not danger of war with the United States over Taiwan?" "If the U.S. uses H-bombs on us when we don't have them," Chou responded carefully, "in the eyes of the world they are defeated. True, some of our cities will be destroyed, but this will not be left unanswered. We have friends." Chou added that they did not expect war, quoting Mao that the "East Wind now prevails over the West Wind."

The talk moved to Rittenberg's arrest. Chou explained that Sidney had been accused of spying for the Americans, but this had been determined to be a mistake. Then Sidney himself arrived, dressed as always in a rumpled corduroy suit. Anna Louise told him that "Chou has just been telling me what you went through." Chou explained, "We could not keep secret something we had done wrong." The group was joined by an American whom Anna Louise did not know: Frank Coe, who had recently come to China with his young wife, Ruth. Coe had been a senior economist in the Treasury Department and a major architect of the International Monetary Fund but was forced to resign in 1952 when he took the Fifth Amendment on party membership before the Senate internal security subcommittee. He had been without a regular position until the Chinese had quietly recruited him in late 1957. Frank and Anna Louise took to each other instantly.

As the reception came to an end, Chou invited Anna Louise and Emily, Sidney, the Coes and Lu Ting-yi to dinner. During the banquet, Anna Louise told the story of her arrest. She finished by revealing that she had been half consciously preparing to leave Russia for good in 1949. She had no hard feelings toward the U.S.S.R., but "the social experimentation underway in China is the most exciting and the most important thing taking place anywhere in the world. I feel at ease here."

Lu Ting-yi came the next afternoon as promised. He told Anna Louise that *The Stalin Era* had sold 110,000 copies in China, and that her analysis had been highly praised for its fairness. "But what did you mean," he asked, "by the 'Great Madness'?" Anna Louise floundered for words: "It just seemed to fit." Lu replied, "It does fit, but do you understand the source of the madness?" Stalin, he explained, was a great revolutionary but was "too metaphysical" in his concept of "opposition." He thought that any opposition must be liquidated. "This is the way of death. Life requires opposition and contradiction and not liquidation." The explanation suggested that she could do "by instinct" what the Chinese did "by analysis." Here in Peking were a group of people who had a conceptual understanding of the world but did not get lost in "mere abstraction." "How is it that the Chinese understand these things?" she asked. "We study philosophy," Lu replied. "When Chairman Mao first met Dr. Ma Hai-teh, his question was 'Have you studied philosophy?' In Shansi Province alone, one million people are studying Hegel, Marx and Mao."

Suppertime approached, and Lu made excuses for departure. Anna Louise would have none of it: "Go out and buy supper, here's some money, and bring it back." Lu returned with food and talked until late in the night about the major issues confronting the People's Republic. The Communists understood the conflict over the offshore islands as a continuation of the civil war with Chiang and thus found it important to keep the United States outside the conflict. Domestically, the central committee had decided the previous July to push rapidly ahead with the development of the people's communes in order to rationalize and reorganize agricultural production. In June only 30 percent of Chinese peasants had lived in communes; now the figure was close to 75 percent, and by the end of the year it would be around 90 percent.

Anna Louise was instantly worried. "How do you get the peasants to join? In Russia, they went much too fast, and it caused great dislocation and misery." Lu hastened to assure her that the groundwork had been laid in the pre-Revolutionary "land to the tiller" campaigns and more fully in the development of farming cooperatives in the 1950s. Mao himself had proclaimed that "people's communes are good" and that they were "a basic unit of society, whose task it was to man all industrial and agricultural production and educational work and political affairs." Anna Louise asked about iron and steel. Here too, Lu told her, the commune made what it needed, even ball bearings.

As the evening wore on, Anna Louise seemed to be trying to find a question that Lu would be unable to answer, and she grew testy as he carefully elaborated each problem area. Later he realized that she had been looking for an excuse to ask for an interview with the chairman and kept him so late in a search for a gap that his thorough explanations could not fill.

The excitement of her return culminated on National Day, October 1. She was invited to sit on the high dais with Mao and other dignitaries for the celebration, and she made her way through a bright maze of arched streamers and multicolored paper flowers to the top of the high wall at the north of T'ien-an Men square with Tang Ming-chao and Chu Po-shen. After the parade and the traditional fireworks display, Mao, Chu Teh, Chou En-lai, Liu Shao-ch'i, Lu Ting-yi and the other top leaders came over to her. Somewhat shy in the presence of the chairman, she greeted him awkwardly, wanting to ask for an interview but knowing that it was inappropriate. Mao shook her hand, asked after her health and said, "If we had known that it would take this long for you to return to China, we would not have asked you to leave Yenan." It was close to absolution.

Shortly before Anna Louise's return, Mao had republished her 1946 "paper tiger" interview with him. This plus a published photograph of Anna Louise shaking Chairman's Mao's hand led representatives of Hsin-hua, the China news agency, to interview her at the Peking Hotel. Anna Louise told them of the years during which she had yearned to return to China and of the pleasure she took at finding the present-day ambience still that of Yenan. Indeed, she remarked, the spirit was evident in the way that high party officials regularly went to work in local backyard steel furnaces as part of the "Great Leap Forward"; she herself hoped to have a try at steel production. She spoke with admiration of the "brilliance of Marshal P'eng" and recalled the foresight of Mao on paper tigers. At the end of the interview she brought out the long fur-lined greatcoat Lin Piao had given her in Manchuria in 1946 and the trousers of quilted silk she had bought at the same time. When the story was written up for *Ren Min Ri Pao* (*People's Daily*), her acquisitions became fused into a "pair of fur-lined silk pants given to her by Lin Piao." Anna Louise wondered dryly to Frank Coe "what Mrs. Lin must have thought."

The joy of her return to China and Emily's care of her were so beneficial that she was soon able to discard the crutches on which she had depended for almost a year. She still had what her friend Dr. Ma called a "wobble walk," like an oversized two-year-old, but the energy of her earlier years returned. She made a trip to the Evergreen People's Commune outside of Peking and recognized it for the showpiece that it was, but the excitement of the development of a new form of social organization made her want to see more. Tang arranged for her and Emily to take a trip to Chengchow in Honan province with her old friend the economist Chi Ch'ao-ting and his wife, Luo Ching-yi.

The Chengchow commune was the earliest to have been established in China, and its apparent success convinced Anna Louise that her first major project should be the commune movement. On her insistence, the group visited a number of different kinds of communes, where Anna Louise posed detailed questions about every aspect of life. Each night her companions heard her typing her day's notes as they fell asleep. Anna Louise had resumed her role as a reporter.

The party returned to Peking at the end of October, and within a few days Emily departed for the United States. The first stage was over; Anna Louise was alone again without a regular job. All the foreigners she knew in China were employed in productive positions that seemed to occupy sixteen hours of their day. That her hosts insisted on picking up the tab for her room, board and transportation only added to her embarrassment. She was unable to return to the United States to lecture on the material she had just acquired because to do so would endanger her passport. She wrote repeatedly to Ruth Aley, the literary agent she had acquired after the return of her passport, urging her to find some kind of journalistic connection with a mainstream American publishing firm or a newspaper chain like Cowles. Ruth worked hard at it, but nothing developed; only the *National Guardian* carried her as a correspondent.

Without a regular job, she had no regular contact with others. Elsie Cholmeley arrived at her room one afternoon to find Anna Louise sitting at the desk, tears pouring down her cheeks. "I just can't stand it, I'm so lonely," Anna Louise confessed, dashing over to the bed and starting to crawl in. Elsie was taken aback; she was a forceful, unflinching woman who tolerated little nonsense. "You have to make yourself a program," she said to Anna Louise. "Organize your life so that you see people." She suggested an Italian friend who might dine with her once a week. Anna Louise liked the idea and henceforth made sure that she ate with others.

Elsie described the scene to other friends, and eventually the party leaders decided to make Anna Louise a resident rather than a guest. Chou En-lai suggested to her in early December that she would be welcome to stay and work as long as she wanted to in order to write articles for the foreign press. Mindful of her experiences on the *Moscow News*, Anna Louise had enough sense to realize that she would need to "consult" with someone on any material sent out of the country and asked for a "reliable comrade with international experience." Chou suggested that she work with Tang Ming-chao on substantive questions and submit material through Wang Ch'u-liang, an important party member with excellent English and experience in the United States. A few days later, when she complained about living in a hotel, Elsie mentioned that a suite of rooms would soon be available in the Peace Compound just around the corner from the hotel. The compound had once been the Italian embassy and now served as the headquarters of the Peace Committee, the organization in charge of foreigners residing and working in China. Anna Louise found that she could move in the next March; in the meantime, she was advised to go south to Canton to avoid the harsh Peking winter. She added a request for a competent interpreter who could type in English.

As the New Year approached, she began to feel more at ease. She started work on a book on the communes. Her new secretary, Chao Feng-feng, was a highly intelligent, vivacious twenty-seven-year-old with a receptive smile, excellent English, infinite patience and the ability to resist being pushed around. She was also able to move easily from conversations about a political event to discussions of Anna Louise's health or her dress for a party. Social events also impressed on Anna Louise how fully accepted she was in this new world. On December 30 she went to a dinner party at the Peace Compound and then played bridge with Chu Po-shen, Tang and Sidney Rittenberg. "Believe it or not," she later wrote to Emily, "they have plastic cards in China and use the Blackwood convention." Political teasing flew around the table. "Look out for Chu, he is a left deviationist in bidding, too adventurous." Tang was a "dogmatist" because "whatever he bids first, he sticks to it against the world. But you see what happens. He goes down and down."

The next night, Sidney and Anna Louise were the only foreigners invited to a New Year's Eve dance at the Peking Hotel. It was like

Saturday night in Yenan. Anna Louise danced with the head of the air force, with Ma Si-wu, the chief justice, and with the mustachioed Marshal Ho Lung, now a vice-premier. Around ten-thirty, she went up to her room, asking Feng-feng to call her in an hour. Feng-feng fetched her with the words: "The best dancer of Yenan has arrived." When she returned to the ballroom, she saw Chou En-lai besieged by requests for a dance. He turned down two girls but accepted a third in a scarlet sweater. Sidney whispered to Anna Louise: "She is a minority nationalist. The premier can turn down Chinese girls, but he mustn't refuse a national minority."

After that dance Chou came over to Anna Louise's table. The loud-speaker announced: "The great and glorious year of 1958 is about to leave us; the greater and more glorious year of 1959 is arriving. Let us greet the happy new year." Chou turned to Anna Louise, kissed her on the cheek and wished her a happy new year in English. Feng-feng was so flustered by this that she translated his words into Chinese. Chou asked Anna Louise to dance. The orchestra began the New Year with a fast tune, so fast that Anna Louise wondered if she could possibly keep up. But she did, in front of 800 people, "all of whom knew that I was getting Chou En-lai's first dance of the year." Anna Louise was so excited that when she returned to her room shortly after one o'clock she wrote ten single-spaced pages of letters to friends.

She had much to write about, and many people who wanted to hear from her. Her close friends received duplicate carbon copies of letters, but some wanted specific questions answered. James Aronson at the *Guardian* pressed her for an interview with Mao. Anna Louise was coy to the point of shyness. She wrote to Aronson that she would ask to see Mao only when she had either some "intelligent questions to which only he could give a reply" or when some "serious important news agency sent questions to which Mao's answers would be an important event." Harrison Salisbury, who had won both a Pulitzer Prize and expulsion from the U.S.S.R. for his reporting on socialist countries for the *New York Times*, wrote inquiring if there was any possibility of his being allowed a visit. He had been the first regular *Times* correspondent in Moscow after World War II. Anna Louise passed the letter along to Chou En-lai; she would not "presume to advise," she noted, but thought that he should know of the *Times*' interest. When no answer came—the Chinese equivalent of a long-term, though not necessarily permanent, refusal—Anna Louise wrote Salisbury that the answer was either no or unclear. She responded to his request for a comparison of Russia and China with three detailed pages in which she noted particularly that while she found no overt censorship in China, she was expected to police herself, which was perhaps, she admitted, "a more difficult task."

In addition to all the correspondence, Anna Louise worked on the communes project. She had doubts about the efficiency of the communal approach to organization of industry, but in agriculture she found an extraordinary rate of change and experimentation. Dr. Ma explained the incentive: "Free rice." Anna Louise was determined not to cast too gentle an eye: "Slaves and servants always got their food and lodging. Why should 'free food' be so revolutionary?" Now they controlled the food supply, Ma pointed out, and Anna Louise was quickly converted.

She contrasted what she found in the communes to her experience in the Soviet Union some thirty-five years earlier. In China most of the local cadres were drawn from the area in which they worked; there were no urban missionaries who knew nothing except their "line." And on the national level, unlike the U.S.S.R., where only kulaks and peasants had come under the policy of collectivization, all citizens—especially the leaders—were expected to follow the same line. The congruence between the two levels was assured, she thought, by the activities of Chairman Mao. "When Mao came back from his September trip around the country," she wrote to the Tompkins, "he found that the Peking big shots weren't making steel. So he said at the first session with them, 'A short while back it was decided that steel should be made by the whole people, wasn't it?' 'Yes,' they replied, expecting some comment from Mao on the success of the drive. Then Mao asked: 'Are the ministries of the people's government going to be part of the whole people or not?' Steel mills were up within twenty-four hours. Believe me, no bureaucracy is going to flourish while Mao lives."

And while she was aware that "peasants who do not agree with the new line feel overworked and complain," she found the same pioneering enthusiasm she had encountered forty years before in Seattle. She wrote to American friends that "good social engineering suggests that in such a movement a local leadership does *not* stop the drive by regulations, but lets it run until its natural end begins to appear and only then intervenes to tidy up details."

In February, while she was still in Canton, where she had spent the hard part of the winter, Anna Louise learned that her old friends W. E. B. Du Bois and his wife Shirley Graham had arrived in China for an extended visit. Du Bois was ninety-one years old. Anna Louise sent off a welcoming letter but did not see them until she returned to Peking on

March 7 and gave a dinner party in their honor. Toward the end of the meal, Chou En-lai dropped in for a visit and told Du Bois that he would arrange an interview with Mao. Anna Louise resisted the impulse to ask to be included—"I've learned some manners," she wrote to Warwick Tompkins later. The next day, however, a call came from Liao Cheng-chih, inviting her to join the meeting.

Mao was spending much of his time inspecting the communes by quietly touring the Chinese countryside. He always arrived unannounced, spoke with local officials and the populace, then departed for the next unknown destination. When Anna Louise left Peking with Feng-feng, Tang, and Pu Shou-cheng, Chou En-lai's official interpreter, she did not know where they were headed.

The group joined Du Bois and his wife in Wu-ch'ang in Hupeh Province and went to East Lake, a resort developed from a swampy lake. Early on the morning of the thirteenth they were told that Mao would receive them at 9:45. When they arrived at the stone villa where he was staying, Mao was descending a long flight of stairs to greet them. He was dressed in a gray wool suit and moved with notable energy. As he shook Anna Louise's hand, he said, "How do you do," in English at the same time that Anna Louise said, "*Nin hao.*" They both laughed. Greeting Du Bois, Mao expressed surprise at his color: "You are no darker than I. Who could tell which of us is darker?" The group proceeded up the stairs, Anna Louise by Mao's side. He began to count the years since Yenan; Anna Louise interrupted: "Twelve years this month." Mao seemed surprised and was visibly taken aback when Anna Louise remarked that the present occasion was the first interview he had granted to any American correspondent since Liberation. "It seems this is right." Anna Louise surmised that he had thought of their meeting not as an interview, but as a reception for his personal guests.

The company entered a large room with windows on three sides overlooking the lake. Du Bois sat opposite Mao, Anna Louise and Shirley at the other two ends of the small table. Mao turned to Anna Louise with the precise grace of Chinese etiquette. "You are an old friend and will be with us long. You are Chinese. You are the hostess. These are new friends; they are the guests." Mao referred to Anna Louise as *chung kuo jen*—Chinese by culture as opposed to race—and Anna Louise remembered that in China, the guest always takes precedence over the host. Mao's remark was a courteous notice that she should assist with Du Bois' and Graham's questions and refrain from raising her own.

Talk began with light laughter about age. Mao expressed admiration at how well Du Bois carried his years. "You are old enough to be my father," he remarked. "But even I feel my years, though I still have spirit and some strength. I can swim the Yangtze each year. This is my swimming partner." Mao turned to the first secretary of the Hupeh provincial committee and then mentioned other rivers he had swum—the Pearl River near Canton and the Yellow River. He wanted to swim the Hei-lung Chiang. Anna Louise remarked that if he did that he would be in Russia. Mao looked at her as if she had given him new information and laughed: "Ah, you are quite right."

As always the banter hid a point. "If you three would allow it," he continued cheerfully, "I would like to swim the Mississippi. But maybe three others would oppose it—Eisenhower, Nixon and Dulles." Du Bois was a bit taken aback and remarked grimly that he thought those three would like Mao to swim the Mississippi, "especially if it were downstream where it is very wide."

"Really?" said Mao in apparent delight, ignoring Du Bois' implication. "Then if they agree I could start in just a few days as a tourist."

"Like Mikoyan," interjected Anna Louise, referring to the Soviet foreign minister's recent visit.

"Oh, no," Mao protested, "Mikoyan talked politics. I would not talk any politics. I would just swim the Mississippi and then I would like to watch President Eisenhower play golf; and then maybe call on Mr. Dulles in the hospital."

Du Bois, who was perturbed at Mao's levity, made an attempt to get into the mood. "That might give Dulles a stroke."

Mao was immediately solicitous. "I care very much for Mr. Dulles' health. I hope that he recovers and continues to be secretary of state. In that work he is quite beneficial to us. Also he is useful to the American people and to the working people of the whole world." Mao's foreign audience looked puzzled. He explained his conceit: "This is quite true. I often say it. Dulles is useful because he sticks to his principles. He is firmly against Communism, against the Soviet Union and against China. To this end he suppresses people's movements and sends troops and establishes military bases all over the whole world. All this is useful to the whole world. I hope they do not change this policy." He turned to Du Bois: "Do you believe this?" Du Bois was upset: "It depends on how many people are intelligent enough to understand what Dulles is doing. Very intelligent people seem to be befuddled and turning away from decency. I tremble at this and don't want this situation to go on too long."

"I think otherwise," Mao responded. "The period is not too long, it is too short."

"You have not suffered the disadvantages of this period as long as I have," retorted Du Bois. Mao replied that he hoped Dulles would remain secretary for ten years longer. "We very much hope that for ten years we will have no diplomatic relations with the United States and no trade. This will be very beneficial to us. As to occupying Taiwan, let Dulles continue as long as he likes. The U.S. troops are bound to leave Taiwan eventually, but we want them there as long as possible as teachers to our people. Once they leave, there is less advantage to us. What better education is there for our people and the people of the world? The events of the Middle East are also very educational. I had hoped that the U.S. troops would stay in Lebanon for at least half a year. One or two years would have been better." He ended on a tone of mock complaint: "Why did they pull out so soon?"

Mao continued, listing several events in the previous fourteen months that Dulles' policies had provoked. Most important was the shelling of Quemoy: "Our war with Chiang has lasted thirty years; yet the U.S.A. sent half its aircraft carriers here just because we shelled our Quemoy." His tone implied regret that the U.S. fleet should have been so bothered over so trivial a matter, and he noted that the Chinese had perhaps performed a "volunteer service" for the American Democrats by the extra-heavy bombardment of the offshore islands the day before the congressional elections, thereby reminding the voters of Dulles' inability to settle the situation. As he had twelve years earlier in Yenan, Mao made a model on the table, using a teacup for Quemoy, an ashtray for Chiang's approaching vessels and a packet of cigarettes for the U.S. fleet steaming a careful distance away.

Du Bois interrupted, uncomfortable with Mao's lighthearted treatment of brinksmanship. "While such policies go on, the people in Taiwan suffer, the American Negroes suffer. I fear extermination of the American Negro."

Mao reassured him: "There are eighteen million Negroes in America. It is impossible to exterminate them. It is the bourgeoisie that will be exterminated, not you. The bourgeoisie is already gone from the U.S.S.R. and soon will be gone from China. Mr. Dulles and his kind will be exterminated. And Mr. Dulles is doing all he can to exterminate himself. That is why I appreciate him so much."

"Would you vote for him?" asked Du Bois dryly.

Mao laughed with the appreciation of a point scored. "Personally I would not vote for him."

Du Bois persisted. "Many of my family have been exterminated." Mao gravely revealed that six of his own family had been killed—his two brothers, his former wife, sister and nephew by the Kuomintang and his eldest son in the Korean War. "In spite of all this, they can never kill all the Communists. There may be fewer members in my family, but in China as a whole there are more Communists."

Mao turned to other problems besetting the United States, especially Cuba: "The Cubans are right under the United States. Yet they do not worry about A-bombs and H-bombs. This is not a matter of the size of the country, but of the political awakening of the people. In the past our people feared American imperialism. This was one disease. They had another disease: they admired American imperialism. When you have these two diseases, you get a third: fear and admiration become worship. In China, even the working people were affected. In the last eight or nine years we have been able to change this mentality."

For Mao, this was indicative of a broader political problem. "These diseases affect the American people, and the Negroes among them." Du Bois interrupted that the working people in America were not affected by fear or admiration but by income. A sharp argument followed on whether the economic factor or the "power of superstition" prevailed. Du Bois insisted on the former. Mao responded that when people whose class position should make them take one side take the other, they are affected by superstition. "Did you ever eat dog meat?" he concluded. "I am sure that if people would offer you dog meat, you would feel unhappy even before you ate it. But can you give me a reason? You have never tasted it, you have no experience, no practice. Your refusal is hearsay from the influence of social environment. It was the same with me. Then in the guerrilla war it was offered to me. I took it very reluctantly. I didn't vomit, but I felt uncomfortable for some time. Gradually I became accustomed. Here you see the force of social custom."

Mao rose and suggested they go for a walk. Anna Louise thought they had come to the end of the interview, but after a leisurely stroll, Mao led the way back upstairs into a dining room set for a meal. A two-hour lunch began. Midway through they were served sea cucumbers, a species of sea slug relished by the Chinese for its odd combination of slimy and crunchy textures. Mao offered Anna Louise some, but she refused. "And is this superstition or experience?" he asked. Anna Louise, who had never tasted them but found them repulsive, lied: "I tried them once."

During lunch Anna Louise finally had the chance to ask Mao some questions of her own. She asked if she might accompany him on one of his tours of the countryside, to be able to show Americans that it was not true that a "small group in Peking ran everything." Mao thought that would be possible. He was very involved, he observed, with the development and correction of the "organizational roughnesses" of the communes.

As their meal came to an end, Mao turned his thoughts to death. "I am sixty-six, and I can die of disease or in an airplane accident or from some agent of Chiang's coming to kill me. But there is no use in the fear of death. It does not stop death to fear it, it only provokes death. I do not wish to die: I hope to see the end of imperialism. But if I must die, I am not afraid." Du Bois wondered puckishly about his own afterlife, since although his friends and enemies thought him to be a Communist, the party knew that he was not one. Mao told him not to worry: "You are now ninety-one years old, and when you meet Marx, he will accept you as a comrade. It is always possible, of course, that I may precede you, in which case I shall be glad to recommend you."

The interview ended. As Anna Louise wrote up a preliminary version that night, she reflected on her vague sense of dissatisfaction. Mao had seemed relaxed and confident. But she had the sense she often had after talking with Mao, that she had to work to find the core.

Nobody on earth is as easy to listen to as is Mao, but few people do I find as hard to put down on paper. I can explain this most easily by a comparison to Chou En-lai. Chou . . . has specialized in interpretation, so that he puts his ideas in foreign terms and only the bare words need translation. But Mao, beginning as a peasant of China and becoming a poet, a philosopher, a Marxist, a leader of armies and of government, still specializes, by constant contacts and conscious effort, as the soul and analyzing brain of the Chinese people. In talking with Mao, one feels a great expansion of vision, a lightning thought that flies easily over the world, a philosophy that accepts life and death and the long travail of man through countless ages and countless millions of human beings, a hard-won, costly advance, always imperiled by accidents of nature and conflicts of men, yet always moving forward in a reach that may conquer the stars. One becomes aware of the many thousand years in which the Chinese peasants revolted against oppression and were bloodily suppressed by the millions, yet arose again. And beyond this, of the millions of years in which man rose from the naked link between man and ape— "Humanity is only in its childhood," he once said. . . . Always one feels that this is the scale of the reality within which Mao is thinking: that he knows from childhood the Buddhist thought and from student days the Taoist thought and now he has accepted the Marxist thought on this ultimate reality, and has found his own place in this reality, both his unimportance as one individual and his supreme importance as the carrier forward of life. Because of this he can talk easily and lightly about serious things and seriously about trivial things. But his thought, whether joking or serious, is always Chinese.

Anna Louise was very distressed when Tang told her the next day that the talk had been "among friends" and was not for publication.

She finished the book on the communes soon after her return to Peking—without the material Mao had given her—and began to look for another project. Her immediate time was occupied by the move into the Peace Compound. Her new residence, on the first floor of an old European-style building, had a large living room and study opening up through four windows onto the well-kept garden, a bedroom, and a dining room from which she could exit to a small porch, beside which stood a magnificent pomegranate tree. The apartment was furnished with pieces from old imperial residences: an enormous wardrobe covered with five-clawed dragons ("five for the emperor's household," Anna Louise noted with pleasure), a mahogany writing desk inlaid with marble, rugs in Chinese blue and white. She had a housekeeper to herself and shared a cook with the other families in the compound.

The Peace Compound was the fulfillment of the dreams that had followed her since Chicago's Hull House. She lived by herself, yet there were always people available, even a small flock of children who called her Granny. She was completely freed from the details of housekeeping; if she wanted to entertain, she simply asked Feng-feng to tell the cook. The cook quickly learned to prepare bland western food for Anna Louise, prompting Sidney Rittenberg to quip that Anna Louise's most astonishing achievement was to have ruined an excellent Chinese chef.

About forty people lived in the compound; in her building were Sai Onji, a member of the Japanese imperial family frankly sympathetic to the Chinese, the Chilean José Venturelli, and Rewi Alley. Anna Louise and Rewi quickly became fast friends, and the two of them had breakfast regularly on the porch when the weather allowed. It was the most comfortable living arrangement Anna Louise had ever had. She wrote to her Russian friend Valentina: "I think life is nearly as perfect as human beings can make it. It is certainly fixed to ensure maximum efficiency for my age. The only lack is that I am somewhat lonely."

Her loneliness derived in part from the consuming commitment of her friends to their jobs. Anna Louise read the *New York Times*, the *Wall Street Journal*, the *New York Herald Tribune*, various news magazines, and the daily sixty-page summary of Chinese and foreign wire services that Hsinhua distributed, but she needed people with whom to discuss her opinions and analyses. She complained to Tang; eventually a system was worked out. Every evening a different set of her friends, both Chinese and foreign, would come for dinner: soon it was recognized around Peking that there were no good reasons for missing supper with Anna Louise Strong. She always dressed, often in a long gown of brocaded Chinese silk with a carefully selected piece of jewelry on her breast, and gave the meals a certain ritual formality. During the day she gathered and sorted information; the evening was for analysis. She waited for the comment that seemed to encapsulate the group's discussion and used that as a building block. One participant remembers, "You didn't really talk with Anna Louise, you were there to help."

But she still had no regular job. Her Chinese friends tried to find activities for her. Liao Cheng-chih asked her to evaluate the visa applications of Edgar Snow and Walter Lippmann, both of whom were trying to come to China. Anna Louise was neutral on Lippmann and generally in favor of Snow, even though he "had developed an inclination rather strong toward Gandhi and even Tito, as well as a disquieting tendency to quote historical figures like Litvinov and Soong Ch'ing-ling verbatim about things they certainly did not say for the public. . . . But . . . he can write and get an audience."

The prospect of Snow's visit brought home to Anna Louise her own need to have a publicly recognized job. She continued to Liao: "I very much do not want Snow to know how much I get for free here, for he is not discreet with facts that seem to him to make a good story." Anna Louise was nervous that she might come under the statutes of the "trading with the enemy" act and had tried to use as little as possible of her foreign currency in China, living off the royalties from *The Stalin Era*, but she was becoming increasingly dependent on the generosity of her hosts.

Then, in the middle of March, a rebellion broke out against the indirect Chinese rule in Tibet. Both the Kuomintang and the Communists claimed Tibet as part of Greater China, and the government of the People's Republic had slowly started to restructure the feudal theocracy by which the lamas maintained their rule. In exchange for assured military control of the southern border with India, the Chinese had agreed in 1956 not to upset the system of serfdom for at least six years, pending local reforms. Peking had, however, welcomed escaped serfs into China and trained them in administrative and technical skills. In response to pressure from a majority of his advisors, the Dalai Lama on March 10, 1959, attempted to recover full control of Tibet and assert its total independence of China. Tibetan forces surrounded and bombarded Chinese army headquarters in Lhasa. After a short fight they were suppressed, and the Dalai Lama fled to India. China immediately moved to take fuller control of the "autonomous region."

In this complex situation Anna Louise dashed off an article which held out hopes for reconciliation with the Dalai Lama and sent it to the *National Guardian*. Her Chinese friends soon made it clear to her that her hopes were unlikely, and she was forced to modify some of her claims. Whatever the source of the rebellion, the Chinese had taken the opportunity to change substantially the structure of governance in Tibet. Local government was dissolved and its functions transferred to a central committee. Anna Louise admitted to Aronson that more was now at issue than "restoring order," but with the horrific conditions of serfdom, she saw little to regret in the passing of the control of the lamaseries.

Central to the plans of the Peking government were the runaways who had been trained in China. Anna Louise interviewed both serfs trained in Peking and the Panchen Lama, now the highest-ranking lama able to return to Tibet, and produced a book, *Tibetan Interviews*, that was published by the New World Press in Peking. Again no mainstream American press would publish her work, and Anna Louise wrote to ask Carey McWilliams at the *Nation* "if she should give up hope writing for the general U.S.A. press."

Before she received a response, she was presented with an opportunity to get material that might well prove irresistible to western editors. Hsinhua was organizing a trip to Tibet for a select group of journalists; Anna Louise insisted to Chou En-lai that she be allowed to join. At first Chou was dubious: the journey was difficult and the group would stay for a month at an altitude of over 12,000 feet. But Anna Louise was so determined that he agreed she could go if she passed a physical examination. Her blood pressure proved to be 130/65 and her pulse a steady sixty beats a minute. She found out that she would be the first American woman and the oldest American ever to visit Lhasa.

Unfortunately, the first plane they took was not pressurized, and Anna Louise was so sick when they arrived at their first stop, Hsi-ning, that she went to bed, "lest I topple over." The next day they were supposed to board small military planes, also unpressurized, to cross the 20,000-foot Tanglha range. Fortunately for Anna Louise, the departure was postponed because of a storm. Lying in bed while the rest of the group made preparations to use the delay to visit the famous Gumbum monastery,

Anna Louise admitted to herself that the time was approaching when she would be too physically weak to get information herself. She had become increasingly fond of Feng-feng; she would train her, she decided, to do firsthand research. She commanded Feng-feng to go to the monastery and told her what her own mother had said to her when she was twelve: "Be able to say who it is, what they look like, what they want, and what you think of them." Anna Louise was happy with the results when Feng-feng returned, although she scolded her for not giving enough physical details.

By the end of the three-day storm, Anna Louise had fully recovered and she and Feng-feng boarded a plane with Tang Li of the *People's Daily*, Alan Winnington of the *London Daily Worker* and M. Domogadshik from *Pravda*. The last passenger was a doctor. Anna Louise's first glimpse of the plane's interior made her think it has been designed for a "high dignitary." In fact it had been specially prepared for her: a luxurious sofa covered by a royal blue down coverlet had replaced three rows of seats on one side; an oxygen mask lay incongruously between two pillows edged with pale blue lace. The moment Anna Louise lay down on the sofa, Winnington pulled out his camera and started to photograph her. "It's fixed for a prime minister," he said. "No, for the Queen of Sheba," she retorted. "Take all the pictures you want. I get the bed."

The Tibet airport was a half day's journey from Lhasa, and it was evening before the travelers caught sight of the red-and-white Potala Palace, the traditional residence of the Dalai Lama. With some amusement Anna Louise gratefully accepted the stretcher that had been provided to carry her up the hundreds of steps to the Potala. By the next morning, however, she was full of energy and eager to begin exploring. Although she wrote glowingly to friends of the spread of literacy, improvements in agriculture and the introduction of small industry to Tibet, she also reported that 45 percent of the lamaseries had supported the rebellion against China and the occupying military forces had to exert considerable control to break the hold of the monks. Between trips to places of political interest, there were performances by local groups and displays of extraordinary skill on horseback: "With their dark skin and sharp profile, wild horseback riding and craze for primary colors, the Tibetans remind me more of American Indians than anyone I have ever met," she wrote the Tompkins.

Anna Louise maneuvered as best she could to be the first back to Peking so as to scoop her colleagues, but she did not succeed and returned with the others on September 10. Even with genuinely new and exciting material on Tibet, she continued to have difficulty placing articles in American publications. Carey McWilliams of the *Nation* had answered her letter assuring her that he would be receptive to anything she sent him, providing that her articles contained a "critical self-awareness . . . toward the subject matter." She should be "on guard even against her own enthusiasms," he wrote. It was an honest letter, but it upset Anna Louise. She had not realized that she was coming across as "oblivious or convinced by propaganda."

Eleanor Roosevelt's answer to a letter from Anna Louise concerning troops in Korea helped to explain the problem with the American press. Mrs. Roosevelt wrote to Jessica Smith, who had forwarded Anna Louise's letter: "I am afraid that Anna Louise Strong's letter does not impress me a great deal. She says all the things one would expect a convinced Communist to say, and she must be a very convinced Communist or she would not have returned to those countries after her imprisonment and having to seek protection at home in this country." Mrs. Roosevelt considered it "useless" to respond directly to Anna Louise. Instead she devoted half of one of her newspaper columns to excoriating Anna Louise's position on Korea. Anna Louise was angry and hurt; Mrs. Roosevelt, she wrote Emily, had treated her "as would the Duchess of Upper Hudson snubbing the servant who came to the front door." She immediately wrote to Mrs. Roosevelt again, noting that other Americans like Harrison Salisbury at the *New York Times* never used her letters to attack her in public. She concluded: "You and I derive from the same source: the democratic Christian America of the turn of the century. From that beginning we have both journeyed far, as has America. But if it is 'useless' for us to seek understanding, . . . peoples and nations far more alien than we ever were must achieve it. . . . All of us must fight the [closed mind], beginning in our own souls."

The rejections from the United States were somewhat compensated for by the full life she was now leading in Peking. In November, when Che Guevara came to China to buy $40 million worth of factories, he called on her to ask for the right to translate her book on the communes into Spanish. "It will be very important for Latin America," he assured her. He also invited her to come to Cuba whenever she wished. As she was leaving his farewell banquet, Foreign Minister Ch'en Yi invited himself and his wife to her place for the evening. Anna Louise wrote happily to Emily: "This invitation turned into a dinner party for sixteen people, to which I invited my American friends and Rewi Alley, and to which Chou En-lai also came. Rewi had just received a lot of old Boxer [Rebellion] trophies from New Zealand. . . . We made Chou En-lai put on the Boxer officer coat and he was a handsome pirate chief in an opera."

Her seventy-fourth birthday party on November 24 was also a major celebration. During the day many people dropped in to see her and leave presents, and in the evening there was a banquet with forty guests. She had been told to hold the seat on her right for a late guest, and at nine-thirty Chou En-lai arrived. Her birthday parties became rituals at which high officials always appeared.

Feng-feng was her constant companion. When Anna Louise went south to Hainan Island in the winter, Feng-feng went too and left her two sons with their father in Peking. In addition to being more and more her researcher, Feng-feng scheduled Anna Louise's appointments and pro-vided the physical therapy necessary to keep her legs from cramping; she also took charge of the Toblerone chocolates that were shipped from Zurich. All that was lacking was Anna Louise's confidence that Feng-feng really liked her: "I still think that Feng-feng is doing it out of *duty*," she complained to a friend once after Feng-feng had administered a soothing leg massage.

While she and Feng-feng were in Hainan, Chou and his wife came to visit her. Chou had just concluded an as-yet-unannounced border treaty with Burma, but he told her that Nehru had refused any settlement, so he would go to Delhi in a month to try to work it out. This was real news, and Anna Louise could not restrain her journalistic enthusiasm. She dashed off a long letter to Jim Aronson, who wrote back that he might put part of her letter into the "Spectator" column. Anna Louise was terrified. She cabled him immediately and followed it up with a long letter: "I have never doubted that the catastrophe to me in Moscow . . . came not only by the evil of Beria, but also by my own character which drew attention to me—and not favorably. Nor do I doubt that the same thing could happen to me in China in a politer way. If I should reveal personal contacts in public that would be bad enough; but if I should say anything that caused diplomatic trouble, then I would want to take cya-nide." Similar statements went to Emily: "I am praying to God, yes actually to God, to put it far, far out of Jim's mind until I myself actually get word to Jim." Aronson considered her fears exaggerated but printed nothing. In the third week in April, Chou did visit Delhi, but the border problem was not resolved.

The period of official pluralism epitomized by the slogan "Let a hun-dred flowers bloom, let a hundred schools of thought contend" had ended. The more the Chinese leaders came to see Anna Louise as unofficial spokesperson for official policy, the more troublesome became her encounters with censorship. Whereas her book on the communes had been printed in sixteen days, her book on Tibet took over two and a half months to get into print, most of it spent in negotiation over the "opinions" of various comrades, all duly "approved by the leadership." At the end, the foreign language publishing house called her at midnight with a final change that had to be accepted before they could go to press. She told them to bring her the pages. After almost two hours of argument she had met all their demands except that she change her characterization of the Living Buddha Geda from "pro-Chinese" to "pro-Han." Tibet, she was told, was a part of China; thus no Tibetan could be "pro-Chinese." Geda's fault in the eyes of the British could only have been that he favored the Han ethnic majority that dominates China politically and socially. It was too much. "There never was such a thing as 'pro-Han,'" she yelled, "and certainly Geda never was." When the press representatives refused to accept her protestations, she began to cry and wept almost without stopping for twenty hours. She then took to her bed for nine days and did no work. Finally Israel Epstein came to dinner and solved the problem by substituting "loved the people" for "pro-Chinese." Anna Louise was reminded of her old fights on the *Moscow News*, and it depressed her.

To add to her unhappiness she was again having physical problems. She had cataracts in both eyes that prevented her from seeing clearly beyond ten feet. Most nights she required two sedatives to sleep at all. The massive amounts of vitamins A, B-1, C and D she was taking to alleviate the symptoms of Paget's disease were exacerbating the progressive calcification of internal organs the disease causes. She had to have Novocain injections several times a week for the pain in her limbs.

There was some relief when in the summer of 1960 Emily returned for a visit. The two friends took a vacation at Pei-tai-ho, a seaside resort about six hours by train from the capital. Anna Louise took short swims and followed her Chinese friends' advice to heap warm sand over her legs to improve circulation. Her room was full of fresh flowers and plants; the gardener had even brought her several night-blooming cereus when he discovered how much she liked them. She and Emily fought as much as they talked, especially over the nightly games of bridge; everyone in Pei-tai-ho except Emily apparently knew that to beat Anna Louise at bridge was to risk her wrath, but to lose too easily was to rouse suspicion that could explode at any moment. Rewi Alley took them on several trips up the coast to the beautiful small temple at Ch'in-huang-tao and to Shan-hai-kuan—"the first pass under heaven"—at the beginning of the Great Wall. Anna Louise especially loved the temple at Shan-hai-kuan dedicated to the Lady Meng, who had jumped to her death in the sea when she learned that her husband had been one of those sacrificed in the building of the Great Wall. The story went that the Lady Meng's tears had so moved the gods that they had caused the wall to crack at the point where her husband was immured.

In late July, while Emily was still there, the Russians withdrew a major portion of their industrial aid to the Chinese. Gasoline was soon in such short supply that buses were converted to propane gas. All of her Chinese friends assured her that rupture with the Soviet Union was impossible. Anna Louise kept her peace, but she had trouble reconciling herself to the dismissal from his army posts of P'eng Teh-huai, who in contrast to his replacement, Lin Piao, had favored a more conciliatory attitude toward the Russians.

She tried to pursue the matter through her contacts and met with bland nonresponses. Annoyed at vague answers from Lu Ting-yi to further questions posed by Aronson about Sino-Soviet relations, she wrote him heedlessly: "The trouble is that at the slightest breath of a suggestion that anyone in China would possibly differ from Mr. K[hrushchev], they rear like a Victorian damsel threatened with rape. Mr. K is perfect; Chairman Mao is perfect. No disagreements anywhere. No deviations anywhere, and even my suggestion of a 'division of labor' in which Russia does the diplomacy and China the arousing of the colonial peoples was much objected to." Within a week she regretted this letter, too, and cabled Aronson that her comments were "for orientation only" and she was not to be quoted on the subject of Moscow-Peking.

She was caught between her passion for a story and her fear of repeating the trauma of the Russian experience. She first agreed to write an article on the Chinese-Soviet conflict for the *Guardian*, and then backed off on the excuse that "all the people I might consult are out of town." Tang had told her that there was no problem with Russia that would not be resolved. She closed her letter reneging on the article with a parable: "If a husband has a temper and his wife wants to save the marriage, what does she do when he throws his weight about because she is not quite his echo and says, 'I'll show you who is boss in this family. I have canceled that dress of yours from Paris and put all those jewels I bought for you in my own safe deposit until you beg for them properly.' Now if the lady gets mad and answers in anger, and especially if she reveals her husband's actions to her neighbors, then the man is caught in a trap of his own making and the way leads toward separation . . . but *if* the lady smiles and says, 'Well, dear, if you feel that way I must try to make my old clothes do and string a few beads and sew a nice dress for the next party,' presently when anger cools, as it always does, the husband thinks, 'My God, if my wife goes to that diplomatic party in hand-made clothes and without the jewels the neighbors know I have bought for her, *what* will they think of me? They might even think me bankrupt.' So maybe the jewels come out of the box after all. And the lady, if wise, never admits that there was any trouble at all. This is just a story that might be.''

After Emily's departure, she continued to worry about China's relations to the Soviet Union. She finally told Chou that the economic consequences of the Soviet withdrawal alarmed her far more than the ideological differences, only to be admonished, "We do not consider it so. An economic loss can be made up in a relatively short time, but a mistaken line could curse our children's children. The First International was broken by a wrong theory and so was the Second. Results would be worse today." She appreciated Chou's argument about the importance of the party line and gained increasing respect from her Chinese advisors for her ability to be "reasonable if given reasons."

But more and more she felt unsatisfied with her lot. Edgar Snow came for an interview with Mao, and she found herself as jealous of his American contracts as of his time with Mao. She decided unkindly that he was arrogant, "as if he had made the Revolution himself," and wrote nastily to a relative that Snow's behavior was "pathological. . . . He brought five fine cameras and broke them all and borrowed two more and broke them, and sat down on a friend's eyeglasses and broke them. I can't quite explain it."

She was fair enough to defend Snow's long article in *Look* against Emily Pierson's criticism and the integrity of his reporting to Lem Harris, but the publicity and income he was deriving from his China connections provoked her to write to Jessica Smith: "Every time that I have offered free labor, or failed to collect for my labor, my work has been undervalued." She would no longer write gratis; perhaps if she started to charge for her reporting, her work might be taken more seriously in magazines of broader circulation.

She spent the winter of 1960–61 in Hainan again, worrying about the harvest and the situation in Laos. The lack of snow promised the third poor crop of winter wheat. She did not make the mistake of ignoring the famine as she had in her writing from Russia in 1931, but she did attribute most of the problems to natural disasters. When the foreign press and the Russians pointed to a failure of the commune system, Anna Louise reminded her western friends that before the revolution three years of drought would have meant over ten million deaths.

Meanwhile, the American government was preparing to try to stem the tide of revolution in Southeast Asia. A large contingent of American advisors had been sent to Laos shortly after John F. Kennedy's election and was meeting with at best mixed results against the Pathet Lao insurgents. Anna Louise decided to investigate the situation herself. She left for Laos on March 28, 1961, expecting to interview top Laotian leaders. Instead she found more political confusion than she had seen since the twenties in Mexico. The previous August a captain of a parachute battalion named Kong Le had astonished the world by taking over the capital and bringing back Prince Souvanna Phouma, a "pro-western neutralist." Kong Le was, she discovered, "an incredible mixture of naive youth, military brilliance, and political ignorance plus modesty. He believes . . . in omens: 'Whenever I dream I see Prince Souphanouvong (along with Phouma, the most powerful politician) on a white horse, I know that day I'll have a victory.' The Pathet Lao are no more Communists than were the Americans before Jefferson. They are very primitive democrats." When a supposedly progressive woman deputy told her that there was no land reform because there was plenty of land and that "although it was true that the minorities had been called 'kha' or slave, that was an impolite term and should not be used," Anna Louise threw up her hands.

She spent three weeks in Vietnam and Laos and saw enough to convince her that Laos was not going to be the tinderbox of Indochina. She wrote a short book on her trip, *Cash and Violence in Laos and Vietnam,* which concluded with a chapter looking sadly forward to the coming conflict in Vietnam. Here, for the first time, Anna Louise used the term "American imperialism," as if the policies pursued in Indochina were a quality of the United States as a country and not simply of some rulers.

Nonetheless, she maintained an ardent interest in both American politics and her own personal affairs in the United States. She worried about the status and fate of her properties, especially Rim Forest. When Grace Nelson proved to be an inadequate steward of her accounts, she became at first despondent and then furious and badgered Fritchman with repeated long, pedantically detailed letters about points of law, title deeds and the smallest minutiae of ownership, to the degree that Frank Coe told her that she should have been a banker. At one point she wrote, but did not send, a seventy-five-page diatribe against Fritchman and the church, threatening to break off all relations. Fritchman was long-suffering and knew her mood swings; he protested gently against such anger, but at times it seemed to him that Anna Louise thought he had nothing to do but take care of her affairs. He finally managed to extricate himself by suggesting that she deal with the church lawyers directly. She in turn depended increasingly on her nephew Tracy, Jr., and his wife Dolphine, who gradually took over the administration of her affairs in California.

That summer she was invited by the Soviet Writers' Union to go to Moscow. She had maintained almost no contacts there, but various American friends, including Emily Pierson, were going, and there were matters of money and her files to resolve. She was received personally by the ambassador at the Russian embassy in Peking and assured that there would be no problem. But there was. When on her next visit to the embassy, she was told, "Your request to visit the Soviet Union is still under consideration," she snapped back angrily: "I did not request; I was invited." Sidney Rittenberg found her fuming at home and suggested that she call the Writers' Union directly. As soon as Anna Louise announced herself to a secretary, the line went dead. All attempts to call again were met with claims of "difficulties" on the Russian end. The trip never came off, and she decided to try again the following summer.

In September and October tensions between China and the U.S.S.R. increased when relations were severed between the Albanian party and the Warsaw bloc. Chou En-lai made a speech at the Twenty-second Party Congress in Moscow deploring any public one-sided censure of a fraternal party, and after pointedly laying a wreath on Stalin's grave, left the congress before its conclusion. On November 7, the anniversary of the Russian Revolution, the Chinese sent fraternal greetings to both the Russian and the Albanian parties, attaching a note to the latter that read, "No force on earth can shake the Chinese-Albanian alliance."

Anna Louise had several long talks with Tang about these developments and then sent to her friends a private report revealing that she might not be able to come to Moscow the next summer either. In a note to Emily she added that the American Communists' automatic obeisance to Moscow over the question of Albania showed that they still had to learn that "the U.S.S.R. is not invulnerable to mistakes and that the duty of the world's Communists is not thinking 'yes, yes,' but careful thought."

At the turn of the year China launched a campaign of protest against the "oppression of the American people" by their own government. Rallies were held in major Chinese cities against the Smith and McCarran acts. "More than anything else," Anna Louise wrote to Fritchman, "this campaign resembles the old 'prayer meeting' campaigns of my childhood.

It has the same fervor and faith that the God on whom they call is mighty to help. But it is not God the Chinese call upon, but the Mighty People." It seemed to her that she heard a whole nation saying: "America has not only imperialism. It also has good people. . . . Meanwhile be wary. Do not be deceived by the agents of Kennedy, by his 'peace corps' with its tales of the American ideal. This is no more the America of Jefferson, Lincoln and Roosevelt. This is the America of Kennedy and the Iron Heel!" Her claim that the Peking campaign was "the biggest ever made in history for justice in another land" notwithstanding, the *Guardian* did not print her report. When she realized that Aronson had only taken one out of the last twelve pieces she had sent him, she asked him directly why. He assured her that the American Communist party had nothing to do with *Guardian* editorial policy. "To be frank," he wrote, "I feel your stories—while they are honestly felt and in many cases movingly reported—still lack a sense of journalistic detachment and attribution which is essential for the American reader today."

Anna Louise was grateful for Aronson's straightforwardness: "I know that the tendency appears when one stays too long in a different country. . . . To speak from one land to another is always hard. . . . I solved this problem in the U.S.S.R. by going nearly every year to the U.S.A. to lecture, with special intent to keep contact with American audiences and editors. Each time it was a shock, like a cold shower. Then when in three or four months I grew accustomed to American ways of thinking, I returned to Moscow with a lot of bright ideas from editors, only to find my husband thought me crazy even to mention such ideas to the Press Department, so alien were they. . . . This annual double shock helped keep me aware of the way to write for Americans. In China this contact is impossible." Her letter continued for three single-spaced pages, trying with great lucidity to analyze her obstacles but with a growing consciousness that it might not work out.

Her isolation increased. In March 1962 her brother Tracy wrote that he was going to accompany an American delegation to the Disarmament Conference in Moscow that July and would very much like to see her. She made new inquiries at the Soviet embassy and was not only received warmly but invited to visit Siberia on her return. Wanting to keep the visit personal, she turned down an invitation to address the conference on Sino-Soviet relations. Such a talk, she wrote to Emily, would have become known as her "famous last words."

When her brother called her on June 30 from Leningrad with the news that he would not come to Peking because of American passport restrictions, she told him she would meet him in Moscow: she had now received delegate credentials from both the American Russian Institute and the Fellowship for Social Justice. Many of her California friends were attending the Congress; Anna Louise looked forward to her trip. On July 3, she applied to both the Chinese and Soviet authorities for the proper papers.

In six hours the Chinese produced a neat little folder entitled "Exit and Reentry Permit #043." The Soviets delayed. She could not take the plane on July 6; despite the fact that her credentials had been accepted at the conference, no visa came. She got in touch with both her brother and Holland Roberts by phone; Roberts promised to push harder in Moscow. On Sunday she went back to the embassy. A new acting consul met her, as arrogant and discourteous as the previous one had been welcoming and polite. He began by reminding her of the recent victories of the U.S.S.R. over the Chinese in volleyball, and when Anna Louise attempted to change the subject by saying she never attended such events because of failing eyesight, he gloated that "youth is indeed better than age" and boasted that he was "one of Lenin's replacements," having been born in the year of Lenin's death. On her best behavior Anna Louise managed to restrain herself from pointing out that "Lenin's replacements" referred properly to workers who had joined the party in 1924, and not to babes in arms. After forty minutes he finally told her that her visa had been turned down because "the Soviet Writers' Union was unable at this time to give her the tour which she had requested." "For the first time," she later noted, "I failed to be fully polite." A fight ensued, with Anna Louise loudly proclaiming that she had never wanted their tour, and that over two thousand visas had been granted.

On Tuesday, Tracy phoned from Moscow to tell her that the visa had supposedly been cabled from Moscow an hour earlier. Anna Louise kept a man up at the embassy until midnight waiting for it. She could not take the plane the following day; the next one was on Saturday the 14. Holland Roberts told her that she should come anyhow, that he had been told two days earlier that her visa had been sent. Anna Louise suggested as a fallback plan that he gather a group of friends for an extended phone conversation should the elusive visa fail to appear. After this conversation, Anna Louise began to have trouble establishing telephone contact. On the twelfth, she tried to place three calls to her brother's room between 6:30 and 7:00 A.M. to be told each time that he was out. Six hours later he called from a phone outside the hotel and told her he had been in his room the whole time. When Holland and the California group tried to reach her that Saturday, the line went dead.

The experience confirmed her evolving suspicion that her arrest in 1949 had actually been an assault on her support of the Chinese. She wrote to Holland Roberts a few days after the fiasco: "Stalin also tried to stop China's revolution. He ordered Mao to submit to Chiang else China would perish in a world war. This is the period I was arrested. The reason in retrospect is clear. Russia would not permit independent contact between China and the world; Moscow must dictate revolution everywhere. . . . Khrushchev has now abandoned the revolution entirely . . . to make Russia rich."

Anna Louise's consciousness of having burned her bridges was strong. One of the questions Roberts had asked over the telephone was "Why do you live in Peking?" In the last week in July she tried to write out an answer. She was not completely happy with the result and did not send it, but the text makes clear that China satisfied her long-term desires. "It is the way I have always wished to live. In the U.S.A. I attained a life similar to this when I lived in Hull House or Henry Street Settlement, or when I worked abroad with the Friends service. A life in which chores are handled by others, but without the cost inherent in personal servants." When Foreign Minister Ch'en Yi asked one day if she was lonely in China, she thought a minute before she replied: "Everyone is lonely at times, but I am less lonely in China than I have been elsewhere."

During a dinner with Chou En-lai in August, Anna Louise mentioned her anxiety about publishing outlets in the United States. Chou suggested that she write a monthly general letter to all those who sought information about China. The suggestion was strikingly similar to one her father had made to her forty years earlier about Russia, and she took to it immediately. She and Tang worked out the financial and physical details. A letterhead showing T'ien-an Men and the inscription "Letter from China by Anna Louise Strong" was printed and the first mimeographed letter went out on September 17, 1962.

The possibilities of the letter became apparent with the second issue. On October 12, after a long period of tension, the Sino-Indian border war started when Nehru ordered his troops to occupy a disputed region. Anna Louise wrote a lucid analysis of the Chinese position and followed it with a longer one a month later. Her Chinese friends were quick to see the advantage of a nonofficial regular vehicle for propaganda and analysis.

She used her rota of suppers to prepare the newsletter. Friends, including Tang and Wang Ch'u-liang, would suggest topics. After data was gathered, she wrote a draft and read it aloud for comments and criticism. The fifth issue, dated January 12, 1963, was printed rather than mimeographed and carried short articles by all the Anglo-Americans working in China.

Response to the *Letters* in the United States and elsewhere was very positive. They were republished in some newspapers in South Asia and used for discussion groups elsewhere. When Anna Louise returned from her winter vacation in Hainan, she was encouraged by Chou and others to make the *Letters* a regular part of her routine. Elsie Cholmeley became assistant editor.

Just after the Cuban missile crisis, in November 1962, Anna Louise received a letter from Cuba:

Dear Comrade,
We invited you to Cuba fundamentally for the happiness you would afford us by having you among us and so that you could know our Revolution. . . . The situation here in Cuba is that of a state of alarm or combat; the people await the aggression on a war footing. Nobody thinks of taking a step back. Everyone is ready to carry on his duty. If we ever perished . . . one could read in each corner of our land some message like that of the Thermopylae. At any rate we are not studying the posture for the final gesture; we love life and shall defend it. Please accept a revolutionary greeting, from your friend,

FATHERLAND OR CONQUER

Che
(Major Ernesto Che Guevara)

Anna Louise wanted very much to visit Cuba, but she was trying to finish her book on the Sino-Indian conflict. She wrote back to Guevara, postponing her visit. She was having trouble with the book. At her birthday party, Chou had told her that the Chinese army had trapped about 20,000 troops and then let them go, a few thousand at a time, taking care not to mistreat them while they were imprisoned. Anna Louise asked Chou how many troops the Chinese had used. He would not tell her. "Not that we care about saving Nehru's face, but the dignity of the Indian people is involved." He did not want to shame his "Asian brothers" before the world. To the Chinese, the victory had been sufficiently clear and the justice of their position obvious enough that they would not permit any significant investigative reporting of the event. Emboldened by her exchanges with Aronson, Anna Louise protested to Liao Cheng-chih that what she had written so far "could not convince any honest opponent, or even a careful expert."

It does not even convince *me*. I have many holes in this letter, and I have papered them over to make a good case, and I think I have done so. But in a book, the holes would become too big and would ruin my reputation and my case. The trouble lies where I have always found it in China's present propaganda, that you demand that no picture of actual hard struggle be shown. . . . I cannot do the good articles that might be done on the reduction of mortality or crime in China's cities in comparison with—for instance, New York— because you permit no admission that anyone in China ever dies or commits crime. I cannot show the struggle for grain and a sound agriculture, because I am not allowed to admit that anyone in these three years ever starved to death.

And the same is the problem when it comes to the Indian border. According to the picture thus far given me, the Chinese on the border sat virtuous and restrained like Buddha and never fired a shot in anger until the massive Indian offensive began October 20, and then they went into counterattack at some unknown moment, and found themselves as if by magic 30 or 40 kilometers away with the Indians scattered before them. Somehow or other all the gains made by India in three years, all the territory taken on the western border, as well as that beyond the MacMahon line, got so fast into Chinese hands that it was done by God. China is an unsullied virgin who wins the world and brings it to her feet by virtue, chastity, and the aid of heaven alone. Now I agree that there is something in that view, but it is a view that cannot convince anybody. . . . If one can make a real contribution to the future by a book, it is worth doing. But just to copy *Hsinhua* is not enough.

Liao did not reply.

The Sino-Soviet split and the protectiveness of the Chinese made her task more difficult. The American Communist party denounced China in terms harsher than those used by the Kennedy administration, and many of her old friends in the American party once again severed relations with her. She continued to present the Chinese case with vigorous righteousness. Harrison Salisbury wrote in the *New York Times:* "Strong indication that Peking has abandoned real hope of even a paper compromise of the dispute was seen in the fact that Anna Louise Strong . . . appears to have been given the assignment of presenting China's case to Western Communists"; he then devoted fully half his article to detailing her analysis. Similar reports appeared by Paul Wohl in the *Christian Science Monitor.* Ruth Aley sent copies of both pieces to Anna Louise, who was amused by the fact that she had at last made the mainstream American press:

> . . . Commentary by Paul Wohl
> Analyzed, buttressed
> By quotes . . .

from Anna Louise Strong's
"Letter from China"
ME, no less!
You sure get around, writes Ruth.
I couldn't get into
That *Monitor*
If my agent tried
A year of Sundays
But there I am
an AUTHORITY
   Sitting on a beach
Admiring
The blue Pacific
Off Hainan
  ME
And the round round world!

Her life settled into a routine. She produced the *Letter* about ten times a year, summered at Pei-tai-ho and spent winters in Hainan. She worried constantly about the growing U.S. involvement in Vietnam and followed with interest and enthusiasm the development of the civil rights movement in the American South. In July 1963, at Pei-tai-ho, she taped a speech supporting the resistance of American blacks to racial and class oppressions; it was played at a major rally in Peking on the occasion of Chairman Mao's "Letter to the American Negroes," his first published work in several years. "This Negro struggle," Anna Louise claimed at the end of her speech, "is not yet the American revolution, but it may spark it. As more and more of the American working class and progressives join to support the Negro movement for 'Freedom now,' this may win a new birth of freedom for all exploited Americans and reinforce the anti-imperialist struggles of the world."

She began to see herself as the Chinese leaders did: as China's mouthpiece to English-speaking countries. When in September 1963 she "heard from a friend that China is about to make some nuclear history," she hastened to write Liao with advice on how to publicize it. "China's usual habit seems to be to encourage her enemies to do all their talking first . . . and then reply herself last. . . . This technique has its points, but not with a bomb explosion." She went on to suggest the wording of a short paragraph that would defuse potential criticism. The twelfth *Letter* on December 8 included just such a statement of the "Chinese platform on nuclear weapons." For whatever reason, the People's Republic did not in fact explode an atomic weapon until October 16, 1964, a year later, and when the explosion came, it was coupled with an announcement that followed the broad outlines of the text suggested by Anna Louise.

She also made repeated attempts to de-ideologize Chinese rhetoric. The extent of her actual influence is not clear, but the leaders continued to use her as an important conduit of information. The thirteenth *Letter,* published on December 30, 1963, contained a long interview with Vice-Premier Bo I-bo, the chairman of the State Economic Commission, who announced important information about changes in overall policy and used the occasion to press one of the hardest public attacks the Chinese had made on Khrushchev. Thus Anna Louise was infuriated when her left-wing American friends continued to ask her for "inside information" on China, as if the *Letters* could be ignored as the casual opinions of an old-lady ideologist. Ironically, the *Letters* were receiving closer and closer scrutiny by the U.S. State Department as it became clear that they often closely anticipated official policy.

On January 15, 1964, Anna Louise suddenly received an invitation to have lunch with Chairman Mao two days later. The senior Anglo-Americans in Peking had also been invited: Frank Coe, Sol Adler, Israel Epstein and Sid Rittenberg. Accompanied by K'ang Sheng, Mao met them in one of the reception halls of the old imperial palace in Peking. He began to reminisce about the days in Yenan and his development as a revolutionary. "After you left us," he said to Anna Louise, "and after we left Yenan, some of our friends, both in China and abroad, thought it was all up with us. You know, we don't need to be afraid of any reactionary force, no matter how powerful, because they have to split up. . . . The reactionaries are always trying to catch ten fleas by using all ten of the fingers. Have you comrades ever tried? I suggest you get yourself a few fleas, place one firmly under each finger, get someone to give the signal and let go and try to catch them."

Mao seemed most concerned with impressing on his guests the necessity for change in Chinese life: "You mustn't think that in China today there is no one who opposes us. There are many who did not accept socialism at first. . . . There are also some who want socialism in their hearts, but their idea of it is not real or scientific. Under communism, if we ever reach it, will there be no more opposition, no more political struggle, no more social revolution in any form? I don't believe it. People will always polarize into advanced, middle and backward, and it will always be necessary for the advanced elements to do the political work."

Anna Louise remarked that life would be very dull otherwise. Mao laughed: "Yes, otherwise people like us would find very little to do."

The conversation turned to "revisionism" and Khrushchev. The first face-to-face clash, Mao recalled, had come in 1958. Khrushchev had come to Peking to press for naval bases in China; Mao had refused, and when Khrushchev had pushed harder, Mao had remarked ironically that "he had better take the whole seacoast of China." When Khrushchev asked what China would do then, Mao said that he would go again to the hills and fight guerrilla war. Khrushchev snorted that such tactics were of no use in the modern world. "Well," said Mao, "I told him, 'If you insist on stopping China's nostrils up, what else can be done?' "

Mao wanted to give his listeners the full history. In 1959 Khrushchev had again come to China, fresh from his talks with Eisenhower at Camp David. He immediately requested the release of certain Americans imprisoned in China as spies. "That would be difficult," Mao had said to him. "You know, we have laws in our country." Khrushchev reddened. He had promised Eisenhower, he said, that these men would be released, even though the American president had doubted that the Chinese would agree. Khrushchev had also urged Mao to yield the "frozen wastes" on the Indian border on the ground that this might "win Nehru to fight imperialism." Mao had refused.

The problem with Khrushchev, Mao said, was that he, like the imperialists, saw the world as divided between two great powers with a third world as spectator, a view that left little space for revolutionary activity. "We see rather a realignment of forces," Mao explained. "There are the Marxist-Leninists promoting world revolution, and the imperialists trying to suppress it. Then there are the revisionists who fear imperialism and try to make a deal with imperialism; the three continents [Asia, Africa and Latin America] in the throes of anti-imperialist nationalist revolutions; and lastly, the 'northern tier,' France, Canada, Scandinavia and others who are part of the capitalist world but have contradictions with the United States and therefore find concrete agreement with the left."

Frank Coe asked Mao what role he was playing personally in the fight against revisionism. A sardonic laugh preceded Mao's response: "I myself have done very little in the fight against revisionism. I've just written a few poems. I don't have any other weapons personally; my poems are my weapons." There was more truth to Mao's disclaimer than the company perhaps knew, for Mao was in a minority on the central committee, with K'ang Sheng one of his few consistent supporters.

As the group moved into the dining room, Mao mentioned that the final rupture with the Soviets had come the previous July with the publication in Moscow of an "open letter" attacking China. "Since then we have been like the 'Monkey King Upsetting Heaven' in the old play. We have thrown away the Heavenly Rule Book." Mao laughed and then became very serious. "Remember this. Never take a Heavenly Rule Book too seriously. One must always go by one's own revolutionary rules."

As the group sat down to lunch, Mao started to rehearse his analysis of Russia, which he would later publish as *Khrushchev's Phony Communism*. There was no possibility of stopping the debate with the Russians, he said. "A comrade from the Communist party of the Soviet Union visited me recently, bringing a letter from the Soviet leadership. He said to me: 'Comrade Chairman, we Soviet Communists have at times been too severe in our criticism of the Chinese party.' 'Oh, no!' "—Mao smiled at the memory—" 'I can't agree. Just think: "Trotskyites, dogmatists, sectarians, anti-Soviets, racists"—how can such people not be criticized?' This Soviet comrade responded: 'Comrade Chairman, I must remind you that this is a very serious matter.' I told him," Mao continued, " 'Don't worry, comrade. A war of pen and ink doesn't wound the human body. There are at least four things I can guarantee. No matter how you criticize and attack us, the sky will not fall in, mothers in China will not stop bearing children, the trees and the grass will not stop growing and the fish will not stop swimming in the rivers.' Again the Russian comrade looked surprised, and I said: 'You don't believe me? Get to some river and see for yourself: are the fish still swimming or not?' "

At the end of the meal Mao accompanied them to the car in the traditional gesture of the host. Standing without a coat in the freezing weather, he congratulated Anna Louise on the success of her *Letter*. "We couldn't do our job without you," he said and suggested to K'ang Sheng that arrangements be made to translate it into other languages.

Anna Louise was very excited. Much of what Mao had said constituted an important policy statement on differences with Russia. Mao's vision of the Monkey King who made its own rules as it went along implied that the Chinese party was about to undertake policies for which there was no clear historical antecedent. Anna Louise, Eppie and Sid Rittenberg wrote up a first draft of the interview and submitted it to Wang Ch'u-liang for clearance. He made some "suggestions" and a revised version was submitted, written almost exclusively by Anna Louise. No permission came. Over the summer, Anna Louise rewrote some of the material for her *Letter* but again failed to get clearance. She found herself somewhat embarrassed. In February she had written to Aronson of her coming scoop. Now she had to file the material away. In retrospect, it seems likely that the problem lay not with Mao but with others in the central committee. Mao was a minority on most important issues, and it is unlikely that he could have obtained permission to have his talk published as policy.

During the year Anna Louise's attention turned more and more to the spreading war in Vietnam. She abbreviated her vacation in Pei-tai-ho to write a *Letter* on the Tonkin Gulf incident, devoting a special box to Vice-Premier Ch'en Yi's warning to the United States about the conditions that would lead to China's active entry into the war. In November she went to Hanoi for an International Conference of Solidarity against U.S. Imperialist Aggression and in Defense of Peace, accompanied by Rittenberg, Coe, and Robert and Mabel Williams, American blacks who had fled from legal charges in the United States first to Cuba and then to China.

Political tensions ran high. Anna Louise's presence in Vietnam was an embarrassment for the Russians. It appeared to the Chinese that the Russians wanted to make a deal whereby Americans would withdraw troops from Germany in exchange for the neutralization of South Vietnam, Laos and Cambodia; the North Vietnamese, aware of this policy, were trying to play their friends from other countries off against the Russians.

The day before the conference opened was Anna Louise's seventy-ninth birthday. Her hosts presented her with rich cakes at breakfast and lunch. At three P.M. the Americans were told that Ho Chi Minh wished to receive them. They were ushered into a small room that Anna Louise recognized as the room where she had met Ho in 1961 on her way to Laos. A third cake appeared, somewhat less ornate and rich than its predecessors. There was a light knock at the door. Rittenberg opened it to admit the president himself. He wished Anna Louise a happy birthday and then, as he cut and passed the cake, recalled in excellent English how he had worked his way around the world as a pastry cook and merchant seaman just after World War I.

Ho then brought in a thirteen-year-old South Vietnamese boy named Ho Van Bot who was horribly scarred from napalm burns. He thought that it might be a powerful gesture to introduce this victim of American aggression to the conference the next day. As the president left, he gave Anna Louise an ornately carved cane that he had received from Prince Sihanouk; now that Sihanouk was a friend of the Chinese, he thought

Anna Louise might like it. She did, and said with a laugh that if she dared she would call him "Uncle Ho," as the North Vietnamese did. Ho looked surprised and retorted, "But you are my older sister."

Back in her rooms, Anna Louise was a bit nervous about the responsibility for introducing the boy to the conference. Nor was she soothed by the insistent hovering of Li, the North Vietnamese president of the peace council and one of the most Soviet-oriented of North Vietnamese. For longer than seemed necessary, he bustled about in a manner that annoyed Anna Louise. After he left, she finally started to relax. She took out her false teeth, a new acquisition that summer, and lay down for a rest. Half asleep, she suddenly felt a hand on her arm. Without thinking, she swung her other hand, hitting the intruder in the jaw. It was Li, returning to talk with her. Hearing the resultant commotion, Rittenberg and Coe came in. Anna Louise kept shouting: "That man came in when I was lying down resting, with my teeth in the basin, with my hair all askew, while I was lying down resting, and began to paw me."

It took some while to quiet her and restore Li's dignity. Anna Louise eventually pleaded pure reflex and spent the rest of the afternoon with Coe and Rittenberg preparing for her talk the next day.

Texts of speeches had to be submitted for clearance beforehand; Anna Louise's was cleared. Rittenberg had submitted nothing. When they arrived on the platform with the boy, Anna Louise told Hoang Quoc Viet, head of the North Vietnamese delegation, that they wanted to introduce the young South Vietnamese to the audience. Hoang opposed it because they had not cleared the speech of introduction. Anna Louise responded, "Well, the U.S. delegation is obviously not going to be able to do this; that is too bad because Ho Chi Minh asked it of us himself." Permission was granted.

Anna Louise's speech was a high point of the conference. She retraced the changes she had experienced in America: "In my seventy-nine years I have seen my country grow from a young anti-imperialist nation to the strongest imperialism on earth." She recalled the reception of the *Shilka* and the actions of workers in Seattle in support of the new Soviet Republic in 1917; they had dropped a caseload marked "sewing machines" to reveal stacks of rifles for the "whites," hoping to inspire similar actions in ports around the world. In closing, she appealed directly to American women, to "those mothers who already courageously challenge the White House." Pointing to the maimed child on the platform: "Mothers of America, is this the task for which you raised your sons?"

The impact was stunning, and the political message became clear when

Rittenberg rose to introduce Bot to the almost 900 delegates, observers and newsmen. He closed with the challenge the American group had worked out beforehand: "Let the scars of Ho Van Bot be a challenge to us all, through which we judge and distinguish between true friends and false, between comrades-in-arms and hypocrites." The point was underlined when the chief Russian delegate was slow in rising to applaud and had to be dragged to his feet by his associate.

As the meeting broke up, Mrs. Cam, whom Anna Louise had met the previous year and who was the first woman lawyer in Indochina, asked Anna Louise if she would speak to the South Vietnamese children gathered outside in the yard. Anna Louise walked out with her through the tangle of tents and autobuses to where the children were preparing to leave. A dozen youngsters came toward her, the oldest girl, who was about fourteen, holding out a bar of chocolate with a stiff embarrassed air. Anna Louise was ill-at-ease with Mrs. Cam's effort to get the refugee children to accept "American people" as friends. She started to say that chocolate was more for young people than for old, then realized it would be ungracious and removed the wrapper, broke the chocolate into pieces and suggested they share it.

With this the girl who had offered the gift burst into tears and clutched Anna Louise, and all the other children started to cry as well, clinging to her clothes. Soon Anna Louise and the interpreter were weeping with them. Anna Louise brought back some control by telling the children that "we are eating this chocolate together because we are all going to work together to liberate South Vietnam, and the chocolate will make us a little stronger."

The final reception was in the presidential palace. Long tables had been placed in a rectangle for the delegates. Ho sat at the center of one long side with Anna Louise on his left, a South Vietnamese on his right. The Chinese and Russian delegations were farther away, one on each side. Anna Louise thought that the arrangement seemed to say: "This conference most directly concerns South Vietnam and the American people." Anna Louise quietly congratulated Ho on the deftness with which the conference had given the appearance of unanimity. He replied with a proverb, "It is not easy to satisfy every man and his wife," but added, "The question here is really very simple."

Exhilarated but very tired physically, Anna Louise returned to Peking the first week in December. The news that greeted her disturbed her greatly: Emily had fallen while alone in her house in Cromwell and spent the night on the floor with a broken hip, unable to move. Her daughter

Ann had found her the next day. The episode made vivid to Anna Louise both her distance from old friends and the physical decay of old age. Her own legs were increasingly painful. Feng-feng walked with a hand just off her elbow in case she slipped; there was a special guardrail around her bath.

In June Anna Louise was back in Vietnam for a world trade union conference. The same politics prevailed. Shortly after her arrival she was told that the Russians did not want her to address the conference. She was furious, the more so when the Vietnamese also tried to dissuade her. She threatened to cause a major scandal, and a session of the conference had to be postponed to work out the problem. When Hoang Quoc Viet came to inform her that the U.S.S.R. had challenged her credentials because she was not a trade unionist, she sat quietly for a minute and then said, "I understand. Our Vietnamese friends are in difficulty. A very powerful delegation; international commitments. Of course I have not been closely associated with trade unions in recent years. But I can remember when the Seattle trade union council sent me to Moscow, and Lenin spoke and gave me my card. Of course," she continued with perfectly genteel exaggeration, "that was a long time ago, and these things don't count for very much." Hoang "went gray to the roots of his hair" and when she had finished said in a genuine burst of emotion, "You will not only speak, but have unlimited time and no one will stop you."

Together with twenty other delegates, Anna Louise had a talk with two American prisoners, pilots of planes that had been shot down. She was cautious about what she said and what agreements she made. When the National Liberation Front ambassador asked her to be a mailing station between American POWs and the United States, she refused, not wanting to be used by the Vietnamese. Contrary to later reports, she did not broadcast to American soldiers in South Vietnam, but when a tape of her address to the conference was rebroadcast, she found herself attacked by the right-wing commentator Fulton Lewis, Jr., as "an octogenarian Axis Sally." After a predawn visit to the port of Haiphong, recently the target of major U.S. bombing, she returned to Peking, exhausted, as she wrote to Fritchman, by "the conference and by the heat, both atmospheric and polemical."

When Anna Louise went to Pei-tai-ho in the summer before her eightieth birthday, her life seemed to have settled into a hectic but satisfying routine. She was still able to renew her energy with short rests and vacations. Symbolically, the FBI in the United States suddenly realized that she was drawing social security payments and moved to stop them.

As for her disposition, she wrote to Emily in answer to a short article on her that had appeared in the *Philadelphia Sunday Bulletin:* "Sid tells me that my temper now is not a patch on what it was twenty years ago, and in general my disposition is improved by living in China. But Feng-feng, always a careful analyst, says that when I travel I get irritable in adjusting to new places. I agree with her. The irritations of not remembering where I put my comb or cold cream, etc., can induce quite a temper of frustration which I take out on anyone handy. Chinese are very understanding about what they consider an almost inevitable characteristic of age; nonetheless, I must take care. I have told Dr. Ma that I want to consult him about it; he laughed and said he did not think my mind showed signs of being crotchety at all."

15

The End of the Visit

My motto remains, "I'm off to die with Odin," from a story in
which it appears that the devil is winning and the rich man
and the virtuous man have deserted, but the rover keeps on,
liking a good flight and liking Odin. That's me.

—Anna Louise to Ruth Aley, December 12, 1962

Shortly after the talk with Mao, Wang Ch'u-liang brought word that the
Foreign Languages Publishing House was interested in editing a complete set of Anna Louise's works. When she protested that she had
written over thirty volumes, even Wang was stunned. They settled on a
six-volume edition of *Selected Works on China's Revolution*, the first of
which was to be *China's Millions*. Anna Louise undertook to write a new
preface for the first volume.

In June 1965 she sent an early draft of the new preface to her sixtieth
Oberlin reunion. She explained that she remained in China not only
because she had found her widest audience there but also because of "the
same clear comradeship and clear thinking that had stimulated me in
Yenan." She also spoke of her desire to return to some future reunion, to
see not only her classmates but the new Oberlin youth. "I congratulate
Oberlin that the president of the Students for a Democratic Society,
which pulled off that spectacular April 17 march [against the Vietnam
War], was Paul Potter, a recent Oberlin graduate. If any classmates care
to write to me, I want to know what share Oberlin took in that march,
and in similar events now going on. For these are the natural sequence
from Oberlin's great history with which Oberlin has not always kept faith,
a history that fought for the great values of mankind, even against government rules."

Feng-feng's two boys, aged eight and six, accompanied their mother to

Pei-tai-ho that summer, on Anna Louise's invitation. The vacation was spent happily and quietly, mostly editing the text of *China's Millions* and integrating a new first chapter that had previously been published as "Canton Prelude." After their return to Peking, Anna Louise and Feng-feng took a spectacular boat trip down the Yangtze gorges, investigating flood control and electrical power resources.

During the fall a number of important political changes took place in China. Lo Jui-ch'ing was replaced as army chief of staff by Lin Piao. Lin was much more hostile to the Russians than was Lo and firmly committed to a concentration on domestic political matters. In early November the Shanghai *People's Daily* published an article sharply critical of a 1961 play which had been seen at the time as a veiled attack on Mao's policies. That the rebuttal had been published in Shanghai, which was known as a center of the forces supporting Mao, and not in Peking, was a subject of considerable discussion.

On November 21, three days before her birthday, Tang brought Anna Louise two cards. One, from Mao, was bound in red ribbon and covered with flowers; the other, from Chou, was bright red. Both were invitations to birthday parties for her. As Anna Louise expressed her pleased surprise, Tang explained that eightieth birthdays were traditionally major days of celebration in China, so much so that many families never recovered from the drain. The lavishness seemed confirmed when the next day she was informed that a special plane had been chartered to take her and thirty of her friends, foreign and Chinese, to an unnamed destination. Mao, as usual, was not in Peking; he was, the group soon found out, in Shanghai. At the Ch'in Ch'iang, an elegant old Shanghai hotel in the former French quarter, a large and comfortable suite awaited Anna Louise. Her guests were given rooms on the same floor.

The next day was spent sightseeing. Anna Louise was first told that Mao would receive only her, but she demurred: "All my friends have come this long distance with me," she proclaimed. "If Chairman Mao sees me, he should see them too." The following day, November 24, word came in the late morning that the time had come to visit the chairman and that he would see the whole party. Mao was waiting at the door to receive them with his wife, Chiang Ch'ing, at his side, an unusual gesture, for she traditionally stayed away from public functions.

As they entered the large room set with thirty white slipcovered chairs arranged in an oval, Mao shook hands with each of the guests. He seemed in excellent humor. In contrast, Wu, the editor of the Peking *People's Daily*, sat somewhat dourly in a corner with a few high officials from the propaganda ministry who looked equally glum. Anna Louise was escorted to a chair at the head of the oval. As Mao made his way to the vacant seat beside her, he pulled out a cigarette and remarked jokingly that as a smoker he was "of one faction, whereas Comrade Strong," and he gave her a teasing look, "was of the opposite faction, a nonsmoker." As often, Anna Louise was taken aback by Mao's opening gambit.

Dr. Ma came to the rescue and challenged him directly: "Are you making this a factional affair?" "Certainly," replied Mao. "The doctors say I should not smoke; I say I do. How many of you people smoke? Let the smokers raise their hand with a cigarette. To have a cigarette in the hand will be taken as a sign of the smoker." He said this in a light tone, but in what only a few of the foreign members of the group recognized as very cryptic classical Chinese. Those who understood that an allusion was intended looked at one another, perplexed. Others thought it a strange beginning. "Well," Mao chuckled, "it seems that in this too I am in the minority," and he looked over at the group from the propaganda ministry. "Nevertheless, I shall smoke and urge you to also."

Mao asked the group their opinions on the world situation. He received a few hesitant replies to which he listened with only half interest. The group pressed him for his thoughts. "All right, since you all agree," said Mao, again in the diction of the classics, "I see that you have had a meeting in advance and have passed a resolution on how to handle me. It would have been nice to have a divergent opinion." Another look shot over to those in the corner. "But since you all have such a firm front against me, I have no choice but to tell you what I think." With this exchange, again directed over the heads of his audience, Mao turned to more obviously substantive matters, beginning with the recent massacre of Indonesian Communists.

After almost two hours of talk focused on his prophecy of a 10,000-year ideological debate with the Russians, Mao interrupted himself by saying to Dr. Ma: "You health department folks don't look after people's health. See how late it is for eating. My wife has invited us all to lunch." Chiang Ch'ing had come out from behind a screen that hid a door to another room. The group returned to their rooms to wash and then went to the banquet hall. Mao entered a few minutes later and stopped silently before each of the ornately carved bamboo screens, seemingly lost in his thoughts. Suddenly his concentration cleared, and he turned to lunch. With the traditional gesture of the host, he placed some of the first appetizers on Anna Louise's plate.

As the dinner drew to a close, Mao showed no signs that he wanted to leave. Finally he said: "I see that Comrade Liao [Cheng-chih] is looking at his watch; it means that Liao wants me to leave for another meeting." For some minutes Mao made no move to go. Liao looked more insistently at his watch. Mao threw down his cigarette grumpily: "Well, I wanted to finish this cigarette, but Liao won't let me."

The next evening there was another birthday party, this time hosted by Chou En-lai. In his toast Chou said that foreigners had a way of halving the value of everything by interpreting them *kung ts'e*, metrically. But this meant that Anna Louise was in fact only "forty metric years old and that we will celebrate her birthday for many years to come." He presented her with the first copy of the new edition of *China's Millions*, for which she had finished reading proof only some ten days before. It was handsomely bound in grey with gold lettering and came in a Chinese-red jacket.

Anna Louise beamed and stood with some difficulty, though without assistance, to reply. She had decided to read the preface to the new edition as a response to her hosts. The talk kept her on her feet for a long time, and at one point a Chinese official, seeing her obvious discomfort, rose to bring her a chair. Chou En-lai sternly but almost imperceptibly waved him off. Just as she finished, Chou rose and seated her himself.

Even Chou's dinner was not without the symbolic politics that had marked the banquet with Mao. After Chou had thanked their hosts with the encomium that many thought that the capital of China should be moved to Shanghai, a choral group came in to perform the "Long March Cantata." In the middle of the song Chou jumped to his feet: "Wait a minute, why do you skip the stanza that Hsiao Hua wrote?" Hsiao Hua was a director of political indoctrination in the army, friendly to Chou but an enemy of Lin Piao. The conductor of the group protested that they could not do the verse because it had not been rehearsed. Chou said that he could sing it and, displaying a surprisingly good tenor, proceeded to teach it to the chorus and then conduct it himself. Chou closed the celebration with a little speech about the importance of teaching the young the traditions of the old.

After all the excitement, Anna Louise spent the next month in bed with an inhaler and medication. The doctors did not find her well enough to travel south to Canton until almost the last week in January. Even in Canton she still spent most of her time in bed. While she was there, she received a letter from her brother Tracy. Since his retirement in 1955, he had written, taught, lectured and toured for the World YMCA. Now seventy-eight years old, he was traveling around the world with his wife, still mainly on YMCA business. "It would be interesting," he wrote, "some time to have a long talk together as to both of us sharing father's idealism and faith in the Kingdom of God and mother's sacrificial death penetrating the world at large. You have gone deep into the uprising of the masses for status, freedom and a new world, while I have touched the youth of the world looking through the eyes and heart of faith in Jesus Christ and a loving father God at work everywhere in the hearts of men."

"I am much intrigued," she wrote back to her brother, "at your desire for a long basic talk with me about our roads in life, and basic views on life. . . . I think you should plan . . . to take in Peking." The YMCA connection might help, she thought, even though, "the Chinese feel more at home with Americans who come without benefit of passport just because they long for China: but Edgar Snow gets in even though they know that Harriman will drop in on him later to pump him about what he saw. . . . I must tell you that your concept of the universe with a loving father is one I have not considered for many years."

These were also months of increased anxiety about her relations with the United States. In April she sent three articles to the *National Guardian* and was outraged in May when she saw that they had been edited. She accused the *Guardian* of "very skillful malice, . . . (a) most serious evil, . . . mutilation and distortion," and demanded they publish her letter "correcting the past." Aronson had troubles of his own. The staff at the *Guardian* was increasingly influenced by the views of the New Left. The younger members thought Anna Louise and Cedric Belfrage, as well as Julio Alvarez del Vayo, all still on the masthead, unnecessary burdens from the past and were demanding their ouster. Aronson had defended his old friend against these attacks but did not feel that her present efforts were sufficiently objective to print without editing. He shielded her from the knowledge of the staff attacks but wrote back honestly, "I am profoundly shocked at the violence of your reaction." He requested that she withdraw her public letter, for if the *Guardian* printed it, "I would have to write a long response and I am afraid that you would not come out very well in the last analysis." Anna Louise was just as angry at Aronson's response as she had been at his editing and was dissuaded from placing an angry advertisement only by the ever-watchful Liao. She remained petulant and wrote Elsie Cholmeley from T'a-ch'eng oil field in July: "Here I am, the only foreign visitor yet allowed at T'a-ch'eng; Jim Aronson might have had the story, but he won't get it now."

Anna Louise was still fuming when she arrived in Pei-tai-ho for her summer vacation. Elsie sent another urgent letter telling her that Tang wished her to do nothing more about the *Guardian* until she got back to Peking and to take as complete a rest as possible.

Most of the *Letters from China* in the first five months of 1966 were devoted to the war in Vietnam, including a special supplement on "When and How Will China Go to War" that detailed the limits beyond which China could not be pushed in Indochina. But even more important developments were going on inside China. In the last week in March, Mao had moved against the Peking branch of the party, and by the beginning of May some of his gnomic comments at her birthday party began to make sense. P'eng Chen, the mayor of Peking, was dismissed and Lu Ting-yi and Marshal Lo Jui-ch'ing were removed from all responsible offices. More dismissals followed quickly: the presidents of Peking and Nanking universities and the entire editorial boards of the two major Peking daily newspapers among them. On June 13 it was announced that the old system of competitive examinations for university admission was abolished and the enrollment for 1966 delayed by half a year.

In her June 30 *Letter*, Anna Louise spent eight and a half pages on the Cultural Revolution, as the massive changes were now called. It was not, she hastened to assure her readers, "a fight for succession" but a dream she had supported for fifty years for "the remaking of man's mind and the creation of the world." The tone of her letter was one of hope and enthusiasm, except for a clause that "it would be prudent" for her to withhold comments until autumn. "However, the roll of drums and the clang of cymbals and the thunder of marching feet . . . kept me awake for weeks until I grew used to them as the background of daily life." Emily Pierson found this *Letter* "hard to digest," and Anna Louise, quietly bothered by the fact that an old friend like Lu Ting-yi had been cast aside, could only protest that "I do the best I can. . . . We shall see what we shall see." At a hastily called meeting of the central committee of the Chinese Communist party during the first twelve days in August, it became clear that Mao was now in full practical command of the party, rather than the minority voice he had been for the previous five years.

The report of the central committee reached Anna Louise in Pei-tai-ho just as she finished a talk on the oil fields of T'a-ch'eng to a visiting group of French Communists. The executive director of the resort read out the new directives: "to struggle against and crush those persons in authority who are taking the capitalist road, to criticize and repudiate reactionary bourgeois academic authorities, to transform education, liter-

ature and art and all other parts of the superstructure that do not corre-
spond to the Socialist economic base." At the end everyone clapped, and
then the bewildered foreigners present whispered to one another.

Shortly afterwards young Red Guards in khaki uniforms with red arm
bands began to appear on the streets of Pei-tai-ho; on August 18 news
reached the contingent of foreigners that a rally of one million Red Guards
had met in Peking and been received by Mao and Lin Piao, who had
themselves joined the organization. During the meeting of the central
committee, Lin had emerged as the second member of the hierarchy;
Liu Shao-ch'i was lowered to eighth.

Anna Louise returned to Peking at the end of August and immediately
sought Sidney Rittenberg to find out more about the new developments.
He arranged an interview for her with some Red Guards on September
12. Together with Feng-feng, they made their way to the Working People's Palace of Culture near T'ien-an Men; it had been given as headquarters to the new organization. Even with Feng-feng, they came under
immediate scrutiny and were barred entry at a second gate. They turned
to go; then Rittenberg whispered, "Don't hurry. You have been recognized as Shih Teh-lang, to whom Mao gave the paper tiger interview."
(The twentieth anniversary of the interview had been celebrated in the
Peking Daily the previous August 24.) Before they went far, they were
called back and brought to a center courtyard for the interview. Anna
Louise spoke mainly with a young firebrand who had given up the name
of "She Who Loves Literature and Studies It" for a Red Guard name of
"Fighting Red Banner." Anna Louise asked Fighting Red how names
were changed. She replied, "Each one can make his own rebellion about
his name."

As the talk proceeded, Fighting Red said that Chairman Mao had de-
fined the future of the Red Guards as "an armed revolutionary youth organization." There were nods all around. "But you haven't any arms," Anna
Louise protested. "Not yet," they said somewhat ominously. Rittenberg intervened, "Oh yes you have"; he held aloft a copy of the *Quotations from
Chairman Mao*. The young leader of the Guards continued, "With Chairman Mao as our leader . . . we will make the whole world red." As if
this were not enough, she added: "And then the whole universe."

Anna Louise noticed that some whispering had been going on between
her interlocutor and the fifteen-year-old who sat on her other side. Rittenberg later told her what was being said. Fighting Red had planned to
give Anna Louise an armband and accept her into the Red Guards. The
fifteen-year-old was protesting. "Don't be silly," said Red, "she is an

international comrade, and we can make her an honorary member." "It is you that is silly," retorted the younger girl. "People have to volunteer, and she hasn't applied." Red was somewhat nonplussed until she found the answer. "She hasn't thought of it, and she doesn't know the rules." Red finally pinned an armband on Anna Louise and said, "You were the first foreign comrade to talk to Chairman Mao about the paper tiger, and now you are the first to be admitted to the Red Guard." The whole group applauded.

"Now," said Fighting Red, "what are your instructions to us?" Anna Louise made a short speech. She told them that they were the successors to Chairman Mao, that they were the backbone of a self-defense force and, most important, that their criticism of the educational system was of central importance. She urged them to remember that Mao had said to concentrate on real enemies and take care to see that people who make mistakes be given the chance to correct themselves.

Her membership in the Red Guard did not remove Anna Louise's hesitations about the new stage of the revolution. She called the closing of the schools "the most upsetting feature," but claimed that the youth was "educating itself with terrific initiative". Feng-feng's increasing involvement with the Red Guard occupied so much of her time that Elsie Cholmeley took over some of her duties. When Feng-feng came in with her long hair cut and said that she had asked the guards if it were a sufficiently nonbourgeois style, Anna Louise remained silent, but the next morning at breakfast she angrily denounced the incident to Rewi Alley.

The gardener who took care of the grounds disappeared, and the flowers went to seed; Anna Louise was told that Chairman Mao thought that flowers were counterrevolutionary. "Well," she sniffed angrily, "Chairman Mao smokes, and I don't intend to start," and she wrote an angry letter to Liao that was not answered. On October 16 she stood with a friend looking down from T'ien-an Men on the crush of over two million Red Guards frantically waving little red books at Mao and Lin Piao, and started counting ambulances taking away the injured. When the total reached eighteen, she declared: "I've had enough. Let's go." But she came back that evening for the fireworks and managed to meet Mao and have him sign her copy of the little red book. "You must be tired," she said solicitously. "No, I'm not," Mao responded and vanished in the crowd.

She expressed some of these worries in a letter to Tang Ming-chao, who replied tersely: "A newborn baby is always a mess. But you don't throw it away." She tried to write a long article for the *Guardian* on the

Revolution, but it was rejected by Wang Ch'u-liang and Liao with the comment that she had made the Red Guards sound "too much like Boy Scouts." They were, she was informed, "marching to train for the next step in revolution." On January 6, 1967, she composed a letter to Frank Coe about her anxieties, now heightened by the dismissal and condemnation of Liu Shao-ch'i: "Last night I sat until nearly 1:00 P.M. in a kind of coma, unmoving at my desk, thinking among other things that I no longer felt safe in China, that the wonderful sense I had for so long . . . was displaced by a sense of chaotic unease, in which I felt that, just as Russia once jailed and threw me out, something similar could happen here. I was imprudent enough to tell this to Feng-feng, who said these were wrong thoughts, and I replied that I knew it."

She had found out from Israel Epstein that her long article on the Cultural Revolution had in fact been killed because with the attack on Liu almost everything she had written was out of date and insufficiently political. She gathered new material for another article, which she now hesitated to write. She felt, she confided to Frank, "a tinge of heresy in my soul. It was clear that [the Red Guards] were uniting the nation on the basis that Mao was God: that his works were the one and only ultimate and absolute standard: that any deviation from Mao was 'the bourgeois line' and to be eradicated. And I think it may be well for China to be thus united around a God-image. But I do not believe in it myself. I am willing to believe that Mao's works are the greatest and best yet appearing for the present epoch, that he is 99.99 percent god, but not 100 percent. That little difference till now seemed to be negligible. But from what is done to the head of state in China, it appears that any shadow of deviation is death. Do I put this too seriously? Or not?"

Her first writings on "The Thought of Mao Tse-tung" had been drawn from interviews with Lu Ting-yi and Liu Shao-ch'i. "So I ask myself, What drew me to China? Was it Mao? And I answer: Yes—and no. It certainly was not Mao alone. Nobody is ever 'alone.' It was Mao as met in a few talks, but especially Mao as explained to me by two persons both of whom are now being downgraded. It was Mao not as God, but as the leader recognized as chief by a galaxy of very able devoted people, all of whom I admired. And now, if Mao is going to get rid of people like these and substitute Lin Piao and the Red Guards, I feel that the picture of Mao himself thus changes. It may be more revolutionary, but I do not think that it inspires the confidence I felt when Mao was supported by a galaxy all the way from Chu Teh to Chou En-lai. And I feel that if the present head of state is thrown out or even seriously downgraded in dignity, China loses thereby and Mao loses thereby." In the past, she noted, when she had been perplexed by some new move on China's part, she was "convinced into at least tentative acquiescence not by reading Mao's works" but by speaking with those like Lu Ting-yi who supported him. "Now, if some of those able people are jettisoned, this forces me to ask: In what way did they disagree? I want to know, for possibly I might think they were right."

Paradoxically, she recalled that "one of the truest things that Stalin ever said" was that decisions should be made by committee, not individuals; but at present in China, "*nobody*, but *nobody*, is expected or permitted to have ideas except Chairman Mao." She had asked Feng-feng what the criterion of bourgeois was, and received the expected troubling reply: "If it does not accord with Chairman Mao's thought." The threat of being outside was as troubling as the cost of remaining in

> I wonder whether God, if there is a God, would like being worshipped? I doubt it: I think it would bore any sound mind. All that one knows of Mao indicates that he appreciates dissent. But the drift in China is towards a religion, a deity, whose every word is of equal weight. This may be needed by people faced by a possible big war. But it leaves me a heretic, and hence restless and even unsafe.

Probably on Feng-feng's advice, Anna Louise did not send the letter to Coe, although her last paragraph indicated that she thought she would. When she got back to Peking, the *People's Daily* called asking for a picture of her "studying the works of Chairman Mao." Anna Louise refused because, as she told Rewi Alley, "all my friends would know it was a fake. I read Chairman Mao, I learn from Mao, but I do not *study* him." She was irresolvably of two minds about the Cultural Revolution. She saw clearly that the Red Guards were not only *not* under the control of any given central authority but also not in control of themselves. The effect of the Red Guard movement was to release an enormous amount of energy that was then available as a power source to various competing groups. Anna Louise was attracted to the free energy and the practical experience gained by the roaming bands of youths who traversed the country from border to border, touching, as one of them put it to her, "every person in his soul." She was not happy with the deification of Mao, or with the struggles between the various competing groups to see which organization, if any, would receive the mantle from the Red Guard.

Little of this analysis got into the *Letter from China*, except indirectly, as when she noted that People's Liberation Army soldiers were taking

over many basic tasks in industry. She continued to write about successes
in production and innovations in industry and minimized the conflicts,
disruption and outright violence that occurred in many areas of China.
But in private she told a friend: "Mao appears to be playing this one by
ear, and I am afraid he may be tone deaf."

As had been the case in the thirties in Russia, it was a good time to
turn her energies elsewhere. The *Letter from China* began to include
long articles from friends, especially Israel Epstein, and much of her
attention became focused on writing her reminiscences of her arrest and
concerning past friends in the United States.

Letters from Warwick and Helen Tompkins distressed her. They had
moved to Morongo, a conservative Southern California town, and had
become devotees of the writings of Jacques Ellul, who argued that Marx
had ignored the technological and bureaucratic rigidities structured into
modern society. Anna Louise not only was appalled by their new allegiance but also became embroiled in a sour dispute over money the
Tompkins owed her on some property. In response to what she considered a gentle letter of reproof about the minor debt, they remonstrated
with her for lack of sensitivity: "Really, Anna Louise, you test the bonds
of friendship to their very limit, and if we did not both know and care so
much for you . . . we would have terminated contacts long, long ago. It
is a great pity you have so very little insight into the psychological mechanism of both Anna Louise Strong and other people, and we can both
regret that your far-reaching curiosity and intellectual ability never drove
you to investigate that most interesting of subjects, yourself."

Anna Louise did not know what to reply, especially since their daughter Ann was in Peking and intimately involved with the development of
the Cultural Revolution. She wrote worriedly to Fritchman, who could
only confirm their old friends' move away from politics. In her last letter
to the Tompkins, in mid-March 1967, she observed that "the cultural
revolution has plowed much deeper than perhaps was originally intended." Sidney Rittenberg had become increasingly involved with the
ultra-left—the most radical—faction of the Cultural Revolution and had
become a leader in the Mao Tse-tung Thought Combat Corps. With the
cooperation of the most left-wing elements in the so-called Cultural Revolution Small Group, he had taken effective control of Peking Radio, a
highly unusual step for a foreigner. Rittenberg had maneuvered with skill
and, according to some, with duplicity, but was now under "mass arrest."
This meant that he could not go anywhere without permission or the
accompaniment of "representatives of the masses"—i.e., a Red Guard.

The arrest was lifted a few weeks later when Rittenberg published an extensive self-criticism in *People's Daily,* but Anna Louise felt her contact with her friends increasingly threatened.

In the midst of this, she received another letter from her brother Tracy, raising the possibility of his coming to China by himself, since Edith did not want to enter a country against the wishes of the U.S. passport authorities. She wrote to Liao about a visa but received no answer and reluctantly admitted to Tracy that conditions in China had become so unpredictable that "I no longer know where to inquire." An attempt at a meeting with Tracy in Ulan Bator, Mongolia, fell through as well.

She wrote Tracy in Geneva, asking if he could find out what had happened to Prousse, the watchmaker whom she had persuaded forty years ago to come to Moscow. "I have felt somewhat responsible for what happened to him, and still more to his family. . . . He was arrested and then dropped from sight: his wife came to me for help and I tried to inquire." Tracy looked, but there was no trace of Prousse or his wife.

May Day arrived, and Anna Louise celebrated with a trip to the high dais at T'ien-an Men, but her mind remained elsewhere. A few weeks earlier she had received a letter from James Aronson saying that the New Left faction of the *Guardian* editorial board had taken control of the newspaper and that he had resigned in protest. Their old quarrel still rankled, and she was unkind in her reply: "You have doomed the paper." Aronson, decent to the end, responded immediately with a stiff gentleness that he had been forced out after trying his best to maintain harmony and order. Anna Louise had also turned her sights from her old friends to the New Left—the Students for a Democratic Society and the rising radical movement among blacks. She had sent $500 to the Student Nonviolent Coordinating Committee (SNCC) the previous year and now sent the same amount again, plus $200 to the Cambridge Neighborhood Committee on Vietnam, a grass-roots antiwar mobilization effort.

The summer brought relief from the pressure of the *Letter* but not from five separate loudspeakers broadcasting slogans day and night at the intersection of Ch'ang-an Chien and Wang-fu-ching, less than a block from her home. With a proud petulance, she declared that she was "taking *no* work" to Pei-tai-ho, intending "only to do a bit of swimming and to learn a bit of Chinese." Feng-feng, who was deeply involved with her political activities and probably not eager to spend too much time with a foreigner, announced that she would not accompany Anna Louise that summer.

Anna Louise did do a lot of swimming. Despite the warnings of Dr.

Ma not to overexert herself, on a calm day she swam over one hundred meters. She tried to learn Chinese guidebook phrases from the "nice little girl" who had been assigned to her in lieu of Feng-feng, but succeeded only in provoking discreet giggles from her companions when she insisted on mispronouncing words with great vigor. Anna Louise was disturbed: the reason for trying to learn Chinese was the anticipation of being alone and "helpless in an emergency" with no one to translate as simple a demand as a glass of water.

Her contacts with the leadership became less and less frequent. Ch'en Yi, still foreign minister, was the only member from the upper echelon who came to a dinner party after her return from Pei-tai-ho. In August he had been severely criticized in a meeting with Red Guards, and he told Anna Louise in a half-joking tone that he had had to go from the criticism meeting to a reception at the Foreign Office. A dunce cap had been placed on his head, so instead of calling for a car, he had called for an open truck. Anna Louise laughed, not quite sure how to take the story; she did notice that a contingent of guests, of whom Rittenberg seemed to be the nominal leader, was openly avoiding the room in which the foreign minister sat. As Dr. Ma came over to them, Anna Louise remarked, "Things are vivacious," apparently responding both to the tenor of the evening and the continuing activity outside on the street. Ch'en retorted grimly, *"Luande tsai hou tou na"* ("Chaos lies for certain in the future").

A further distressing sign of the preoccupations in China came when, for the first time, no one from the leadership appeared for her birthday. Indeed, there was no party at all, although some of her friends dropped in during the late afternoon. She felt the world closing in upon her; her contacts were limited to people in the Peace Compound and the few friends who still came to dinner. One evening in early March Sidney Rittenberg did not arrive for his Sunday-night supper. Two days later she was told by the Miltons that he had been arrested as "anti-party." Within a few weeks, Israel Epstein and Elsie were also "taken," and the paper seals that signified official control were placed across the door of their apartment.

Rittenberg's arrest troubled Anna Louise in many ways. She depended on him and his contacts for inside analysis and gossip, and he had assured her and other foreigners that he was in no danger. If Rittenberg, who had always seemed to have a special relationship to the Chinese because of his intelligence and command of the language, could be swept away so easily, no one was safe. There were also problems of work: without Feng-

feng, Anna Louise had depended on Eppie for help with editing the *Letter* and Elsie for typing. Finally she turned to Donna Schuman, an engaging, intelligent young American who took over some of the typing duties and came to spend time with her in the afternoons. Her isolation grew, but despite reports to the contrary in the foreign press, she was never criticized or attacked. Her relationship to Mao and Chou protected her.

On March 5, 1968, at the Ts'ung-hua resort near Canton, Anna Louise received a cable from her nephew Robbins: "Dad died March 3 Service Valparaiso March 9 Robbins." Anna Louise cabled back "Deeply shocked please convey deepest sympathy Edith and arrange suitable wreath honoring devoted life." It was another hard blow, especially after her failure to reach Moscow. Anna Louise elaborated her feelings to Robbins in a letter the day she received the telegram: "I do not know how to phrase it, but I do not know anyone who more honestly gave his whole life to the service of God and man, as he saw them both. I shall always regret the fact that we did not succeed in meeting last winter. . . . I would have given much for two or three days talk on ultimate subjects of life." She offered Edith the use of any of her residences in California, a gesture that was appreciated, although Edith chose to remain in Olympia, Washington, in an old-age home.

In Peking more and more of her friends found themselves "stood aside." Wang Ch'u-liang was sent to a May Fourth Cadre School for hard labor and "reeducation." Shortly after her brother's death, Anna Louise informed the readers of the *Letter* that she could no longer promise them ten issues a year. Her excuse was the infirmity of eighty-three years, which was real, but actually she was more frustrated by her lack of access to new material. She was effectively isolated in the compound, and the *Letter* was now either a repetition of Hsinhua or written by others.

In February 1968, Ken McCormick had written her that he wanted to work out a contract for a second volume of autobiography. He asked for a copy of her 157-page reminiscences on "Why the Russians Arrested Me"; she refused to send it to him "because one of my most trusted friends [Frank Coe] says that it should never be shown for publication until it has been carefully edited to remove parts that might seriously injure individuals now alive." But the suggestion of an autobiography became a welcome "motive for refusing many demands."

McCormick became an important symbolic link with home, and she exchanged letters with him at the rate of one every three weeks for the next several months. Some of her old imperiousness returned, and she ordered him to find copies of books, articles and reviews of her writing. She started to dictate accounts of portions of her life, mainly to Donna Schuman, but was slowed down by a medical checkup in which doctors ordered her not to talk for more than three hours a day. An inflammation had been detected on a vocal cord, and although it was not malignant, the doctors wanted to ensure rest. She was ordered "never to equal her previous year's production."

She was writing, or wanted to write, about her "own experience in living and searching." But the material she sent to McCormick was mainly a compilation from her previously published books, linked together by transitions that were not always coherent. McCormick was quietly uneasy, especially after John K. Fairbank, the dean of American China scholars, wrote back a sad note after reading drafts of the first chapters: "Unfortunately, these pieces are . . . benign beyond belief." McCormick, who was probably hoping to get an account of her arrest and the interviews with Mao, thought that it might be helpful to bring in an editor who knew Chinese affairs. When he forwarded Edgar Snow's suggestion of Ilona Ralf Sues, Anna Louise was insulted: "I believe that she is not competent and my experience with her [in 1938] makes me distrust her emotional temperament. . . . I never . . . want contact with her again." She suggested instead Maud Russell, but added that there was no one outside China who was competent to "dispense with having all my chapters read by some authority in Peking."

A little later, a mysterious forged *Letter from China* appeared as a "reprint" in various left-wing journals in Southern Asia. The forgery was well done; it raised questions about the good relations between China and North Vietnam and attacked the National Liberation Front as "bourgeois." In India, Chester Bowles thought it important enough to communicate the contents of the forgery to the State Department with commentary. The actual source of the letter was never determined. Anna Louise promptly sent out rebuttals to all the progressive journals she knew who reprinted her material and wrote an early *Letter No. 60* denouncing the forgery to her 40,000 subscribers.

The end of the year found her ill-at-ease and suffering from chronic bronchitis. She had lost fifteen pounds and weighed less than she had in fifty years. She began to dispose of her stocks, placing the funds in accounts in Nassau and Canada in order to minimize the amount that would need to pass through probate court in the United States. She wrote to Leonard Boudin, who had been instrumental in helping her get a passport, about the difficulties of appointing an executor in China. She was concerned about what to do with the extensive files Fritchman had kept for her in his house. Robbins had suggested that she consider giving them to the University of Washington in Seattle, which already had both her father's and brother's papers. After extensive negotiations between Fritchman and Richard Berner, the curator of the archives at Suzzallo Library, an arrangement was worked out whereby some sensitive files were to remain closed to the public for an indefinite time because of their political content.

Anna Louise was slowly putting her house in order. In late October she wrote out a new will, appointing Frank Coe her executor. She bequeathed her funds in Nassau equally to "the National Headquarters of the Black Panther Party . . . for whatever uses Huey Newton or his successors may direct" and to the "pastor's fund" at the First Unitarian Church for civil rights projects. She also left her property to the church. The money in Canada was left to "Frank Coe, for purposes of supporting the world revolution and specifically the revolution in the United States of America." Her new friends David and Nancy Milton, who had arrived as the Cultural Revolution was starting, were witnesses.

Strain and age were beginning to tell. Anna Louise grew less certain about priorities. When she discovered in the fall of 1968 that the San Francisco branch of the U.S. post office was not forwarding mail to China unless it was addressed to "People's Republic of China," she railed for days and wanted to write an entire *Letter* on the topic. She asked Corliss Lamont to research the subject for her in New York and was not dissuaded from making a major issue out of it until Tang told her that it was not worth her while.

She went south again in January 1969, expecting to spend most of her time on her autobiography, which she now projected as three volumes: "*I Change Worlds* (done), *Roving to Revolutions,* and *What I Found in China.*" By February, she was constantly short of breath with considerable loss of voice and frequent choking, especially when she swallowed. Anxious doctors put her in the hospital, then sent her back to Peking for more intensive treatment. On the plane trip she had a mild heart attack, which the doctors concealed from her. They also found fluid in her left pleural cavity, and her left vocal chord was paralyzed. The infection of her lungs led to pneumonia, and her legs swelled up alarmingly. The doctors did not expect her to recover and were surprised when in early June she regained her health sufficiently to insist that she be sent home. Dr. Ma later said that it was as if she had "decided" not to die then.

Part of what drew her back was the work for McCormick. He continued to press her for the interviews with Mao, but Anna Louise's journalistic conscience required that she get direct permission from Mao to publish them. She decided that her best chance would come on National Day at T'ien-an Men. Both Feng-feng and Tang tried to dissuade her, but she went ahead with her plan. Over the previous summer she had produced a thirty-four-page account of the three interviews. "I am aware," she wrote in the draft of a letter to Tang, "that you are against my writing anything at all, but I nonetheless intend to put this material into the best shape I can, while my memory is still clearer than it may be in another year, because I consider it a duty I owe future history." She also wrote to Mao himself, explaining that she needed the articles for a book "in which I intend to develop the thesis that past revolutions have always tended to relapse because they changed only the political and economic power but not the minds of men," whereas China, through the thought of Mao, had discovered a way to keep the revolution "continuous."

The issue of the interviews became central when she received a letter from McCormick toward the beginning of August responding to a question she had raised about copyrights on her previously published material. McCormick passed on his lawyer's judgment that if the new work was "simply a scissors and paste job," there might be a problem, whereas "a conscientious rewrite" would pass all legal tests. Anna Louise boiled over, in part from bad conscience, for the material *was* in fact "a scissors and paste job." She wrote back that given what the lawyer had said, "the only chapters that have a chance to be copyrighted will be the one (*sic*) on Talks with Mao Tse-tung, which I may not be able to write at all. . . . I think then we should just forget this book, rather than work a year and a half on a non-copyright book." McCormick hastened to assure her that she should not worry about the technicalities.

Anna Louise began preparation for October Day by taking short walks in the compound. She had not left her bed between February and July except to go to the bathroom, but she slowly worked her way up to six- and seven-minute practice walks. She was invited to the premier's banquet on September 30 and attended in a wheelchair. Despite "a fine seat at the premier's own table," she had to leave early. The next day she made her way to the top of T'ien-an Men; after the parade Mao came over to shake her hand. She addressed her question about publication to K'ang Sheng, who said that he would look into it. By force of will, she even made it back to the evening fireworks.

On October 13 a council of six doctors delegated Dr. Ma to tell Anna Louise that she would not be allowed to go south for the winter. He broke the news gently: "We took into account the fact that you hate the Peking dark winters, that the southern sun brings you out to walk. But the variations of atmospheric pressure in the south have in the past two winters given you asthmatic shortness of breath. Moreover, you cannot again chance a plane flight as you did last winter, and the train would wear you out."

Anna Louise raged and fumed. "I will not change the dictatorship of the proletariat for the dictatorship of doctors."

Ma responded, "We are not dictating; we merely advise."

"Like hell you merely advise," snapped Anna Louise. "You know perfectly well that at your advice the Peace Committee will not give me an interpreter to go south or rent a place at the Hot Springs for me or buy me a ticket on the plane. You know that I cannot walk to the station and carry my baggage and buy my ticket in Chinese. You know I have to submit.

"George," she concluded, "you know that Chairman Mao says that one should do only fifty percent of what doctors say."

"Well," Ma retorted, "why don't you start, then?"

In the midst of her angers, the act of putting her affairs in order brought back old memories. On the first day of November, she wrote to Corliss Lamont: "I wonder if you can tell me if Roger Nash Baldwin is still alive. . . . If he is living, I should very much like to be put in touch with him. I knew him very well more than fifty years ago when he was in jail in New York. . . . I should like to write to him and perhaps send my *Letter from China* to him if he wants it. He was always much interested in international affairs." Lamont responded a bit stiffly with the address, noting that he had not forgiven Baldwin for his decisive role in the expulsion of Elizabeth Gurley Flynn from the American Civil Liberties Union in 1940. But when Anna Louise received the information she was too involved with a family affair to write to Roger.

John Strong, Robbins' youngest son, had just graduated from Oberlin and was traveling through Southeast Asia on a Watson Fellowship. He asked Anna Louise if he could visit her, and she applied for a visa for him. When he wrote to her from his father's house in Geneva that he had gotten his passport validated for China in accord with a new general rule permitting academics and other professionals to travel to the People's Republic, she was delighted. But her pursuit of a visa was met with evasion, and she wrote angrily to Robbins, "The Chinese have a habit that we Westerners cannot understand or like: they never say *no*. Hence I have asked for five months for John's permit and get no final answer, but finally my secretary blows up and tells me that the American government is rotten. I argue that China is supposed to distinguish between U.S. imperialism and the American people, that I am an American and so is my nephew and we intend to remain so."

On November 2, Tang told her that John would not be admitted. Anna Louise promptly started to make plans to meet him in Phnom Penh, Cambodia, and on the 17 she wrote coldly to Tang about "my present plans." She would go to Cambodia in March to meet John and then return to the United States for at least a year:

> This is because I shall not stay in a country which, as China does today and indefinitely, refuses to admit any of my American kin or friends. I want to see some of them before I die. I am not as young as the chairman, nor as optimistic. I do *not* expect to live to see the end of U.S. imperialism. Therefore I had better put in what strength I still possess in doing a bit of fighting against U.S. imperialism in the only land where it counts, i.e., the U.S.A., where already there is far greater revolutionary upsurge than has occurred in my lifetime. If I live long enough, which seems unlikely, I might like to return to China, but probably not.
>
> I admit that it is largely the refusal of contact with my grandnephew that has started this train of thought. But the thought itself has widened. I have asked myself *why* I am in China at all. Everyone else has a job but I don't. . . . I came because Mao in Yenan invited my return and because ever since I met him I felt that the answer to the world's revolution was here. I still feel that way.

She was resentful, she added, that she was out of touch with developments taking place among the youth in the United States and that Tang had forbidden her to invite Black Panther leader Eldridge Cleaver to visit her in China. Several days later she returned to the theme she had raised with Robbins. "Am I expected to wait until I die for a non-answer? After all, there are limits to the torture one can take." It was "unreasonable," she said, to think that her great-nephew could be a spy or do any spying. Finally, "it seems to me that if China intends to shut out all Americans until America makes a revolution, my job is not in China, but over there." To add to her distress, her friends the Miltons were on the point of leaving for the United States. She asked Tang how long it would take her to get an exit permit; it had taken them a year and a half.

John was in Ceylon during this blowup. After receiving Anna Louise's letters with the report of Tang's refusal, he cabled her that they should meet in Cambodia and sent a detailed itinerary. Anna Louise promptly wrote back with arrangements and suggestions of a hotel, but spent the first paragraph of her letter pointing out to John where he had wasted money on superfluous words in his telegram.

When the possibility of making the trip to Cambodia was eliminated because of the spreading war in Southeast Asia, Anna Louise turned somewhat unwillingly to the one source left to her. She wrote to Chou En-lai in December 1969 apologizing "for taking your time in a purely personal matter, but you have several times in the past intervened to help my personal situation, and I do not know to whom else I might turn." Chou, busy trying to hold the various factions of the Cultural Revolution in check, did not immediately respond.

With the new year, Anna Louise's condition rapidly deterioriated. Her memory betrayed her again and again. She ate little and was insomniac to the point that she no longer distinguished well between day and night. When Donna Schuman came for her dictation sessions, she found Anna Louise listless and more interested in reminiscences about her childhood than in writing. She spent considerable time arranging her jewelry collection. Doctors who visited her wanted her to go to the hospital, but she persistently refused. Two nurses were sent to her house on a regular basis. They were especially worried that her weight had continued to fall and now stood at just over 100 pounds. To encourage her to eat, they made certain her remaining friends came for dinner.

Even with company, Anna Louise refused both food and medication. Each day at suppertime yet another nurse would arrive dutifully bearing a vial of medicine. The nurse would stand by Anna Louise at the table, waiting for her to drink the medication that had been poured into an elegant slender wineglass. And each evening, with all present fully aware of the gesture, the Lao Tai-tai would find a moment in which the conversation was so animated that her arm would fling the contents of the glass over her shoulder, or with a surprisingly agile flick of the wrist, dump it to the left or the right. Silently, the nurse would leave.

With little food and less medication, Anna Louise's strength ebbed markedly in February. Rewi Alley no longer heard the rattle of her typewriter; even the new electric one from Hong Kong was beyond her ability. Too tired to write, she would sometimes sit at her desk tearing paper, methodically placing each piece in an orderly pile. Unable to speak more than a few sentences, she asked Rewi one afternoon to put a Strauss waltz on the phonograph and danced a few times around the room, as she had so often done when she needed a break from work. Rewi noticed that there was still grace in her steps.

In March her breathing became increasingly strained. Nurses Yao and

Chang urged that someone be present day and night; Anna Louise raged against the imposition on her privacy and the implication of dependency. She began to sort through her drawers, placing the tokens of her life in order. Nurses and doctors were compassionate but uneasy. There was no possible hope that Anna Louise's condition would improve alone at home. If left to her own devices, she would will the ending of her life as she had determined its living. Hospitalization was ordered on March 20.

Anna Louise accepted the fiction that she was going to the hospital "for her teeth." She had resisted because she was afraid of being isolated from people with whom she could talk; the orderlies and nurses spoke no English. But she had not counted on her friends. Within hours of her hospitalization, they were in attendance, reassuring her that one of them would always be at her side. Rewi Alley, Frank and Ruth Coe, Sol and Pat Adler and the Schumans took their turns visiting, and despite the demands of politics and the growing xenophobia of the Cultural Revolution, Feng-feng planted herself firmly within reach of Anna Louise's call. Soothed by their presence and by the chocolate ice cream they miraculously brought to her each day, Anna Louise regained some of her composure and defiance. She adamantly refused intravenous medication or any food except the treasured chocolate ice cream, which she insisted on sharing.

On March 28, 1970, Robbins Strong received a cable in Geneva. "Anna Louise very ill in hospital urgent you cable John he fly Hong Kong immediately contact China Travel Service for flight to Peking. Signed Tang Ming-chao and Frank Coe." John was at this point without an address in Indonesia. Robbins forwarded the contents of the cable to a family friend in Indonesia and sent details in a letter to Hong Kong. He did the same with Tang and Frank's cable the next day, announcing Anna Louise's death and indicating that John should still go to Peking.

It was not a propitious time for a public funeral for a foreigner in Peking. The Cultural Revolution had entered a more violent phase, and pitched battles were now reported from various cities in China. Nevertheless, arrangements were announced to the foreign community that surprised even the most optimistic. The funeral oration would be given by Kuo Mo-jo, vice-chairman of the National People's Congress, a distinguished revolutionary and one of the foremost poets and calligraphers in China. Cautious negotiations took place when Ruth Coe pointed out that no women were on the list of those who would accompany the urn. Eventually Ruth Coe and Teng Ying-ch'ao, the wife of Chou En-lai and herself a member of the presidium, were included.

The ceremony was held on April 2. A large black banner stretched across one end of the hall inscribed in both English and Chinese: "May Anna Louise Strong Live Forever in Our Memories." Centered beneath the banner and draped with black crepe was a large photograph of Anna Louise. Directly below, on an altarlike stand, was the urn containing her ashes, flanked by large wreaths from Chairman Mao and Lin Piao. The symmetry continued both politically and aesthetically; to the sides of the urn were wreaths from Chou En-lai and Vice-Premier Li Hsien-nien, as well as ones from the more left leaders of the Cultural Revolution, Ch'en Po-ta, K'ang Sheng and Mao's wife, Chiang Ch'ing. Additional wreaths came from Teng Ying-chao, Kuo Mo-jo and other prominent personalities, from the Premier of North Vietnam, the National Liberation Front of South Vietnam, and multitudes of organizations and diplomats.

Kuo Mo-jo's address began with an acknowledgment of the "grief that we all have, gathered here today to honor her memory." After noting that Anna Louise "visited China six times," he concluded: "The life of Anna Louise Strong was a glorious life, a fighting life. . . . We can tell Comrade Anna Louise Strong: 'Rest assured, the present world situation is excellent. The days of U.S. imperialism and all reactionaries are numbered. And it is certain that a new world will soon come into being, a world that you long looked foward to and fought for all your life, a world that will ring emancipation for all mankind.' May you rest in peace, Comrade Strong! Your memory will be cherished forever by the Chinese people, the American people and the revolutionary people all over the world."

More than 500 people filed past the urn to pay their respects. Chou En-lai, looking pale and drawn from months of unrelieved political activity, wore a black armband and openly wept. After the ceremony, Anna Louise Strong was interred in the Babaoshan Cemetery of Revolutionary Martyrs on the outskirts of Peking. The handsome gravestone was inscribed in Kuo Mo-jo's rich calligraphy: "Progressive American Writer and Friend of the Chinese People."

Of all those in Peking, perhaps Rewi Alley felt the absence of his friend the most. He returned home after the funeral, painfully conscious of the now-vacant flat beneath him. The next morning he woke early and stepped downstairs to the porch where he had shared so many buoyant breakfasts with Anna Louise. He glanced out and found, somehow not to his surprise, that the pomegranate tree they had both loved had died. He knew then, as he said ten years later, that when he tried to plant another, it would not bloom.

Notes

We have omitted from these footnotes any citations that can be easily deduced from the body of the text. A large amount of background material is silently present in the text; when we have been directly informed by a particular work, it is mentioned below. Books are cited by author; see the bibliography for the complete citation.

I Change Worlds was Anna Louise's public presentation of her life until 1935. It is invaluable but less candid than it often appears. In the Peking Library is an uncompleted manuscript, *My Later Years*, most of it excerpted from the books that she had published after 1935. There is also a long essay on her arrest by the Russians which she entitled *Why the Russians Arrested Me*. This is candid and detailed, written not for publication during her lifetime but for posterity.

The major archival collections of Anna Louise's papers are in the archives of the Peking Library and the Suzzallo Library, University of Washington, Seattle, Washington. In addition, we have made use of the relevant material in the Philip Jaffe archives, Emory University, Atlanta, Georgia; the Social Welfare Archives of *Survey* magazine, the University of Minnesota Library, Minneapolis, Minnesota; the Peace Collection at Swarthmore College Library, Swarthmore College, Swarthmore, Pennsylvania; the American Board of Missions archives, Houghton Library, Harvard University; the Roger Baldwin archives in the Seeley Mudd Library, Princeton University; and the Raymond Robins archives in the State Historical Society in Madison, Wisconsin (courtesy Lynn Lubkeman).

We have additionally used the archives of Sydney Dix Strong and Ruth Maria Strong, and the relevant portions of the Tracy Strong archives, all in the Suzzallo Library at the University of Washington. The archives of the University of Washington have detailed descriptions of their holdings.

Anna Louise herself gave a good collection of her published material to the Hoover Library, Stanford University, Palo Alto, California.

We are grateful to the following individuals who made available part or all of their private files of correspondance with Anna Louise: Reverend Stephen Fritchman, Jessica Smith, James Aronson, Emily Pierson (courtesy of her daughter, Ann Tobey), Corliss Lamont, Carey McWilliams (courtesy of Iris McWilliams), Lement Harris, Kenneth McCormick (courtesy of Sheila Cole), Cedric Belfrage (courtesy of Sheila Cole), Tracy Strong, Jr. and Dolphine Strong, Robbins and Katherine Strong, John Strong, John Niederhauser.

We are also grateful to the following people for the interviews which they granted us:

Pat Adler, August 19, 1980, Peking
Sol Adler, August 19, 1980, Peking
Rewi Alley, August 13, 14, 15, 1980, Pei-tai-ho
James Aronson, October 3, 1980, New York City
Roger Baldwin, May 18, 1981, Oakland, New Jersey
Julia Older Bazer, October 18, 1981, New York City

Dorothy Borg, February 26, 1980, New York City
Angus Cameron, May 14, 1983 (telephone)
Chang Hsue-ling, July 30, 1980, Peking
Chang Ts'ai-chen, July 26, 1980, Peking
Chao Feng-feng, August 20, 1980, Geneva, Switzerland
Chen Han-seng, July 24, 1980, Peking
Jack Chen, November 18, 1980, San Francisco
Elsie Cholmeley, July 17, 1980, Peking; August 14, 15, 1980, Pei-tai-ho
Joseph Clark, June 15, 1982 (telephone)
Ruth Coe, July 12 and 22, 1980, Peking
James Davies, April 4, 1982, San Diego, California
Israel Epstein, July 17, 1980, Peking; August 14, 15, 1980, Pei-tai-ho
Edward Falkowski, October 20, 1980, New York City
Dr. Fang Ch'i, July 26, 1980, Peking
Stephen Fritchman, February 24, September 19, 1980, Los Angeles
James Gale, January 23, 1983, La Jolla
Talitha Gerlach, August 6, 1980, Shanghai
Han Suyin, October 20, 1980, New York City
Robert Harmon, May 16, 1981, Weems, Virginia
Ruth Strong Harmon, May 16, 1981, Weems, Virginia
Lement Harris, May 19, 1981, Norfolk, Connecticut
Dorothy Healey, June 20, 1982, Los Angeles
Joan Hinton, July 30, 1980, Peking
Philip Jaffe, June 12, 1980, New York City
Bernard Koten, October 20, 1981, New York City
George Lanyi, April 4, 1979, Oberlin, Ohio
Liao Meng-hsing (Cynthia Liao), July 20, 1980, Peking
Li Chou-jen, July 23, 1980, Peking
Li Pang-ch'i, July 24, 1980, Peking
Ling Ch'ing, July 24, 1980, Peking
Liu Ning-yi, August 18, 1980, Peking
Lu Ting-yi, July 21, 1980, Peking
Luo Ching-yi, July 29, 1980, Peking
Dr. Ma Hai-teh (George Hatem), August 15, 1980, Pei-tai-ho
Jan MacKinnon, November 18, 1982, Tempe, Arizona
Steven MacKinnon, July 24, 1980, Peking; November 18, 1982, Tempe, Arizona
LaRue McCormick, May 6, 1983
David Milton, June 1–2, 1980, Eugene, Oregon
Nancy Milton, June 1–2, 1980, Eugene, Oregon
Grace Nelson, November 13, 1980, Los Angeles
John Niederhauser, May 15, 1981, Orange, California
Sidney Rittenberg, June 4, 11, 1980, New York City
Maud Russell, October 4, 1980, New York City
Harrison Salisbury, July 24, 1980, Peking
Sao Ch'ih-p'ing, August 7, 1980, Nanking
Donna Schuman, November 17, 1981, San Francisco
Julian Schuman, November 14, 1982, Tempe, Arizona
Jessica Smith, October 5, 1980, New York City
Harry Steinmetz, October, 10, 1980, San Diego
Dolphine Strong, December 3, 1980, Orange, California
Edith Robbins Strong, May 16, 1981, Kilmarnock, Virginia

John Strong, December 28, 1981, Lewiston, Maine
Katherine Stiven Strong, December 5, 1981, Claremont, California
Robbins Strong, December 5, 1981, Claremont, California
Tracy Strong, Jr., December 3, 1980, Orange, California
Tang Ming-chao, July 14 and August 19, 1980, Peking
Gerald Tannebaum, October 2, 1980, New York City
Ann Tobey, June 27, 1981, Townshend, Vermont; June 30, 1981, Amherst, Massachusetts
T'u Chien-kuo, August 1, 1980, Yenan
Nym Wales, November 17, 1982 (telephone)
Wang Ch'u-liang, July 17, 1980, Peking
Allen Whiting, March 3, 1981, La Jolla, California
Leonard Woodcock, August 19, 1980, Peking
Wu Pei-fang, August 6, 1980, Shanghai
Yang Tsao (Sid Engst), July 30, 1980, Peking
Yao Chin-fang, July 26, 1980, Peking
Yu Shi-lian, July 30, 1980, Peking
Correspondence with the authors is cited by the sender and the date.

Documents that appear in the material obtained from the FBI, the U.S. State Department, the Federal Communications Commissions and the Bureau of Investigation under the Freedom of Information Act are cited by agency and date of filing.

We have kept a modified Wade-Giles system of romanizing Chinese characters on the grounds that Anna Louise used it and that it is still the least confusing for most Western readers.

1

LAO TAI-TAI

Most of the material in this chapter comes from interviews with those who were present in Peking during the last months of Anna Louise's life: Ruth Coe, Julian and Donna Schuman, Rewi Alley, Joan Hinton, Yang Tzao, David Milton, Nancy Dall Milton, Sol Adler, Pat Adler, Chao Feng-feng, Dr. Ma Hai-teh (George Hatem), her doctors at the hospital, Fang Ch'i and Li Pang-ch'i, and nurses Yao Chin-fang and Chang Ts'ai-chen.

Ruth Coe and Dr. Ma Hai-teh told us of her anger in the hospital. The great-nephew to whom she wrote is John Strong, and the citation is from a letter in his files, dated November 5, 1969. The story about her Chinese name comes from our interview with Sidney Rittenberg, and that of her exchange about obeying doctors from our talk with Dr. Ma Hai-teh. All those in the hospital attested to Chou's distress at Anna Louise's condition; Ruth Coe told us of the request that he made of her husband that he find John Strong. Sidney Rittenberg, who was present at the Yenan bridge game, recounted those events to us. Our interview with Rewi Alley is the source of the account of Chou En-lai's command that she eat. John Strong recalled for us her last words; Drs. Li and Fang told us of the efforts made to resuscitate her and of their contact with Chou En-lai.

In addition to the obituaries cited here, an important one was written by Allen Whiting in the *Washington Post*, April 12, 1970. A transcript of the memorial service at the First Unitarian Church was in the Fritchman files. Additional memories of the service came from our interviews with Dorothy Healey and LaRue McCormick. The letter from Lincoln Steffens is in her archives, University of Washington, dated late 1933, and the final passage is from *I Change Worlds*, p. 422.

2
CONSPICUOUS ORIGINS

In addition to Chapters 1–3 of *I Change Worlds*, biographical material was drawn from Albert Strong, *The Strongs of Strongsville*, and Frederick Strong, *A Biography of John Stoughton Strong* and *The Tracy Lineage*. Anna Louise evinces her pleasure with her ancestor John Russell in *I Change Worlds*, p. 6. Sydney's description of his wedding trip is in his archives at the University of Washington. The letter from her grandfather (November 25, 1885) is in the University of Washington archives. Her analysis of her own childhood is on p. 414 of *I Change Worlds*. The important letter to Helen Tompkins (January 9, 1961) is in the Peking Library.

A major source for this chapter are the diaries that Anna Louise kept from 1896 to 1906 and the letters she exchanged with her family and her teacher Miss Farrell. All of them are preserved in the University of Washington, as are the "Doings of the Strong Family" written by Sydney for the family and now in his archives.

Anna Louise's difficulties in public school appear in *I Change Worlds* on pp. 9–10. The poems are cited from the collection that Uncle Del put together, which is in the authors' possession. Ruth Maria's letters to Sydney are in her archives at the University of Washington; the letter about their distance is September 12, 1886. Ruth discusses Anna Louise's attitude toward the 1896 campaign in a letter to Sydney during October 1896. Anna Louise's allegory about the campaign is found in her diary from that month. A good account of the women's club movement can be found in Rothman (1978), pp. 64–73. Anna Louise kept diaries between 1896 and 1906; they are all in the University of Washington archives. Her mother's lesson on "taking your share" is in *I Change Worlds*, p. 17, and her account of her separation anxieties comes on pp. 10–11.

Anna Louise's family had printed her *A Trip to England by a Little Girl* (in the University of Washington archives). Ruth Coe and Chao Feng-feng each told us of how Anna Louise learned to be a journalist. The trip to Switzerland is derived from her diary and letters back to her father. The complaints and analysis of Germany and Rome went to her father on July 29, 1901, and October 21, 1901; both are in the University of Washington. Her worries about performance in college are in a letter to her grandmother of December 27, 1901, at the University of Washington.

3
ADOLESCENCE AND THE KINGDOM OF GOD ON EARTH

Information about courses the family took at Oberlin College comes from college transcripts of Anna Louise and her parents obtained from the college archives. Physical descriptions are drawn from yearbooks and Tracy B. Strong's personal recollections. Anna Louise passes over her college days in a few pages in Chapter 3 of *I Change Worlds*. Sydney's letter to Ruth about Anna Louise attending Oberlin (February 27, 1902) is in his archives, University of Washington. All letters between Anna Louise and her father for this period are in her University of Washington archives, unless otherwise noted.

Her diary (at the University of Washington) while at Oberlin and Bryn Mawr is the major source for this chapter. Unless noted, citations are from this diary. In a letter of February 18, 1903, her father urges her to improve the moral condition of Bryn Mawr (in the Sydney Dix Strong archives). The letter to her parents about Aunt Sarah (August 4, 1903) is also in Sydney's archives. An account of Sydney's and Ruth's difficult journey can be found in Sydney's diary at the American Board of Missions archives, Houghton Library, Harvard University.

Anna Louise's analysis of her parents comes in a letter to Grace Nelson, November 2, 1959, in the Peking archives. The vision of her mother is from *I Change Worlds*, p. 19, and the distress with the president of Bryn Mawr is on p. 22.

Some additional details about her time at Oberlin come from reminiscences reported in interviews with Elsie Cholmeley, Israel Epstein, Grace Nelson and Donna Schuman. Miriam Corbin died in China in the early 1970s, and Paul remained until his death shortly before World War II.

After she left Oberlin and until 1906, Anna Louise's diary remains a major source. Her play *The King's Palace* is psychologically very revealing, as are many of her poems published in *Storm Songs*. Though she was editorially constrained, it is possible to discern the focus of her interests in her writings for *The Advance*, September 1905 until April 1906. Copies are in the Washington archives. *I Change Worlds*, Chapter 4, is not always reliable, as Anna Louise was trying to emphasize how little she knew about the world and is both prudish and politically discreet about her involvements with men.

She describes her labors for *The Advance* in *I Change Worlds*, pp. 27–28. The draft of her long letter to Miss Fitch is in the University of Washington archives, as is the unsent letter worrying about getting a Ph.D. The intensity of relations between upper-middle-class women during this time is well described in Smith-Rosenberg (1974). Anna Louise's marginal notations to Kant are in her copy of the *Critique of Pure Reason*, in the authors' possession. Her experience in the factory is sketched in her diary and elaborated as an unpublished story, "Fit to Survive," in the University of Washington archives. Some of her essays for her classes in literature are in the University of Washington archives and reflect her anxiety that her academic role was only pretense.

We have taken our understanding of settlement houses from Rothman (1978) and Wald (1934). Wald includes some memories of Anna Louise. Both the thesis version and the published version of *A Consideration of Prayer from the Standpoint of Social Psychology* are important; the first is more revealing and forms the basis for our comments. The citation about thought confusing action is in her thesis, on p. 108. The exultation about "bluffing God" after her thesis defense comes in *I Change Worlds*, pp. 32–33.

4

THE CONTAINMENT OF MULTITUDES

In our interview with him, Roger Baldwin confirmed the reservations Anna Louise had about social work as a vocation. We drew our knowledge of Judge Lindsey from Larsen (1972) and from Lindsey's obituary in the *New York Times*, March 27, 1943. Neither source mentions the romantic interest between the two.

Anna Louise's analysis of the National Child Labor Committee comes in *I Change Worlds*, p. 36. During this time she worked on Luther Gulick's book, *A*

Philosophy of Play (1920); occasionally one sees her hand. Roger Baldwin told us of Anna Louise's "philosophical-ethical outlook." Her anxieties about firing workers are in *I Change Worlds*, p. 40. The letter from Lindsey that supports her positive feelings about socialism is cited in Larsen (1972), p. 70.

Much of the detail of her romance with Baldwin comes from his account to us. Their letters are in the University of Washington and in the Baldwin archives. Anna Louise wrote to her father about the kiss on April 12, 1912. Roger's supposed jealousy comes from a letter she sent to her father on May 19, 1913. We were helped by the biography of Baldwin by Lamson (1976), especially pp. 42–43.

The letter from Ayres warning her about the politics of her job is December 19, 1912, and in the University of Washington archives. Julia Lathrop is discussed in Rothman (1978). We were informed about Jane Addams from our reading of Davis (1973), especially pp. 57–75, and Levine (1971).

The wish that David Thompson were a girl is in a letter to her father, November 19, 1914, to whom, on April 16, 1915, also goes her relief that they will not marry. The ecstasy of mountaineering comes from *I Change Worlds*, pp. 48–49. Her sister in law Edith told us of her never-forgotten anger at Anna Louise's presumptions.

5

A GLIMMER ON THE HILLS

Our understanding of Seattle's history at this period derives from Sale (1976), O'Connor (1964), Friedheim (1964), and *The Seattle General Strike*, a pamphlet issued by the Strike History Committee and written by Anna Louise. We learned about labor politics during this period from Morgan (1951), Foner (1980), volumes 3 and 4, Weinstein (1969), as well as from the *Seattle Star*, the *Seattle Daily Call*, and the *Seattle Union Record* for the years that Anna Louise was in Seattle and an unpublished analysis of the Industrial Workers of the World that Anna Louise wrote in 1917 and which is at the University of Washington. She hopes that Baldwin can arrange for publication in a letter to him on December 11, 1917 (in the Baldwin archives). The files of the Bureau of Investigation contain the story of her cheering for the "bolsheviki."

Anna Louise's platform for the school board election appears in the *Seattle Star*, November 27, 1916; her archives at the University of Washington contain letters of congratulation, mainly from upper-middle-class liberals and labor union members. Copies of the articles she wrote on the Everett massacre are in her papers in Washington. Her own account of her time in Seattle is covered in Chapters 5, 6 and 7 of *I Change Worlds*.

Anna Louise and Roger Baldwin corresponded throughout this period and until about 1921. The surviving letters are in their archives; her letters are noticeably warmer than his. Baldwin told us about his reunion with Anna Louise after the outbreak of the war. She describes her escape into the mountains in *I Change Worlds*, on p. 57. The support statement from the longshoremen is in her archives in Washington, and her resignation statement from the school board appears in the *Seattle Star*, March 8, 1918. Her letter to Ayres and the note from Baldwin after her defeat are also in the University of Washington archives. The rather chaotic files of the Bureau of Investigation on the Seattle region in 1918 contain a list of IWW members and their membership numbers, among them one for Anna Louise.

Tom Mooney remained in jail and was pardoned by Roosevelt in 1934. Anna Louise gives an accurate history and an interesting analysis of the failures of the strike, though the pamphlet (issued by the strike history committee of the labor unions) is written to show labor in the best light. See Friedheim (1964) for a more complete rendering and especially (p. 112) for Harry Ault's account of the publication of Anna Louise's February 4 editorial.

The story of the *Shilka* is generally known, but details were provided to us in our interview with Harry Steinmetz; Harvey O'Connor also drew our attention to it in a letter to the authors. The text of the indictment is in Anna Louise's archives (University of Washington) and in Friedheim (1964), pp. 185 f.

Edith Robbins Strong and Roger Baldwin gave interviews that filled in Anna Louise's personal life during this period. Correspondence resumed with her father after he left for Australia. The letter to her father about Tracy's rent is April 18, 1921, and that about her worries with the *Record* went also to him on March 26, 1921. We learned about Steffens' travels from Steffens (1958), Stinson (1979), Palermo (1971) and especially Kaplan (1974); we have reconstructed what he said to Anna Louise about Russia in Blanc's Café from *I Change Worlds*, pp. 86 ff., and Steffens (1918). The letter about Waldo went to her father on July 5, 1921 (in the University of Washington archives); she describes her experiences in Poland in *I Change Worlds*, p. 91.

6

CROSSING THE BAR

The letters Anna Louise wrote to her family during this period are at the University of Washington, both in her archives and in those of her father and brother. Some of those to her father were bound and circulated among friends. Only those letters whose addressee and/or date is not apparent from the text will be cited specifically.

Her own account of her time in Russia during the work with the AFSC is in Chapters 8 through 11 of *I Change Worlds*. On the ARA and the Quakers, we consulted Fisher (1927), Hoover (1961), Scott (1964) and Weissman (1974). Anna Louise describes Samara to her father on December 13, 1921. William Mandel, in a letter to the authors (November 26, 1980), told us about Anna Louise and her chocolate bars, a story reported to him by Albert Rhys Williams. "Creators in chaos" appears in *I Change Worlds*, p. 112; see also *The First Time in History*, pp. 17–18. She takes notice of the dedicated heroes of the Revolution in *I Change Worlds*, p. 103. The long account of her delirium is in *I Change Worlds*, pp. 117–118. Weisbrod (1968) reports the unfortunate story about Mary Pattison. See Anna Louise's letter to her father, February 18, 1922, for her account of her illness.

Anna Louise refers to Katterfield (the American representative to the Comintern) by his party name, "Carr," in *I Change Worlds*, p. 127. We learned about American Communists in Moscow at this time from Draper (1957), pp. 267 ff., and from Jessica Smith. Anna Louise informed her father of her intention to return to Russia as a correspondent on April 2, 1922. The interview with Trotsky in *Izvestia* is reprinted in Weissman (1974), pp. 105–106. She wrote to her father about Trotsky on December 14, 1922, and again on December 17, 1922. See Draper (1957), pp. 381 ff., for a description of the Comintern and Profintern congresses, as well as Deutscher (1963), pp. 1–74, and Fischer (1964), pp. 625 ff., for an analysis of Trotsky's position and personality at this time.

Anna Louise expressed her psychological ease in the U.S.S.R. in a letter to her father on January 27, 1923, and reported her banter with Trotsky on January 11, 1923. She described the trip with Rakovski to C. J. France on March 10, 1923 (in the University of Washington archives), and to her father on March 1, 1923. The American miners were the main focus of another letter to Sydney on March 20, 1923. Her relationship with Hal Ware was described to us in interviews with Israel Epstein, Elsie Cholmeley, Maud Russell and Jessica Smith.

She spoke of Borodin to her father in a letter on May 31, 1923; that Borodin returned to the U.S.S.R. via Seattle clears up a detail in Holubnychy (1979), pp. 29–31. Our portrait of Borodin is informed by Holubnychy (1979), Jacobs (1981) and Chen (1979), as well as our interview with Jack Chen. The story of her visit with her brother comes from our interview with Robbins Strong. Anna Louise announces the refusal of permission for the club to her father on July 16, 1923. Borodin's "consolation" is in *I Change Worlds*, p. 188.

A letter describing her mania for things Russian was sent to her father from London on December 10, 1923; six days earlier she had announced to him the signing of the contract with Boni and Liveright. The article on "What Makes Lenin Great" is in *Hearst's International* magazine (January 1924), pp. 100 ff; "Russia's Leading Politician: J. V. Stalin" is in the April issue, starting on p. 65.

The letter admonishing her father to get a job was sent on March 2, 1924. Her disappointment over Hal Ware and her return to Moscow were detailed to Sydney in letters of April 30, 1924, May 17, 1924, and June 1, 1924. Deutscher (1963), p. 161, provides an unflattering portrait of Ruth Fischer; Anna Louise told Sydney of the source of Ruth's problems in a letter of July 2, 1924. Problems with the bread in the camp were discussed with her father on October 10, 1924; she wrote to Lipp on September 7, 1924 (in the University of Washington archives). The hope for the colony is quoted from *Children of the Revolution*, p. 8.

Anna Louise's quarrel with Tracy was recounted to us in separate interviews by all of Tracy's children (Robbins, Tracy, Jr., and Ruth Strong Harmon), as well as by Edith Strong. See Anna Louise's letter to her father February 9, 1925, for a milder version. Her distance from Jessica Smith is the subject of a letter to her father, May 13, 1925. The attacks by the DAR and the pamphlet mentioned are in her Washington archives. Her distress with *Cosmopolitan* is in *I Change Worlds*, p. 207. The rejection slip from *Survey* magazine is in the Social Work archives at the University of Minnesota.

7
TWO CHINA TRIPS

We have used a number of sources for historical background: Akimova (1971), Chan and Etzold (1976), Chang Kuo-t'ao (1971), Chiang Kai-shek (1969), Gillan (1967), Jacobs (1981), Holubnychy (1979), and Wilbur and How (1972).

Anna Louise's account in *I Change Worlds* is in chapters 19 through 21. Her letters to her family and friends, all in the University of Washington archives, continue to be central sources and will be cited only when important or when the text does not provide the chronology.

The citation from Akimova (1971) is on p. 62. Anna Louise's declaration of love for Peking reappears in the preface to the new edition of *China's Millions*. On students, see the article by Ka-che Yip in Chan and Etzold (1976). Chen Hanseng recalled his first encounter with Anna Louise in our interview with him.

The citation from Fanny Borodin about Canton appears in "New Women of Old Canton," *Asia*, June 1926. Her visits with the warlords was written up in "Chang, Feng and Wu," *Asia*, July 1926.

In addition to Anna Louise's articles mentioned above and the "Canton Prelude" in *China's Millions* (1965), we learned about Canton in 1925 from Chang Kuo-t'ao (1971), vol. 1, pp. 77 ff. and 467 ff., and from our interview with Cynthia Liao, who also described to us how she picked up Anna Louise from the Shameen steamer. The quotation from Mrs. Liao is from "New Women of Old Canton," p. 557. The climbing of White Cloud Mountain was told to us by Cynthia Liao. Anna Louise wrote up her Japan trip in "Three Men of Japan," *Asia*, March 1926.

After she got back to the United States the FBI began to pick up her movements. A later summary of previous reports, dated January 19, 1929, mentions that she addressed local Communist party chapters. She wrote to her father about her visit with Swope on April 30, 1926. A letter from February of that year contained her anger at the situation at John Reed; her letter to Yavorskaia is February 8, 1926 (in the University of Washington archives). *I Change Worlds*, p. 214, mentioned her distress with Amtorg.

There is further discussion of her desire to join the party in *I Change Worlds*, pp. 392–393. The letter from Paul Kellogg was dated May 15, 1926, and she replied on June 8, 1926, and July 18, 1926; all three are in the *Survey* archives at the University of Minnesota.

Her distress with the Babins was in a letter to her father on September 2, 1926, and her relief about giving up John Reed in one to Ellen Hayes, September 20, 1926. The long letter to her father about Roger Baldwin and marriage was dated November 3, 1926. *I Change Worlds*, pp. 238–245, contains her account of the trip to Mexico. She mentioned the painting in 1949 (in *Events in Moscow and New York*) when detailing the contents of her confiscated files in Moscow. Alix Holt's introduction to Kollontai (1977) and Porter (1980) helped us with a description of Kollontai and her time in Mexico. Kollontai became famous in the West for her views on sexuality and in particular her proclamation that the sex act was equivalent to a "drink of water."

Anna Louise wrote her father of her desire to return to China on March 14, 1927, and of her departure from San Francisco on April 30, 1927. Her article on Stalin was published in the *New York Times Sunday Magazine* on April 24, 1927, and her arrival in Shanghai was noted by the *China Courier* on May 23, 1927. She recounted her church visits in "Five Churches in Shanghai," a manuscript in the University of Washington archives. The description of T. V. Soong is from *China's Millions*, p. 16, and the quote from Von Salzman is on p. 15.

In his interview with us, Jack Chen provided not only the story of the *People's Tribune* but general background on Hankow in 1927. On Rayna Prohme, see Sheean (1934) for his account of his time in Hankow. Anna Louise gave an account of her visit to Hankow in *I Change Worlds*, pp. 260–261. We have drawn on Jacobs (1981), pp. 261–271, for background.

The account of the departure to Chengchow is from *China's Millions*, pp. 48 ff., as is the account of her time there. The story of Wang Su-chun was published in *Harper's Magazine*, November 1927, pp. 749 ff. Anna Louise published an account of the lot of lower-class women in Hankow in "Some Hankow Memories," *Asia*, October 1928. The time around Feng's headquarters is described in a manuscript, "Feng's Headquarters," in the University of Washington.

Jack Chen described to us in detail his memories of the motor trip across the Gobi Desert. The story of the "Internationale" comes from Chen (1979), pp.

136–137. Jack Chen told us of Anna Louise's horror at Voroshin's greed, and of her protection of the automobile. Anna Louise wrote an account of the trip for *Asia* (September 1928), from which we take Borodin's tirade against Russians. *China's Millions*, p. 335, contains the story of the child and the shepherds, and the story of Anna Louise's dream of a man on a white horse comes to us from our interview with Jack Chen. Chen (1979), p. 163, tells of the problems getting the car rolling on the sand, and Jack Chen also told us of Ningsia and of Anna Louise's insistence on knowing what was going on at all moments. Chen (1979), p. 168, has the story of Anna Louise getting lost. We have also been informed by the "Letters from China" she sent to *Unity* (a church magazine) for September through December 1927; copies are in her archives at the University of Washington.

8

MARKING A TIME AND PLACE

We were helped in our understanding of the background of this period by Jacobs (1981), Holubnychy (1979), Isaacs (1961), Deutscher (1963), Serge (1951), Fischer (1941), Fischer (1964), and Sheean (1934). In *I Change Worlds*, this period is covered in chapters 22 to 31. The description of the China trips is amplified in *China's Millions*. Her letters to her father (all in the University of Washington archives) provide a further running commentary.

Anna Louise expressed her hope for the festivities to her father on October 9, 1927. Trotsky's problems are described in Serge (1951), pp. 246–247; Deutscher (1963), p. 376; Fischer (1941), p. 92. Details of Rayna Prohme's death come from Anna Louise's letters to her father and Sheean (1934), pp. 299–302, who recalls Fanny Borodin and the lemons. Jack Chen in our interview and in Holubnychy (1979), p. 229, remembers Fanny as a "typical Jewish mama." The letter in which Anna Louise announced that she would not return for Christmas was sent to her father on November 30, 1927.

She described her ascent of Mount Kazbek in *I Change Worlds*, pp. 270–272, to her father on September 30, 1928, and to her brother Tracy on October 1, 1928 (in the Tracy Strong archives, University of Washington).

Anna Louise's difficulties with housing and guests and a sense of her life are drawn from a letter to her father (October 26, 1928), from Allan (1938) and from a letter written to an undisclosed correspondent on August 31, 1933, which Ms. Allan shared with the authors. Among the few reviews of *China's Millions* is one in *Survey*, Vol. 61, p. 311 (December 1, 1928).

An account of the First Five-Year Plan in Soviet Central Asia that confirms some of Anna Louise's assertions is Massell (1974). Anna Louise's letter to Walter Duranty is dated December 3, 1928. The story about the murdered organizer is in *Red Star in Samarkand*, pp. 255–256. *Red Star* was reviewed in the *New York Herald Tribune* (December 15, 1929); *Christian Century* (January 15, 1930); and the *New Republic* (November 20, 1929).

The meeting in Boston is reported in the FBI files on January 27, 1929, as are her troubles with the DAR. The "Sherlock Holmes test" is in a letter of May 9, 1929, to her father. Anna Louise's relations with Dubenko and the first part of the trip are described in a letter to her father (May 28, 1929) and to the secretary of the British Labour Party James Middleton (July 13, 1929—in the University of Washington archives) as well as in *The Road to the Grey Pamir*, pp. 16–17. Dubenko was shot during the purges in the late 1930s. The stories of her trip to

Murgab all come from *The Road to the Grey Pamir;* she writes to her father about the adventure on August 9, 1929.

Background on collectivization has been drawn from Moshe Lewin (1966), who cites *The Soviets Conquer Wheat,* pp. 438–440, to show how *bad* collectivization was. The importance of the attitudes of the organizers, on whom Anna Louise lays most of the blame for the excesses, has been argued by Sheila Fitzpatrick in Fitzpatrick, ed. (1978), pp. 8–40 and discussed by Solomon (1977) and by Roger Portal in his introduction to Lewin (1966). Anna Louise cited Kollontai's dictum to her father on November 26, 1929. Her appreciation of the kolkhoz is from *The Soviets Conquer Wheat,* p. 33; the story about Shevchenko comes from our interview with Lement Harris, though not that she was disturbed by what she saw there. The letter to her father describing her distress was dated January 26, 1930. Lyons (1941), pp. 120–121, reports Sydney's distress. The analogy to the man on skis was sent to her father on April 13, 1930; that about injustices on February 15, 1930. The difficulty in making a judgment on collectivization is in *The Soviets Conquer Wheat,* pp. 70–71; there is similar material in Lewin (1966), pp. 393 ff., and Serge (1951), pp. 274 ff. Her letter to her father about the injustices was February 15, 1930. The judgment on Stalin is from *I Change Worlds,* p. 289. She wrote to Dwight Waldo, the McClure features editor, on November 22, 1929 (in the University of Washington) about Stalin as a symbol of unity.

Anna Louise described her Russian pamphlets to her father on February 16, 1930, and in a joint letter to her father and brother on February 21, 1930. The pamphlet on farming was published in English as *Modern Farming—Soviet Style* by International Publishers. The story of the eggs in Kiev is in the letter to her father and brother, February 21, 1930, and she complained about getting fat to her father on February 28, 1930.

For an account of Borodin during this period see Jacobs (1981), especially pp. 314–315. Her response to his question about an English-language paper is from *I Change Worlds,* p. 301. The text of her prospectus for the paper is in her archives at the University of Washington; she announced the project to her father on July 6, 1930.

The identification of Joel Shubin as the press officer is made in the interview the Passport Division conducted with Anna Louise on October 30, 1956, p. A8 (University of Washington archives). Details of the first weeks of the *Moscow News* come from our interviews with Jack Chen and Edward Falkowski; Falkowski reported the phrase about "Anna Louise and the four dwarfs."

Her difficulties with Jimmy Duncan were described to her father on December 25, 1930, where she also reported crying in Oakland. The story of her return to Moscow comes from our interview with Edward Falkowski. She wrote to her father on April 4, 1931, that her resignation had been refused. Lement Harris told us of the early days of Anna Louise's and Joel's courtship. Jack Chen, Israel Epstein, Elsie Cholmeley, Julia Older Bazer and Bernie Koten attested to Anna Louise's fears of becoming an old maid in their interviews with us, as well as to other details of the relationship with Joel. Interviews with Philip Jaffe, Maud Russell, Jessica Smith and Robbins Strong also helped develop our sense of Joel. Anna Louise's best account of the development of their relationship appears in her passport interview, p. A7. The detail of the new apartment is mentioned in "We Soviet Wives," *American Mercury,* August 1934, p. 422; Edward Falkowski told us the address. Her vision of marriage as companionship is also from "We Soviet Wives," p. 423.

Vacsov's censorship was recounted to us by Jack Chen. The meeting with Stalin is described in *I Change Worlds*, pp. 333 ff. The vision of Stalin as the "best committee man" had been with her since her *Hearst's International* article in 1924 and reappears in *The Stalin Era*, p. 21. Some of our analysis of what Anna Louise understood about Russian socialism from her meeting with Stalin is influenced by Malcolm Cowley's review in the *New Republic*, May 1, 1935, pp. 345–346. Joel's suggestion that she was getting ready to join the party is in *I Change Worlds*, p. 385. The long letter Seema Allan wrote to her friend is dated August 31, 1933, and was given us by Ms. Allan.

Her hopes for an active role in the United States appear in *I Change Worlds*, p. 385. The account of her meeting Emily Pierson is from our interview with Ann Tobey. The correspondence with Steffens is collected in the University of Washington archives; the long discussion of what she was attempting in *I Change Worlds* is in a letter from Steffens to her in late 1933.

In *Events in Moscow and New York*, in the University of Washington archives, Anna Louise singled out for mention the confiscation of the corrected manuscript of her interview with Stalin. Her "Hearst's soul" is in *I Change Worlds*, p. 387; her exchange with Borodin comes thirteen pages earlier. The claim that there are "two truths" is from the preface to *This Soviet World*, pp. x–xi. Her anguish with Kollontai and Yavorskaia are in *I Change Worlds*, pp. 396–402; the musing over the nature of discipline is sixteen pages later. The account of her membership in the American Communist party is taken from her passport interview, p. A81, which can be found in the Washington archives; in our interview, Dorothy Healey confirms that the arrangement Anna Louise describes would have been possible in terms of the party and that Anna Louise gave her an account similar to this one in 1953.

In our interview, John Niederhauser described his arrival in the U.S.S.R. and some of Anna Louise's feelings about his sister. See also Tracy Strong to Sydney Dix Strong, August 5, 1933, in the Tracy Strong archives for additional material about his nephew's and niece's times in Russia. In a letter to Raymond Robins, October 25, 1950, in the Robins archives, she made clear that the troubles in Russia were such that she decided to go elsewhere, without speaking her anxieties about Russia.

9

OLD FRONTIERS AND NEW DEALS

I Change Worlds covers until 1934; the fragments of a second volume of autobiography, *My Later Years*, are in the Peking Library. The first trip to Spain is described in *Spain in Arms* and in the first chapter of *My Later Years*. Her meeting with Contreras is in *My Later Years*, pp. 87–88, and *Spain in Arms*, pp. 41–48. The little boy who wanted to fight fascism appears in *My Later Years*, p. 22.

The *Newsweek* article appeared January 23, 1937; a copy of the banquet invitation is in the University of Washington archives; the account of her speech in Canada is in *My Later Years*, pp. 27–28.

Anna Louise's letters to Eleanor Roosevelt and the responses are collected in the University of Washington. The letters about Spain to Mrs. Roosevelt are dated February 1937; from Mrs. Roosevelt, February 24, 1937. Her anger at missing the vacation with Joel is in *My Later Years*, p. 28. Robbins Strong told us of his conversation with Ducia. Anna Louise's review of Trotsky is in *Soviet Russia Today*, May 1937, p. 36. The journal was edited by Jessica Smith, and

Anna Louise wrote regularly for it during this time. Robbins reports urging Anna Louise to go to China in a letter to his family on July 6, 1937 (in the Robbins Strong files).

For an account of the Long March, see Snow (1978), especially pp. 470–473, and Selden (1971), especially pp. 93–108. All figures on the Long March vary depending on sources. Nym Wales told us of her and Edgar Snow's meeting with Anna Louise in Shanghai.

The material involving Sues is taken from her book (1944), pp. 8, 188. On Marshal Yen, see Gillan (1967), pp. 273 ff., 152 ff., and especially p. 161 for an account of his hoped-for economic reforms. The account of the meeting with Chu Teh is drawn from *One-fifth of Mankind*, pp. 127–137, 151–159, and *My Later Years*, pp. 47–60. The story about Yao's return is from Sues (1944), p. 189. Philip Jaffe told us of Anna Louise's continuing anger at Ms. Sues. The meeting with Teng Ying-ch'ao was filled in with Anna Louise's notebooks from the interview (now in the University of Washington). We have learned about Agnes Smedley from our interviews with Jan and Steven MacKinnon; the detail about Yenan is from their introduction to Smedley (1976), p. xxvi. Anna Louise wrote an introduction to Smedley (1938), in which she suggested that Agnes organized better than she wrote. Rewi Alley also provided us with an account of Smedley in Hankow; our interview with Chen Han-seng filled in some aspects of her overall character. The story of the dinner party with H. H. Kung comes from *My Later Years*, pp. 40–41. Isaacs in Isaacs (1961) does not mention his relation with Smedley or the *China Forum*. Emily Hahn, who met Anna Louise at a party in Hong Kong after her departure from China, remembers thinking that her support for the U.S.S.R. seemed moderate, since she prudently remained as quiet as she could whenever the subject came up (letter to the authors, September 22, 1981).

Anna Louise wrote to Eleanor Roosevelt on her return on February 24, 1938, and again in March, 1938, and on June 25, 1938. Philip Jaffe told us of the writing of *One-fifth of Mankind*.

Anna Louise's observation about suspicion in the U.S.S.R. appears in *The Stalin Era*, pp. 136–137; the account of her distress about the purges which follows is drawn from an interview with Manlio, a Japanese correspondent, the text of which is in her archives in Peking. She told the story of her forced trip to Minsk in "How I Saw Minsk," *Soviet Russia Today*, February 1939. The letters in which she worked out with Eleanor Roosevelt the plan to write about the New Deal were sent to Mrs. Roosevelt on January 29, 1939, and March 8, 1939; Mrs. Roosevelt responded February 2, 1939, and April 10, 1939. Anna Louise mentioned the "hot soup" of California in *My Native Land*, p. 18. The title of the book she wrote about her trip (*My Native Land*) recalls the famous book of her relative Josiah Strong, *Our Country*, written to defend America against immigrants, and the left-wing film *Native Land*, popular during the 1940s. Relations between Anna Louise and the Niederhausers were attested to in interviews with Tracy and Dolphine Strong, as well as one with John Niederhauser. Most of the stories of her trip come from *My Native Land*: the dead baby is on pp. 95–97; her arrival in Seattle, on p. 142. The visit with Lem Harris in in *My Native Land*, pp. 185 ff. and was recalled in our interview with Mr. Harris. An account of the work which Harris was doing has been recently published in Dyson (1982). Anna Louise's analysis of the TVA is in *My Native Land*, p. 216, and her conclusion about the New Deal on p. 224. The end of her trip was filled in from *My Native Land*, with details provided by Ann Tobey.

Granville Hicks wrote to her on October 2, 1939; the letter is in her archives in Washington. The cautious but sympathetic editor was at *Asia* magazine, November 1939; see p. 647. Eleanor Roosevelt's reservations were in a letter of August 28, 1939 (University of Washington). In a letter to the authors (February 23, 1983), Franklin D. Roosevelt, Jr., warned us that many of those who took lunch with Eleanor Roosevelt would later claim to have also seen the president and additionally assume that Mrs. Roosevelt was serving as a conduit to her husband. Anna Louise seems in fact finally to have had lunch with both FDR and his wife; she also seems to have assumed that Mrs. Roosevelt was passing on her information, as Mrs. Roosevelt indicated.

Ann Tobey provided the information about Emily Pierson's steadfastness after the Nazi-Soviet pact. See also Anna Louise's article in *Soviet Russia Today*, November 1939.

Katherine Strong is the source of the detail of the lemon meringue pie. Ruth Niederhauser's advice about investment was sent to Anna Louise on September 23, 1939 (in the University of Washington archives). *My Later Years*, pp. 134 ff., contains the story of her return to Russia and her excitement about the arrival of the Red Army into Lithuania. She told the story at the time in a pamphlet called *The New Lithuania*. Robbins Strong is the source of the account of her encounter with her brother Tracy in Kaunas. Joel's farewell comes from *My Later Years*, p. 140.

10

LANDS REVISITED

My Later Years continues to be a major source of information for this period. We have used Schaller (1979) for background. Rewi Alley and Israel Epstein provided accounts of their meetings with Anna Louise in Chungking. We were also helped by the reminiscences of many of the journalists present at the "War Reporting in China during the 1940s" conference held in Tempe, Arizona, November 17–19, 1982, especially those of Annalee Jaccoby Fadiman.

The stop in Ha-mi, the meeting with Johnson, her arrival at the house of Sir Archibald, and the meeting with Chou are in *My Later Years*, pp. 164 ff. The material Chou gave her is in the University of Washington archives. Chou's message for Borodin is from *Why the Russians Arrested Me*, p. 139. The letters to Morgenthau, White and Davies are in the University of Washington archives.

The dream for a Hull House on the Palisades is mainly in *My Later Years* and in her correspondence with Joel (in the University of Washington archives). She wrote to Joel on April 2, 1941, in response to a letter from him dated March 17, 1941; she wrote again on May 31, 1941, promising Christmas presents. They corresponded in English. The confused FBI agent reported on April 3, 1941. Her next letter to Joel was in August 1941.

Her defense of the Nazi-Soviet pact is in *The Soviets Expected It*, p. 279. She wrote of the death of her father in *My Later Years*, p. 108. Her first bout with Paget's disease is described in *My Later Years* and is also drawn from our interview with Ann Tobey. Dr. Alexander Keyssar helped us with the etiology of Paget's disease.

The correspondence with Willner is in the University of Washington archives. Some accounts of left-wing screenwriters and agents (including Willner) can be found in Caute (1978), in Ceplair and Englund (1980), and especially Navasky (1980).

The letters surrounding Joel's death are in the University of Washington archives, including the one to "Herb" on August 4, 1942, in which Anna Louise suggested that Joel might have married again, and the one to the Litvinovs, August 5, 1942. The letter announcing that Moscow could no longer be a home was sent to Jessica Smith on August 7, 1942.

The account of her life in California after Stalingrad was mainly provided by our interview with Sidney Rittenberg. She recalled her meeting with him in a letter to the CIO about October 1946, which is in the University of Washington archives. The scenario for *Wild River* and her correspondence with Willner are in the University of Washington archives. The scenario Anna Louise and Edgar Snow wrote is in the Washington archives, with a letter signed by "Bill" indicating Welles' interest. Our interview with Angus Cameron helped on the publication of *Wild River*.

Anna Louise's next book, *Peoples of the U.S.S.R.*, is patterned after Nicholas Mikhailov's *Land of the Soviets* (New York: Furman, 1939), of which she owned a copy. A copy of the will she wrote is in our possession from the papers of Ruth Niederhauser. Much of the correspondence surrounding her departure exists in FBI photostats. Ladd's memo to Hoover is dated July 23, 1944.

The details of her return to Moscow are in *My Later Years*, pp. 233 ff., and in the book she wrote on the trip to Poland, *I Saw the New Poland*, which contains the story of her crossing the border on p. 35. The important letter to Jessica Smith in which Anna Louise despairs of working in the U.S.S.R. is from an FBI transcript, which dates the letter April 15, 1945, and is itself dated August 31, 1945. Her consternation with the Russians is also in *My Later Years*, pp. 279–280. The friction caused in high circles in the United States by the end to lend-lease is attested to by Stettinius (1949), pp. 318 ff. Harry Hopkins' intervention to allow Anna Louise's manuscript diplomatic passage is duly recorded by the FBI on the March 1, 1946, report, p. 4.

Jessica Smith has told the story of their sea voyage in the last chapter of Smith (1948) and in our interview with her. The FBI recorded their arrival in a report of March 1, 1946. In his interview Philip Jaffe filled us in on Anna Louise's activities after the return. In his *Amerasia Case from 1945 to the Present*, especially on p. 26, Jaffe discussed material relevant to his political situation. See also John S. Service's account, in Service (1971).

The FBI collected the circulars denouncing Anna Louise, and their files on her provide full details on her speeches and activities. They record her obtaining State Department permission for the NATS flight. The source of that authorization is not completely clear. Anna Louise had known John Paton Davies when he was secretary of the embassy in Moscow; he originated the recommendation that a U.S. military advisory group (the Dixie Mission) be dispatched to Yenan. He knew of her connections to Chou En-lai. He was impressed enough with Anna Louise to recommend in 1949 that the CIA use Anna Louise (and Edgar Snow, John Fairbank, Agnes Smedley) as consultants on China. See *Interlocking Subversion in Government Departments* ("Jenner Report") (Washington, D.C.: U.S. Government Printing Office, 1953, p. 46). We were unable to find out if Mr. Davies had any contact with Anna Louise over the NATS flight. Anna Louise had also been in touch with Harry Dexter White and Henry Morgenthau after her 1940 trip and had caused quite a stir then with the information detailing the split between the CCP and the KMT. She had also spoken with Stanley Hornbeck and had renewed her contact with him by letter as late as February 27, 1941 (in the University of Washington).

11
YENAN: THE CITY IN THE HILL

Anna Louise published three accounts of her time in Yenan: *Dawn over China*, *Tomorrow's China*, and *The Chinese Conquer China*. Her notebooks on Yenan are in the University of Washington archives and constitute an important source of information about this time.

The frontispiece poem is in the Peking archives. The account of her life in Peking was provided by Robbins Strong. Some of the physical details of Yenan come from our visit there in 1980. Anna Louise's account of her own project is from *Tomorrow's China*, p. 8; the quote from Chu Teh is in her notebooks in the University of Washington archives. The first interview with Mao was reconstructed from interviews with Ling Ch'ing, Lu Ting-yi, T'u Chien-kuo, and Dr. Ma Hai-teh. The material in *Tomorrow's China*, pp. 31–32, proved especially useful. A carefully edited version of the "paper tiger" interview appears in Volume 4 of Mao Tse-tung's *Selected Works*. We have presented the interview verbatim as closely as possible, drawing on Anna Louise's field notes (University of Washington archives), her first write-up and the hand corrections by Lu Ting-yi (in our possession), the revised write-up (in our possession), the account she published in *Amerasia* and the version that appears in Mao's *Works*. That the "paper tiger" interview had the Soviets among its intended audiences was confirmed in our interview with Ling Ch'ing, her "official" interpreter at the time.

The quotations from Lu Ting-yi are taken from Anna Louise's write-up of their talk, which is in the University of Washington archives; those from Liu Shao-ch'i are from a similiar manuscript in the Jaffe files. See also Anna Louise's article in *Amerasia*, June 1947.

Material relating to Sidney Rittenberg comes from our interview with him and from his manuscript "Cross Country" in the Jaffe archives. Details of her trips to the liberated areas are drawn from her notebooks in the University of Washington archives, but the story about the naval intelligence officer comes from Rittenberg.

For worries by American officials at the appointment of J. Leighton Stuart, see Melby (1971), pp. 155 ff. Anna Louise's arrangements with Evans Carlson and De Lacey are mentioned in a letter to her sister (October 25, 1946) that was photostated by the FBI.

Anna Louise's pursuit of Chou was recalled by Sidney Rittenberg and Ling Ch'ing. The bridge game was recalled by Rittenberg, and the score is in her University of Washington archives notebooks. The general sources of the dancing episode are *The Chinese Conquer China*, pp. 25 ff., *Tomorrow's China*, pp. 15 f., *Dawn over China*, and our interviews with Ling Ch'ing and Sidney Rittenberg, who is responsible for the detail about the drummer. The excitement caused by the articles Anna Louise wrote on Mao's thought is mentioned in her letter to Philip Jaffe, March 11, 1947, in the Jaffe archives. Similiar information is in *Why the Russians Arrested Me*, p. 14, the notebooks in the University of Washington archives, and from our interview with Lu Ting-yi.

Mao's judgment about the capture of Yenan is in the notebooks in the University of Washington archives. Details on the evacuation comes from a manuscript in the Emily Pierson files and our interview with Dr. Ma Hai-teh. The account of the last days in Yenan and the departure comes from interviews with Dr. Ma, Sidney Rittenberg, Yang Tsao, Ling Ch'ing, T'u Chien-kuo; from the notebooks in the Unviersity of Washington archives; from *Why the Russians Arrested Me*, pp. 1–5; from a letter to Lu Tsui, February 22, 1949 (FBI transcript); from William Hinton's memoir of Anna Louise in the *National Guardian*, May 9, 1970, p. 9. Dorothy Borg's interview provided information on events in Shanghai. The letters from Chou, Huang Hua and Dr. Ma are in the University of Washington archives. The publication of *Dawn over China* is discussed in *Why the Russians Arrested Me*, pp. 7–10. The exchange with Ambassador Stuart was recounted to us by Robbins Strong.

12

ARREST IN RUSSIA

Details of Anna Louise's difficulties leaving Shanghai are in a letter to Philip Jaffe, August 1947, in the Jaffe archives. Her distress with the Russian treatment of the Communist Chinese appears most clearly in *Why the Russians Arrested Me*, pp. 10–13, and is hinted at in her pamphlet *Inside North Korea*, pp. 6–9. We have been informed about the Russian treatment of their China experts by Harrison Salisbury's review of three books on the topic in the *New York Times Book Review*, September 19, 1971. The most complete account of her efforts to break the story about China in Russia is in *Why the Russians Arrested Me* and in the internal memorandum, February 7, 1958, for the RAND Corporation that Allen Whiting wrote after his interview with Anna Louise in California. We thank Professor Whiting and Richard Solomon of the RAND Corporation for making the memorandum available. The quote from Borodin about her reputation is from this memorandum.

Her Chinese contacts in the United States were attested to by Liu Ning-yi and Tang Ming-chao in interviews. The FCC files contain all the radio intercepts. The article by Elizabeth Gurley Flynn is in the *Daily Worker*, January 12, 1948. The FBI took down the text of Anna Louise's speech on China (dated February 9, 1948), and James Davies and George Lanyi reported to us the story of her speech at Oberlin.

We have used the three volumes of MacDougall (1965) as well as Caute (1973 and 1978) for background on the Progressive party. Anna Louise's letter to Glenn Taylor is in our possession, and the comment from Harry Steinmetz comes from our interview with him, as does the judgment that Communist party members were suspicious of Anna Louise.

Chen Han-seng described his relations to Anna Louise in our interview with him. The FBI was regularly intercepting Anna Louise's mail; the "Hans" letter was filed on May 21, 1948.

Tracy Strong, Jr., and Dolphine Strong as well as John Niederhauser told us of the disintegration of Anna Louise's relationship with her sister; the letter in which Anna Louise analyzed it to her brother is in the Peking archives (February 7, 1966). The radio link her sister helped her with is discussed in a letter to Carey McWilliams (early 1948, in the McWilliams files). She spends a few pages on the question in *Why the Russians Arrested Me*.

The FBI distressfully reported that she received her passport in a memo dated June 3, 1948; Anna Louise mentioned it in the letter to C. B. Baldwin (University of Washington archives).

The developments inside the American Communist party surrounding the publication of the Duclos letter are described in Dennis (1977), pp. 162 ff.; Jaffe (1975), pp. 53 ff., Isserman (1979) and Starobin (1972). Mao's telegram to Foster is in his *Selected Works*, Vol. 3, pp. 287 f. Jaffe (1975) points out that Foster asked for the telegram. The memorandum Anna Louise wrote about the CPUSA became an FBI photostat, July 28, 1948. The ultimatum she gave Epstein is from *Why the Russians Arrested Me;* we have identified Epstein. A discussion of this episode can be found in Philip Jaffe's chapter on Anna Louise in his unpublished memoirs, pp. 132 ff. Among other things Epstein changed the phrase about Mao changing "Marxism from a European to an Asiatic form" to a reference to Mao's "application of Marxist thinking to Chinese problems." Mr. Jaffe was kind enough to discuss this topic with us and make available the relevant chapter from his memoirs. He published an earlier version in *Survey.*

Our interview with Liu Ning-yi continues to be an important source for the period after Anna Louise returned to Paris, as does *Why the Russians Arrested Me.* In addition, after her arrest Anna Louise wrote herself a kind of long personal memorandum, *Events in Moscow and New York.* It is dated December 1949 and was probably intended as an argument to the CPUSA; it is in the University of Washington archives. Anna Louise did not have access to this when she wrote *Why the Russians Arrested Me,* but the two versions go together remarkably well.

A State Department memorandum, October 6, 1948, took note of her articles in *Glos Ludu.* We have reconstructed events after she arrived in Moscow up until her arrest from the following sources: *Why the Russians Arrested Me; Events in Moscow and New York;* "Statement for O. John Rogge" in the University of Washington archives; interviews with Dolphine Strong, Harrison Salisbury, John Emerson (a councilor at the embassy at the time), and Tang Ming-chao. The fury at Simonov is best described in the manuscript version of the second article she published later in the *New York Herald Tribune,* which is in the University of Washington archives. The letter from Fred Field is mentioned in *Events in Moscow and New York;* in a letter to the authors (January 24, 1983), Mr. Field indicates that he does not remember this letter. The phone call to Elsie Cholmeley was mentioned to us in our interview with Maud Russell, although the identification of Cholmeley comes from *Events.* Borodin's phone conversation with the publishing house is both in *Why the Russians Arrested Me,* pp. 29–30, and in the Whiting RAND memorandum. The possibility of a separate peace between the KMT and the CCP that the U.S.S.R. would negotiate is in *Why the Russians Arrested Me* and in Department of State (1949), p. 293. The story about Harry Eisman was reported to us in a personal communication from William Mandel, November 26, 1980. Anna Louise's own account of her efforts in Moscow are in her nightly write-up of her testimony before the grand jury, in her archives at the University of Washington.

Details of her locating Liu Ning-yi come from our interview with him; from *Why the Russians Arrested Me,* pp. 27–33; from a dispatch from the U.S. embassy to the State Department, February 15, 1949; from Anna Louise's article in the *New York Herald Tribune,* March 29, 1949; from *Events in Moscow and New York,* p. 3; and from our interview with Rewi Alley. Liu remembers only the second visit.

The time Anna Louise spent in jail and her interrogation were reconstructed from *Why the Russians Arrested Me,* pp. 34–43; from the drafts of the *New York Herald Tribune* articles in the University of Washington archives; from the account in the *New York Times,* February 18, 1949.

Her expulsion is described in *Why the Russians Arrested Me* and *Events in Moscow and New York;* the letter she sent to Lu Ts'ui in Paris was dated February 20, 1949, and is in her FBI files. Her arrival in New York is also described in *Why the Russians Arrested Me;* the identification of Jack Lotto was in the FBI report of the occasion. Cedric Belfrage wrote up the sad events in Belfrage and Aronson (1978), pp. 87 ff. The Associated Press dispatch was cited from the *Washington Star*, February 24, 1949.

The major source of events as Anna Louise left LaGuardia Airport is *Why the Russians Arrested Me*. Fred Field has a dim memory of the phone call (letter to the authors, January 24, 1983); the account is taken from *Events in Moscow and New York*. The citations from Lem Harris are taken from Anna Louise's account. Her statement to the press after her first appearance before the grand jury is taken from the *New York Herald Tribune*, February 26, 1949, and the UP dispatch in the *Washington Times Herald*, February 26, 1949.

Emily Pierson's files contain the letter certifying Anna Louise's condition. Belfrage expressed his relief at Anna Louise's intentions not to "play the Judas" in the *National Guardian*, February 28, 1949. However, Foy Kohler wrote on February 17, 1949, from the U.S. embassy in Moscow that the State Department should "exploit to the maximum" the fact that Anna Louise's "enormous left-wing following must be considerably shaken."

The FBI wiretap on the conversation between Harris and Anna Louise was filed on March 4, 1949. Belfrage's hope for Anna Louise's article was expressed in a letter he wrote to Emily Pierson (March 3, 1949), which is in his files. The events up until Anna Louise's visit to the CDFEP are drawn from *Why the Russians Arrested Me*, *Events in Moscow and New York*, and the FBI wiretaps on Emily Pierson's house. In a letter to the authors, John Abt wrote he has no memory of the episode with Henry Wallace. The quote from Wallace was given by Blumenthal to Anna Louise and taken down by the FBI wiretap. The episode with the mysterious visitors is from Anna Louise's accounts, and her bitter thoughts about Abt are in *Events in Moscow and New York*, p. 10. John Abt, in a letter to the authors (March 17, 1983), denies Anna Louise's allegations.

The long conversation with Blumenthal about the publication of the articles was taken down by the FBI (March 11, 1949); it corresponds to Anna Louise's own memories in both *Why the Russians Arrested Me* and *Events in Moscow and New York*.

Memories differ considerably on what happened at the offices of the Committee for a Democratic Far Eastern Policy. The version given in the text is basically that which Anna Louise gives in *Why the Russians Arrested Me*. Maud Russell, in a letter to the authors which elaborates on the interview she gave us, says that Anna Louise boasted about the splash she was going to make with her articles and ordered her to take a message "downtown."

Ms. Russell, who remembers being in a hurry to leave, does not know where Anna Louise wanted her to take the message and indicates that she had in any case "no contact" with the Communist party. Whatever Anna Louise's feelings about Maud Russell during this time, she welcomed her in China a decade later. The only thing that is common to both versions is that Anna Louise was trying to get Maud Russell to take a message somewhere, and that Ms. Russell did not.

The exchange with Abt about publication is also from Anna Louise's account in *Events in Moscow and New York*, pp. 12–25, and *Why the Russians Arrested Me*, pp. 67 ff. The article she published in the *National Guardian* is discussed in a letter she wrote to Cedric Belfrage, April 12, 1949 (Belfrage files); some indications of the problems the *Guardian* incurred can be found in a letter from Belfrage to Anna Louise, February 9, 1950, also in his files.

Anna Louise wrote on September 19, 1949, to Lem Harris that she "really doesn't know if her interpretations [of why she was arrested] are true." Harris' response (November 2, 1949) is in her files in the University of Washington. She had also written in the letter of September 19, 1949, an earlier version of her reflections on the modern state. Those in the text are taken from *Events in Moscow and New York*, p. 17.

The difficulties she had with Chen Han-seng about "peasants" and "farmers" were mentioned by Gerald Tannebaum in our interview. Corliss Lamont provided us with a copy of the collective letter of protest (April 12, 1949) to Soviet ambassador Vishinsky. We have cited the editorial Jessica Smith wrote from the copy she provided us. The letter from Maud Russell is dated April 7, 1949, and is in the University of Washington archives; Anna Louise's response (April 11, 1949) is in the Emily Pierson files.

The encounter with William Patterson is drawn from *Why the Russians Arrested Me*, pp. 76–77, as well as from an FBI wiretap on a conversation between Anna Louise and Emily Pierson, April 15, 1949. The letter to Chen Han-seng (September 25, 1949) is in the University of Washington archives, as is that to Belfrage (November 4, 1949), as well as the letter about the "auto accident," which is to Harry F. Ward (May 8, 1949). The letter to Cameron is also in the University of Washington archives and is dated March 6, 1949.

13
PUTTING DOWN ROOTS: SALVATION OR A CHURCH

The information about her anger is in a letter to Raymond Robins, September 11, 1949, in the Robins archives. Similar sentiments went to Ella Winter on September 14, 1949 (University of Washington archives). Her hopes for China were expressed in letters to Raymond Robins on May 17, 1949, and September 1, 1949, from which the comparison between Communist parties is taken. Both these letters are in the Robins archives. She took great comfort from the publication of the Department of State (1949) "White Paper" on U.S. relations with China, which she wrote to Robins (n.d., 1949, Robins archives) "convinced her of her own propaganda."

Starobin reports his boycott of her in Starobin (1972), p. 301n. The "nest of Titoists" comes from an internal party document that the FBI quotes in a report of April 4, 1952, p. 92. Anna Louise reports the episode in a letter to Raymond Robbins on April 20, 1949 (Robins archives), and describes in *Why the Russians Arrested Me*, pp. 82 ff.

Fritchman (1977), pp. 102 ff., gives an account of the First Unitarian Church. We draw the story of their meeting from our interview with him. Jaffe (1975) and Jaffe (1979) tell the story of *Amerasia*. He told us of Anna Louise's apology in our interview.

The letter to Joseph Starobin about the Grossman article (itself in the *Daily Worker* of January 25, 1950) is attached to a letter Anna Louise sent to Holland Roberts on June 11, 1950, in the University of Washington archives. Anna Louise wrote of the episode in *Why the Russians Arrested Me*, pp. 99–100. The Washington archives also contain the letter to Pauline Schindler on November 24, 1950, proclaiming that she is not going to "kneel" any more; she mentioned stopping her "contributions" to the party in *Why the Russians Arrested Me*, pp. 92 and 102a.

We learned of Rogge's changing role in Shannon (1959), pp. 204–205. Anna Louise mentioned the McCormick cable in a letter to Corliss Lamont on September 12, 1950 (Lamont files) and wrote to Chou on August 4, 1950. The interchange with Willen is described in Willen (1955), in a letter from Mr. Willen to the authors on November 22, 1980, and in our interview with George Lanyi. Starobin's reply to Belfrage was dated May 25, 1950, and is in the Aronson files. The event is reported in Belfrage and Aronson (1978). Anna Louise responded to Morton Schrag on May 6, 1950; a copy is in the Aronson files.

Anna Louise's speech on Korea is drawn from *I Saw North Korea* in the authors' possession. Her letter to Ambassador Vishinsky was sent October 1, 1950, and is in the University of Washington archives.

The first two issues of *Today* contain an analysis of Mao in Russia. Anna Louise had recognized these problems in a letter to Raymond Robins on October 9, 1949 (Robins archives); see the account in Starr (1979), pp. 298 ff. In China, we were told, the story spread that Stalin kept Mao waiting for six weeks before seeing him for negotiations.

Anna Louise cited the *Wall Street Journal* in *Today*, January 5, 1952. Her credo appeared in *Today* on January 17, 1952. The story about the car running out of gas is from our interview with Grace Nelson. The long letter to Emily Pierson about her "inner transition" is dated July 1, 1952, and is in the Pierson files. Anna Louise's pleasure with Hardiman's trip appeared in the December 1952 issue of *Today;* she wrote to Emily about Hardiman's treatment of her on January 10, 1953 (Pierson files). Her distress with 1952 appeared in *Today*, mid-January 1953; her distress with Eastern Europe comes from a letter to Emily Pierson in June 1953, in the Pierson files.

Starobin (1972), p. 205, makes the same point about the *Monthly Review* that Anna Louise does. Anna Louise writes to Emily on November 30, 1953, about her visit to Milton Lester. Tracy Strong, Jr., and Dolphine Strong told us of Anna Louise's acquaintance with Marta Miller; Grace Nelson told us of her first meeting with Anna Louise as well as the stories of their work together. John Niederhauser recounted her visit to Mexico.

The U.S. embassy in Guatemala sent a dispatch to the State Department on January 13, 1954, describing reaction to Anna Louise's visit there. The activities of Winiewicz are told in Belfrage and Aronson (1978), pp. 101–102, and in Aronson's interview with us. Aronson's letter is from his files, December 2, 1954. Anna Louise pleaded with Emily for silence about her profits in a letter dated December 11, 1954, in the Pierson files.

Anna Louise described the news of her exoneration in *Why the Russians Arrested Me*, pp. 110–111, and in a letter to Lem Harris, March 24, 1955 (Harris files). The letter to Belfrage that she is no longer "bound" was written in 1956 and is in the Belfrage files; the letter about "Jimmy Jones" went to Emily on March 18, 1955, and is in the Pierson files.

Anna Louise remembered her conversation with Zarubin in *Why the Russians Arrested Me*, p. 125. Bernard Taper in the *San Francisco Chronicle*, June 8, 1955, p. 9, reported on her news conference.

Anna Louise's reaction to Khrushchev's secret speech was told to us by Dorothy Healey. The "great madness" of the purge trials is from *The Stalin Era*, pp. 64 ff. Anna Louise's interview with the Passport Division of the State Department (October 30, 1956) is in the University of Washington archives, p. B39. Dulles' decision is also in the Washington archives. Her letter about her psychiatric problems was sent to Aronson on March 20, 1957, and is in the University of Washington archives.

Her departure from the United States and her stay in Stockholm are described in *Why the Russians Arrested Me*, pp. 128 ff. The scene at the airport comes from our interviews with Grace Nelson and with LaRue McCormick, Anna Louise's appearance in Stockholm from our interview with Rewi Alley, and the problems at the registration desk from our interview with James Gale.

She wrote to Grace Nelson from Moscow about the plumbing on July 26, 1958; the letter is in the Peking archives. The rest of the material is taken from *Why the Russians Arrested Me*, pp. 144 ff. It is possible that she may have left her files with Arthur Adams rather than with Surkov; we have been unable to find out.

14

THE SPIRIT OF YENAN

Anna Louise described her arrival back in Peking at the end of *Why the Russians Arrested Me*. Sidney Rittenberg described his reunion with Anna Louise in his interview with us. Rittenberg thinks that his arrest in 1949 had something to do with his relation to Anna Louise; in a private communication Harrison Salisbury has told us that Huang Hua denies this and says that the arrest was precipitated by something Rittenberg wrote. The account of the first meeting with Chinese leaders is taken from her notebooks, which are in the Peking archives, from a letter she wrote to Chou En-lai (November 4, 1958), also in Peking, and from an article she published in *New Times* on "Chinese Strategy in the Taiwan Strait," Vol. 46 (1958), pp. 8–11. Rittenberg is the source of the story about his arrest; Ruth Coe told us of the first meeting between her husband and Anna Louise. The first encounter with Mao was described to us by Ruth Coe and Tang Ming-chao and by Anna Louise in a letter to Harrison Salisbury (November 10, 1958), in the Peking archives.

Anna Louise recounted her interview with Lu Ting-yi in a letter to Helen and Warwick Tompkins (October 14, 1958), which is in the Peking archives. More details were filled in by our interviews with Tang Ming-chao and Lu Ting-yi, by Anna Louise's letter to Ruth Aley (January 1, 1959) and by Anna Louise's notebooks, both of which are in the Peking archives. Lu told us that he was at that time less enthusiastic about some aspects of the Great Leap Forward and the communes than Anna Louise was, but could not say so.

Ruth Coe reported the story of Anna Louise's interview with the *People's Daily*; our interview with Luo Ch'ing-yi filled in the account of the trips to the communes that was in Anna Louise's Peking notebooks. Elsie Cholmeley's interview with us is the source of the story of Anna Louise's initial loneliness after Emily Pierson's departure. The account of the New Year's Eve dance was drawn from our interviews with Chao Feng-feng and Sidney Rittenberg, as well as from letters to Emily Pierson (January 1, 1959) in the Pierson files and Ruth Aley (January 1, 1959) in the Peking archives.

The letter replying to Aronson's suggestion that she interview Mao (November 10, 1958) comes from the Aronson files; his interview with us provided more information on Anna Louise's ongoing relations with the *National Guardian*. The letter to Chou En-lai (November 4, 1958) as well as her reply to Salisbury (November 10, 1958) are in Peking. Dr. Ma Hai-teh told us the story of her initial attitudes toward the communes; the letter to the Tompkins about the steel mills is dated January 18, 1959, and is in the Peking archives.

The account of her first interview with Mao has been put together from the unpublished account called "Three Talks With Mao Tse-tung," which is in the Peking archives; from a letter to the Tompkins (April 14, 1959); from Anna

Louise's "Notes on the East Lake Interview" in the Peking archives; from her initial write-up of those notes, also in Peking; and from our interview with Tang Ming-chao.

The account of her suppers is reconstructed from our interviews with Sidney Rittenberg, David and Nancy Milton, Dr. Ma Hai-teh, Rewi Alley, Ruth Coe, Sol Adler, Israel Epstein and Elsie Cholmeley. See also Milton and Milton (1976), pp. 101–102.

Anna Louise's letter about Edgar Snow is dated March 6, 1959, and is in the Peking archives. The account of her writing about Tibet comes from our interview with Rewi Alley, a letter she wrote to Carey McWilliams (May 28, 1959) in the McWilliams files, her books *Tibetan Interviews* and *When Serfs Stood up in Tibet*, a letter to Lem Harris (September 15, 1959) in the Harris files, our interview with Chao Feng-feng, a letter to the Tompkins (September 15, 1959) in the Peking archives.

Her difficulties publishing in the American press comes out in letters from Carey McWilliams to Anna Louise (July 16, 1959) and from Ruth Aley to McWilliams (July 11, 1959), both in the McWilliams files. Her difficulties with Eleanor Roosevelt appear in letters from Anna Louise to Emily Pierson (December 7, 1959—Pierson files); to Lem Harris (November 25, 1959—Peking archives); and to Jessica Smith (November 1, 1959—Smith files); in the letter Mrs. Roosevelt sent to Jessica Smith (December 29, 1959), also in the Peking archives, that was forwarded to Anna Louise; in Mrs. Roosevelt's column in the *New York Post*, December 21, 1959; and in Anna Louise's responses to Emily Pierson (January 10, 1960) and Eleanor Roosevelt (January 26, 1960), both of which are in Peking.

Her everyday life during 1959 and 1960 was described to us by Rewi Alley, Chao Feng-feng, Tang Ming-chao, Ruth Coe and Wu Pei-fang; much of it can be gleaned from her notebooks on her trips, in the Peking archives.

Her crisis about telling too much is revealed in letters and a cable to James Aronson (April 17, 1960; July 23, 1960; July 30, 1960), now in the Peking archives; a letter to Emily Pierson (April 13, 1960) in the Peking archives; an internal memorandum on the issue circulated to *National Guardian* editors by Aronson, now in the Aronson files; and some "Notes for later use" by Anna Louise dated August 25, 1960, in the Peking archives.

Anna Louise spoke of her troubles with her characterizations of Tibet in a letter to her friend in Moscow, Dorothy Adams (July 22, 1960), in the Peking archives; the required changes discussed in the text appear on pp. 186–188 of *When Serfs Stood up in Tibet*. It should be noted that at this time Anna Louise also pressed successfully for the publication of Rewi Alley's book *China's Hinterland*, which some in China thought had an out-of-date line on communes.

The description of her medication and health problems comes from a letter to Emily Pierson, March 7, 1961 (Pierson files); further information comes from interviews with Dr. Ma Hai-teh, Dr. Li Pang-Ch'i, Dr. Yao Chin-fang, and Chao Feng-feng.

Chou's analysis of the problem of "line" appears in her letter to the Reverend Stephen Fritchman (November 6, 1960—Fritchman files); similar ideas appear in a letter to Lem Harris (September 24, 1960), in the Peking archives. The difficulty that the Chinese sometimes had in keeping Anna Louise in line were quietly attested to in interviews with Wang Ch'u-liang and Tang Ming-chao.

Anna Louise's unkind words about Edgar Snow appear in a letter to the Tompkins (November 11, 1960) and one to Robbins Strong (December 13, 1960); her defense of Snow to Emily Pierson was written February 12, 1961. All of this material is in Peking. The letter (November 27, 1960) to Jessica Smith about writing henceforth for a fee is from the Smith files.

The Laos trip is the subject of *Cash and Violence in Laos and Vietnam,* but the description of Kong Le comes from a letter in the Fritchman files (May 9, 1961). Her problem with "American imperialism" was discussed in interviews with Han Suyin and Sidney Rittenberg. See the opening pages of *Cash and Violence in Laos.*

Her anxieties about the First Unitarian Church and her property occupy a disturbingly large portion of the Dolphine and Tracy Strong, Jr., files, as well as the Fritchman files. The particular question about the ownership of the Rim Forest property appears in her letter to Fritchman (October 18, 1961) and Fritchman's reply (November 21, 1961), both of which are in the Fritchman files. This information was supplemented by interviews with Ruth Coe and Sidney Rittenberg.

The development of the Sino-Soviet conflict and Anna Louise's comments on the Twenty-second Party Congress appear in letters to Emily Pierson (September 11, 1961; December 6, 1961—Pierson files); in "Notes on talk with Tang" (November 19, 1961), which is in her Peking archives; and in the privately circulated "A personal view of what hit the world at the Twenty-second Party Congress." This latter report eventually reached a newspaper correspondent in Warsaw who also used Ruth Aley as a literary agent. He or she allowed the American embassy there to look at it, though not to copy it, and an account made its way to the State Department.

Her troubles with Aronson and the *Guardian* appear in letters to her from Aronson on (April 5, 1962—Aronson files) and (August 13, 1962—Peking archives) and her response on September 1, 1962 (Peking archives). An interview with Aronson filled in the circumstances.

Most of the account of her attempt to get to Moscow in the summer of 1962 comes from her account "For the Record," which she circulated privately to friends and a copy of which is in Peking. The letter to Holland Roberts is dated July 17, 1962, and is in Peking; the manuscript she wrote in response to Roberts' question about living in Peking dates from the same month and is also in Peking; the quotation of Ch'en Yi is from there.

The story about Chou and Nehru is in a letter to Grace Nelson (December 12, 1962—Peking archives) and in an unused (and probably censored) draft of the third *Letter from China.* The letter from Guevara (November 19, 1962) is in Peking. Her troubles with Liao come in a long letter she sent him on November 3, 1962 (Peking archives). Salisbury's article drawing from Anna Louise appeared in the *New York Times* (September 1, 1962). It contained an implication that the *Guardian* was Anna Louise's American "vehicle," which disturbed Aronson enough that he wrote complaining to Salisbury (January 24, 1963—Aronson files). Anna Louise's poetical fancy went to Ruth Aley in a letter of February 20, 1963 (Peking archives).

The text of her speech on the racial situation in American is in the Peking archives and forms the subject of her reflections in a letter to Frank Coe (August 11, 1963—also in the Peking archives). The advice on how to publicize China's nuclear program went to Liao on September 7, 1963 (Peking archives).

The interest the State Department (or portions of it) showed in Anna Louise's *Letter* was attested to by Allen Whiting in his interview with us. See, for instance, a memo from the Bureau of Intelligence and Research in the State Department, April 2, 1964. Her anger at her left-wing American friends appears in her letter to Holland Roberts, April 1, 1964 (Peking archives).

The account of the second talk with Mao is reconstructed from "Three Talks with Mao Tse-tung"; two drafts of the interview sent to Wang Ch'u-liang (April 2, 1964; October 8, 1964); the "Material on Khrushchev" appended to "Three Talks"; her letter to Aronson (April 4, 1964—Aronson files); and from interviews with Sidney Rittenberg, Sol Adler, Ruth Coe, and Israel Epstein.

The transcript of the peace conference in Hanoi was published in 1964. In addition, we drew upon our interviews with Sidney Rittenberg and Chao Feng-feng. The story of Anna Louise hitting peace council president Li comes from Rittenberg, as does that of Mrs. Cam and the chocolates.

The problems surrounding her second Hanoi trip were described to us by Ruth Coe and Sidney Rittenberg and form the focus of her letter to Stephen Fritchman on July 11, 1965 (Fritchman files). The letter about her disposition to Emily Pierson was written September 25, 1965, and is in the Pierson files.

15

THE END OF THE VISIT

Wang Ch'u-liang told us of the project to publish the works of Anna Louise, and she herself writes to Beryl Wheeldon about it, August 23, 1964 (Peking archives); in addition the Peking archives contain a draft outline of the project. The letter she sent to her Oberlin reunion is in the Peking archives and appears as part of the preface to the new edition of *China's Millions* and again as part of the double *Letter from China* (December 20, 1965).

Malraux says in *Antimémoires*, p. 365, that at this time Mao told him that he now "was alone." Milton and Milton (1976) and Lee (1978) are among the few who have seen the importance of this interview.

The account of the eightieth birthday parties is drawn from our interviews with David and Nancy Milton, Sidney Rittenberg, Rewi Alley, Julian Schuman, Ruth Coe, Tang Ming-chao; from *Three Talks with Mao Tse-tung;* from Milton and Milton (1976), pp. 98 ff. The point that Anna Louise required Mao to see all the guests comes from Sidney Rittenberg; Mao's gambit about smoking is attested to by everyone we interviewed; Mao's classical references come from our interview with Sidney Rittenberg, as does the point about Mao's departure and the stories about Chou and the "Long March Cantata." David and Nancy Milton told us of Anna Louise's after-dinner speech.

Anna Louise told what the birthday celebration cost her in a letter to Grace Nelson, December 10, 1965 (Peking archives). Her brother's letter to her is dated January 18, 1966, and her reply February 7, 1966; both letters are in the Peking archives. Anna Louise wrote Liao Cheng-chih in distress when she could not obtain a visa for Tracy (March 22, 1966).

Her anger at Aronson was in a letter dated May 21, 1966 (Peking archives). His response is dated June 8, 1966 (Aronson files). Anna Louise's petulant sour-grapes letter was sent to Elsie Cholmeley on July 31, 1966 (Peking archives). Our interview with Aronson filled in this occasion.

The information about the beginning of the Cultural Revolution comes from Lee (1978). Anna Louise responded to Emily Pierson's distress of her initial account in a letter dated August 7, 1966 (Peking archives). The announcement of the Cultural Revolution directives in Pei-tai-ho were described to us in an interview with Sao Ch'ih-p'ing, who was the translator for the group of French Communists. Anna Louise spoke to them in French.

The interview with the Red Guards appears in *Letter from China*, No. 40; our account was filled in by our interview with Sidney Rittenberg. Anna Louise expressed some of her doubts in a letter to Beryl Wheeldon on September 25, 1966 (Peking archives); the gnomic letter from Tang was written on October 22, 1966. More information was provided in interviews with Rewi Alley and Tang Ming-chao, as well as by Anna Louise's letter to the Tompkins, January 13, 1967 (Peking archives). The long and important draft of a letter to Frank Coe written May 6, 1967, is in the Peking archives; the story about "studying" Mao comes from our interview with Rewi Alley. An appraisal of Anna Louise and her attitude toward the Red Guards may be found in Reece (1968).

The sense that she wanted to turn her attentions elsewhere comes up in a letter to Israel Epstein, February 3, 1967 (Peking archives) and even in *Letter from China*, No. 48 (April 26, 1967). Her anxieties about her relations with the Tompkins are expressed in her letter to Stephen Fritchman (March 6, 1967) and to them (March 11, 1967), both of which are in the Peking archives, as is the protestation from the Tompkins to Anna Louise (January 28, 1967).

The difficulties in meeting her brother are apparent in her letter to him, January 31, 1967 (Tracy Strong archives), and to one of the authors, December 21, 1967; the sad request to find Prousse was written March 12, 1967, and is in Peking.

She expressed her anger at Aronson in a letter on May 3, 1967; Aronson's reply was written a week later. Both of these letters are in the Aronson file. The interview with Aronson filled out this episode. Anna Louise's anxieties about her lack of Chinese were expressed to Han Suyin (August 18, 1967—Peking archives).

The story about Ch'en Yi comes from our interview with Dr. Ma Hai-teh. Anna Louise's anxieties about the world "closing in" were attested to by a number of people we interviewed in Peking. Details of Rittenberg's situation and arrest came from interviews with David and Nancy Milton, Chao Feng-feng, Dr. Ma Hai-teh, and Rewi Alley. See also Milton and Milton (1976), pp. 302–303. The Epsteins (and David Crook, an Englishman also arrested at that time) were released after three years, with special apologies to Crook. According to anonymous sources, the Epsteins were deemed to have been "misled" by Rittenberg; Rittenberg was viewed as a "special case" and not released until 1978. Sidney Rittenberg remains one of the most fascinating and enigmatic characters in the U.S.-China relations. His fate is not unusual among foreign advisors to the Chinese: see Spence (1969). Of Anna Louise's other friends in Peking, Rewi Alley was never in personal trouble during the Cultural Revolution, although his adopted son was severely beaten and survived being pushed out a window in what was supposed to look like suicide. Dr. Ma received some criticism but suffered mainly in that his work was disrupted, his medical teams were disbanded and his equipment fell into disrepair.

The letter to Ken McCormick refusing him the account of her arrest is dated February 28, 1967; she wrote to him that she had been asked to limit her output on June 6, 1968, and described what she wanted to write about on July 9, 1968. All these letters are in Peking. The letter from Fairbank to McCormick is dated August 1, 1969, and is in the McCormick files. Anna Louise reported her weight loss to McCormick on January 9, 1969 (Peking archives).

The question about where to place her archives was occasioned by a request to Fritchman by Robert Pringle, a graduate student in history, to use her files for a dissertation. Fritchman recommended that Anna Louise turn him down on political grounds, which she did through Fritchman. See Robert Pringle to Stephen Fritchman, November 3, 1968; Fritchman to Anna Louise, November 30,

1968; and her reply, December 10, 1968, all in Fritchman's files. Pringle eventually wrote a master's and a Ph.D thesis at the University of Virginia, both on Anna Louise, but without any of the material now in the Seattle archives.

Anna Louise wrote to Corliss Lamont about the post office issue on November 30, 1968 (Peking archives); Tang told us of the incident. The expanded project of the autobiography went to McCormick on January 9, 1969 (Peking archives). Her angry letter to Tang was composed August 27, 1969, and is in the Peking archives; her letter to Mao was written September 23, 1969. It is interesting that she described Mao's revolution as continuous, a word associated with Trotsky's doctrines. See Starr (1979), pp. 209 and especially 302 ff., for an analysis of the similarities and differences between Mao and Trotsky. In our interview, the Miltons indicated that Anna Louise knew the basic accuracy of the "scissors and paste" accusation.

Anna Louise wrote to K'ang Sheng about the Mao interviews on October 11, 1969 (Peking archives). Dr. Ma's attempt to persuade her to be a reasonable patient comes from his interview with us. The exchange with Lamont about Roger Baldwin was initiated by her letter of November 1, 1969; he replied on November 11, 1969. Both these letters are in the Lamont files.

Her angry letter to Robbins (October 18, 1969) is in the Robbins Strong files; that to Tang (November 2, 1969) in the Peking archives, as is her follow-up about her "job" (November 17, 1969). The letter to John Strong comes from his files (December 4, 1969); that to Chou asking once more for his intervention is dated December 9, 1969 (Peking archives).

The story of the medication comes from our interview with Donna Schuman; Anna Louise's physical condition in her home from the interview with nurses Yao and Chang.

The funeral was described to us by Rewi Alley, Ruth Coe, Dr. Ma Hai-teh, Donna Schuman, Julian Schuman, Chao Feng-feng, Sol and Pat Adler. The eulogy by Kuo Mo-jo was reprinted in the last *Letter from China*, No. 70.

Bibliography

PRIMARY SOURCES

Books and Pamphlets by Anna Louise Strong:

Storm Songs and Fables. Chicago: Langston Press, 1904.
The Song of the City. Oak Park, Ill.: Oak Leaves Press, 1906.
The King's Palace. Oak Park, Ill.: Oak Leaves Press, 1908.
The Psychology of Prayer. Chicago: University of Chicago Press, 1909.
Boys and Girls of the Bible. Chicago: Howard-Severence Company, 1911.
Child Welfare Exhibits: Types and Preparation. Washington, D.C.: Government Printing Office, 1915.
The Seattle General Strike, issued by the History Committee of the General Strike Committee; Anna Louise Strong, historian. Seattle: Seattle Union Record, 1918; reprinted by the Shorey Bookstore, Seattle, 1972.
Ragged Verse. Seattle: Seattle Union Record Press, 1920.
The First Time in History: Two Years of Russia's New Life, Preface by Leon Trotsky. New York: Boni and Liveright, 1924.
Children of Revolution: The Story of the John Reed Children's Colony on the Volga, Which Is as Well a Story of the Whole Great Structure of Russia. Seattle: Pigott Printing Center, 1925.
China's Millions: The Revolutionary Struggles from 1927–1935. New York: Knight Publishing Company, 1935; expanded from 1928 edition, New York: Coward-McCann. New edition, Peking, 1965.
Red Star in Samarkand. New York: Coward-McCann, 1929.
The Soviets Conquer Wheat: The Drama of Collective Farming. New York: Henry Holt and Company, 1931.
The Road to the Grey Pamir. Boston: Little, Brown, 1931.
I Change Worlds: The Remaking of an American. New York: Henry Holt and Company, 1935. Reprinted with an Introduction by Barbara Wilson by Seal Press, Seattle, 1979.
This Soviet World. New York: Henry Holt and Company, 1936.
The New Soviet Constitution: A Study in Socialist Democracy. New York: Henry Holt and Company, 1937.
Spain in Arms. New York: Henry Holt and Company, 1937.
One-fifth of Mankind. New York: Modern Age Books, 1938.
My Native Land. New York: Viking Press, 1940.
The Soviets Expected It. New York: Dial Press, 1941.
The New Lithuania. New York: National Council of American-Soviet Friendship, 1941.
Wild River. Boston: Little, Brown, 1943.
Peoples of the U.S.S.R. New York: Macmillan, 1944.

I Saw the New Poland. Boston: Little, Brown, 1946.
Dawn over China. Bombay: People's Publishing House, 1948.
Tomorrow's China. New York: CDFEP, 1948.
The Chinese Conquer China. Garden City: Doubleday, 1949.
The Stalin Era. Altadena, Calif.: Today's Press, 1956.
The Rise of the Chinese People's Communes—and Six Years After. Peking: New World Press, 1959, 1964.
When Serfs Stood up in Tibet. Peking: New World Press, 1960.
Tibetan Interviews. Peking: New World Press, 1961.
Cash and Violence in Laos and Vietnam. New York: Mainstream Publishers, 1962.
Letters from China, Nos. 1–10. Peking, 1961–1962.
Letters from China, Nos. 11–20. Peking, New World Press, 1963.
Letters from China, Nos. 21–30. Peking, New World Press, 1966.
Letters from China, Nos. 31–70. Peking, 1966–1970.

SECONDARY SOURCES

Akimova, Vera Valdimirovna Vishnyakova-. *Two Years in Revolutionary China, 1925–1927.* Translated by Steven I. Levine. Harvard East Asian Monographs. Cambridge: Harvard University Press, 1971.
Allan, Seema Rynin. *Comrades and Citizens.* London: Gollancz, 1938.
Barrett, David D. *Dixie Mission: The United States Army Observer Group in Yenan, 1944.* Chinese Research Monographs. Berkeley: University of California Press, 1970.
Belfrage, Cedric, and James Aronson. *Something to Guard.* New York: Columbia University Press, 1978.
Brecher, Jeremy. *Strike.* San Francisco: Straight Arrow Books, 1972.
Caute, David. *The Fellow Travellers.* New York: Macmillan, 1973.
———. *The Great Fear.* New York: Simon & Schuster, 1978.
Ceplair, Larry, and Steven Englund. *The Inquisition in Hollywood.* New York: Doubleday, 1980.
Chan, F. Gilbert, and Thomas H. Etzold, eds. *China in the Twenties.* London and New York: New Viewpoints, 1976.
Chang Kuo-t'ao. *The Rise of the Chinese Communist Party, 1921–1938.* 2 vols. Lawrence: University Press of Kansas, 1971.
Chen, Percy. *China Called Me.* Boston: Little, Brown, 1979.
Chiang Chung-cheng (Chiang Kai-shek). *Soviet Russia in China. A Summing up at Seventy.* Taipei: China Publishing Company, 1969.
Committee on Russian American Relations. *The United States and the Soviet Union: A Report.* November 1, 1933.
Dawson, John. *The Life and Thought of Sidney Dix Strong.* M.A. thesis, Department of History, University of Washington.
Davies, Joseph P. *Mission to Moscow.* New York: Simon & Schuster. 1941.
Davis, Allen F. *American Heroine: The Life and Legend of Jane Addams.* New York: Oxford University Press, 1973.
Dennis, Peggy. *The Autobiography of an American Communist, 1925–1975.* Westport, Conn.: Lawrence Hill, 1977.
Department of State. *United States Relations with China ("White Paper").* Washington, D.C.: U.S. Government Printing Office, 1949.
Deutscher, Isaac. *The Prophet Unarmed. Trotsky: 1921–1929.* New York: Vintage, 1963.

Draper, Theodore. *The Roots of American Communism.* New York: Viking, 1957.
————. *American Communism and Soviet Russia: The Formative Period.* New York: Viking, 1960.
Duke, David T. "Anna Louise Strong and the Search for a Good Cause," *Pacific Northwest Quarterly,* Vol. 66, No. 3 (July 1975), pp. 123–137.
Dyson, Lowell K. *Red Harvest: The Communist Party and American Farmers.* Lincoln: University of Nebraska Press, 1982.
Fischer, Louise. *The Life of Lenin.* New York: Harper and Row, 1964.
————. *Men and Politics.* New York: Duell, Sloan and Pearce, 1941.
Fisher, H. H., *The Famine in Soviet Russia: The Operations of the American Relief Administration.* New York: Macmillan, 1927.
Fitzpatrick, Sheila, ed. *Cultural Revolution in Russia, 1928–1931.* Bloomington: Indiana University Press, 1978.
Foner, Phillip. *The American Federation of Labor in the Progressive Era.* Vol. 3 in *The History of the United States Labor Movement.* New York: New World, 1980.
————. *The Industrial Workers of the World, 1905–1917.* Vol. 4, *The History of the United States Labor Movement.* New York: New World, 1980.
Friedheim, Robert L. *The Seattle General Strike.* Seattle: University of Washington Press, 1964.
Fritchman, Stephen H. *Heretic: A Partisan Authobiography.* Boston: Beacon Press, 1977.
Gillan, Donald. *Warlord: Yen Hsi-shan in Shansi Province, 1911–1949.* Princeton: Princeton University Press, 1967.
Gornick, Vivian. *The Romance of American Communism.* New York: Basic Books, 1977.
Gulick, Luther. *A Philosophy of Play.* New York: Scribner's and Sons, 1920.
Hollander, Paul. *Political Pilgrims: Travels of Western Intellectuals to the Soviet Union, China and Cuba.* New York: Oxford University Press, 1981.
Holubnychy, Lydia. *Michael Borodin and the Chinese Revolution, 1923–1925.* Unfinished dissertation, Columbia University, 1979.
Hoover, Herbert. *An American Epic. Famine in Forty-five Nations. The Battle on the Front Line, 1914–1923.* Volume 3. Chicago: Regnery, 1961.
Isaacs, Harold. *The Tragedy of the Chinese Revolution,* 2nd rev. ed. Stanford: Stanford University Press, 1961.
Isserman, Maurice. "The Half-Swept House: American Communism in 1956," *Socialist Review,* Vol. 12, No. 1 (January–February, 1982), pp. 71–101.
————. *Peat-Bog Soldiers: The American Communist Party, 1939–1945.* Ph.D. dissertation, History Department, University of Rochester, 1979.
Jacobs, Dan. *Borodin, Stalin's Man in China.* Cambridge: Harvard University Press, 1981.
Jaffe, Philip. *The Amerasia Case from 1945 to the Present.* New York: self-published, 1979.
————. *The Rise and Fall of American Communism.* New York: Horizon Press, 1975.
————. "The Strange Case of Anna Louise Strong," *Survey,* No. 53 (October 1964), pp. 129–139.
————. "The Strange Case of Anna Louise Strong," chapter in Philip Jaffe's unpublished autobiography.
Jones, Mary Hoxie. *Swords into Plowshares: An Account of the American Friends Service Committee, 1917–1937.* New York: Macmillan, 1937.
Kaplan, Justin. *Lincoln Steffens.* New York: Simon & Schuster, 1974.

Kirsch, Botho. *Sturm ueber Eurasien: Moskau und Peking im Kampf um die Weltherrschaft.* Stuttgart: Seewald Verlag, 1970.
Kollontai, Alexandra. *Selected Writings.* London: Allison and Busby, 1977.
Kuusinen, Aino. *Before and after Stalin. A Personal Account of Soviet Russia from the 1920s to the 1960s.* London: Michael Joseph, 1974.
Lamson, Peggy. *Roger Baldwin: A Biography.* Boston: Houghton Mifflin, 1976.
Larsen, Charles. *The Good Fight: The Life and Times of Ben B. Lindsey.* New York: Quadrangle, 1972.
Lee, Hong Yung. *The Politics of the Cultural Revolution.* Berkeley and Los Angeles: University of California Press, 1978.
Levin, N. Gordon. *Woodrow Wilson and the Paris Peace Conference: America's Response to War and Revolution.* Lexington, Mass.: Heath, 1968.
Levine, Daniel. *Jane Addams and the Liberal Tradition.* Madison: State Historical Society of Wisconsin, 1971.
Lewin, Moshe. *La paysannerie et le pouvoir soviétique, 1928–1930.* Paris: Mouton, 1966.
Long, Edward Robert. *Loyalty Oaths in California, 1947–1952: The Politics of Anti-Communism.* Ph.D. dissertation, History Department, University of California at San Diego, 1981.
Lyons, Eugene. *The Red Decade.* Indianapolis: Bobbs-Merrill, 1941.
McAuliffe, Mary Sperling. *Crisis on the Left: Cold War Politics and the American Liberals, 1947–1954.* Amherst: University of Massachussetts Press, 1978.
MacDougall, Curtis D. *Gideon's Army,* 3 vols. New York: Marzani and Munsell, 1965.
Malraux, André. *Antimémoires.* Paris: Gallimard, 1967.
Mao Tse-tung. *Selected Works,* Vols. 1–5. Peking: Foreign Languages Press, 1966, 1977.
Mason, Pamela F. (Hull). *Lineage of the Tracy Family.* 1895.
Massell, Gregory J. *The Surrogate Proletariat: Moslem Women and Revolutionary Strategies in Soviet Central Asia, 1919–1929.* Princeton, N.J.: Princeton University Press, 1974.
Melby, John F. *The Mandate of Heaven: Record of a Civil War, China 1945–1949.* New York: Doubleday, 1971.
Milton, David, and Nancy Dall Milton. *The Wind Will Not Subside: Years in Revolutionary China—1964–1969.* New York: Pantheon, 1976.
Morgan, Murray. *Skid Road.* New York: Viking, 1951.
Moseley, George. *China Since 1911.* New York: Harper and Row, 1968.
Navasky, Victor. *Naming Names.* New York: Penguin, 1980.
Nearing, Scott. *The Making of a Radical.* New York: Harper and Row, 1972.
O'Connor, Harvey. *Revolution in Seattle: A Memoir.* New York: Monthly Review Press, 1964.
O'Neill, William. *Better World: The Great Schism: Stalinism and the American Intellectuals.* New York: Simon & Schuster, 1982.
Palermo, Patrick F. *Lincoln Steffens.* Boston: Twayne, 1971.
Pepper, Suzanne. *The Civil War in China: The Political Struggle, 1945–1949.* Berkeley: University of California Press, 1978.
Porter, Cathy. *Alexandra Kollontai: A Biography.* London: Virago, 1980.
Pringle, Robert. *The Making of a Communist: Anna Louise Strong, 1885–1925.* M.A. thesis in history, University of Virginia, 1967.
Reece, Bob. "An Octogenarian Red Guard," *Far Eastern Economic Review,* Vol. 69, No. 11 (March 14, 1968), pp. 456–458.

Rothman, Sheila. *Woman's Proper Place: A History of Changing Ideals and Practices from 1870 to the Present.* New York: Basic Books, 1978.

Sale, Roger. *Seattle, Past to Present.* Seattle: University of Washington Press, 1976.

Salisbury, Harrison. *An American in Russia.* New York: Harper and Brothers, 1955.

———. *Moscow Journal.* Chicago: University of Chicago Press, 1961.

———. "Review of Books on China," *New York Times Book Review,* February 17, 1971, pp. 2 ff.

Schaller, Michael. *The U.S. Crusade in China.* New York: Columbia University Press, 1979.

Scott, Richenda C. *Quakers in Russia.* London: Michael Joseph, 1964.

Selden, Mark. *The Yenan Way in Revolutionary China.* Cambridge: Harvard University Press, 1971.

Serge, Victor. *Mémoires d'un révolutionnaire.* Paris: Editions du Seuil, 1951.

Service, John S. *The Amerasia Papers: Some Problems in the History of U.S.-China Relations.* China Research Monographs. Berkeley: University of California Press, 1971.

Shannon, David A. *The Decline of American Communism.* New York: Harcourt, Brace and Company, 1959.

Sheean, Vincent. *Personal History.* Garden City: Doubleday, 1934.

Smedley, Agnes. *China Fights Back* (with an introduction by Anna Louise Strong). New York: Vanguard Press, 1938.

———. *Portrait of Chinese Women in Revolution,* edited and with an introduction by Jan and Steve MacKinnon. New York: Feminist Press, 1976.

Smith, Jessica. *People Come First.* New York: International Publishers, 1948.

Smith-Rosenberg, Carrol. "The Female World of Love and Ritual: Relations between Women in Nineteenth-Century America," *Signs: Journal of Women and Society,* vol. 1, no. 1 (1974), pp. 1–29.

Snow, Edgar. *Red Star over China.* New York: Bantam, 1978.

Solomon, Susan Gross. *The Soviet Agrarian Debate: A Controversy in Social Science, 1923–1929.* Boulder, Col.: Westview, 1977.

Spence, Jonathan. *To Change China: Western Advisors in China, 1620–1960.* New York: Viking Press, 1969.

Starobin, Joseph R. *American Communism in Distress, 1937–1957.* Cambridge, Mass.: Harvard University Press, 1972.

Starr, John Bryan. *Continuing the Revolution: The Political Thought of Mao.* Princeton: Princeton University Press, 1979.

Steffens, Lincoln. *The Autobiography of Lincoln Steffens.* New York: Harcourt, Brace and World, 1958.

———. *The Letters of Lincoln Steffens,* 2 vols., ed. by Ella Winter and Granville Hicks. New York: Harcourt Brace, 1938.

———. "The Rumor in Russia," *Nation* 107, December 21, 1918.

Stettinius, Edward R., Jr. *Roosevelt and the Russians: The Yalta Conference.* Garden City: Doubleday, 1949.

Stinson, Robert. *Lincoln Steffens.* New York: Ungar, 1979.

Strong, Albert. *The Strongs of Strongsville.* Fort Dodge, Iowa, 1931.

Strong, Tracy B. "Taking the Rank of What Is Ours: American Political Thought, Foreign Policy and the Question of Human Rights," in Paula Newberg, ed., *The Politics of Human Rights.* New York: New York University Press, 1980.

Sues, Ilona Ralf. *Sharks' Fin and Millet.* Boston: Little, Brown, 1944.

Vladimirov, Peter. *The Validmirov Diaries*. London: Hale, 1975.

Wald, Lillian. *Windows on Henry Street*. Boston, 1934.

Wales, Nym. "The Classic Fellow Traveler," *New Republic*, April 1970.

Walzer, Michael. *The Revolution of the Saints*. Cambridge: Harvard University Press, 1965.

Weinstein, James. *The Corporate Ideal in the Liberal State, 1900–1918*. Boston: Beacon Press, 1969.

Weisbrod, Marvin H. *Some Forms of Peace: True Stories of the American Friends Service Committee at Home and Abroad*. New York: Viking Press, 1968.

Weissman, Benjamin M. *Herbert Hoover and Famine Relief to Soviet Russia, 1921–1923*. Stanford: Hoover Institution Press, 1974.

Wilbur, C. Martin, and Julie Lien-ying How, eds. *Documents on Communism, Nationalism, and Soviet Advisors in China, 1918–1927: Papers Seized in the 1927 Peking Raid*. New York: Octagon Books, 1972.

Willen, Paul. "Anna Louise Strong Goes Home Again," *The Reporter*, April 7, 1955, pp. 28–29.

Index

Random House: *Strong*

ABOUT THE AUTHORS

TRACY B. STRONG, who is Anna Louise Strong's great-nephew, was born in China. Both he and his wife, HELENE KEYSSAR, teach at the University of California at San Diego. He chairs the Department of Political Science, and she, the Department of Communications. While researching this book, they spent several months in the People's Republic of China, studying the archives on Anna Louise and talking with people who had known her.